Kalm's Account of his Visit to England

On his way to America in 1748

Pehr Kalm

(Translator: Joseph Lucas)

Alpha Editions

This edition published in 2019

ISBN : 9789353923648

Design and Setting By
Alpha Editions
email - alphaedis@gmail.com

KALM'S

ACCOUNT OF HIS

VISIT TO ENGLAND

ON HIS WAY TO AMERICA IN 1748.

Translated by JOSEPH LUCAS.

WITH TWO MAPS, AND SEVERAL ILLUSTRATIONS.

𝔏𝔬𝔫𝔡𝔬𝔫:

MACMILLAN AND CO.

AND NEW YORK.

1892.

LIFE OF KALM.

PEHR KALM was born in March, 1716, in the Swedish Province of Ångermanland, three months after the death of his father, Gabriel Kalm, Minister at Nerpes, in Österbotn. His mother's name was Catharina Ross. Kalm became a student at Åbo in 1735, where Professor Brovallius directed his attention to Natural History.

Brovallius introduced him to Baron Bjelke, who not only received him into his own house, but sent him to travel; in 1740 to Tavastland, Savolax, and Karelen, and in 1741 to Upland and Vestmanland. On setting out for the latter he entered as a student at Upsala, under the guidance and instruction of the great Linnæus. In 1742 he travelled through Vestgötha and Bohuslän, and published his "Vestgötha och Bohuslänska Resa" in 1746. In 1743 he visited the Skjärgård, or Archipelago on both sides of Stockholm, in Roslagen and Södermanland.

His contributions to the *Flora Svecica* of Linnæus

from these home journeys were honorably acknowledged by Linnæus (*De Peloria*, Ups. 1744).

In 1744 he went with Baron Bjelke through Russia and part of the Ukrain; and in 1745 explored the southern half of Vestergöthland.

In 1745, Kalm, still a student, was elected a Ledamot, or Member, of the Swedish Academy of Sciences, and in the following year was appointed *Docens* in Natural History at the Academy at Åbo. In 1747 he was nominated as the first Professor of Œconomie at Åbo.

The same year, at the instance of Baron Bjelke and Linnæus, he was commissioned by the Government and the Vetenskaps Academi, or Academy of Science, with the joint subsidies of the Universities of Åbo and Upsala, and the Manufactur Kontor of the Swedish States, to visit North America, for the purpose of describing the natural productions of that part of the world, and of introducing from thence into Sweden such useful plants as might be expected to thrive in the North of Europe.

Kalm himself says in his Preface (p. 7) :—

" In the autumn of 1747, after His Majesty had granted me permission to leave my duties, and license to travel abroad on the errands of the Royal Swedish Academy of Science, and after His Majesty had not only given me his own Passport, but also had most graciously given orders to his Ministers at the French, Spanish, and English Courts, as well as those at the United Provinces in Holland, to obtain for me the Passports of these Powers, I commenced on 16th October [New Style, which is everywhere used in this preface] the voyage from Upsala down to Götheborg.

" I had chosen as my assistant the Horticulturist (Trägårdsmästaren) Lars Jungström, who was quite at home in the science of Horticulture and the cultivation of plants, adroit in delineating all sorts of things by mechanical drawing, indefatigable on journeys, and in the highest degree trustworthy. We remained at Götheborg on account of a continuous adverse wind to the 11th December, when we sailed from thence, but being driven by a fearful storm we were obliged to seek Norway. Here we remained till the 8th February, 1748, when we sailed from thence to England, and arrived at London the 17th of the same month. For want of a vessel to cross to America we were obliged to remain in England till the 5th August, when we went on board at *Gravesend*, and on the 11th of the same month we lost sight of England. . . . ."

" [On the return Voyage] 1751.

" After a bad voyage, unusual storms, and being often in peril of our lives, on the 23rd March we caught sight of England. On the 27th of the same month our ship ran aground at the mouth of the river Thames so hard, that with two pumps we could not pump out as much water as poured in through the bottom of the ship, but were obliged to seek the nearest land, from whence I travelled by road to London, where I arrived on the 29th March, and had the pleasure some days later to see our ship and goods arrive there, after it had been repaired. On the 5th May we left London, and on the 16th of the same month reached Götheborg, and on the 3rd June arrived at Stockholm.

" From notes which I made on these Travels, the first Volume [1753] is communicated to the public. It contains various observations made in Norway and England. [The first 111 pages of the second volume, 1756, contains the remainder of the English notes].

" As far as regards *English Rural Economy* (Landt hushållningen), I have omitted much in order that the work might not become too bulky, but think, please God, of giving it to the Swedish Academy. When I have been speaking of England, I have sometimes come to use some English words. I do not see why it should be accounted in me a fault more than for others to use French words. They are however nearly [p. 11] all explained by me in one place or another.

" Many who have more pleasure in reading books for diversion than for instruction, will perhaps soon be weary of seeing Aker, Äng (arable fields and meadows), and various matters connected [p. 12] with agriculture, so often named in this description of travels (Resebeskrifning) which is unusual in most descriptions of travel which have hitherto appeared, if I except those of the great Linnæus, and those who have followed his *method*, and some few others, but it was just the object of this journey and my principal business to collect such. I wish that we had, not only of the whole Kingdom and each Province, but also of every Härad, and even Parish (Socken), an accurate description of the Rural Economy, as by that means we should have a clear light and guide for improving our agriculture. [This seems to be the original suggestion for an Agricultural Survey such as was carried out in England towards the end of the century, forty to fifty years later]. By that means we get to select the best of everything, and to reject that which we find in our agriculture to be less profitable than another; we are thereby led to devise still better, when the science of Agriculture is thoroughly set going.

"When a number is quoted after the name of a plant without any book being named, the *Flora Svecica* of Linnæus is always meant.

"When any particular thing has been told me which I had no opportunity of seeing for myself, I have commonly named my Sagesman (informant), partly to

express my gratitude to the person who has communicated anything, and not to give out as my own that
which belongs to another, partly that it may stand to my
informant's [p. 14] own account, in case it be found to
be little in accordance with the truth. In reference to
that which I have not seen myself, but have been obliged
to rely upon the accounts of others, I have in addition
commonly used the word **berättades** or **sages** or **skal,**
but that which I have either seen myself, or all have
related with one mouth, I have said that it is so.

"I have studiously omitted descriptions of plants,
animals, and rocks, **örters, djurs, och stenarters.**
Most readers regard them as wearisome ; besides they make
the book larger and dearer ; but I have always introduced
where I have got to know of any, the *uses* of plants,
animals, and minerals. The descriptions I will, please
God, communicate in a Latin work at some future time.
.   .   .   .   .   Âbo, the 13th July, 1753."

Kalm, who had married in America, in 1750, a lady
from Sweden, died on the 16th November, 1779, without
completing his account of his travels. Thus says Odhelius
(*Â minnelse Tal*, p. 25) : "The description of the American
"travels which he published by degrees during the same
"period, gave him additional occupation. We have in his
"lifetime seen three parts of it come out (1753-56-61), and
"the fourth which he had ready and written with his own

"hand, his successor in office (Kreander) has promised
" immediately to place in the hands of the public."

This promise was never fulfilled. Professor Kreander
obtained possession of the manuscript of the subsequent
parts under the will, but was prevented by his early
death from publishing them. Previously to the lament-
able fire of 1827 they were preserved in the library at
Âbo.

TRANSLATOR'S PREFACE.

Of the now exceedingly rare
three volumes, not much more
than one-half relates to America.
The first 137½ pp. of Tom. I.
bring up the account to Kalm's
departure from Grömstad for
England.

The wonderful account of
England occupies from p. 138 in
Tom. I. to p. 111 in Tom. II.—in
all 458 pp. 8vo. The American portion was translated into
English last century by John Reinhold Forster, but the

English portion has never before been translated. It is totally unknown in this country, but far transcends in completeness and accuracy of description any work of its age on England known to the present translator. Kalm's work in England was carried on from four centres: Gravesend, London, Woodford, and Little Gaddesden. Few subjects have escaped his scrutiny; but whether social or natural, town or country, each has been described with the minute and delicate accuracy of a man of keen observation, of refined taste, and of high scientific training.

The botanical names used by Kalm are mainly those of Caspar Bauhin, and of Linnæus in the *Flora Svecica,* Stockholm, 1745, 8vo. The identification of the plants would have been a hopeless task but for the existence in the British Museum of two volumes, with MS. notes, from the library of Sir Joseph Banks. The first of these is the copy of the *Prodromos Theatri Botanici* of Caspar Bauhin, Basileœ, 1671, 4to, with press mark " 448 p. 3 (2) " ; and the second the copy of the *Fl. Svecica,* with the press mark " 450 f. 2." On the margins of these two copies are written the Linnæan names of many if not most of the plants enumerated in those two works, as given by Linnæus in the 13th Edition of the *Systema Naturæ* (Vindobonæ, 1767—1770, 3 Tom. 8vo), which from its publication superseded the works of the older botanists and the earlier works of Linnæus himself.

Kalm's agricultural notes are full of vivacious and picturesque descriptions and of valuable information and suggestions : the scientific portion is of the very highest order of excellence, as witness his measured geological sections of tertiary strata, his description of the *Chalk*, the *Portland stone*, or the *Totternhoe stone*, &c., and his careful enumeration of the genera and species of grasses found in grassfields and haystacks. For the rest, his acuteness of observation and faithfulness of description have been verified by the translator on the ground.

The head-pieces and tail-piece and the ornamental capitals are reproductions of the originals. The legend on one of the head-pieces should read ' **Ljusare ändå**,' ' Lighter yet.'

In this translation the circumflex has been used instead of the Swedish ° over the letter " a," as was done by Linnæus in his *Flora Lapponica*, 1737, 8vo.

The figures, with the exception of that of the archæological mystery on p. 402, and the plan showing its site, are reproductions of Jungström's figures, some of which have, however, been omitted. Mr. F. W. Lucas, the author of the magnificent work on America, "*Appendiculæ Historicæ;* or, Shreds of History hung on a horn," 1891, 4to, has contributed a learned note on the identity of the Frisland of the *Zeni* with Faerö, a proof that may be strengthened by the names of several other places in

Faerö. He also contributed the note on p. 19, and that on p. 20, on Angria, the Sea Rover, concerning whom, Robert Bloomfield writes in the little poem on Shooter's Hill :—

> " This far-seen monumental tower
> Records the achievements of the brave,
> And Angria's subjugated power
> Who plundered on the Eastern wave."

He has also contributed facsimiles of the portions of Rocques' survey, showing Wanstead Manor, and Chelsea as they existed at the date of Kalm's visit.

The sections on pp. 406-7 have been published by Mr. Whitaker, F.R.S., in the Memoirs of the Geological Survey of England (*Geol. of London*, 1889, pp. 174-5) as condensed by him from the M.S. of this translation.

J. L.

TOOTING GRAVENEY,
     December 4th, 1891.

KALM'S ENGLAND.

THE VOYAGE FROM GRÖMSTAD TO ENGLAND.

[T. I. p. 138.]

N the 28th January, 1748, at 10 o'clock in the morning we committed ourselves in the Lord's name to the seas between Grömstad in Norway and England. On the passage nothing especially remarkable occurred, beyond that on January 30th, at 4 o'clock in the afternoon, a very large fish appeared, which for more than an hour swam before the ship on

the surface of the water. When its back-fins stood
above the water they looked in the distance like a sail.
The weather was beautiful and the wind moderate, and
after a fair passage, on the 4th of February, we caught
sight of the English coast and *Foreland* lighthouse, and
at night we cast anchor off *Margate.*

Thermometrical Observations were made this day both
in the air and in the sea water. In the air, or in the
shade on the south side of the ship the Thermometer of
Celsius at 10 o'clock in the morning stood 4½° above 0°
[40·1° Fahr.] I had several whole buckets full of water
drawn up from the sea, and set the Thermometer in them
directly, when the Mercury shot up like an arrow to 8° *Cels.*
[46·4° Fahr.] where it always remained stationary and
went neither higher nor lower : but when I took it out of
the water and held it in the open air, it again fell in two
or three minutes to 4° or 3° above 0° *Cels.* [39·2° or
37·4° Fahr.]

[T. I. p. 139.] At sunrise on the morning of the 5th
February, we took a pilot on board, when we at once
began to sail up to the River Thames, near and in whose
mouth there lies an endless number of banks.

On the left hand, the English coast was now continuously in sight, and consisted of white chalk, which at
the water's-edge was nearly perpendicular. At a distance,
as seen from the sea, this country was like enough to the
coasts of Estland [Esthonia] although the kind of rock
here was altogether different.

The water was whitish, which was due to the chalky
bottom; for when we drew up the anchor, all that adhered
to the anchor-fluke was bare white chalk, mostly dis-
integrated and soft like a thick mud. Although small
pieces of hard chalk, **Krita,** occurred amongst it, we
did not see any flints or *Testacea* therein.

On the land appeared one church after another, with

towers all of stone, as well as beautiful houses, **gârdar,** windmills, etc.

Bankarna vid Segelleden. The banks near the navigable channels are marked by black or white buoys, which float on the surface of the water.

In this river there is the Ebb and Flood, which goes right up beyond London. Seafarers avail themselves of it in this way, that when it is flowing upwards, the ships and boats which are bound for London go with it, but directly the Ebb begins to go, these all cast their anchors and lie still; then, on the other hand, those coming from London lift anchor, and drive outwards with the Ebb as long as it continues to run, and when it stops they drop their anchors. In this way vessels come both to and from London without particularly [T. I. p. 140] caring about the wind that is blowing, so long as it is not too strong. It is impossible to express the untold multitude of ships and vessels which sail up and down this river daily, especially in the summer time, when ships in some of the narrower places can hardly avoid running into each other, and often at the same time cause each other great damage.

Themse Floden. *The River Thames.*—On the 6th February in the morning we continued our voyage. At mid-day we sailed past the town of Gravesend on the left hand, which is commanded by a little fort in its midst.* The width of the river for about a mile above Gravesend was about three to four musket shots.

Bâtars Styren. *The steering apparatus of boats.* In

---

* *The Blockhouse* erected 1539 by Henry VIII. "Upon which certain "piece of land called ' Le Grene' a certain house and tower called a Block- "house by our Lord the King, is just now built and constructed." (*Deed of Conveyance* of "Le Grene," 3rd June, 1543). "This Blockhouse remains "at the waterside in front or north of the terrace at the west side of Terrace "garden and pier." (Cruden *Hist. of Gravesend* 1843, 8vo. p. 163). [J. L]

some boats they had so arranged the steering apparatus
that one could sit forward in the boat and steer it. On
the top of the rudder was set crossways, a ' tiller ' or board
of some two feet long, which was parallel with the stern-
panel of the boat, when the rudder was directed end
backwards or in *linea recta* with the boat's keel. On to
both ends of the tiller was fastened a small cord or
' tiller-line,' **tåg,** wherewith they turn the rudder where
they will. Thus one could tie the tiller-ropes to his arms
and steer, but equally do what he liked with his hands.

Landets beskaffenhet omkring Themsen. The
landscape around the Thames where we were sailing was
pleasant, and one of the prettiest I had ever hitherto seen.
The Thames was for the most part three to four musket-
shots wide. On both sides the strands, **Stränderna,** were
sometimes rather high and steep, especially farther down
towards Gravesend, sometimes quite low, remarkably so
farther up towards London. Next to the river there
lay for the most part meadows, **ängar.** Farther up
[T. I. p. 141] from the Strand, the country was sloping
from the hills down towards the river, and on these
slopes appeared ploughed fields, **åkrar,** which were consequently very favourably situated.

No dikes, **diken,** could we see; but in place of
gärdesgårdar (fences) there were mostly **häckar,**
hedges of different kinds of bushes.

Beautiful buildings, mostly of brick, **sten,** made a
show everywhere, yet we saw some small houses of cross-
beams covered with boards. A number of churches
adorned the country in many places along by the river,
all of stone, and with more or less high towers.

A great number of church towers were built in the
same way as the city gates of Moscow, viz.: the walls
were cut off horizontally a little above the church, so as
to leave the section square at the top.

In other respects, the country sometimes appeared hilly but without any rocks except the chalk, **Krit-bärgen.** On the hills, and also in many other places, there appeared leafwoods* and beautiful plantations, **löfskog och sköna lundar,** whose trees were in some places tall enough.

Krittbrott. A chalk pit was also remarked here and there on the banks of the river, as at Cliffe and Purfleet.

Får och hästar. Sheep and horses appeared everywhere on the ploughed fields and pastures, **betesmarker,** though the weather was still chilly enough. The ground was everywhere bare, so that not the smallest sign of snow was seen, but the fields began in some places to look tolerably green.

Arundo, 99, *vulg.* [*A. Phragmites,* L., now *P. communis.*]

The Reed grew in abundance near the banks of the river. We also saw it cut, bound in sheaves, and laid in great heaps on the river banks. Wooden houses were in many places thatched with it.

There were walls, **vallar,** on the edge of the river's bank, between the river and the adjacent meadows and ploughed fields, about 4 feet high, which consisted of earth, **mull,** with planks outside towards the river to prevent [T. I. p. 142] the river from overflowing the ploughed fields and meadows when a very high tide occurred. In some places these walls were of earth only, **af bara jord.**

In the sequel they shall be fully described.

---

* A natural observation for one coming from a land of pines. [J. L.]

LONDON AND SUBURBS,

INCLUDING

HAMPSTEAD, CHELSEA, FULHAM, WIMBLEDON COMMON,
PECKHAM, DULWICH, GREENWICH, &c.

In the evening at sunset we arrived at *London*.

Immediately upon my arrival I addressed myself, according to the instructions given me by the Royal Academy of Science of Sweden, to *Mr. Abraham Spalding*, a Swedish merchant in *London*, who afterwards, during the whole of my visit to England gave me every imaginable information, help, advice, and explanation of various things; recommended me, partly himself, partly through his friends, to all the places I had occasion to visit, or where there was anything remarkable to see; lent me all the money I required for the whole of my foreign travels, and besides that, showed me manifold kindness.

The 9th February, 1748.

Note respecting *Concha* (1333) *Subviol.* [*Mytilus Edulis,* Mussel] omitted.

The 11th February.

Ärter. To make peas still more wholesome and agreeable, a mill, **en qvarn,** is used to grind them in,

so that they are split in two, and the thin pellicle or
scale which surrounds them is detached. [T. I. p. 143.]
It is well known that all peas split naturally into two
parts as soon as the outer cuticle is removed from them.
Afterwards the loose skin is farther winnowed away with
a winnower or fan, **Vanna eller dryfta.**

[Paragraph on pickling Cucumbers, **Gurkor** omitted.]

The 15th February, 1748.

Thermometrical observations were made yesterday. [T. I. p. 144.] The room which the people lived
in had a fire in it the whole day from morning till night,
although most of the heat went away through the chimney, because in London they neither use a **spjäll,** nor
know what a **spjäll** is, for which reason also there is no
name for it in the whole of the English language.* The
thermometer was first set by the side of the window,
when it always stood at 10° Cels. [50° Fahr.] During
my visit to Norway I also made similar observations in
the large hall, **sal,** which we lived in, which was only
warmed by a little iron stove, **järn-ugn,** and that seldom
over twice a day. When it was warm enough in the hall,
the thermometer stood at 19° or 20° Cels. [66·2° to 68°
Fahr.] but when it fell to 15°, 14°, or 13° Cels. [59°, 57·2°,
55·4° Fahr.] we thought it was tolerably cold and chilly.
The observations were carried on both when it was very
cold, and only moderately cold, out in the open air. To-
day the thermometer hung from morning till evening in
the same room in the middle of the wall between the
window and the fireplace, when it ranged through the
day between 8° and 5° Cels. [46·4° and 41° Fahr.] In
the fireplace however nothing but coal was burned. The

---

* *Fr.* "Bouchoir, clapet, de cheminée, de poële." Weste, *Lex.* 1807.
Damper, valve. [J. L.]

following day it ranged between 7° and 4° Cels. [44°6°
and 39°2° Fahr.] It remained thus all the other days
and never went above 10° Cels. [50° Fahr.]. In Sweden
the fire is commonly lighted as soon as the thermometer
falls as low as 10° Cels. There, 15° Cels. [59° Fahr.] is
considered very moderately warm, but 20° Cels. [68°
Fahr.] is too hot for most people, that is when the thermometer hangs on the window frame.

[T. I. p. 145.] *The 19th February*, 1748.

Köks-Kryddgârdar.—*Market-gardens* appeared in
several places, together with very large fields which the
market-gardeners rented, and had sown with everything
that is required in the kitchen. The length and breadth
of the beds was such as is usual in kitchen gardens, some
with thin planks round them. They sloped, although a
very little, towards the mid-day sun. Most of them were
at this time covered over with *glass frames*, which could
be taken off at will. Under these they had sown *cauliflower*
seed, **Blom-kâls-frö,** which was already come up four
inches high. The cauliflowers, **Kâlen,** stood in even rows
across the beds, **sängen,** about eighteen inches between
each row, and each plant. As cold and snow had come,
they had placed the frames over the beds, afterwards
Russian matting over these, and straw over that, four inches
thick. They had stood thus till to-day at noon, or a
little before, when the straw and mats were cast off, and
the frames raised quite up, so that the sun and air could
play freely over them. On some of these beds there were
no mats over the frames, but bare straw lay on the glass.
Otherwise the beds were arranged inside in the way
which is usual with *forcing beds*, **drif-bänkar,** viz. :
horse-dung down at the bottom and fine good mould on
the top. Of the rest of the field, a great part was filled
with large *bell-glasses*, **glas-klâckor,** under which also

cauliflower plants were set, three or four under each bell-glass. Besides the afore-named beds, there were here long asparagus beds. Their height above the ground was two feet. They had at the sides, either boards, or only straw. On the top they were similarly covered with glass, matting, and straw, which had just been all taken off at mid-day. The *Asparagus* under them was one inch [T. I. p. 146] high, and considerably thick. On the field stood a number of bell-glasses with Asparagus under. All these bell-glasses had not any straw, matting, or anything else over them on account of the cold and snow, but stood quite bare. They were all of one piece.

Rädisorne. The *Radishes* were also sown in beds, which nearly lay horizontal with the ground. In the snowy weather they had been covered over only with a mat, which was taken off at mid-day. They had now begun to come up. For shelter against the north wind, there were set up by some beds on the field, small fences, **hägnader,** of *reeds* arranged perpendicularly, and of about 2 inches thickness.

[Kalm was at Woodford from 28 Feb. to 16 Mar.]

[T. I. p. 166.]　*The 16th March,* 1748.

In the morning I went in to London from Woodford, to get certain information as to how soon any ship would go from thence to America.

Husens byggnad. *The construction of houses.* At all the places I passed through in *Essex*, brick houses were used, **brukades Stenhus.** They were all built of brick, **tegel,** but in some of the farm houses the brick-work was built between crossbeams of wood, **var teglet muradt emellan Kors-verk af trä,** which were erected both *ad angulos rectos et acutos.* Some out-houses only, such as **Lador och Logar,** 'lathes' and 'lodges,' to thrash corn in, horse-stables, **häst-stall,** etc., were so far of wood, that

the walls were built of boards, nailed horizontally over
one another. The ordinary houses in which the folk
lived, consisted often of two or three stories, **våningar,**
seldom of one only. I speak now of *Farm-houses* or
Bonde-gårdar. The roofs of the houses were all of
tiles, **tak-tegel,*** both of the square and flat sorts, and of
that which resembles gutters, **rännor,** such as are
used with us in Sweden. The former, or the square
sort, was most used. This seemed to have the advantage of the [T. I. p. 167] *concava,* or gutter-like tiles,
because if one or more tiles of this sort cracked, the
water could still not run down through it, as almost
always happens with the concave. In some places, in
laying the roof with such square and flat tiles, they had
smeared clay under the tiles by which means it was made
impossible that either rain or snow could be, by wind or
blast, driven into the loft. The chimneys were commonly
built in one of the gable-walls, often so far out, that the
gable-wall formed one side of the chimney, and the three
others were altogether outside the building. This had
the advantage, that if the soot were to take fire in the
chimney, and the chimney cracked, there was still seldom
any fear of fire in the building.

The 17th March, 1748.

Huru Hästar Spännas före, Köras, etc.

How horses are put to, driven, &c. The vehicles, **åkdon,**
which are used here in England, are wagons and carts,
Vagnar och Kärror. As has been said before, they
do not know of the *Sled,* **Släda,** because the snow, which
seldom lies on the ground over a couple of days, does not

---

* "THACKTILES. Roof tiles; opposed to wall tiles, or bricks. *North.*"
Grose. *Prov. Gloss. Supp.* 2nd Ed. Lond. 1790. 8°· but wrongly explained
in Bailey *Eng. Dic.* Ed. 1753. 8°· [J. L.]

give them the opportunity of using it. For ordinary
Coaches, **Kusk-vagnar,** a pair of horses are harnessed
abreast, **spännes i bredd,** as with us in Sweden; or,
when they are heavier, two, three, or more pairs, one
after another; but for other wagons on which all sorts of
things are carried, and for carts, where they are large,
the horses are harnessed or spanned in quite a peculiar
manner, viz., not in pairs or abreast, as for the
coaches, but all in a single row the one after the other.
I have once seen as many as eight such horses spanned
all in a row after one another, nevertheless, it is rare to
see so many. Commonly five or six horses are used for
one of the large baggage wagons, **tross-vagnar** [T. i. p.
168], so harnessed *tandem,* **i rad.** They are bound to and
after one another with strong iron chains, **järn-kädjor,**
one of which goes on each side of the horse, and where it
comes sometimes to rub against the horse's side it is covered
with leather, so that it may not gnaw the horse, **gnaga
hästen.** The weight and thickness of these chains is
such that any other than English horses would with
difficulty be able to support it, for the horses which are
used here in England for these wagons, are as large as
the largest cavalier-horses, **Ryttare-hästar,** in Sweden,
fat, and of an uncommon strength. By the collars,
lokarna, the horses drew the load or the wagon, **lasset
eller vagnen,** which is fastened on to these iron-chains;
and the chains are supported by straps, **remmar,** four
inches broad, which lie across the horse's back. There
are seldom any reins, **tömmor,** used in the whole length
of this long row of horses, but they were accustomed
to be steered wherever he wished, or to stop or go faster,
only by the various and particular calls of the driver,
Kuskens. Also one never sees more than a single carl
accompany and drive a wagon and six horses spanned all
in a row.

All English horses, at least as many as I saw, have had the tail, **svantsen,** cut off about six inches from the root, so that the whole stump of the tail was only four or six inches long. On my asking the reason of this, some Englishmen have answered that it is the custom of the country to have the horses so bob-tailed, **stump-svantsiga.**

But must it not be considered a reason that the tail has been docked, because, when they are harnessed all in a row, and close behind each other the horse going before may not strike the next in the eyes with his dirty and muddy tail? The wagons which are used here are frightfully large, with very high wheels, and are loaded with an [T. I. p. 169] astonishing weight.   Hence it happens that no roads in this country can stand against them, **stå bi,** but the large and heavy wagon and cart-wheels cut deep ruts in the road, in the same way as happens on the roads with our rocks, **Bergslagor,** in Sweden. [Defoe's advice was not carried out till some years after this date].

The 18th March, 1748.

Påfoglars nytta.—*The use of Pea-fowls.*   Some English *gentlemen* kept at their own houses a great many Peafowls, Peahens, but particularly Peacocks, which they did, partly because these fowls are very beautiful and showy, partly and principally because their young are one of the best flavoured steaks, **stekar,** which can be desired.   They are fed in the winter time with corn in the same way as hens.

Rena gålf, etc.—*Clean floors, etc.*—English women generally have the character of keeping floors, steps, and such things very clean.   They are not particularly pleased if anyone comes in with dirty shoes, and soils their clean floors, but he ought first to rub his shoes and feet very

clean, if he would be at peace with them in other things.
Hence it is that outside every door there stands a fixed
iron, on which the men scrape the mould, and other dirt
off their shoes before they step in. The women leave in
the passage their *pattins*, that is, a kind of wooden shoes
which stand on a high iron ring. Into these wooden
shoes they thrust their ordinary leather, or stuff, shoes
(when they go out) and so go by that means quite free from
all dirt into the room. In the hall or passage, and afterwards at every door, though there were ever so many one
within the other, there lies a mat, **matta, täcke,** or something else, to still more carefully rub the soil off the shoes,
so that it is never, in short, sufficiently rubbed off.

[T. I. p. 170.] *The* 19*th March,* 1748.

Frukost, *Breakfast,* which here in England was
almost everywhere partaken of by those more comfortably
off, consisted in drinking Tea, but not as we do in
Sweden, when we take a quantity of hot water on an
empty stomach, without anything else to it, but the
English fashion was somewhat more natural, for they ate
at the same time one or more slices of wheat-bread,
which they had first toasted at the fire, **half-stekt vid
Elden,** and when it was very hot, had spread butter on
it, and then placed it a little way from the fire·on the
hearth, so that the butter might melt well into the bread.
In the summer they do not toast the bread, but only
spread the butter on it before they eat it. The cold
rooms here in·England in the winter, and because the
butter is then hard from the cold, and does not so easily
admit of being spread on the bread, have perhaps given
them the idea to thus toast the bread, and then spread
the butter on it while it is still hot. Most people pour a
little cream or sweet milk into the teacup, **brukas, at
slå litet grädda eller söt mjölk i Thee-kuppen,**

when they are about to drink the tea. The servants in
London also commonly get such a breakfast, but in the
country they have to content themselves with whatever
else they can get.

Middags-måltiden. *Dinner* did not here consist of
one particular kind of food, any more than it does among
other peoples : but still the English nation differed somewhat particularly from others in this ; that butchers'
meat formed with them the greater part of the meal, and
the principal dishes. The meat is prepared in various
ways ; yet generally speaking it is either boiled or roasted.
When I say that it was boiled, let no one imagine that it
was made into soup, **lagt i såppa,** for what we in
Sweden call **supan-mat** seems hardly ever to be in use
among Englishmen. [T. I. p. 171.] Thus, all kinds of
soups, **soppor,** call them what you will, as well as **gröt,**
välling, and nearly all kinds of **mjölk-mat,** &c., in the
houses of most Englishmen, are entirely unknown. Thus,
it is that in England at dinner-time they hardly ever use
spoons, **sked,** for anything but pouring the *sauce* on the
" steak," **än at ösa** "saucen " **på stek ;** to take turnips,
potatoes, carrots, &c., from the dish, **fatet,** and lay them
in abundance on their plates. It is indeed true that one
sometimes gets a kind of **köttsoppa,** or *broth*, as it is
called, but it is more nearly a **kött-spad** than a **kött-**
soppa. Boiled meat, **kokadt kött,** is here used in the
same way as we use a **kokadt skinka** (boiled ham)
bringstycke (brisket), etc. **Oxkött** is called *beef ;* **kalf-**
kött, *veal ;* **får-kött,** *mutton ;* **fläsk,** *pork.* No *Ragouts,*
Fricasees, **Plåckfink** (Ortolans), &c., does one ever
see in their houses, but the meat is cooked in large
pieces. Roast meat, **Stek,** is the Englishman's *delice*
and principal dish. It is not however always roasted,
stekt, to the same hardness as with us in Sweden. The
English roasts, **stekarne,** are particularly remarkable

for two things. 1. All English meat, whether it is of Ox,
Calf, Sheep, or Swine, has a fatness and a delicious taste,
either because of the excellent pasture, **betet,** which
consist of such nourishing and sweet-scented kinds
of hay as there are in this country, where the cultivation of meadows has been brought to such high
perfection, or some way of fattening the cattle known
to the butchers alone, or, for some other reason.
2. The Englishmen understand almost better than
any other people the art of properly roasting a joint,
konsten, at väl steka en stek, which also is not
to be wondered at; because the art of cooking as practised
by most Englishmen does not extend much beyond roast
beef and plum pudding, **stek och P.** *Pudding* in the
same way is much eaten by Englishmen, yet not so often
as butchers' meat, for there are many meals without
pudding. I do not believe that any [T. I., p. 172]
Englishman, who is his own master, has ever eaten a
dinner without meat. *Puddings* are prepared here in
manifold ways, with or without raisins, **Russin;** currants,
Corinther, and such like things in it, but they all deserve
the credit of being well prepared. *Potatoes* are now very
much used together with the roast meat, **stek.** They are
cooked as we cook turnips, and either put on the same
dish as the meat or on a special one. A cup of melted
butter stands beside it, to pour on to them. When they
have *boiled meat,* whole carrots are laid round the sides of
the dish. Cucumbers, **gurkor,** are much used with their
roast meat as before described; also several kinds of
green vegetables, as lettuce, **lactuc,** salad, **sallat,**
sprouts, **grön-kål,** and other cabbage, **kål,** prepared
mostly like lettuce or spinach, **spinat,** &c. Turnips are
here used in exactly the same way as potatoes. There
is also eaten much green peas when they can be had;
but otherwise than green, beans and peas are very

seldom eaten. *Cider*, **äppel-mos,** is also much drunk with roast meat. Their *pies*, which are mostly a kind of **tärtor,** *tarts* and *pastry*, are also sometimes seen. Cheese, **ost,** nearly always concludes the meal, **måltiden.** Commonly, there is set on the table, whole, a large and strong cheese, and each person cuts what he likes from it. **Mjölk-mat** is hardly ever seen at their meals, either dinner or supper, except what is taken in puddings, and in *tea* in the morning. Butter, **smör,** is seldom placed on the table. Their drinks are various. Those who can afford it mostly drink wine, others ale, **öl,** cyder, " swag," or small beer, **svagdricka,** but the favourite drink —**lifdryk**—of all the Englishmen is *Punch.* After meal times one generally sits for an hour at the table, or at least as long as till certain toasts, **skålar,** have been drunk by all, such as the King's health, the Prince [T. I., p. 173.] of Wales, the Royal Family, absent friends, &c.

Afton-måltid, *supper,* is taken by some Englishmen, but by others, never. It is, however, with those who eat it, a very sparing meal. It seldom consists of more than one dish, which is commonly butchers' meat, for the most part roasted, and a little cheese after it. It often consists only of cold meat, and that which is over from dinner, **middagen.** As Englishmen eat a late breakfast and a late dinner, **sent Frukost och sent Middag,** they do not require such a heavy supper.

[Kalm was at Woodford and Little Gaddesden from Mar. 20, to Ap. 21, 1748.]

[T. I. p. 366.] *The 21st April,* 1748.

In the morning I went from Woodford into London. *Mr. Abraham Spalding* then introduced me to *Mr. Ellicot*, F.R.S., who was now reckoned one of the best clock-makers in London, both for watches for the fob, **Byx-säck-Ur,** and other clocks. In one of his rooms he showed me several of the clocks he had made, the ingenuity of some being exceeded by that of others. Towards evening, I accompanied him to the great patron of Natural History and lover of learned men, *Mr. Peter Collinson,* F.R.S., who afterwards took me with him to the Royal Society, which meets every Thursday at five o'clock in the afternoon. A little time after I had entered, the Secretary read out a notice, **sedel eller** *Bill,* containing the announcement that " a Swedish *gentleman* of " the name of KALM had been introduced to see the Royal " Society by *Mr. Collinson,* Fellow of the same Society." Here were read out " Observations on the variation of " the Magnetic Needle " [by Mr. George Graham, F.R.S.] " observations on a *Coccionella,* which had damaged trees " in Ireland " [by the Revd. Philip Skelton.] A communication from *Mr. Bradley* that he had seen a comet, etc. [This last is not recorded in the *Phil. Trans.* for 1748. J. L.]

A little after 7 o'clock the meeting was concluded, when the Fellows went home by degrees. Mr. Collinson at once introduced me to Dr. Mortimer, secretary of the Royal Society, and to *Mr. Catesby,* author of the precious and costly work on the Flora and Fauna of Carolina in America. [In the Brit. Mus. the only edition is Catesby (M.) *Nat. Hist.* of Carolina, 2 vols., folio, London, 1771.]

[T. I. p. 367.] *The 22nd April,* 1748.

A great part of this day was devoted to seeing rarities in *London.* *Mr. Warner* gave me his company the whole day to show me the same. Among several other noteworthy objects, I reckon in particular the following: King Charles the 1st on horse-back, all in bronze. The place where King Charles I. had his head cut off. King James II. in bronze. Westminster Abbey Church, where

c

the kings of England are crowned and buried. We saw here the royal tombs, among which Queen Elizabeth's and the beheaded Scottish Queen Mary's, King Henry VIII.'s and King William III.'s tombs were well worth seeing. An old chair, **stol,*** was shown in this church, which was very badly made, on which all the later English kings, for a period of several centuries, have sat when they were crowned. Many a poor old woman with only one room has a better and more handsomely made chair, **stol,** than this; but for the sake of its great age, because it had been brought from Scotland as long ago as the 13th century by King Edward I., and on account of the prophecy about the stone, **sten,** which lies in this chair, **stol :**

Ni fallat fatum, Scoti quocunque locatum,
Invenient lapidem Regnare tenentur ibidem.

it is held in so high esteem. There is seldom anyone, who now sees it, who has not the curiosity to sit upon it. At the coronations this chair is overdrawn with costly cloths. Another chair stands beside it, which was made when King William III. and his Queen Mary were both crowned at one time. Besides this we saw Sir Isaac Newton's tomb, **graf,** and the monument erected near it to his memory. One thing struck me particularly—[T. I. p. 368]—that they not only erected here monuments and epitaphs to such well-deserving men as had been buried in this church, but also in honour of such as had their resting place elsewhere; even for such as had not been of the English nation, and perhaps had never been in England, but either through heroic actions, or their learned writings, had won the love and esteem of the English nation.

We afterwards saw both Houses of Parliament, the upper and the under. The place where they impeached,

---

* " *Solium regale* " Ov. Fasti. VI. 353, and in four other places. [J. L.]

anklagade, the Scottish lords [Lovat, Kilmarnock and Balmerino] for the late rebellion was examined; St. James's Park, the Royal Palace, &c., Chelsea *Hortum Botanicum*, which is one of the principal ones in Europe. Here we found the learned Mr. Miller, who is *Horti Præfectus* of the same.

In the evening I was at the house of Dr. Mortimer, secretary of the Royal Society. Here I met the great *Ornithologus* Mr. Edward, who had published a book on birds in the English language, with matchless copper plates, all in life-like colours, so that it looked as if the bird stood living on the paper. He had now with him several drawings of a number of rare birds from several districts, which he had hit off incomparably well, and intended to publish. *

To write with a lead pencil, so that it may not be rubbed out.

Mr. Warner told me that if one writes with a lead pencil on clean paper, and, as soon as he has written, dips the paper softly and carefully in clean water, and afterwards leaves it to dry thoroughly, all that has been written with the lead pencil will be very difficult [T. I. p. 369] to rub out, but sticks to the paper nearly as fast as if it had been written with ink.

[Paragraph about **Liktornar**, omitted.]

The 24th April, 1748.

Sjö-Rofvaren *Angria. The device of the Sea-rover Angria to make ships sail fast.*

Captain Shierman, who had lived in the East Indies for a period of fourteen years, had in the same period had the ill luck to be once taken by the notorious sea-rover

---

*George Edwards (c. 1693—1773), F.R.S. 1757, began to publish his "Natural History of Birds" in 1743. He presented to the Brit. Mus. the Dutch picture containing a drawing from life of the Dodo, from which most modern representations are taken. [F. W. L.]

*Angria,** in which captivity he had been for more than
two years [T. I. p. 370.] before he had made his escape.
He told us what means this sea-rover used to make his
ships sail very fast, so that no European ship could get
away from him, so that he could not overtake it, **med
mindre han ju skulle fâ det fast,** which consisted in
this, that he never kept any of his ships in the sea over a
month; after the lapse of which time he had it carried
into some dock, tapped off the water, and afterwards
made them polish the ship quite smooth and slippery
with cocoa-nuts which were cloven in two.   With these
cocoa-nuts the ship was polished on the outside, that is
to say, the part of the ship which was under water,
so long that there was not much left of the cocoa-
nut; and as the cocoa-nut has at the same time an
abundance of oil in it, so the surface of the ship was
doubly polished and made slippery, **glatt och halt.**
First the cocoa-nut, by its hardness, made the ship in the
polishing quite smooth and polished, **slätt och glatt,**
and secondly, the oil of the cocoa-nut made it so slippery,
halt, that it went incredibly fast through the water, and
had from it very little resistance.   After the lapse of a
month the oil began to diminish, and a number of *Testacea,*
or snails, **snäckor,** mussels, **musslor,** and such-like
shell-fish, **skal djur,** fastened on to the ship, from which
cause the ship took to going somewhat slower; wherefore
he at once had it drawn up on the land, or carried it into
a dock, made them scrape off that which had fastened
upon it, and polish it, as has been said.   In this way he
put himself in a position that no European ship could

---

*The piratical state, founded by Konna Ji Angria, in the middle of the
XVIIth century, flourished for more than 100 years, though the English,
Portuguese and Dutch tried to destroy it.   Col. Clive and Admiral Watson
at last succeeded, and on the 13th February, 1757, took Geriah, then the chief
stronghold of the Angrias, and broke their power.   [F. W. L.]

escape him, after he had once caught sight of it. All his ships were of oak. His strong castle on the land made him and his ships safe, if any naval power, **sjö-magt,** should attempt to chastise him. In outward appearance he was very handsome, was somewhat cruel, **grym,** especially towards the captives, whose [T. I. p. 371] heads he very often had cut off for his amusement. He died when he was only 30 odd years old, and left his trade to his brother, and to his sons, whom he had by his many wives.

The 25th April, 1748.

Description and use of the White Stone which is here called Portland Stone.

This kind of stone is much used, particularly in London and the neighbourhood, for house building and other purposes, and takes its name from the Isle of *Portland.* It is a white, or white and slightly inclining to yellowish, and sometimes a grey stone, a species of lime-stone, and is very like the *Freestone* which has been described above at *Tatternel,* in Bedfordshire. Doubtless it has the same origin as this. In this *Portland Stone* there is also found a very great abundance of *oyster* and *mussel shells,* and other *testacea.* It has also the property that when it is sawn or broken, it smells strongly of stink-stone, **orsten.** Everywhere in London where there are masons' yards, one sees carls, who sit and saw this stone asunder into different shapes. Their saw, which they use for this purpose, looks exactly like any other saw, but has no teeth, instead of which they employ sand, which effects the same purpose as teeth. The operation is thus: they take the sand which is found here near London, and sift it tolerably fine. After that it is blended with a little clay moistened with water, laid on a board, which is placed above the stone they intend to saw, so that the board slopes towards the *score,* **skåran,** or *rift,* **remnan,** which the saw makes. On the upper side of

[T. I. p. 372] the board there stands a can or bucket full of water, **kanna eller ämbare.** This vessel, **käril,** has a little pipe at the bottom, through which the water softly runs across the sloping board past the fine sand, a little of which it carries by degrees with it down into the score or saw cut, **i skåran,** when the saw requires it. Then the water carries down the sand which had lain in its way, but when all the sand has run off the board, the carls push more sand with a stick down to the water that it may bear it in the same way by degrees down into the saw score, **såg-skåran,** under the saw. Meantime, the carl draws the saw forwards and backwards, when this fine sand keeps continually falling, **faller alt för et,** under the saw blade, and thus performs the same service as teeth, to wear away and saw the stone. They said the reason why they do not use teeth on their saws, is that the teeth would bite so hard and fast, that no one would be able to keep up the sawing. With other tools used by masons, **sten huggare,** they prepare and fashion this stone in manifold ways. The greatest part of St. Paul's Church is built of this stone, right up to the top; also, the Abbey Church of Westminster; indeed, nearly all other Churches, as well as the high so-called *Monument.* Of this stone, also large and magnificent gentlemen's houses are built, in London as well as out in the country. Besides that, grave-stones, outside window-frames, and the lintels, jambs and arches of doors, paving stones for floors, and curb-stones for footpaths at the sides of streets where no one drives, are made of this stone. It is used also to cover garden walls with, and walls round properties, for posts along the sides of the streets to prevent coachmen and carters from driving on to the path where people walk, for posts round fireplaces, chimney-posts, for window sills of buildings, for garden rollers [T. I. p. 373], for posts under ricks, and for stone steps, **trapp-stenar.** Of this stone, also, those wonderful bridges, London Bridge and Westminster Bridge, are built. Also, all milestones are made of it. In short, this *Portland Stone* is here used for everything for which the stones of Gottland,* **öland,** and the flaggy firestone, **tälg-stenen,** of Kinnekulle can be used.

The 26th April.

[Paragraph " *Præservativ* mot **Rödsot** " omitted.]

Dikes-broar af Tegel. *Brick Bridges over Ditches.*

I saw nearly everywhere in the places which lie around London, that where any water came to run under the highway, **landsvägen,** or also any other road, they had instead of any other bridge, made a bridge of brick, **en bro af tegel.** They had dug there a very deep ditch, walled and arched a bridge with bricks, and afterwards filled up with earth the part over the arch, so that the road was even and flat all the way across it, so much so that there was little sign of any bridge. [T. I. p. 374.] They had also managed in the same way, when any little beck or runnel, **bäck eller rännel,** came to flow though any earth-wall, **mull vall,** which had been cast up round meadows, arable fields and market gardens, or when it passed under any house, &c., so that the water there always ran under and through small arched channels of brick. It were much to be wished that we, in Sweden, should follow the same custom, for experience here shows that brick bridges last a long time, and from this it is clear that their arch, when it is properly made, is strong enough, **kunna nog hålla,** to drive upon.† There can

---

* "Civility and courtesy, *en passant,* are indigenous to the limestone strata of Gottland." Sylvanus. *Rambles in Sweden and Gottland.* London, 1847, 8vo. p. 156. [J. L.]

† This now reads as a gentle satire. There are few such "country bridges" without a notice that they are only strong enough for ordinary traffic, as distinguished from traction engines. [J. L.]

hardly be any land where larger carts and wagons are used, and heavier loads are laid on them than in England, where three times as much, if not more, is loaded on a public coach, **en for-vagn,** as in Sweden. However, I have seen such bridges everywhere in use where I have travelled in England, in Hertfordshire, Bedfordshire, Buckinghamshire, Essex, Middlesex, Surrey and Kent. We could scarcely make a better use of our abundant granites, **grå-stenar,** than they if they were employed for this purpose.

The 27th March, 1748.

To-day I went up inside the *Monument*, as it is called, in London, and inspected the same. Many would shudder to look down from such a height, and wonder how so high and narrow a pillar of stone, which is hollow within, so that one can go up by steps inside it to the top, has been able to stand for so many years steady and firm. It seems, however, that those who live round about it on all sides, have difficulty in controlling their fears for the same in heavy storms, but further on more shall be given about this.

[T. I. p. 375.]

To get an abundance of Kitchen Garden Plant Seeds.

The market gardeners around London have commonly the custom that they do not employ their time in sowing and cultivating all sorts of garden and kitchen garden produce, but they mostly keep to something special. Thus some are only used to sow beans, peas and spinach, **spinat,** and leave out the other vegetables. Others again do not trouble themselves about those, but propagate other plants. Some do not devote themselves to **fråga ej efter,** the planting and cultivation of any particular plants to sell for household use, but devote all their time and labour to sowing all kinds of plants tor kitchen and flower market gardens, **för köks och blomster kryddgården,** so as to provide themselves with seed, which they afterwards sell, and make their living out of that alone. Other gardeners, **trägårds mästare,** only make it their business to keep **träscholor,** or *nurseries,* in which they have all kinds of young trees to sell, and so forth, so that it often happens, for example, that one of the gardeners who has only laid himself out for tree-planting, has not sown vegetables in his garden. Amongst those who exclusively devoted themselves to sowing all kinds of plants for the purpose of getting their seeds for sale, was Mr. Gordon, who had before been gardener to the famous *Sherard.* While I was in his market garden I noticed that the earth and mould, which he mostly used for his plants, was meagre enough in comparison with what is generally used in a kitchen garden, **köks-krydd-gård.** This was that the plants might not shoot much in leaf, but give a large quantity of seed, for a fat earth causes the plants to grow luxuriantly in stalk and blade, but there result therefrom few or no seeds, and *vice versâ,* for the same thing happens here as in *regno animali,* a fat hen lays few eggs.

[T. I. p. 376.]

At rätt *propagera Arbutus* **af frön.** *The proper way to raise Arbutus from seed.*

Mr. Gordon told me that there are very few nurserymen who can raise, **fort planta,** *Arbutus folio serrato,* C. B. from seed, for it comes up well enough after it has been sown from seed, but when it is transplanted it commonly dies. Mr. Gordon's plan for this was that he sowed the seed in a forcing bed, **dref-bank,** and as soon as its plants came up, he transplanted them; for if he waited longer, they commonly died when they were moved to another place, a thing which few people know.

[T. I. p. 378.]   *The 29th April, 1748.*

Hattar of Tagel.   *Hats of horsehair.*

Several ladies in this place had hats which were made
of snow-white horsehair and looked incomparably well.

The dome of St. Paul's.

At mid-day I went with Mr. Warner and Captain
Shierman up *St. Paul's* **Kyrko-torn** to see the *prospect*
round London from thence. We ascended the same
right up to the top by steps, **trappor.** The tower is all
built of white Portland stone which is full of all sorts of
petrified bivalve shells, **musslor.** Farther on more
shall be given about St. Paul's Church and Tower.

From the highest gallery, **Från öfversta** *galleriet,*
of this tower was a matchless view on all sides if only the
air had got to be clear, but the thick coal smoke, which
on all sides hung over the town, cut off the view in
several places. From it we could count a very large
number of Churches in London, that is to say, something
over 60, all of which had towers, and could be distinguished from the other large houses.

**Innanhvalfvet eller kåpan på detta stora
torn, som är inne uti Kyrkan,** the inside of the dome
of this great tower, which has galleries round about it on
the inside, is particularly remarkable for this, that if one
sets his mouth close to the wall and whispers something,
hviskar någon ting, at one of the doors, which go
in to the dome, and another person at the same time sets
his ear to the wall at one of the other doors which are
on the opposite side of the dome, he hears every word
that is whispered, **hör den hvart ord, som hviskas,**
very plainly and distinctly, as when one speaks through
a long small pipe or *tube*; but if he takes his ear from the

wall, nothing at all is heard, **höres alsintet,** although the other person whispered as loud as before.

[T. I. p. 379.] *The 30th April,* 1748.

Mull-vallar omkring ängar, köks-krydd-gårdar, etc. *Earth-walls around meadows, market gardens, &c.*

A number of small enclosed meadows, pastures, and market-gardens, lie on all sides round and close in to London, and part of them also in the suburbs. Instead of fences, plank-fences, walls or other kind of hedge around all these, high and thick earth-walls were cast up. These earth-walls consist of the same soil, **jordmon,** as is found on the meadows, &c., viz., of a brick-coloured clay, **tegel-färgad lera,** with much *gravel* and *Pebble-stones* amongst it. In one place and another in the suburbs they had cast up walls around the market-gardens, for the most part merely of the dirt which had been shovelled together on the roads close by. The height of these earth-walls was various, mostly 6 feet, sometimes, though seldom, as much as 8 feet, yet often only 4 feet or 3 feet, but few below that. There was commonly a ditch on the outer side of them. The wall was broader at the bottom, but afterwards narrowed more and more up to the top where it was sometimes scarcely 6 inches broad. The breadth or thickness down at the ground, 8, 6, 5, or 4 feet, according to the height of the wall. When such a wall became old, it fell down in some places, for which reason it should be very often repaired. The height and inclination of the wall, together with the ditch outside it, prevented any cattle from getting over it as long as it was whole. By this means wood was spared, and no more time or trouble was required for repairing these earth-walls than with us

in Sweden is yearly occupied with our **gärdes-gårdar.**
Still it seems that such mud walls would not do well for
fences with us, because our great cold [T. I. p. 380] in
winter and the thaw, **tjälen,** would tear them down, so
that they would require too much repairing. When these
English mud walls began to tumble down in any place,
they took some of the earth which was dug up in the
ditch beside the wall, and daubed it over the sides of the
wall till they were quite flat, or if the hole was large it
was filled up with the earth just named. They are very
anxious about this, that grass and plants should grow on
the sides of the walls, for it hinders rain and frost in the
winter from injuring the walls so much; because these
plants and their roots bind the earth, and besides that
overgrow it so that it then tumbles down less.

The 1st of May, 1748.

Meadow-inclosures round London and their grass-growth.

We said just now that on most sides of London, close
in to the town, there lie among other inclosures several
inclosed meadows or pastures, **ängs-täppor eller
beteshagar,** with high earth-walls round them. The
grass-growth in them was very thick and luxuriant,
nearly everywhere, and was now a foot high or more.
We saw here to-day plants of *Alopecurus culmo erecto*, 52 [*A.
pratensis*, Meadow Fox-tail grass], which was nearly two
feet high, and its spikes, *spicæ*, were everywhere out in
flower. The grand opportunity for getting all kinds of
choice manure here in London to spread on these
meadows is the thing that especially contributes to this
fertile growth. Their owners derived a very large profit
from this source, for some of these pastures were let to
those who kept cows, to supply the town with milk;
others were hired out to butchers, to keep there for a

time the cattle they had bought for slaughter; some to
brewers or others, to turn their horses in. [T. I. p. 381.]
A fixed charge was paid per day for every animal that
had freedom to go there, which for the whole year
mounted up to a considerable sum. On the north side
of London in particular there were the most meadows, in
which there was the most beautiful grass-growth which
can be. By the 18-20 May, the grass-growth was as long
as in our best meadows in Sweden at the close of July.
It was also at the afore-named time in May that they
everywhere began to mow those meadows, which through
the spring had not been baited by any animals.
Bromus panicula erecta coarctata (Linn. *Flor. Svec.* 87)
[Banks. MS. "varietas secalini;" **Sw. Raklosta**].
And the above-named *Alopecurus* formed nearly all the
beautiful growth on these meadows, although red or
white clover, **väpling,** had sometimes mixed with it.
It is said that the owners commonly manure them every
autumn, in September and October, with the dung and
dirt which is collected in London in the streets, and is
laid outside the town in large heaps, from which they
afterwards carry it out on to their meadows, which particularly contributes to this their luxuriant growth.

The 2nd May, 1748.

To hinder thieves from climbing over garden walls. /

The fence, **hägnad,** which was seen here around
gardens and kitchen gardens, was commonly walls of
4, 6, or 8 feet high. In some places, though seldom near
London, there were hedges of several thorny trees. In
some places only were plank fences seen; but walls were
most used, partly because they were the most durable,
and could best fence off violent and cold winds, partly
because the twigs of several fruit trees could best be

spread out and fastened on to them when one wished to
force them to fruit early [T. I. p. 382] which has been
treated of above. But to prevent thieves from being
able to climb over the walls, they had daubed clay,
smetat ler, on the top of it 6 inches high, and 6 inches
to a foot wide. In this clay, when it had only just been
laid on the wall, they had everywhere stuck at random,
a large number of bits of broken bottles, **bouteiller,** glass,
glass-decanters, **glas-flaskor,** and such like, which turned
their sharp edges, **hvassa kanter,** upwards and towards
all sides, and prevented anyone who had the desire to
climb over the wall from taking hold of it with the bare
hands, lest these sharp and edged glass-bits should cut
his hands all to pieces ; and when he in climbing over
should get so far as to sit on the wall, he might get so
much cut that he would not be so soon cured after it. In
England it is very easy to get such broken glass-bits at
inns and beershops, of which there are here so large a
number.

The 3rd May, 1748.

Hjelp för Präst-barn. *Help for Priests' Children.*

To-day *Vocal and Instrumental Musique* was performed
in St. Paul's Cathedral, by more than 100 performers,
where a considerable number of people assembled to
hear it. No one was admitted who had not paid a fixed
charge, which was regulated according to the place he
wished to have in the church. The money thus collected
was distributed to poor priests' children for their main-
tenance and education. The *London Gazette* related that
they collected to-day in this way something more than
£400 sterling. This which took place to-day was only a
Præludium to a great *Musique* which was fixed for the following Thursday, or the 5th *hujus* in St. Paul's Cathedral,
when the Archbishop [T. I. p. 313] of Canterbury, nearly

all the Bishops who were in London, together with an innumerable concourse of people, were assembled there to hear the beautiful *Musique*, which was esteemed the principal of all *Musique*, which are held yearly in London. The Friday's *Gazettes* afterwards made known that they collected somewhat over £700 sterling in the day, which was all devoted to the education and help for both sexes of poor priests' children.

Ceremonies at the beginning of May.

Now was seen at many places in the streets a custom, **plägsed,** which milk-girls practise here in London, at the beginning of May, or at the advent of summer. They had bound together several vessels, **käril,** such as cans, pint pots, drinking-cups, **kannor, stop, skålar, &c.,** which were mostly of silver, but sometimes also of tin, **bleck eller tenn,** and made with them a device, **skapnad,** either like a *Pyramid*, or like a man, or most frequently like a woman, or also in some other fashion. Some of these images, **bilder,** were decked with a number of flowers. They were carried either on a barrow or on the head. A spelman, or fiddler, who played the viol, always accompanied them, together with several girls. They mostly stood in front of each house where they were accustomed to offer milk for sale, when the fiddler fiddled, **då spelmannen spelte,** and one or more of the girls danced. The usage was that after they had done this, they received pence from the persons at whose house they danced. They began this on the 1st May, and kept it up for some days.

The 4th May, 1748.

In the morning I visited the Duke of Argyle, a man who was a very great lover of *Mathematique* and Natural Science [T. I. p. 384] but in particular of *Botanique*, and the branch of that science which is called *Dendrologie*, which treats of trees. After that I spent a great part of the day at the house of *Dr. Mitchell*, who was born in Virginia, in North America, and had spent a great part of his life there, and was thus well acquainted with all the circumstances of that country. Among other things he gave me the following account, which I afterwards found was correct, when I went to America.

[**Vax af et slags Pors**. Deferred. *See* AMERICAN NOTES below.]

[T. I. p. 393.] *The 9th May*, 1748.

In the morning I returned to London.

Arundo vulgaris **til skjul i köks-krydd-gârdar.**
Reeds as screens* in market gardens.

Instead of other fences it was here a very common practice to employ *reeds*, **rör,** as a shelter or screen, **til skjul eller skärm,** for the plants which might grow in the heat of the sun, **i solbaddet.** To this end they had taken reeds, Arundo, 99 [Banks, MS., Phragmites], set them up perpendicularly, and made of them as it were a paling-fence, **et plank,** in a straight line to the length required. The reeds were here laid quite close together, and nearly two inches thick. Above and below were two thin rods, **smala stänger,** between which the ends of the reeds were set and bound fast with bast. The ends of these rods were bound fast to poles, **pâlar,** driven down into the ground. Often instead of any other fence, **hägnad,** around the kitchen gardens they had nothing but these reeds set up in the way just described.

Huru vägar omlagades. *How roads were repaired.*

I have before said that the roads cannot last long on account of their heavy carts and wagons, which with

---

* " Screen, skreen, a device to keep off the wind, hail, &c." Bailey's *Dictionary*, 1753.

their wheels soon cut deep ruts, **hål,** down into the ground. To mend these after they have once been made, all the road was hacked up with pickaxes, **hackor.** After that they took a large harrow on which a weight was laid, with which they afterwards harrowed all the road smooth and even, so that when the horses come on to it walking, they often chose a new track, **spår,** so that the wheels thus came to go on harder places than before. The road is also often harrowed without being first hacked up, but this is only done when the tracks of the cart wheels, **spåren efter kärr hjulen,** are not particularly [T. I. p. 394] deep. Else it was much the practice here that when the road became uneven it was hacked up, and the hacked-up ground was carried to the wheel-ruts, **hålen efter hjulen,** and filled into them.

The 10th May, 1748.

Köks-krydd-gårdar, deras hägnad, ans, etc.

Market-Gardens, their fences, cultivation, &c.

I have named above (p. 386 *orig.*) that the land around *Chelsea* is almost entirely devoted to nursery and vegetable gardens. The same is true of the land on all sides round about *London*, that it is mostly used as pleasure-gardens, nurseries, and market gardens: because **det Stora** *London* (the vast L.) and the frightful number of people which there crawl in the streets, **krälar på gatorna,** pays the market gardeners many fold their labour and outlay. These nurseries and market gardens are surrounded either with earth-walls or walls, **mull-vallor eller murar,** or wooden fences, **trä-plank,** or living hedges of trees, or with walls of oxhorn, of which more below. The earth-walls have been described above (p. 379 *orig.*), the walls, **Murarna,** on p. 381 *orig.,* although the greatest part of them have not such glass-

D

bits inlaid on the top. All these walls are built of brick.
Plank-fences made of boards were also used here in many
places, but the boards which were used for this purpose
were no other than those they had bought from old
broken up ships and boats, **Skepp, farkostar, och
båtar,** which were still quite full of nails. Thus they
knew in this woodless district how to make use of old
ships and boats after they had become useless for the sea.
They also availed themselves very much of hedges as
fences. Hawthorn was the tree of which most hedges
consisted; but besides this I also saw hedges of elm,
especially of a [T. I. p. 395] small kind of it, also of yew,
maple, sloe, and several others, **Barrlind, Äfvenbok,
Slån, &c.** In gardens no tree was so much used for
hedges as yew, **Barrlind,** *Taxus,* which admitted of
being clipped and managed in various ways. How they
used reeds for a shelter has just been told (p. 393 *orig.*).
Besides ordinary vegetables there were planted in the
market gardens which lay nearest the high road all kinds
of flowers, which the passers by bought and carried away
with them. I saw also the whole of this season both
men, old women and girls, **Karlar, käringar, och
pigor,** walk or sit in the streets of London with baskets
full of all kinds of flowers, bound in small bunches,
knippor, which they offered to the passers-by, who also
bought them in numbers. The vegetables which were
most numerous in the market gardens at this season were
beans, peas, cabbages of different sorts; leeks, *Purio,*
Allium porrum, L; **Pip-lök,** *A. fistulosum,* L; **Gräs-
lök,** *A. schœnoprasum,* L., chives; radishes, lettuce (?)
" **Sallad** "; asparagus, **sparis,** spinach. The greater
part of these were sown in rows, so that they could more
easily clear away the weeds between them with English
hoes, **tvära hackor,** and keep the earth loose. Between
the rows of peas, beans and cabbages there was a distance

of 18 inches or 2 feet, and 6 inches to 9 inches or more between the plants in the row. They hoed here entirely with small light English hoes, and the mould was moved on to the stalks of the plants more and more as they grew, so that they stood as it were **i kupor,*** that is " banked up." Peas were growing on pea-sticks. The tops of the stalks were cut off the beans so that they might shoot more into pods of fruit. Between the plants which were sown thicker the earth was cleared of weeds and hoed up with quite small hoes of about 2 inches broad, and with a handle, **skaft,** 2 feet long ; but it cost enough to the one who hoed, who was thus obliged to go very crook-backed, **krokryggig,** and stooping, **luta,** the whole day.

[T. I. p. 396.] *The 11th May.*

In the morning we walked out to see the places which lay on the S.W. side of *Chelsea,* over the bridge at *Fulham,* and went some distance on the other side of the last-named place. At all places between *Fulham* and *Chelsea,* which is a distance of two English miles, and round about Chelsea, we saw little else than mere gardens, **Trä-gårdar,** and especially vegetable market-gardens, **köks-krydd-gårdar.** We have told about them before. Large brick houses, **stenhus,** which belonged to *gentlemen* and others were scattered here and there among the gardens, **Trä-gårdarna,** to which those who lived in London, now and then, especially on Saturday afternoons, went to take the fresh air and to have the advantage of tasting the pleasures of a country life.

Fulhams **Bro.** *Fulham Bridge* [*Putney B.*] Fulham is a *Parish* situated two miles from *Chelsea,* and four from London, to the S.W. In appearance it is a pretty town

---

* " Kupa. Amas de terre autour d'une plante."—Veste. *Lex* 1807. [J. L.]

with several smooth streets. All the houses are of brick, very beautifully built, some of which belong to *gentlemen* and **Herrskaper**, "Lordships," in London, are handsomely built. Round about this place the country is full of gardens, orchards and market-gardens, both for pleasure and use, and it can indeed be said that the country here is everywhere nothing but a garden and pleasance, **Trä och lust-gård.**

The river Thames runs close past this parish on the south side, so that the district can conveniently have *convoi* for passengers from London. Here there is a wooden bridge over the river, built on piles driven down into the bed. All those who walk or drive over it must pay bridge-money, **bro-penningar.** Each person who goes on foot pays a halfpenny, **en** *halfpence.*

[T. I., p. 397.]

Stora fält. *Large Common.*

On the other side of the Thames opposite Fulham there lay a large and tolerably flat and bare common, **fält,** which was abandoned to pastures. It was for the most part overgrown with *genista spinosa*, furze, which was now in its best flower, so that the whole common shone quite yellow with it. In one place only was it cut down, either for fuel or something else. In some places we saw ling here ; but it was quite small. May not the fertility and goodness of the soil be the reason of that ? And may it not rather thrive better on dry and meagre places, **torra och magra ställen.** I also saw small plats with *Reindeer moss*, **Ren mâssa** [*Lichen rangiferinus*], which also was very short. The soil was a brick-colored coarse sand, **tegel färgad grof sand,** with a little soil, **Svartmylla,** on the top. [Wimbledon Common and Putney Heath.]

At förekomma dam på vägar. *To prevent dust on roads.*

From the sun and strong west wind, the roads were now so dry that when vehicles, **vagnar,** and horses went on them there rose from them so much dust, **stoft och dam,** that it was very difficult to get along, for both eyes, mouth and nose were filled with it. Trees and plants by the wayside were covered with it. To remedy this we saw at one place a man driving a cart, **kärra,** which was made like a **bräd-lår,** or large wooden box, but had at the back a transverse row of small holes. This box, **kista,** was now full of water, and when a board at the back which stopped up the holes was raised the water ran out by degrees where the man drove, and made the road quite wet, so that the dust could no longer rise up. It was in front of a *gentleman's* house that he drove up and down the road with his cart. I afterwards saw at several places [T. I. p. 398] such carts used, especially when the King went up to Parliament.

[T. I. p. 403.] *The* 15*th May,* 1748.

In the afternoon I walked out on the North side of the town to see the country on that side. The land here was mostly divided into grass fields, **ängs-täppor.** Beautiful and very well-built villages, farm-houses, and buildings were scattered here and there amongst them These villages and houses were commonly surrounded with beautiful gardens. A multitude of people now streamed out here from all sides of London to enjoy their Sunday afternoon and take the fresh air. In all the aforesaid villages there was a superfluity of beer-shops, inns, and such-like houses, where those who came from the town rested. There were also small summer houses, **lust-hus,** built in the gardens, with benches and tables in them, **med bânkar och bord uti,** which were now all full of swarming crowds of people, **folk-skâckar,** of both sexes.

[T. I. p. 404.] *The 16th May,* 1748.

Ormar handterade med hânder. *Snakes handled with hands.*

We saw to-day as well as on the previous days a common man clad in rags, who had a large collection of living Vipers and snakes, **Hugg-ormar och Snokar,** which he went and carried about in the streets, **dem han gick och bar omkring på gatorna,** to show to folk for money, **at visa åt folk för penningar.** He could handle them with his hands quite quietly, and without the snakes offering in the least to bite him, **utan at Ormarne bödo det ringaste til, at hugga honom.** He had a bag, **påse,** in which he laid them, and when anyone gave him " en *halfpence,*" he took them out with his hands, either one after another or also by the hand-full, as many as he could hold. Often to awaken more astonishment, he stuffed either a viper or a snake whole into his mouth, **antingen en Huggorm eller en Snok helt och hållen in uti munnen på sig,** and kept his mouth shut for a little while, and then opened his mouth and let the snake crawl out of it. When he slipped them on the ground they sought to run away. He said he had sometimes been bitten in the thumb by them when he had caught them ; but he knew such an antidote for it, **et sådant bot derföre,** that it could not do him any harm ; yet he would not make known what it consisted in. That the *snakes,* **snokarne,** did not do him any harm was no wonder, but how he managed with the vipers, **men huru han bar sig åt med Huggor-marna,** I know not. This I saw, that they not only did not offer to bite him but also when a stick was pointed

at them, **dâ en käpp sattes ât dem,** or when some
one poked their heads with the end of his stick they
never bit at the stick. Some of the more forward of the
small crowd, sometimes dared to take hold of them
without the snakes attempting to bite them: whence
there seemed to be reason to believe that this man had
clipped off the teeth with which they [T. I. p. 405.]
bite. Such were our opinions about this, to-day. The
following day Dr. *Mitchel* paid him highly, when he made
known to Dr. Mitchel in what his art consisted, that he
could so carelessly handle the vipers; viz.: in this, that
when he had caught one of them fast, he had cut off the
two large teeth, which they, as a cat with its claws, can
shoot out and bite with, or draw back. After they have
lost them, they can do no further harm. He related that
sometimes when he had caught them, he had been bitten
by them, but that his antidote for that had been Snake-
Oil, **Orm-olja,** which he had made in this way, that he
had boiled the snake-fat, **Orm-ister,** to oil, which oil he
constantly carried with him in a glass bottle, and when
he was bitten, he smeared himself with this oil over the
place where he had been bitten, when he had no further
harm from it, after he had merely rubbed in the oil.*

---

* In M. Morin's *Reptiles et Poissons*, 144 pp., Paris, 8vo., is pp. 62-3 an
" Addition a l'article de la Vipere Commune" consisting of two extracts from
Valmont de Bomare, a contemporary of Kalm, of which the second is
"REMEDES CONTRE LA MORSURE DE LA VIPÈRE. Les remedes vulgaires
" contre la morsure de la vipère (p. 63) sont extérieures et intérieures. Les
" extérieures sont de lier promptement, si l'on peut, la partie au-dessus de la
" morsure, *to tie up if possible the part above the bite ;* d'approcher le plus près
" de cette morsure un morceau de fer rougi au feu, *to hold a piece of red hot
" iron close to the bite,* ou de brûler sur la plaie un peu de poudre à canon, *or
" to burn a little gunpowder on the wound,* ou bien enfin de scarifier la plaie et
" d'appliquer dessus de l'ail, du sel ammoniac pilés ensembles, *to scarify the
" wound and apply to it a mixture of garlic and sal ammoniac pounded together.*
" As an internal remedy, on avale l'alcali volatile pris à des doses assez fortes."
—(Valmont de Bomare.) [J.L.]

He said that among other things, the difference between
a viper and a snake, **Huggorm och en snok,** was
this that the viper when he sees that a human being
wishes to strike him dead, always holds the head higher
than the neck ; but a snake in the same case holds it
lower down than the neck.

[Defer a note on North America.]

[T. I. p. 408.] *The 18th May,* 1748.

At hindra damm på gator. *To prevent dust on roads.*

From the great drought which there had now been
for several days there rose a strong and thick dust in the
streets of the town ; but still more outside the same from
the grinding of horses, wagons and carts, so that one
could scarcely open his eyes, **så at en knapt . . . .**
kunde se up med ögonen, especially outside the
town. To somewhat prevent this in the streets of the
town, there were here and there men or boys who with
shovels cast about the water which had come to run out
of the pumps on to the street, and thus made the streets
wet. Those who had their shops close to each other,
strax bredevid, where there was much wheel traffic,
had the streets sprinkled in this way. On the places in
front of the houses, **platsar utanför hus,** where people
walked backwards and forwards, water was also spread
for the same reason.

[Defer the visit to *Sir Hans Sloane.*]

[T. I. p. 409.] *The 19th May,* 1748.

[Defer Friesland, &c.]

[T. I. p. 410] *Cedrus* **af** *Libanon* **burit frukt.** *Dr.*
Mortimer said that he had been out into the country to visit
an acquaintance, where some cedar trees from Lebanon
had been planted, one of which had now for the first time
borne fruit and had cones, **kottar.** It was planted there

from seed, fifty or fifty-two years since, and from the time
it was sown it has not been moved from the same place.
The others, which had been sown at the same time, but
afterwards moved, had not yet shown a sign of fruit.

The 20th May.

To-day we took a walk down to the Greenwich side on
the south side of the river Thames. In all our walks out
into the country, however often they occurred, we took
care to notice, **som fast ofta Skedde, togo vi noga
i akt,** what the grass growth in the meadows consisted
of, its state of luxuriance, with various things which belong
to the cultivation of meadows, **ängs-skötseln,** but as this
would take up too much room in a description of travels,
en Resebeskrifning, it is left for some other *Academic*
work.

Stängsel omkring krydd-gårdar åkrar, ängar, &c. *Fences around market-gardens, arable fields, meadows, &c.*

The palings and fences, **stängsel oct hägnad,** which
on this side, quite near to London, were used round
nursery and market gardens, arable, and meadows, **trä-
och köks-krydd-gårdar,** &c., were commonly such
mud-walls or clay-walls, **mull-valler,** as have been
previously described [p. 379, *orig.*]. In other places
there was a similar mud-wall, but still not so high,
on which the Elder tree, **Fläder-trä,** *Sambucus,* had been
planted, and which have made a thick and beautiful
hedge. By all these earth-walls there were commonly
ditches, which still, in this drought, had an abundance of
water in them.

[T. I. p. 411.] In some places on these walls there were
Willows, **pilar,** planted, about two or three fathoms from
each other, which had been cut off, or polled, about 12

feet above the ground, after which they had struck out a
multitude of new shoots, **telningar**, which were afterwards cut off again, **å nyo**, as often as they were required.
In other places, and everywhere somewhat farther from
town, here in *Kent*, they had hedges of hawthorn round
their *inclosures*, with which afterwards all kinds of leaf
trees had mingled themselves.

Beskaffenheten af högderna.

About three or four miles S.E. of *London*, there lay in
Kent some high hills side by side. These were long-
sloping on all sides, and consisted of earth, **jord.** I saw
on them, right up to the summit, either arable fields or
meadows all divided into small *inclosures* or **täppor,**
fenced with hawthorn hedges, with a number of other
trees among them. The soil, Jordmon, of which the
upper crust on these hills consisted, was the brick-
colored clay, which is found everywhere round *London*,
den tegel färgade leran som här omkring *London*
öfver alt finnes, blended with a finer or coarser sand
of the same colour. Some of these *inclosures* were sown
with wheat, others with barley ; some with peas and
vetches. A great part with beans. Some were laid
out as meadows, and now stood in an abundant crop of
grass. The earth, **jorden,** on all these hills commonly
looked as if it had been a fine loose *powdered brick,* **en
fin lös sönderstött tegel-sten.** The *prospect* from
them was **behagelig,** delightful. On the west was seen
the whole of London, how it lay and extended itself *in a
crook* along the river Thames, and made a show with its
many towers. [T. I. p. 412.] The top of *St. Paul's
Church* dome seemed to be almost the same height as these
hills. The coal smoke which constantly hangs over
London, sufficiently prevented me from seeing it clearly,
but it stood as in a fog, **tökn.** The ships which sailed

on the Thames could be seen quite well. The country all round resembled a garden, and its many hedges prevented me from seeing much into the fields. In *Kent* the country looked like a collection of wood-grown hills, **skog-beväxta högder,** with ploughed fields among them.

Hvetet. The wheat was sown in *stitches* or small ridges. Commonly, such a *rygg* was ten feet, sometimes, also, twelve feet broad, with water furrows between each rygg. No ditches were used on all the ploughed fields we saw to-day, except by the hedges. The height of the ridges in the middle was six inches, nine inches, or a foot higher than the bottom of the water furrows, and sloped towards both sides. The wheat here stood beautiful, no ears, **ax,** were yet seen. The barley, **kornet,** was sown in the same way as with us in Sweden, in *broad land.*

Ärterna, *Pease,* were all sown in rows, and there was always three feet and sometimes three feet six inches between the rows. They had with *hoes,* **hackor,** cleared away the weeds between the rows, and moved the loose mould, **mullen,** up towards the stalks of the peas. No peasticks, **ruskor,** or anything else had been laid here for the peas to climb up, but they were lying along the ground as they were large. It was a very convenient fashion to sow pease in this way in rows, **i rader,** for one could so very easily take away all the weeds with a rake, **ty en hade ganska lätt före, at med en kratta utöda ogräsen.** In the gardens on this side of the town we saw pease [T. I. p. 413] in the same way sown in rows; but then there was not commonly more than eighteen inches, two feet, or two feet six inches between the rows.

Bönorna, *Beans,* on these fields were all sown in *broad cast,* yet on ten feet wide *stitches,* but in the market gardens at *Southwark* the garden beans were all sown in rows two feet or two feet six inches between the rows. In some places in the gardens there was a number of asparagus beds, and beans were planted in the passages between them. *Vicia Sativa*, tares were always sown in *broad cast*, and not in rows, yet on ten feet broad *stitches*.

Huru får ränsa bårt ogräs emellan Bönor.

How sheep clear away weeds between beans.

In one of the *inclosures* which in the aforenamed manner were sown with beans, we remarked that they had turned in thirty odd sheep, **några och 30 får,** which went there and eat off the weeds between the beans, which weeds they ate up, and bit off quite close to the ground, but did the beans not the smallest harm. We spent a long time in carefully examining, **vi gingo länge och sågo med noga flit efter, der Fåren gingo midt ibland Bönorna,** where the sheep went amongst the beans, whether they had not touched them, but we could not mark a single leaf of them bitten. The weed which grew here in multitudes, and the principal weed was SINAPIS (Linn *Flor Svec.* 548—RAPISTRUM *Flore luteo* C.B. or the common **Åker-senapen** [Sinapis *Arvensis. Linn.*—Lilja, *Skanes Flora.* I 472; BRASSICA *Sinapistrum*, J. Hooker, *St. Fl.* 1870, p. 30. Charlock, at Aldbury, near Tring, "Curlock;" at Whitwell, Herts, "Carlock;" at Rusper, Suss; "Kelk," and in Sussex, generally "Kilk,"] together with some plants of **hvitrot*** (*Triticum*, Linn. *Flor. Svec.* 105), both of which the sheep ate greedily, especially the *Charlock* When the sheep had eaten to repletion they lay down among the beans to rest, **at hvila.†** They thus performed a double service, first,

---

* So on p. 387 *orig.* but elsewhere "Qvickrot" as in Linn *Fl. Sv,* 105.— *Trit. repens.* [J. L.]

† A verb preserved in Eng. "To while away the time." *Fr.* Chômer, to *rest*, 16 *Cent. Chaumer, Provençal,* Chaume, "the time when flocks 'rest:'" [J. L.]

that they cleared away the weeds, and secondly, that they manured the field by their droppings.

Växternas frodighet. *The luxuriance of the plants.*

On all sides around London, both near to the town and also [T. I. p. 414] somewhat farther from it, I remarked that a number of plants were commonly much more luxuriant and larger than with us in Sweden. Thus **karrborre-bladen [kard-borre,** Lilja, *Sk. Fl.* 565, *Lappa ; Arctium Lappa,* J. Hooker, *St. Fl.* 187, *Burdock Dut,* Klissen-kruid ; *Ger,* Klette, *Hoff,* 1791, I. 283 ; *Ital.* Bardana ; *Fr.* Bardane.] *Burdock leaves,* leaves of **kattost** (Malva) *Mallow;* so also Senecio Vulg., *ground-sel,* Aparine Vulg. [Galium Aparine L.] Urtica Urens maxima [U. *dioica.* L.] *great nettle ;* **hundfloka ["gul stormhatt,"** Veste ; *Aconitum Napellus* L. Monkshood] and several other such plants were double as large, if not more, as they commonly are in Sweden, which all seems to be a sign of the soil, and its richness hereabouts, partly natural, partly from long continued manuring and turning over.

The 21st May, 1748. *Sir Isaac Newton's* **Graf.**

Among other beautiful monuments which are erected in *St. Peter's* or *Westminster Abbey* Church here in London, where the Kings of England are both crowned and buried, there is also that which has been erected in memory of the great *Mathematicus* and *Philosophus,* Sir Isaac Newton.* He lies buried in the nave, **i främre delen,**† of the

---

* This touching dedication of KALM recalls the words of Hume—" The "severest scrutiny which NEWTON's theory has undergone, proceeds not "from his own countrymen but from Foreigners, and if it can overcome the "obstacles which it meets with at present in all parts of Europe, it will pro- " bably go down triumphant to the latest posterity."—ESSAY *on the Rise of the Arts and Sciences,* 1742.

† This shows that Kalm must have entered by the West door, now closed. [J. L.]

church immediately in front of the choir, **strax för choret,** where some of the old royal tombs are. Close above the grave and on the side towards the choir his *monument* is erected, where he himself lies carved in white marble, and rests on his right elbow, **och stödjer den högre handen under hufvudet.** Above him is a celestial globe, **himmels-glob,** carved also in white marble, on which the paths of the comets are set out in gilt lines,* **hvårpa** *Cometernas* **gång med förgylte** *Linier* **står utsatt,** also these words: "Dec. 24, 1680."†

Under the right elbow are four books *in Folio,* on which he rests. These books lie one upon another, and there is set forth on one side, **på ena sidan,** what they contain, viz.: on the highest stands the word "Divinity"; on the next under it, "Chronology"; then [T. I. p. 415] "Opticks"; lastly, "Philo. Prin. Math."‡ Down below him stand carved angels, **änglar,** [beautiful little boys], who hold mathematical instruments, &c. §

The inscription on the monument is this:—

H. S. E.
ISAACUS NEWTON, Eques auratus,
Qui animi vi prope divina
Planetarum Motus, Figuras,
Cometarum Semitas, Oceanique Æstus,
Suâ Mathesi facem præferente,

---

* These gilt lines have disappeared. [J. L.]

† This date has disappeared. For the great comet of 1680, see J. Herschel, Astron., Ed. 1867, Art. 573. [J. L.]

‡ These words have all disappeared. From the position of the *Folios,* they must have been gilded on the ends, or what would be the top-edges of the *Folios* if standing upright, as on the books shown in the Frontispiece to the 2nd Ed. of the *Dunciad,* 1729. [J. L.]

§ Mathematics. Thus says Hume: "Religion and Politics, and consequently "Metaphysics and Morals. All these form the most considerable branches of "Science. *Mathematics* and *Natural Philosophy,* which only remain, are not "half so valuable." ESSAY *on the Rise of the Arts and Sciences,* 1742. Time, that proves all things, has given another verdict. [J. L.]

Primus demonstravit ;
Radiorum lucis dissimilitudines,
Colorumque inde nascentium proprietates,*
Quas nemo antea vel suspicatus erat, pervestigavit,
Naturæ, Antiquitatis, S. Scripturæ, †
Sedulus, Sagax, fidus interpres,
Dei O.M. Majestatem Philosophia asseruit,
Evangelii Simplicitatem moribus expressit.
Sibi gratulentur Mortales
Tale tantumque extitisse
HUMANI GENERIS DECUS.
Nat. XXV. Dec. a.d. MDCXLII. Obiit XX. Mar. MDCCXXVI.

Around the Monument itself is an iron railing, **järn-galler.**‡ On one side of the monument there are these words : "Gul. Kent Pict. et Archit. invenit."; on the opposite side " Mich. Rysbrack, sculpsit."

On the grave-stone in the pavement there are these words :

" Hic depositum est

quod mortale fuit

ISAACI NEWTONI."

[T. I. p. 416.] *The 22nd May,* 1748.

In the afternoon I went with some Englishmen and the present Professor of Œconomy at Lund in Sweden, Herr Mag. Burmester, out to *Hampstead,* a little **" stad,"** or *town,* some few miles north of London, in a very delightful place, to which on Sundays, and **"vid vackert väder "** (in fine weather), a great many people ride or drive and walk in the summer to enjoy themselves.

Af hvad jordmon högderna omkring London **bestâ.** *Of what soil the hills round London consist.*

The hills, **Högderne eller jord-backarne,** which

---

* Newton discovered the polarization of light. † Kalm omits the "S" before "Scripturæ." ‡ There are no iron-railings now. [J. L.]

lie in the neighbourhood of *London*, on the Kent side as
well as on the Essex and other sides, resemble outwardly
to a great extent the hills in *Hertfordshire*, which commonly under the top soil, **öfra jord-skårpan,** consist of
bare chalk. Reasoning upon analogy I was inclined to
think that the hills in the neighbourhood of *London* also
consisted lower down of solid chalk,* and that only at
the top lay a thick crust of the brick-colored clay, which
occurs everywhere about here; but several people whom
I consulted about this denied utterly that there is any
chalk under these hills. To-day I got still farther evidence
that this seems to have the truth on its side, for Professor
Burmester told me that he had seen down at *Woolwich*
a shaft, **graf eller grop,** dug to about twenty English
yards down through such a hill, where the strata lay
nearly in this order :—

On the top soil, **svartmylla** . . . .

Then a stratum of the brick-colored clay . . .

Further down a bed of all sorts of mussel and snail
shells . . . .

Next to that a bed of a hard clay full of small round
stones . . . .

Under which a fine white sand which continued
without being bottomed [T. I. p. 417] as far down as the
pit was dug, but no chalk occurs in this hill.† A man,
who lives close to it, was said to be the owner of this pit,
out of which he sells the fine sand to various persons to
use for their brick-making and other purposes.

Vinter-Krassa til Sallad. *Winter-Cress for Salad.*

Erysimum, 557 [E. Barbarea, now *Barbarea Vulgaris*]
or *Winter-Cress*, grows abundantly in England on the

---

* Kalm was right. The chalk underlies the whole of the London basin. [J. L.]

  † This section must have gone close on to the chalk, but did not quite
reach it. [J. L.]

banks of ditches and elsewhere. It is sown here in the kitchen gardens and used in the winter-time and also in the spring while it is still tender, as salad, or more correctly speaking as **gron-kål,** *chouvert,* in the same way as we in Sweden prepare spinach. If they have not planted it in the kitchen gardens they avail themselves of the wild ones.

Ängar och deras gräs-växt. *Meadows and their Grass Growth.*

On the whole of this side of London which we visited to-day there was a great multitude of *inclosures,* or **täppor,** nearly all laid out as meadows. The land around *Hampstead* consisted mostly of hills, long-sloping on all sides. The grass-growth in them was very beautiful, and now as long as any on our very best meadows in Sweden at the end of June, which is principally owing to this, that these meadows are here commonly manured every year. On most of the meadows around *Hampstead* the grass growth consisted almost solely of *Bromus,* 87 [Banks, MS. 'varietas *secalini* '], which here stood as thick as the thickest rye-fields, and every plant was 2 feet 6 inches high or more. When this grass grew on high hills, **kullar,** and on very dry places, it was not longer than it commonly is in Sweden.

[T. I. p. 418.]

Some other kinds of grass had mingled themselves amongst it, but they were so few, that it is not worth while to mention them. Among them, however, *Alopecurus* 52 [A. *pratensis* L.], was the commonest. I also noted however, that in most of the beautiful meadows which are found round London, both these aforenamed kinds of grass have nearly always formed the most plentiful, best, and most luxuriant grass-growth. I should also think that if we in Sweden, especially near to

E

the towns, looked after our meadows with the same care and diligence as the Englishmen around London, our meadows would also yield, **kasta af sig**, as much and as good hay as these, if not more so. The soil was here the same as everywhere around *London*, viz., a brick-coloured clay blended with a finer or coarser sand of the same colour, the surface of which, by the decay of the plants, had got to be mould, **mylla**. A great many of the meadows on this side were now mown, and the hay partly carried, partly also it still stood in rows or cocks.

[Defer AMERICAN NOTE.]

[T. I. p. 419.] *The 23rd May*, 1748.

Hvad Skilnad jordmon gör åt växter.

What difference the Soil makes to Plants.

It is sometimes wonderful to see what a difference the *climate*, as well as the *soil*, and other circumstances, make to one and the same kind of plant. *Medicago*, 621 [M. *lupulina*] covers, **väper på**, the acre-reins **åkerrenar**, of Upland in Sweden, and the roadsides in clay-soil, **ler grund**, where it creeps out of the earth, and often spreads itself out for a length of two feet on all sides. When it gets into vegetable and other kitchen gardens it grows still more luxuriantly and larger. Here around London I found it on the hills and knolls, **på högder och kullar**, where it grows so miserable, small, and slender, **spinkot**, that I had great difficulty in recognizing it. I saw hardly a plant of it which had attained a length of 6 inches, but most were only 4 inches long. Some were also only 1¼ inch. The soil was here a mixture of brick-colored clay, sand, and humus, **svartmylla**, which seemed to be a good earth; but still this plant was here [T. I. p. 420] so small, though at the same time a number of other plants grew luxuriantly enough. *Lolium*,

104 [*L. perenne.*] *Rye grass* had almost the same fate. It grew small and very slender, **spinkot,** while *Bromus* 87 [var. *secalini*] and *Alopecurus*, 52 [*A. Pratensis.* L.] thrive in this earth very well. I particularly noticed in the case of the *Bromus*, that it here formed the longest and principal grass-growth on nearly all the meadows round London, and grew to a length of 2 feet 6 inches or 3 feet, whereas in Sweden, on the dry sand hills, it commonly is not over 4 inches high, slender, and miserable.

[Defer AMERICAN NOTE.]

Vägglös fordom sällsynte i Ängland. *"Wall-lice"* or bugs formerly rare in England.

Mr. Catesby said that about twenty years ago they hardly knew here in England what a "Wall-louse" was; but since that time they had travelled over here in ships from foreign countries, so that there are now few houses in London in which these least welcome guests have not quartered themselves.*

Huru Foglar och Fiskar i en natural Samling bäst *conserveras. How Birds and Fishes are best preserved in a collection.*

Mr. Catesby described the method which he had used on his travels to prepare and preserve birds and fishes, which he designed for his collection. It consisted in this, that when he had got a bird he took [T. I. p. 422] the entrails, **inälfvorna,** out of it, then sprinkled snuff all over the inside, put it in an oven,

---

* "Their original name was *Chinche* or 'Wall-louse'(Ray. *Hist. insect.* 7), and the term *Bug*, which is a Celtic word, Wel. Bwg, signifying a ghost or goblin, was applied to them after Ray's time" [d. 1674]. "Bug" in its old sense *e.g.* "Thou shalt not nede to be afraid of any *bugs* by night" (Mathew's Bible Ps. xci. 5), Winter's Tale, III., 2, 3, also in *King Henry VI.*, 5, 2, and in *Cymbeline* twice, became obsolete. (Kirby and Spence, *Entomol.* Let. IV) [J. L.]

E 2

which was as hot as when bread is taken out of it ; for if
the heat is too great all the fat melts.   When the specimen had remained a short time in the oven it was taken
out to cool.   It was again put in the oven, and left
there till it was quite dry ; for the trick consists in this,
that it must not be dried too quickly, but gradually
. . . . .   Afterwards, if one wishes to carry them
anywhere, they are laid in casks, **tunnor,** or such like,
snuff is sprinkled over and in them, to drive away moth,
mal, and other injurious insects, **skade-kräk.**   Fish
are best preserved *in spiritu Vini.*

[T. I. p. 422.]

Hvart land har Sin Sed.

Each country has its peculiar customs in one thing and
another, and so it is in England.   I believe there is
scarcely a country where one gets to see so many
Peruques as here.   I will not mention that nearly all the
principal ladies, and also a part of the commoner folk,
wear *Peruques,* but I only speak of the men, who in short,
all wore them.   The boy was hardly in breeches before
he came out with a *Peruque* on his head, which was
sometimes not much smaller than himself.   It did not,
therefore, strike one as being at all wonderful to see
farm-servants, **Bonde-dränger,** clodhoppers, **Torpare,**
day-labourers, **dagsverks-karlar,** Farmers, **Bönder,**
in a word, all labouring-folk go through their usual
every-day duties all with *Peruques* on the head.   Few,
yea, very few, were those who only wore their own hair.
I had to look around a long time in a church [T. 1.
p. 423] or other gathering of people, before I saw anyone with his own hair.   I asked the reason for the
dislike of, and the low estimation in which they here
held their own hair ?   The answer was, that it was
nothing more than the custom and *mode.*   Here in

England short *peruques* were mostly used, yet some of the grand people also had "locks" on them, **låckar uti.** They were dear enough. For one guinea it was passable, and did not look very handsome. I should have to give at least a couple of guineas, if I wished to have one of some value, and a good one.

I never noticed that any Englishman used boots, **stöflor,** in any case, except when he was riding and sitting on a horse.* On other occasions shoes, **skor,** were always used. Sometimes, when any snow fell in winter, so that it was dirty in the streets, there was here and there an individual who wore boots.† If anyone in any case walked in the town with boots, he had always a riding-whip, **piska,** in his hand as a sign that he had ridden in, **rest in til häst,** or was just about to mount and ride out of the town. If he did not do this, he was looked upon as a foreigner, at whom the people could stand and stare, as at something extraordinary. I remember that, during my visit to the country in dirty and rainy weather, when I had pulled on my boots, to go drier about the feet, I was asked by one and another if I intended to ride out to any place that day in such bad weather.

The sword, **Värja,** is very seldom worn except by members of Court, or some foreigner.

The 25th May, 1748.

In the afternoon I went with *Dr. Mitchell, Mr. Whatson,* the well-known *Mr. Graham* [T. I. p. 424], and some other Fellows of the Royal Society, out to *Dulwich, in Surrey,* and other places in that neighbourhood, to see what rare plants might be found there, as well as in Kent. The whole of this tract of country was most delightful.

---

* " Rida och sitta til häst." Sitta til häst=Lat. *Equo insidere.* [J. L.]

† "Boots [*Bottes,* Fr.], leather coverings for the legs in traveling." Bailey, *Eng. Dic.,* 15th Ed., 1753. [J. L.]

It went up and down in long sloping hills with valleys between. We had a continuous series of well-built villages, gentlemen's houses, ploughed fields, meadows, orchards and gardens, kitchen - gardens, commons, **utmarker,** &c.

The country was everywhere divided into small *inclosures*, with hawthorn and other hedges round them, so that one could only suppose that he was travelling all the way through a garden. Here and there appeared small woods of all sorts of leaf-trees. When a view of the country was obtained from some of the highest hills, **backar,** it looked pretty enough ; but the great number of hedges caused it to look, a little farther off, as though it were entirely overgrown with woods, through which some brick house peeped here and there ; for as the *inclosures* were for the most part small here, the hedges prevented the ploughed fields and meadows which lay between them from being seen.

[Defer AMERICAN NOTE.]

[T. I. p. 425.]

Gödsel lagd i högar; ängars gödning.

Manure laid in heaps ; manuring meadows.

Nearly everywhere here in England it was the practice to carry out dung and other dirt, which is collected in farms and villages, and lay it in large heaps by the ploughed fields, to lie there for a time and ferment together. Those who live round London buy the dung and refuse which is collected in the streets, and carried out and laid in large heaps outside the town. This manure they afterwards carry out in the spring on to their meadows, market gardens, ploughed fields, &c., lay it in some corner of them, or also on the common close by, in a great heap, where it lies the whole summer under the open sky, and ferments together. On the top it is commonly covered with straw-litter, **halm-byssje**. As a great part of the land round London is laid out in meadows and pastures, and the owners are very careful by all means to cover over the grass-lands with it, because they can thus obtain a larger profit from them, so they commonly manure their meadows once a year, which is done thus. In September or October, or also later, when the cattle are no longer driven on to the meadows or pastures, they take the manure which has lain and rotted in the above-named heaps, carry it out on to the meadow, and there spread it out somewhat thinly. The rain, which at this season of the year commonly follows this, washes the manure down to the roots of the grass, so that it does not evaporate, **at den ej svinner bårt i luften**. Hence it happens that the meadows around London bear so luxuriant and abundant a grass-crop tha t they can be mown so early, and several times a year. [T. I. p. 426.]

This well rotted manure, the time of year when it is spread out on the meadows, and the English climate, in which not much snow falls at a time in the winter to wash away the best and fattest of the manure in melting, cause the meadows to fare incomparably well on it, and accounts for no one here knowing much about what it is for the manure spread on the meadows to burn up the grass.

Råg sällsynt omkring London.

Rye rare around London.

To-day for the first time we saw rye growing here in England, for in all the places we had been at before we had not seen one rye plant, **råg-stånd**, because it is wheat that is grown everywhere here. This rye now stood in the ear, everywhere, and was tolerably fine, so

that rye would thrive here very well, if they had not wheat,
which always has the preference.

Senfärdig Vår. *Late Spring.*

Everyone here in England said that all vegetation
was three weeks later than it had been for many, indeed
for sixty years [1688] in this country ; when we nevertheless thought that it was three weeks earlier than it
could be about Stockholm in Sweden, at this time in
ordinary course.

Hälso-brunnar och hus dervid.

Mineral waters and houses near them.

At one place there were on the side of a hill some pit-
wells dug in the bank, whose water they use to drink in
the summer, like that of any other mineral spring, **sur-
brunnars.** The water had no outlet, and tasted like
the water in ordinary clay-pits, **ler-gropar,** and it seems
that the benefit of this exists only in folks' imagination.
Several cabins, **kojor,** were built close by for the visitors
to the spring. The walls were of sods, the roof of furze,
and the bare ground [T. I. p. 427] served for a floor.

At Dulwich there was a well dug and walled round
deep down into the earth, which had the reputation of
having restored many to health. The water was said to
be purging. The great heat and thirst drove us to drink
a great quantity of it, without the slightest effect.

Matvarors pris i Krigstiden.

The price of provisions in time of war.

I asked whether provisions were dearer here in England in war time than at other times. They answered
" No," but they are then commonly cheaper. The reason
is that it is then forbidden to carry them out of the kingdom. That meat was now dear was due to the cattle
disease which had carried off such a number of animals.

[T. I. p. 439.] *The 28th May*, 1748.

Huru ler beredes til tegel-slåning.

How clay is prepared for brick making.

Immediately outside the town on the north side near the road to *Hampstead*, there were large pits where the clay and sand [T. I. p. 440] were dug up, from which they made bricks close by. The soil here consisted of a brick-colored clay, mingled with a fine sand. This sandy clay, **sand blandadeleran,** was cast together in large heaps in this way, that when one *stratum* of it had been been laid a foot thick, or less, there was spread over it a *stratum* of coal ashes about 4 inches thick or less, then sand and clay mixed, after that coal-ashes again, and so on. Next to that the water was led from the ponds, **vattu-groparna,** to it through troughs, **rännor,** as much, that is to say, as was required. The sand-mixed clay, coal-ashes, and water, were then mixed together for as long a time as was necessary to mingle them thoroughly together. After that this clay so prepared, was thrown into trucks, **kärror,** specially made for the purpose, and carried to the place where the bricks were made.

The 29th May, 1748.

In the morning I went in company with Director Campbell out to the Duke of Argyle's house at *Whitton*, situated ten miles west of London. The Duke himself invited me, and begged me to come there once before I left England, for which visit he himself fixed the day. This Duke's house lies on a great flat common,* **et stort flakt fält.** The soil was very meagre, **mager,** nearly all around being bare ling-heath, **bara ljung hed;** but the Duke has been able to show what pleasure, art, and money are able to effect, and that by their

---

* Hounslow Heath. [J. L.]

means the most meagre places are converted into
fruitful land. The Duke, who had himself the greatest
insight into Botany, as well as Mathematics, and other
branches of Natural Science, **Naturkunnogheten,**
had also had a beautiful garden laid down here. The
first beginning of it was made in [T. I. p. 441] the year
1723, when the Duke first bought, **tilhandlade sig,**
this ground. Here, there was a collection of all the
kinds of trees, which grow in different parts of the world,
and can stand the climate of England out in the open
air, summer and winter. The Duke had himself planted
very many of these trees with his own hand. There was
here a very large number of *Cedars of Lebanon*, which
appeared to have the best opinion of a dry and meagre
earth, and it seems that it might be suitable for planting
on our great heaths and sandy tracts, **stora heder och
moar,*** in Sweden and Finland.

Of North American Pines, **Granar,** Firs, **Tallar,**
Cypresses, Thuyas, all these and many other kinds,
there was an abundance, which throve very well. There
were already small groves of them. Diligence and Art
have not been spared here to make everything delightful.
The Duke comes out here from London as often as he
can find time from his duties. Here is also a beautiful
orangery. There were no more than just sufficient rooms
in the house, though they were very pretty, but not to
be compared with such Castles, **Slott,** and Palaces
which such great lords are used to have, and are
especially common in England. The Duke himself
observed the thoughts, which in consequence of this,
arose in my mind and in that of my travelling companion.
" Your wonder," said he, " probably is why I have not a
" larger and grander house here than this ; but I have
" first decided to prepare this meagre soil, and make it

---

* Mo. *glarea sterilis.* Wallerius, *Mineralogia*, Stockholm, 1747. [J. L.]

" available to plant all kinds of trees in, and after
" setting the trees in the order, and in the positions they
" ought to occupy so that they may grow, then, as I
" have the money, I can always build the most hand-
" some Castle in one year, and even a shorter time,
" when I [T. I. p. 442] choose to do so, which it would
" take a poorer man 10 years to build, but to effect so
" much as that a single tree shall take root and grow as
" much in one year as it would otherwise grow in ten,
" that can I never effect with money, but Nature must
" have its time; therefore he who intends to build a
" house, and lay out a garden round it, ought to make
" a beginning with planting trees to gain time."

In the evening we went back to London, together
with Dr. Mitchell, Mr. Watson, and several other
naturalists, who had been out at the Duke's this day.

The 30th May, 1748.

During the whole of my visit to England, both before
and after the date just given, I made numerous observations not only on the cultivation of meadows, but on the
plants of which the hay and grass growth in their
meadows particularly consists, and which plants are the
most profitable in their meadows on various kinds of
soil; which plants horses, donkeys, cows, sheep, swine,
and other animals usually eat; and which, on the contrary, they reject, and always pass by; with several other
Œconomico-Botanical observations; but, as they would
take up too much room in a description of travels, they
are left for another occasion to be published either in
Academic Disputations or under some other name.

The 2nd June, 1748.

*Plants useful for sowing on the sides of Earth-walls, to
fasten the mould by.*

I have several times before mentioned, that in several

places [T. I. p. 443] around London, high and sufficiently
steep earth-walls are used instead of a fence, **gärdes-
gård,** or other hedge around their ploughed fields,
meadows, and pastures, and market gardens.   When the
earth becomes dry at the sides, especially when there
has been a frost, it is very much given to slip down and
destroy the wall.   I remarked, however, that nature
herself was diligent in remedying this, and that art came
to her aid, which was effected by certain plants that had
taken up their abode on the sides of the walls, and had
bound the earth together with their roots, and by the
shelter of their leaves, **med bladens skugga,** prevented
the sun and frost from doing violence to the mould which
without the plants would be loose.   Among them there
were in particular the following :—

Qvickroten, 105 [*Triticum*], was the best of all
grasses, and was also the commonest on the sides of the
walls.   It grew thickest of all, the most luxuriant, and
the richest in blades, and made the longest grass growth.
The highest was commonly 2 ft. 6 ins. to 3 ft.

Hundexing, 83 [Banks MS., *Dactylis Glomerata*]
stood in some places plentiful enough.

Renlosta, 85, was also a beautiful grass for fastening
earth-walls, especially where the earth is loose.   I saw
it growing in many places on the sides in abundance,
luxuriant and rich in blades, indeed it often stood as
thick as the thickest rye field especially under the shade
of the hedges.   Its height was 2 ft. 6 ins. to 3 ft.   In
some places **Akervinda,** 173 [*C. Arvensis,* L. Ger.
Winde.] *Small Bind Weed,* covered the whole south side
of the high and very steep earth walls, where it had
bound the earth together with its thick growth, plentiful
leaves and shade, **myckna blan och skugga.**

In other places there grew *Hordeum,* 107 [*H. Murinum*] quite alone on both sides of the earth-wall, where

[T. I. p. 444] it stood like the thickest rye-field, but was not taller than about 1 foot high. It seemed as if this grass would thrive best on the south side of the wall. In many places the sides of the walls were covered over either with Quickroot, 105 [*Triticum repens*] or **Renlosta** (85) or *Scandix*, 241, *seminibus hispidis* [*S. Anthriscus*, now *Anthriscus Vulgaris*] *Beaked Parsley*, each of which in its place and by itself made the thickest growth that can be, and certainly seemed to be very profitable and serviceable for sowing on the sides of earth-walls, to fasten the loose mould by. It seemed as if the Quickroot would thrive better on the north side of the walls. These walls consisted of the brick-colored clay found everywhere around London, which has frequently been mentioned before.

The 3rd of June, 1748.

In the afternoon I was at the house of Dr. Cromwell Mortimer, Secretary of the Royal Society in London, where I then made the acquaintance of Mr. Baker, who had written the beautiful book on *Polyps*, in which he recounts the many experiments he had made with them. [Omit a silly note on a child's skull found in a chalkpit.]

[T. I. p. 445.] *Luteola*, 439. [*Reseda Luteola*, *L.*] *Dyers Weed*, *Weld*, grew everywhere outside London on the earth-walls. That it can be contented with the driest earth I noticed from this, that it grew in fissures in the tops of the walls in the greatest heat of the sun where all other plants, even *Poa Murorum* [*P. Compressa*, *L.*] were entirely withered up and killed by the great heat; but this stood there green and in flower, more than 18 inches high. The cattle always left it uneaten.

The 6th June, 1748.

List of births and deaths, &c., in several places. In a printed description of London, in *Folio*, there is a list of births, deaths, and marriages in several of the largest towns of Europe, from which to draw a comparison with London, and to show the size of London. I will in the last volume (D.V.) of these travels give how many are annually born, die, &c., in London. [This promise was never fulfilled.] Now I will only shortly state them concerning the foreign places, as they stood entered in this book. [Pp. 446 and 447 of T. I. contain Tables for Nine towns.]

[T. I. p. 447.]

Several good institutions in London.

In several places, especially in the larger streets, where the people stream backwards and forwards, there sit either men or old women with shoe-brushes, blacking, and such like, ready to clean shoes for anyone who may require their services. Thus when [T. I. p. 448] one walks in the street, and gets muddy about the shoes, he turns to one of those who stand in the street, and allows him to clean his shoes. It is not necessary to take off one's shoes for this purpose, but one sets the feet with the shoes on upon a little table, **stol,** which is put there on purpose, when they are cleaned. A *halfpenny* is paid for each shoe. This is a great advantage in this place, where the women are so very careful about their clean and white floors, besides that, one can go neat about the feet.

In many places, and almost everywhere in the large streets, there stand carriages for hire, **hyr-vagnar,** ready to carry, on payment, anyone who wishes to use them. These hire-coachmen, **hyr-kuskar,** do not get to take payment, according to their own judgment, if they are employed in the town, but they have a certain *Taxa,* how much they shall receive from the one place to another, above which they cannot go without a fine,

utan böter, but where anyone takes a *chaise*, **vagn,**[*] to a certain place outside the town it then commonly depends on a bargain. Besides this there is the law or regulation, **lag eller stadga,** for these hire-chaises in the town, that if one wishes to have the carriage for several hours, a half or a whole day, then it is paid for according to the number of hours, in this way, that two shillings are always paid for the first hour, but after that, only a shilling is paid for each hour. In the same way one can almost anywhere get a *carrier*, **åkare,** to convey anything that may be needed. Similarly there is always a multitude of *porters*, **Bärare,** ready to carry anything from one place to another.

In several places, especially at the west side of the town, where the Court resides, **der Hofvet bor,** there are seen a number of *Post Chaises*, which stand for hire at anybody's service.

At all the *steps* by the river, and in the "lanes," **gränderna,** which run down to the same [T. I. p. 449] there stand whole troops of *rowers*, **Roddare,** who as soon as they become aware of anyone coming a long way off, set up a horrible noise, **et faseligt buller,** so that by shouts and upraised hands they made known their readiness to carry one where he wished to go on the river.†

The Penny Post is also here a useful institution, which consists in this, that if one has a letter or anything else, which does not exceed a pound in weight, to send to anyone in London, or the places situated close by, it is

---

* " We engaged what is termed a *wagon*, but which bears a tolerable resemblance to an ordinary post chaise, to take us to Brill," &c., p. 32, *Descriptive History of Holland.* Grandfather, 1819. 12mo. [J.L.]

† Vincent Bourne gives an amusing description of this in his " Iter per Thamisin."

" At nautae venientem ubi me videre sagaces,
Sese disponunt, omnes clamare parati,
Et jam protensis manibus diversa loquuntur," &c. [J.L.]

sent by *the Penny Post*, which is established at several
places in London, and one pays for it *one penny*, when it
quickly and safely reaches its destination, **snart och
säkert kommer fort.** Besides this, there are
certain men who, every day, when the Post is going to
start from London to any place, go round with small
bells, which they ring. Anyone who has a letter to send
to the Post, can give them to such a man, when he for
one penny safely carries it to the Post, which is a great
convenience in this large town, where many have over
half a mile to walk to the *Post-house*.

[*Water-supply by bored-tree-stem-pipes.*]

About the advantage of having sufficient water at
home in one's own kitchen by means of pipes made of
bored stems of trees, **pip-stâckar,** which bring the
water there underground;* about the streets, which at the
sides are laid with smooth flat stones with posts at the
outside, within which people walk quite safe from all
vehicles and horses; about the *links*, **lycktor,** which
everywhere in the larger streets are lighted at dusk
uptändas i skymningen, and burn the whole night,
together with many other useful institutions, I have either
told before, or am going to speak further on.

The 9th June, 1748.

Vaux-Hall. In the evening I went with some of my

---

* Several of which were to be seen in 1885 lying as excavated at the
northern end of Shaftesbury Avenue close to Oxford Street, of different sizes.
some very large and others quite small, mains and branches. In "Hydraulia,"
By Wm. Matthews, *Lond.*, 1835, 8vo., pp. 66-68, is some interesting
information respecting these wooden pipes from which I extract the following.
The trees were elm; at one time the New River Company alone had 400
miles of wooden pipes, which were entirely renewed in the course of every 20
years. The bore varied from 3 to 6 or 7 inches, and a few near the Reservoirs
10 or 12 inches. Between 1810 and 1820 the whole of the New River Company's wooden pipes were replaced by iron ones. [J. L.]

acquaintances to Vauxhall, to see that much-vaunted pleasure garden, where the youth of London, almost [T. I. p. 450] every evening in the summer, divert themselves. This pleasure-garden lies a little beyond Westminster Abbey, **ofvanför W. A.,** but on the other side of the river Thames. It is full of *allées*, planted with Lime and Elm, **Lind och Alm,** where people can walk about. At one place is a high special *Altan*, built with a roof over it, and benches in the *Altan*, on which the musicians sit. At 6 o'clock in the evening, they begin to assemble, when the music commences at 7 or 8 o'clock in the *Altan*, with a very large number of different kinds of instruments, among which is also an organ [**orgor**, as in French, in the plural.] When they have played for some time, there appear *Chanteurs or Chanteuses*, **Sångare eller Sångerskor,** who also sing from the *Altan*, **låta höra sig från A ;** sometimes only one sings, sometimes two, and sometimes three together.

While they are singing, they are accompanied now and again by instruments. When they have continued for a time, there is an interval, **hålles något up,** both with songs and music, when those who have come out there either promenade, **spatsera omkring,** in the garden or sit down at one of the many tables there are, and have brought to them various foods and drinks, wines, confitures, punch, meat, **stek,** apples, fruits, &c., which are all tolerably dear, so that those who sell them do not seem to lose anything by it. No man or lady enters the garden without paying a *shilling* at the entrance. After that anyone is free to buy anything or not. One can in in the meantime listen to the music, walk about, see and be seen, without any further cost. As soon as it begins to be a little dusk, lamps are everywhere lighted up, which are here in the garden in great multitudes, and which burn for some time after 10 o'clock, when the

F

songs and music cease, and all the guests hurry away.
[T. I. p. 451.] There are here ready all the statues and
ornaments which are used in gardens. Thus the means
of supporting themselves and earning money are manifold. Here the musicians and men and women singers
earn their subsistence. Here those make large profits
who sell various kinds of provisions. Rowers and hire-
coachmen are well satisfied with this institution, because
they have a large profit out of the large number of people
going and coming thither and thence, partly in chaises,
partly in boats, **dit och dädan, dels i vagn, dels
med båt.** The owner, who leases out this pleasure-
garden to those who make all these arrangements, is said
to gather a pretty penny, **vackra penningar,** out of it
in the summer.* I will not now talk about the ruffians,
skälmar, who often plunder and rob those who are
leaving it at night. Meantime, its use by folk may in a
certain way be good, but then it is certain that it is also
in some ways harmful, **men så slår det ej felt at den
ock i somt är skadelig,** because the youth is not a
little ruined through it when he gets into a habit of
coming here every evening. He gets accustomed to do
no work, and, on the other hand, to squander money in
various ways. Young ladies, also, might not always be
improved to the pitch of perfection here.

The 10th June, 1748.

Mr. Peter Collinson's Garden at Peckham.

In the afternoon I went out to *Peckham*, a pretty
village, **en vacker by,** which lies three miles from
London, in Surrey, where Mr. Peter Collinson has a
beautiful little garden, full of all kinds of the rarest plants,

---

* "**Samla vackra penningar,**" it is curious to find this expression,
though in the plural, in the Swedish. [J. L.]

especially American ones which can endure the English climate, and stand out the whole winter. However neat and small this garden was, there was, nevertheless, scarcely a garden in England in which there were so many kinds of trees and plants, especially [T. I. p. 452] of the rarest, as in this. It was here that Mr. Collinson sometimes, as often as he got time from his business, amused himself in planting and arranging his living collection of plants.

Häst knockors nytta.

An use of horse-leg knuckle-bones.

For the border or the outer edge of the flower-beds, Mr. Collinson had set knuckle-bones, **knockor,** of horse or ox-legs, such as the boys with us in Sweden and Finland use to make their so-called **is-läggor,** "*ice-legs,*" with which they run upon the ice. The transversal end, **den tvära ändan,** was set down in the ground, and the round curled end stood upwards. All were the same length, and quite close to one another, which performed the same service in hindering the earth from slipping down from the beds, as if there had been boards set round them. This use of horse-leg bones in kitchen-gardens I have seen before at several places just outside *Moscow,* in Russia.

Huru *Viscum* sås. How *Mistletoe* is sown.

Mr. Collinson told us his method of sowing *Viscum* (Linn. *Fl. Svec.* 816), which consisted in this. The berry is squeezed open, **Bären kramas sönder,** and laid on the smooth places on the bark, **på de släta ställen i barken,** of some tree, when it very quickly fastens itself. But if they are laid in the rimes or cracks, **skråmor eller sprickor**, of the bark of a tree, they will fasten on to it with difficulty.

F 2

Huru Tran-bär kunna sås i en Trägård. How
Cranberries can be sown in a garden.

Mr. Collinson showed me, among other plants, our common **Tran-bärs-ris** *Vaccinia*, 315, *palustria*, Lob. [*Vaccinium Oxycoccos*], Cranberry [*O. palustris*. Pers., Hooker], which are commonly very difficult to transplant into a garden. His method, in which he sought to follow Nature, was this. They were sown in a pot, **kruka,** full of earth ; but instead of leaving the hole at the bottom open, as in other flower-pots [T. I. p. 453] so that the water may run off and not stand at the bottom of the pot and stagnate, **syra,** he had stopped up the hole, so that the water stood and stagnated. The pot was set in the shade, and moss laid upon the earth, in which *Vaccinium palustre* grew. He said that he also got a great number of other bog and water-loving plants to grow by this method.

Trägårds anläggning.
How to lay out a garden.

On this point, Mr. Collinson remarked that one of the principal circumstances in connection with it is, so to arrange that it has the morning sun. No one can believe what an influence it has when the sun gets the first thing in the morning to dry up the vapours, **dunster,** that have fallen in the night.

Then, as regards the shape of a garden, Mr. Collinson held the quadrilateral, **fyrkantiga,** to be the best, and the circular not so good ; for the *Duke of Richmond* had his garden laid out in a circular form, which seemed as if it ought to ward off the drift of the weather more, but the experience was quite otherwise, for when the wind works itself in there, it does more harm than if it were four-sided, because it here courses round the garden, **löper rundt omkring trägården,** because the circular form hinders its escape.

[T. I. p. 406.] *The 17th May, 1748.*

Fences or barriers around meadows, market gardens, &c., of *Ox-horn*. I have above in several places described the fence, **stängsel och hägnad,** which they mostly use near London round their kitchen gardens and meadows, &c., which consists of high cast-up earth walls, **mull-vallar,** but now I will tell about another kind of fence, **hägnad,** which they also avail themselves of here very much, and is such: An earth-wall is cast up in the usual way. The breadth or thickness at the ground is made proportionate to the height of the intended fence, for the higher the wall the broader the *basis.* When the earth has been cast up to a height of about six inches it is levelled all over the top. Thereupon they have ready to hand a multitude of the quicks or inner parts of Ox-horns; for the outer part of the horn itself, is taken off and sold to comb-makers and others who work in horn; or these have, after they have bought the whole horn from the butcher, retained the outerpart, and left the inner and useless part for this behoof. This quick is so cut off that part of the skull commonly goes with it. The quicks are then set quite close beside one another over the earth that has been cast up for the wall, and this so that the larger and thicker ends of the quick, or that to which a portion of the skull is attached, is turned outwards or lies just in the face of the side of the wall. In this way two rows of quicks are laid, viz.: one row on one side of the wall, and the other on the other, so that the small ends of the horn quicks meet in the middle. Over this is afterwards cast earth about six inches thick, when again in the aforenamed manner is laid a *stratum* of double-ranged ox-horn quicks [T. I. p. 407], viz., so that one row turns the large ends towards one side, and the other towards the other. It is thus continued alternately, **skiftevis,** with earth and ox-horn quicks till the wall has reached the desired height. Only it is noted that the wall is battered, or made narrower and narrower the higher it gets. Thus there may often be seen in such a wall as many as six strata of ox-horn quicks. The object of using these quicks is principally to bind the earth in the wall by them, and make it steady that it may not so soon slip down. Sometimes there were less strata of these quicks in a wall, as five, four and three ; but then there was also more earth between each stratum, up to the thickness of one or two feet ; but such a wall was not so lasting as when more layers of ox-horn quicks were inlaid in it. In some few places there were walls of bare ox-horn quicks laid quite thick one upon another, only that they filled up the spaces between the horns with mould. Thus they knew here to make use of that which in other places is thrown away.

[T. I. p. 453.] *The 11th June,* 1748.

Ox-horn Walls and barriers around Market Gardens.

To-day I saw on the north side of the Town a barrier or wall around a market garden, which was built of bare ox-horn quicks. The height thereof was four feet, the breadth [T. I. p. 454] the same. It was not here as in the former place laid strata-wise of ox-horn quicks and earth, but the horns were piled up on one another as thick as ever they could find room, and the interstices only were filled up with mould. The large ends of the quicks were turned outwards. The sides of these walls were quite perpendicular. On the top there was as much earth laid as would lie, **som kunde ligga qvar,** and this was now overgrown with the following plants, which bound it together :—

Convolvulus, 173. [*C. Arvensis.*]

Hordeum, 107. [*H. Murinum.*]

Triticum, 105. [*T. Repens.*]
Senecio, 690. [   ]
Scandio, 241. [*Anthriscus Vulgaris.*]
Cerastium, 399. [*C. Viscosum.*]

The 12th June, 1748.

Quäkarenas Gudstjenst. *The Quaker's Service.*

In the afternoon I was in one of the Quaker's churches
to see their ceremonies at God's service. They had
neither pulpit, **predikstol,** nor altar, but only benches.
The men sat mostly separately by themselves, and the
women on their side also separate, and they did not mix
with each other, as is done in other churches. Nearly
all the men had their hats on their heads, and they only
took them off while prayers were being read. Here there
were no regular priests, but any one of them, be it man
or woman, was a spiritual priest, **en andelig Präst,**
who began to speak and preach in the church, as the
spirit, according to their belief, gave them the inspiration,
**alt som Andan, efter deras tro, gaf dem uppen-
barelsen in.** To-day there preached two old men, of
whom the one who spoke last, delivered a very beautiful
sermon. He scarcely said anything which he did not at
the same time prove from the Holy Scripture. It all
pointed to this, that men [T. I. p. 455] ought more and
more to put off their sins, and seek to enter into fellow-
ship with God. This people is a very paiseworthy body,
because they are commonly more temperate and sober-
minded, **saktmodigare,** more peaceable, **stillare,**
more charitable, **hjelpsammare,** and betake themselves
more to guarding against all resentment, and outwardly
sinful life, than a great part of the Presbyterian as well as
of the English Church, in both of which latter they do
not commit the great fault of neglecting the Sacraments

like the Quakers, who are never baptised, and never go
to God's Holy Communion, **heliga Nattvard,** because
they say that they are spiritually baptised, **döpte på et
andeligt sätt,** and also are spiritually partakers of our
Saviour's body and blood, besides some other points in
which they err.

Further on, in my description of Pennsylvania, which
is a place entirely of Quakers, I have more to tell about
this people, when I shall produce the *Rules* and *Church
Ordinances,* according to which they are regulated, and
which they hold as a *chose sainte,* **en heligdom,** that
only the principal among them have in *manuscript,* but
which are never allowed, with their knowledge, to be seen
by anyone else. [Kalm did not fulfil this promise.]

[T. I. p. 461.]   *The 17th June,* 1748.

Brist på Spring-källor omkring London.

Want of Spring-wells round London.

On all sides of London which I visited I do not know
that I ever saw any springs, **källa,** which spring up out
out the earth, such as occur everywhere in Sweden, but
nearly all the water which they use in London and the
villages round it, is led to the town or villages partly
through underground pipes or tubes from some lake or
river far away, and partly they have dug large pits and
ponds where the rain-water is collected. Thus there is
found in nearly every meadow a large pond, **grop,** with
sloping banks on all sides in which is collected an
abundance of water, which serves for the cattle to drink
when they are kept in these enclosures. Notwithstanding this want of springs around London, yet no place in
the world [T. I. p. 462] suffers less from want of water
than this town, where superabundant water is led through
underground channels to each and every house, or also

by continually pumping and water-forcing machines from
the river Thames. *

The 18th June, 1748.

Nyttan af Ickorns-Svantsar. *Use of Squirrels' tails.*

The hairs which they used here for Artists pencils
Rit-penslar, were taken from squirrels' tails. Those
who prepared them said that those which are taken from
English Squirrels' tails are not much good, but the best
are taken from a kind of squirrel which comes from
Russia.

The 19th June, 1748.

Ox-horn quicks, in addition to walling purposes are
carried out on to the high roads and there spread out,
earth and sand are then laid upon them, which makes
the road firm and durable.

The 22nd June, 1748.

En Sten af Gamla Carthago. *A Stone from ancient Carthage.*

As I was walking through St. Dunstan's Churchyard
in Stepney in company with others, we saw a stone
which was said to have been brought from the Ancient
Carthage, in whose walls it had formerly lain. It was
now built into the wall, on the *East side* of the small projecting [T. I. p. 463] wing or *Church Porch,* which was
on the north side of the Church. On this stone there
was the following legend :—

> " Of Carthage Great was J a Stone
> " O Mortalls Read with pitty !
> " Time Consumes all, it Spareth none,
> " Man, Mountain, Town, nor Citty :

---

* The London Bridge water-works founded 1582, by Peter Morice, and
subsequently augmented. For descriptions and views see Beighton, *Phil.
Trans.* 1731, & Matthews' *Hydraulia,* 1835 pp. 26-28. 8vo. [J. L.]

" Therefore, o Mortalls, all bethinke
" You, whereunto you must ;
" Since now Such Stately Buildings
" Lye Buried in the Dust.

"THOMAS HUGHES, 1663."

Several people had written their names on the stone
here and there, by which they had made the inscription
sufficiently indistinct.

Vitriols-verket och Kökningen.   *The manufacture
and boiling of Vitriol.*

At the Establishment of Herr *Seel*, a Swede, we saw
his *Vitriol*-Manufacture, and the whole process of boiling,
which is shortly this.   The Material of which this Vitriol
is made is a pale *iron-pyrites*, **Svafvel-kes,** of different
shapes.   This iron-pyrites is taken, or found, somewhat
more than 100 miles from London, near *Harwich,* where
it is found on the sea bottom, **på sjö-botten,*** and is

---

* It happens that Urban Hjärne at p. 340 of a work entitled "Den Be-
svarade och Förklarade Anledningens Andra Flock. Om Jorden och Land-
skap i Gemeen." Stockholm, 1706, in a section "Om Jordens Floo," *About
the Strata of the Earth,* has the following : " There is also a noteworthy de-
" scription of the Stratum, floo, in the cliff, **backen,** near *Harwich* in
" England, which has been described in detail by M. S. Buschenfelt.   When
" the sea is at the ebb or low water, this bank, **backa,** is in all 70 feet high
" from the water-line up to the edge of the cliff at the summit, consisting—

	Ft.	ins
" *First*, on the top, of ordinary soil	o	6
" *Next* to that follows a reddish kind of earth . . .		—
" *Next* to that some horizontal beds of broken bivalve shells, "forkrossade **musslor,** sand, and whole bivalve and "univalve shells, **musslor och sneckor,** sand mixed "with pebbles and flint-stones, **Klapur, sand, och,** "**flint-steen,** under one another		—
"Again *coarse sand* containing bivalve-shells, **Mussel-** "**grus,** and sandheds, **sandhvarf,** intermixed as a "streaky mass—in all	10	0

there collected in large quantities and carried to different Vitriol works in England. A great many of these pieces of iron-pyrites, **Svafvel-kes-Stycken,** are exactly like wood, twigs, &c., so that even the medullary rays, **savrändar,** in the branches can be seen. These bits of wood have been so impregnated by the sulphurous spirit or vapour that they are now entirely changed into a **Svafvel-Kes** or lump of iron-pyrites. See Dr. Wallerius' *Mineralogie*, p. 340.*

The lengths of these pieces of iron-pyrites are 6 inches to a foot, as thick as a man's arm, more or less. Oyster shells are also found [T. I. p. 464] in it. But they are mostly unchanged only that they are rusty on the outside.

The lumps of iron Pyrites or Marcasite, **Svafvelkesar,** are not available for boiling Vitriol out of at once,

	Ft.	ins.
" After that, there comes a fine reddish and thin-streaked "mass of shells, **musslemäst,** of clear and clean "stömusslor, to a thickness of	8	0
"and are just as if they had been designedly pounded in a "mortar, and the Englishmen dwelling in the country "round use to burn them to lime after the Dutch manner.		
"*After that* there follows quite another kind of thing, in all "28 feet thick, consisting of an endless number of streaks "and horizontal beds, partly of pebbles and sand together, "and partly of a grey sandy clay, partly of a dark kind of "earth, **mörk jordart,** and so on	28	0
"*After that,* a streaky clay, **en randig lera,** down to the "base and the water, in all 25 feet high. which is like a "network of streaky stuff, distinguished by different "colours and streaks, has the outward appearance of a "dark-brown shale, **skifverberg,** contained in two or "three horizontal bands, **streck,** of 22½ feet thickness. and "extends right through the hill here and there sticking out "like great flat stones, **steen-hällar.**" Hjärne, p. 340. [J. L.]		

* Wallerius, Johann Gottschalk, *Mineralogia*, Eller Mineral Riket indelt och beskrifvit af I. G. W. Stockholm, 1747. 8vo. This was the first of a long series of " Mineralogies." [J. L.]

but they have at first to be prepared for that purpose for a long time, which is done in this way, that they are spread out over a certain shallow pit or "pan," **fält,** to lie out in the open air, so that the sun may get to work freely upon them. Herr *Seel* told me that this place where it is so prepared, has in the first place been fitted for it in this way : they had dug so far into the ground till they came to a solid clay that was able to resist the percolation of the Vitriol-lye, for a looser kind of earth would absorb the most of the Vitriol-lye, but still as they could not trust to that they had laid the bottom with chalk for a thickness of 4 to 6 feet, which had become hard packed together : At all sides of this pit or pan, the banks or walls were similarly made of chalk, to a thickness of 4 to 6 feet ; but to be still more sure that the Vitriol-juice could not escape, **tränga sig bårt,** either through the bottom or the sides of the pit, **dammen,** both the bottom and the sides were rendered with a *plaster* of *gypsum* called *Terras*, which has the property that it afterwards hardens in water like stone. Thus the bottom and sides were so prepared that one could rest assured that the Vitriol-juice or lye, **Vitriolslakan eller luten,** could not pass through them.

The bottom of this pit was not flat or a *planum*, but was shaped like a number of ridges, or roofs of barns or houses, side by side, in the lowest parts of which there were always laid gutters of lead, **rännor af bly,** along which the lye or juice afterwards came to run to the house where the pans were in which the Vitriol was boiled, **kokades.** On this bottom [T. I. p. 465] so prepared the aforenamed *Marcasite*, **Svafvel-kes,** was laid, everywhere a foot thick, when it was left to lie under the open sky, that the sun, rain, and air got to play freely on it. When the sun has been shining for a

long time upon it, this *Marcasite* effloresces to a mould,
vittras sönder til en mull, and that very gradually,
so that the surface of it first begins to effloresce, **vittra
sönder,** and afterwards the remainder. It has to lie
here 6, 7, 8, 10, or even 12 months sometimes, before it
has crumbled to mould. When the sun has worked
some time on it, it becomes quite white and mealy on
the outside, and if one sets the tongue on this meal it
tastes exactly like *Vitriol.* When the rain afterwards
falls on this stone, the mealy part and all that has
become resolved into salt, is washed away from it, and
carried down to the bottom of this dug place, **gräfda
platsen,** when it runs through the canals that are there
to the house where the Vitriol is boiled, where it is collected in a large *Cistern.* Outside the aforenamed dug
pit, **gräfde dam,** where the stone is laid out, there
stand, let down here and there, bottomless tuns, **bot-
tenlösa tunnor,** in which the gutters or pipes which
lead the water to the *Cistern* can be seen down at the
bottom. One sees in them how the Vitriol-lye runs; for
the gutter which comes from the dug pit, ends on one side
of the *tun*, **tunnan,** and on the opposite side commences
the pipe, **pipan,** which leads the water to the above-
named cistern. These tuns are set here for this reason,
that it can be seen in them whether any of the gutters
or pipes have become stopped up, and which pipe it is,
so that the same may be set to rights.

They are very careful here that some rain should fall
on this *Marcasite,* **Svafvel-kesen,** after the sun has
shone upon it for some days. For example, six days'
[T. I. p. 466] sunshine and the seventh rain were here a
beautiful thing; for then the *Marcasite* would soonest
effloresce, **vittra sönder,** and yield the most vitriol-lye;
but as such a succession of weather does not always
happen, the owner has erected at two places in the

square in which the *Marcasite* is spread out, syringes, **sprutor,** to which the water is led through leaden pipes underground. To get the water there, there is a pumping-machine a little way off, which is driven by horses, so that the water is pumped to these syringes by means of three pumps. They can thus, by means of a small long pipe of copper, which is screwed on to the syringe, and can be turned round to all sides, spread the water on all sides over the iron pyrites or Marcasite here spread out, and thus to a certain extent perform the same service as the rain, to wash down the effloresced vitriol-meal or salt. This *vitriol-works* lies close to the river Thames, so that one has the advantage of seeing all the ships that pass up and down the river.

From the Thames there goes an arm up close by these vitriol works; therefore, when the Thames rises at high water, as much of the flood water is collected in the dug channels as is wanted, and is afterwards penned in by a sluice-gate, **dam-bord,** when it is ebb in the river Thames, or the water falls very low. All the water which falls into the effloresced *Marcasite*, **Svafvel-kesen,** either from rain or from the syringes, filters through the same down to the bottom, after it has first dissolved, **löst up,** all the vitriol-salt which it has met with, and carries it with it in the above named way through the gutters or pipes to the *cistern* in the house where the Vitriol is boiled.

From this *cistern* it is pumped by hand up to the *pan* in which it is boiled to Vitriol. This *pan*, **panna,** is of lead, very large, quadrilateral, lies with [T. I. p. 467] its bottom on closely-laid iron bars, and a fire is lighted under it in two ovens close beside each other, entirely supplied with coal.

If they notice that the heat becomes too strong under the pan, they can diminish it by this means—that on the inner side of the oven there go up two or three flues, **korstens-pipor,** in which there are dampers, **spjäll.** When the damper or valve is opened, the flame and heat have freedom to ascend through it, and thus the heat under the pan diminishes, and consequently the degree of boiling; but when the **spjäll** is shut, the heat is increased. The boiling lasts about five, six, or seven days before the lye becomes so thick that it is fit to make vitriol of, which can be proved by means of a special glass globe with holes in it, which they lay in some of the lye, **lut,** which they have taken up. By means of this *hydrometer* it is seen how thick the water or lye, **vatnet eller luten,** is in this boiling-pan. At last, when it is full-boiled, it is tapped off into three large oblong cisterns of lead which stand a little way from the pan, where it is left to stand and cool, when the Vitriol settles on the bottom and sides of these cisterns. The lye which will not give any more vitriol-crystals is poured back into the pan; but the Vitriol that has shot out into crystals is collected.

In the boiling, it is necessary to be particularly careful that the pan is almost constantly full, which is done by pumping more lye out of the cistern into the pan than is boiled in it, because the pan would otherwise melt. Very much and heavy rain on the outspread *Marcasite* is injurious, because the lye which then filters down is so weak that it is not much stronger than mere water, and consequently it requires a great deal of fire, long boiling, and more labour before the Vitriol is produced from it. The owner said he bought every year £100 to £150 worth of this iron-pyrites or Marcasite. As the channels from the Thames [T. I. p. 468] go right into the works, he can lay boats and small barges close alongside, and unload pyrites and coal. He did not employ much more than two or three persons in the whole factory.

[T. I. p. 438.]   *The 27th May*, 1748.

Ängs-bärgningen.*   *Carrying the meadows, or Haymaking.*

The meadows were now everywhere being mown and carried, which lay on the slopes just outside *London.* Some of them were already mown, and the hay carried, **inbârgadt.** The whole process was carried out almost in the same way as with us. The grass was mown with the scythe, and left to lie in the order in which the mowers, **slâtter-karlen,** laid it, till it had become somewhat dry on the upper side. After it was raked out, though seldom with rakes, **räfsor,** but with the here universally used iron-forks, **järn-gafflar,** with a long wooden handle, **et lângt träskaft,** it was so left to dry. Afterwards it was turned once or more with the iron-forks, then raked together into rows, **i sträng,** with ordinary rakes. After that it was cast together with the often-mentioned pitchforks into [**T. I. p.** 439] large cocks **valmar,** getting on for 8 feet high. Afterwards it was laid on large waggons, and carried home. It was very rare here to see any women at the work in the meadows, but the carrying of the meadows was performed mostly by men only. It is incredible what an abundance of grass was now found on those meadows, especially on those which lay on the north side of the town. It nearly

---

* "Ängs-bärgningen" and "Ängsbruket i Middlesex."

In the View of the *Agriculture of Middlesex*, drawn up for the Board of Agriculture: By John Middleton, 1798. London, 8vo. the distribution of "Meadow and Pasture" in Middlesex is shown by a green colour on the *valuable map* at the beginning. It quite substantiates *Kalm's* description, though 50 years had passed away. The subject of "Meadows and Pastures" forms Sec. I., p. 219-225 of "Chap. VIII., GRASS," pp. 219-253. The subject of "Haymaking" or "Ängs-bärgningen" is Sec. III., pp. 237-251 ; that of "Sown-Grasses" so exhaustively treated by *Kalm* forming Sec. II., pp. 226-236. [J. L.]

everywhere stood up to my waist, when I went in the meadows, and was so thick that there could never be any thicker. BROMUS, 52 ["var. secalini"], ALOPECURUS, 52 [A. *pratensis*], POA 78 [P. *Pratensis*], which had now begun to stick themselves up in abundance, made at this time all the beautiful grass-growth that was found here. The meadows were very even and smooth, **jämna och släta,** with not a single hillock, **tufva,** on them. The grass was cut off as near the ground as the scythe could go, so that there were scarcely 2½ inches of stub, **stubbe,** left remaining. When the grass was newly mown, the stub near the ground was nearly white, which was caused by the grass growing so very thick. Also the lower part of the new-mown hay was quite white for the same reason. On account of the luxuriant and thick grass-growth the mower could not progress at each stroke of the scythe, **lie-tag,** farther than a short 6 inches, for the grass was so thick that he was not able to drive his strokes farther in, **at han ej orkade taga djupare in i sänder.** It has been often mentioned above that all these meadows are manured once a year with the choicest manure.

[T. I. p. 468.]   *The 24th June*, 1748.

Ängs-bruket i *Middlesex.   Use of the Meadows in Middlesex.*

Mr. P. Collinson related to me an account of the trade **föd-krok,** and livelihood, **närings-medel,** which the farmers, inhabitants of Middlesex, practise, specially on the side on which Hampstead lies, and beyond or north of that. It consists in this, that the *farmers* or **Landtmännerna** there lay out all the ground and land which they have, only and solely as meadow, without themselves having any ploughed land, or feeding any cattle, excepting some few horses, which they require for

G

cultivating the meadows. The meadow is here all their
food and sustenance. It seems to be wonderful that it
can suffice for that, especially as the *farmers* in this district pay a higher rent yearly than others, but still it is
so. As they live near London they buy and carry home
from thence all their manure, which is collected in the
streets, and afterwards carried outside the town and laid
in great heaps. No farmer who sends in a load of hay to
be sold, allows his wagon to go back empty from the
town, but it is there filled with the above-named manure
only, which after it has lain its proper time by the meadow
and fermented into one mass, **brunnit ihop,** is spread
out in the autumn over the grass-sward in the meadows.
In January, February, or March, the cattle are taken out
of the meadows, and do not get to go on them any longer,
after which the grass is left freedom to grow. In this
state it continues so that the farmer, at the beginning of
May goes for the first time on to it with the scythe, **lian,**
and mows it. A farmer [T. I. p. 469] or **Landtman** on
this side has commonly no more servants than one single
man, **dräng.** Many might then think, How will he with
so little help be able to cut and carry the hay from his
many and scattered large meadows? The answer to this
is that he wins, **bärgar,** all his meadows in the summer
with day labourers, **dags-verks-folk.** In the beginning
of May there come from Ireland over to England a very
large number of Irishmen, who, like our Dalecarlians,
Dalkarlar, in Sweden, go and hire themselves out everywhere to the farmers. The whole of this part of England
which lies immediately north and east of London, carries
on nearly all its hay-making and harvest work with only
this people, who come over at the beginning of May, and
remain there the whole summer, leaving their own dwellings at home in Ireland to the care of their wives and
children; but towards autumn, after the seedtime and

harvest are past, they return home with the money which they have been able to earn.

In the same way as the Irishmen seek their food and income on this side in the summer, so it is the case with those from *Whales* or *Wallis* that they earn their money also on this side of England in *Kent*, for towards the haymaking season, **hö-bärgnings-tiden,** the folk come from thence in very large numbers down to the country parts of Kent to work for wages ; but with this difference that instead of only men coming as from Ireland, there come mostly only women and girls, **bara qvin folk, hustrur, och pigor,** from Wales, all well, cleanly, and very neatly clad. These perform nearly all the summer cropping in *Kent*, both of hay and grain. They also take down and pluck off the hops. They remake the hop gardens. They [T. I. p. 470] gather the various kinds of beautiful fruits which Kent produces. But I will return to the farmers in Middlesex, and their meadow cultivation, **ängs-skötsel.** It is there the afore-named Irishmen, whom they employ in summer to mow and carry all their hay. As soon as the meadow has thus been mown in the month of *May*, and the hay stacked, no cattle are turned into the meadows, but the grass then at once has freedom to begin to shoot and grow, in which it makes such progress that if the weather is good they often get to mow them for the second time by the beginning of *July*. If it happens, then, that they have finished the aftermath or second mowing early, even then no cattle are slipped into the meadows to bait, but the grass is again left freedom to grow, by which they get to mow the meadows for the *third time* in *September*. But if the spring is late, as it was this year [1748] so that they cannot finish the first mowing before the close of May or the beginning of June, and consequently the second not before the second half of July, then they do

not in such a year wait for the third mowing, but as
soon as the meadows have been carried, and the hay
either taken into London or stacked at home, the cattle
are slipped into them to get their subsistence from the
grass-stub on the meadows. As they have few animals
themselves, they either hire out these meadows which
have been mown to butchers in London, who pay them
handsomely by the week for each animal, be it ox or
sheep, which has freedom to go there to bait, i **bet**, or,
as they mostly do, they buy up at the markets a number
of thin oxen or sheep, which they can commonly get for
a moderate price. These they drive on to their
meadows, where they have to go and become fat, till
towards January or February, the time of year, namely,
[T. I. p. 471] in which the places lying farther from
London could not supply it with fat cattle ready to
slaughter, and the cattle or beasts of slaughter are consequently dearest; then these farmers sell them to the
butchers with considerable profit. A great number of
establishments in London keep their own horses, but as
they have no need of them in the winter they keep them
at some of these farmers, and pay three or four shillings
a week for each horse, which is a long way cheaper for
them than if they were to buy hay and keep them in
London in the stable. As there is an untold number of
horses kept in the stable, it is not wonderful that hay is
very dear there, especially at some times of the year, of
which these farmers situated near to London are well
able and know how to avail themselves. And so it may
from this be easily understood to what extent, **huru
vida,** the meadows alone are sufficient to earn for them
and their households, food, clothes, and everything that
they require, and to give them power to pay their heavy
rents without loss.

The 25th June, 1748.

Källare och rum under gator. *Cellars and rooms under streets.*

Notwithstanding the size of London, still they are careful that no spot of ground shall be left useless and waste. In many places there are passages from houses down under the street to the cellars and other rooms which have been built under the street. In one place and another they had dug up one half of a street, and were then engaged either in walling round an old cellar or in building an entirely new one. Under several of the squares there were also built cellars or other rooms.

[T. I. p. 472.]

Små gårdar vid hvart hus. *Small yards to each house.*

At nearly every house in the town there was either in front towards the street, or inside the house and building, or also in both places, a little yard. They had commonly planted in these yards and round about them, partly in the earth and ground itself, partly in pots and boxes, several of the trees, plants, and flowers which could stand the coal-smoke in London. They thus sought to have some of the pleasant enjoyments of a country life in the midst of the hubbub of the town.

The 26th June, 1748.

Huru Sallad tilredes. *How Salad is prepared.*

Englishmen commonly prepare their salad thus: They take *Lactuca,* lettuce, and throw away the outer coarser leaves, because they are bitter, **bäska.** Likewise the coarsest of the stalks are rejected. These lettuce-leaves are cut to pieces very coarsely; afterwards, a little fine salt is taken, two or three knife-points' full, more or less,

according to the quantity of salad one has. This is laid
on a plate, **talrik,** on which vinegar is poured, and is
well stirred about. After that, olive-oil, **bomolja,** is
poured on to it, after which the salt, vinegar, and olive-
oil are mixed well together. This is afterwards poured
on to the cut-up lettuce-leaves, which one puts into a dish,
and so well mixed with one another, when it is ready.
I never saw sugar used here with salad. Green cucumbers are prepared in the same way for salad, after they
have first been cut across into thin slices, **tunna skif-
vor.** Some mix the slices of cucumber with the lettuce-
leaves, and afterwards pour the prepared oil, vinegar, and
salt on to the mixture ; but generally each is prepared by
itself for [T. I. p. 473] the reason that all persons cannot
bear to eat of all the kinds, but have only a relish for one
of them. Some mix together cucumber slices, lettuce-
leaves, mint, *salvia,* **krass,** water-cress, &c., cut them
into large pieces, and prepare salad of them in the
manner described above.

The 27th June, 1748.

Alm. *The Elm.* There is scarcely any tree which
is so much planted in England as the elm-tree ; so that
it can, in a certain way, be called the Englishmen's
*favorite tree.** I saw great numbers of them in London,
and just outside the town. Nearly all the squares in
London were planted round with it. The *Allees* in *St.
James's Park,* outside the Royal Palace, were only and
solely of this tree, excepting that by the water there were
willows, **pilar.** So also around *Moorfield.* Likewise
where the Danish Church stands. This and the willow
were, in short, the only trees which were planted along
the sides of the streets. In the villages outside London

---

* This is only true of the London clay and of the south. The oak mono-
polised the *weald clay* which Wm. Smith called the oak-tree clay. [J. L.]

this tree had been planted on both sides of the road,
where it made a beautiful shade and a pretty appearance
with its widely-spreading branches. Outside most of the
gentlemen's houses there were *allees* or clumps, **lunder,**
of elms. Mr. P. Collinson had, in his beautiful garden
at Peckham, so clipped one of these trees that it, with
its twigs, formed the roof of one of his summer-houses
which stood on one side of the garden, and opposite, on
the other side of the garden, was an *Esculus*, Linn., or
Castanea Equina, C.B., *Horse-chestnut*, clipt in the same
way ; so that its branches spread themselves out on one
side, and formed a roof and shelter over the seat or bench
which was erected beneath it. In *My Lord Tilney's*
garden, which is described under Woodford, there were
high and long *allees*, made only and solely [T. I. p. 474]
of elm. They had there got to grow to some height.
Afterwards they had bent the tops towards one another,
and allowed them to shoot out branches, where they now
made a tolerably thick roof, so that when one stood at
one end and looked along this *allee*, it seemed as though
it were arched or vaulted with green trees. On many
estates these elms were likewise left to shoot out branches
on the inner side of the *allee*, through which they formed
a thick and leafy roof over the *allee*, so that it was very
lovely on summer days to walk along these *allees*, where
it was always shady and refreshing. When I went down
to *Gravesend*, in Kent, and in the part of Essex that lay
opposite to Gravesend, I found no tree, of which there
were so many planted by the streets and outside the
houses, in the towns, villages, and farms, and of which
there was such an abundance in the hedges around the
fields as of this. The reason why they in particular
choose this tree before others is said to be that it gives
the best shade, endures the coal smoke very well, stands
for a long time green, and keeps its leaves till the

autumn, when others are pale and shed them, besides its
manifold usefulness for all kinds of carpenter's and
turner's work, **til allehanda snickare-och svarfvare
arbeten.**

The 28th June, 1748.

Bröd. The bread which here in England was everywhere and exclusively used, at least where I travelled,
was large loaves, **limpor,** baked of wheat-flour, **hvete-
mjöl.** Other bread is next to never eaten. Most
Englishmen had scarcely heard tell of rye-bread, **hört
talas om råg-bröd ;** few had seen it, and still fewer
were those who had eaten it. Many also did not [T. I.
p. 475] know, that anyone was in the habit of baking
bread of rye, but they thought that it was only used as
food for cattle. This ought all to be understood of those
who lived in London and the provinces immediately
round; for several told me that in the north of England
it is common enough to bake bread of rye-meal. Likewise that there are large tracts in the north where most
of the people mostly live on *Haver-bread,* **Hafre-bröd,**
[oatmeal cakes.*] In London they sometimes, at breakfast, **til-frukost,** eat with butter, while they drink tea, a
kind of thin, small, round cakes, which are snow-white,
taste very nice, and are said to be made of the finest
Haver-meal. But still wheat-loaves are the principal
sort.

[T. I. p. 186.]   The 25th March, 1748.

A great *Fire* in London.

To-day there happened the great conflagration in
London in which over 100 houses near the Royal Exchange were burned down. It was generally considered
that there had not been so large a fire in London since

---

* See Lucas' *Studies in Nidderdale* IV., 1872, 8vo.

the great fire in 1666. As regards the fire which happened
to-day, it was remarkable that notwithstanding its size,
there were nevertheless very many in London, both of
my acquaintance and others, who never once knew about
any fire till late in the evening after it was all extinguished,
or they first got to know about it the following day from
the newspapers, **Avisor,** which come out daily in London;
which was partly occasioned by the enormous size of
London, and partly by the thick and voluminous smoke,
which, especially at this time of year, floats over the
town. On our way we did not see any smoke from this
fire, nor did we know to look out for it.

CHELSEA.

[T. I. p. 386.] *The 5th May, 1748.*

Trä-och köks-krydd gårdar. *Orchards and
vegetable market-gardens.*

On all sides round about *Chelsea* there is scarcely
seen anything else than either orchards or vegetable
market-gardens, and beautiful houses as it were scattered
amongst them. The orchards, **Trä-gårdarna,** were
full of all kinds of fruit trees, such as apple, pear, plum,
cherry-trees, &c., which were now nearly all at their best
in full flower. I saw here in many places large fields
which were nothing but **Trä-scholor,** all planted full of
all kinds of small trees for sale. There were here many
gardeners, **Trä-gårds-mästare,** whose only means of
living consisted entirely of these **Trä-scholor,** "tree
schools," or as they are here called *nurseries.* This was
in itself a very useful thing, for when a *gentleman* or any
one else had bought an estate, or [T. I. p. 387] wished
to form a new garden, he was not obliged to wait for
several years before he could rear from seed, small trees
which he could plant out, but he could at once buy all
such of various sizes, well cultivated and clipped, from
the aforenamed nurserymen, so that he could in one year,
if he was otherwise able to afford it, **om han annors
hade råd dertil,** plant as many trees in his garden as
he wished and required, and of whatever kind he preferred. In the same way, if any old trees went off by

Kalm's England]

Extract from Rocque's Surv

BATTERSEA

5. Showing Chelsea, Ranelagh House, etc.

[To face p. 91

any chance, he could always in the above named way easily get others ; and because there were here so many who drove this trade, so it was also easy to get such young trees for a moderate price. The same thing is true of *market garden produce.* Some nurserymen or market gardeners lay themselves out for all kind of market-garden produce, to keep for sale, others trouble themselves only about some few, which they sow in large quantities, and cultivate well. As we to-day wandered out about *Chelsea,* we saw whole tracts, like very large arable fields, sown only with beans, cabbages, and asparagus. The beans were all of the kind which are here called *Broad Windsor Beans.* They were all sown in rows, in *broadland.* The breadth between each row was 21 inches, and often only 1 foot between the rows ; and the distance between the bean plants in each row, 9 inches to 1 foot. They were now everywhere in flower. A boy went with a little iron hoe, **järn hacka,** and cleared away the weeds between the rows, of which weeds **Hvitroten** [T. repens], was the principal and most. In some places they had planted several kinds of cabbages between the rows. In other places there were long beds 3 feet to 4 feet broad, all sown with asparagus. There I noticed a new contrivance [T. I. P. 388], which I had not seen before, viz., how they collected a number of necks of broken bottles. Such a bottle neck was set on each asparagus plant, **Sparis stånd,** so that the asparagus stood and grew up through the neck. The end of the neck was open so that the air had free access to the asparagus. When the sun shone on these glass necks, the glass perforce became very hot, through which the temperature inside the glass or neck was considerably increased, in consequence of which the asparagus came to push up all the quicker, and made haste to grow. All the asparagus plants which were inside these bottle necks were about the thickness of a little finger and were now, as they were at their best, about to be cut. Thus they knew here in England how to make use of nearly everything, often of such things as are regarded by us as useless. It has been shown before (p. 382 *orig.*), how broken bottles and bits of glass can be turned to account, and here it is shown that they also know how to make use of old broken bottle necks.

[T. I. p. 398.] The 12th May, 1748.

Frön ligga länge oskadde i jorden.

Seeds lie long unscathed in the Earth.

Mr. Miller told me, that in a place where *Rhabarbarum verum* had stood for ten years he had this season had it moved from thence to another place where no plant of it had grown for ten years; but now this year where he had had the earth dug up at this place, a new plant had come up from the seeds which had lain there in the earth for so many years, which was now in full flower. Mr. Miller said he had had the same experience with a *Fumaria* (*Fumitory*) whose seeds had lain fourteen years in the ground before they had come up. In the case of the *Fumaria* Mr. Miller mentioned this, that Lobel had made another new species out of *Fumaria bulbosa*, and had called one of them *F. bulbosa viridi flore*, which however is only a variety, for if one takes *Fumaria bulbosa* and buries its bulbs very deep down in the ground, yet so that it can come up, all the flowers come green as Lobel has described it; but if these bulbs are laid nearer up to the surface of the ground it is then an ordinary *Fumaria bulbosa*.

Ugnar i Orangerier. *Stoves in Orangeries.*

The stoves in the Orangeries in Chelsea Apothecaries

Garden are all arranged in the way which Mr. Miller describes in his *Gardeners' Dictionary*, under the word *Stoves*, viz. : that the smoke comes to pass through several bends backwards and forwards in one of the long walls of the orangery. In the largest orangery in Chelsea garden the smoke makes six bends, before it escapes. Mr. Miller said that he had at first [T. I. p. 399] had them made like channels under the floor at the sides of the house, but he had since altered this in the above named way, because he had not found that a good plan. For from the great heat, the tan, **garfvare Barken**, that lay nearest these flues, Canaler, grew so hot, that it became quite dry, and the danger was that it would take fire. He knew two, if not more, examples in which orangeries here in England had been burnt by the tan becoming so hot that it took fire. Coal was burned in the ovens here in the winter, commonly once in the twenty-four hours, viz. : every evening, but if the day is cloudy a small fire is also lighted in the morning. Mr. Miller considered coal the best thing to use for this purpose because they burn so evenly. Peats (**Torf**) he considered to be equally good with coal in this respect ; but they have the disadvantage that the smell of them passes through the wall into the house, so that it smells strong in the orangery, which does not happen with *Coals*. Mr. Miller said that he had at first used *Peat*, but left it off for the reason first named. *Wood*, he believed not to be so good for fuel as coal and peat, because it heats too quickly and strongly. The tan which had lain for a time in the orangery around the pots, **krukorna,** was afterwards used in the garden as ordinary manure. On the mould in the pots in the orangery nothing was laid, neither sawdust nor anything else. In Moscow I have seen saw-dust laid on the mould in the pots in orangeries, to keep them moist longer.

The 13th May, 1748.

To-day the Session of Parliament was closed for this
season, when King George II., at 2 o'clock in the afternoon [T. I. p. 400], went up to Parliament to deliver
part of the Articles of Peace [Treaty of Aix-la-Chapelle]
and to take leave of the House, because His Majesty was
intending to cross to Holland the same or the following
day, and then to go on to his hereditary land in Hanover.
I had one of the best opportunities there could be to see
him both long and well because I stood in the front row
both when he went in and came out of Parliament, just
where he alighted from his carriage. When he had got
out of Parliament and had sat down in his carriage he
remained a short time before he drove away from the
Houses of Parliament, talking to the Duke of Richmond,
who afterwards accompanied him in the carriage.
Besides, when he went in to the Parliament House and
also when he came out and entered his carriage the
crowd raised a cry or shout of joy. Some among them
cried out "God bless the King"—that is, **Gud välsigne
Konungen.**

Ranelagh House.—In the evening I visited Ranelagh
House, which is a little out of *Chelsea* on the London
side, where the youth of both sexes, and the elder people
go to divert themselves. Ranelagh House is reckoned
one of the largest halls in Europe. It is built nearly round,
and has only a pillar in the middle. Here, in the summer
there is *Instrumental* and *Vocal Music* almost every evening,
and now and then in the mornings. Those who wish to
go in there must pay a *shilling*. Round about the house
is a large garden with many *allées* planted with high
hedges on both sides. On all sides within the house
there are built by the wall, as it were, small [T. I. p. 401]
Contoirs, which were quite open to the hall itself.

In the middle of this division, **afstängningen,**

is a table with benches on both sides. Any one who pleases can sit here and be served with all kinds of food and drink, which is here immediately to hand, **som här är strax til hands.** Men and women find nothing else to do here but to walk about in this large hall and listen to the music, or to sit and *faire bonne chère,* **pläga sig,** in the small rooms, or also to divert themselves in the garden, &c. Suchlike pleasure-houses, **lust-hus,** are found in many places, both in and outside of London, where time is killed **förnötes,** in such a way, especially in the afternoons and evenings. In the Town there are held Comedies Oratorios, Instrumental Concerts, **Musique,** Rope-dancing, **Lindansare,** &c. Besides all kinds of pleasure-houses, and according to the time of year, they also avail themselves of one or other of these. If these pleasures were only employed for this purpose, that after one had tired himself out with his duties or business during the day he took his pleasure here once a week in the afternoon to freshen up his spirits, then they would be of great service; but to devote every day to this, seems, *sauf meilleur avis,* **oförgripeligen,** to be nothing else than to waste their youth and lead them to dissipation, idleness, and *libertinage.* Everything has its measure, **Alt har sitt mått.** Here they are accustomed to vanity, ostentation, *inutilité, bagatelles,* **fåfänga,** to waste precious time, to fall by degrees into weakness and indolence and to fight shy of work, **sky för arbete.** Married ladies and Mistresses of Establishments, and the young girls become in many ways altered and ruined, **bårt skämde,** and lose all pleasure in household duties.

Den 14 Maji, 1748.

Rön vid *Larix.*

Mr. Miller told us that the *Duke of Bedford* had had

a number of *Larices*, C.B. [European] *Larches* planted in
his garden, some of which had come to be planted in very
good garden soil, and [T. I. p. 402] others again had to be
content with only a very meagre soil. When they afterwards began to grow, those in the meagre soil had
commonly made double as long shoots as those in the
good garden mould, **trägårds jorden,** and looked very
lively, while on the other hand, the former, which stood
in a good soil looked quite drooping, **matta,** as though
they where obliged reluctantly to force themselves to
grow. The wonder-worthy laws of the Allwise Creator
in respect of plants are proved by this, that the meagre
and poor earth also has its special trees and plants,
which flourish well in it, but thrive badly, **vantrifras,**
in what we humanly speaking, call a better soil. He
said he had found the same with the *Cedar* of Mount
Lebanon, but as I note that he has entered this experience
in his work *The Gardeners' Dictionary*, I will not now say
any more about it, but refer the reader to that work.

Chelsea **är en liten Förstad eller By.**

Chelsea is a little suburb or village, situated a couple
of miles from London towards the west. The river
Thames runs close past *Chelsea*, **stryker tätt förbi C.,**
on the S.E. and S. sides, and on the other sides there is
nothing else besides nurseries and market-gardens, of
which there are here a frightful number. The place resembles a town, has a church, beautiful streets, well-
built and handsome houses all of brick, three or four
stories high. I cannot "just" understand what some of
those who dwell here live upon. Some have small haber-
dashers shops, but that is not saying much. Publi-
cans, innkeepers, coffee-house keepers, brewers, bakers,
butchers, and such like, can here make a good living; because a multitude of people from London in fine weather,

vackert väder, * in the summer come out here, to enjoy themselves, when such people well know [T. I. p. 403] how to charge for what they sell. The principal livelihood of the others seem to be from houses and rooms, which they let to *gentlemen*, who in summer now and again, especially on Saturdays, Sundays, and part of Monday, come out here from London to stay, and take the fresh air. Rooms are here considerably dearer than in London itself, which is said to be due to this, that they have heavy taxes, **utlagor,** and that they get no one in the winter time to lodge there, wherefore they are obliged in the summer time, as it were, to take for both at once to compensate for the loss.

Several houses in this place belong to *gentlemen* who live and reside in *London*, and only now and then journey out to *Chelsea ;* but, in short, a third of the houses are said to belong to *Sir Hans Sloane*, who bought them many years ago, and now lets them to different people.

[T. I. p. 408.] *The 18th May*, 1748.

Sir Hans Sloane.

In the morning I went to Chelsea, and spent part of the morning in Chelsea Apothecaries Garden. Afterwards I accompanied Mr. Miller to Sir Hans Sloane to pay my respects to him. He lay to-day in bed, and looked a picture of old age, and was reported to be now in his 94th year. Mr. Miller gave him to understand, **gaf honom vid handen,** the reason of my journey, that I was intending to visit the places in North America where no Botanist had been before, there to gather and describe all the plants and trees I should come upon,

---

* From Copenhagen to Gottenburg, you have a delightful sail,—if in " vackert väder," as the Swedes say, &c. Sylvanus, *Sweden and Gottland*, 1847, 8vo. p. 44. [J. L.]

H

and make all kinds of observations on Natural History
and Natural Science **Natur-Kunnogheten** &c., which
Sir Hans Sloane approved of very highly, and believed
that I should find there a number of rare things.   *Sir
Hans Sloane* had many years before given up all his public
engagements [T. I. p. 409] and resigned himself now
for the remainder of his life to live in rest and peace
at Chelsea on his estate.   He was now rather deaf, so
that we were obliged to shout loud for him to hear it.
On the tongue he had a swelling, so that he spoke
indistinctly enough and very slowly.   Sometimes a long
time passed by before he got out a word.

[T. I. p. 388].   The 6th May, 1748.

Sir Hans Sloane's Frus Graf.   Lady Sloane's grave.

Sir Hans Sloane had long been a widower.   During
his residence in Jamaica he had married a very rich
widow, which placed him in a position to fulfil his bent
for Natural History, and enabled him to buy the greater
part of the Natural History Collection he now owns.   Ever
since he about eight years ago ceased to be President of
the Royal Society [1740] [T. I. p. 389] he has lived
continually here in Chelsea on his estate free from all
care.   One and all looked upon this man with a particular respect, because he was the oldest of all the
learned men now living in Europe, whose names on
account of their writings and learning, are widely known.
We find in the Philosophical Letters of that learned man,
John Ray, several letters which Sir Hans Sloane had
written as long ago as the year 1684, together with
several of John Ray's answers to them, from which appears what a great insight *Sir Hans Sloane* had even at
that time [aged 29] into all branches of natural science,
not to mention the other sciences.

His wife, whom we have just mentioned, and with whom he had spent the greater part of his life, lay buried in the churchyard here in Chelsea, where Sir Hans Sloane had erected a handsome monument of hewn stone over the grave, which was on the S.E. side of the church against the wall. Round about this carved grave was an iron railing, **järn-galler.** On the east and west sides were Sir Hans Sloane's arms, **vapen.** On the south side there was nothing written, but the hewn stones were there quite smooth. Doubtless Sir Hans Sloane wished to leave others freedom to engrave there his *In Memoriam* and laudatory Epitaph, **åminnelse och låford,** after his dust once comes to be preserved beneath it together with that of his wife. ⌊Sir Hans Sloane died Jan. 11th, 1753, nearly five years after Kalm's visit, and just before this *Tome* was published.⌋

On the north side of this monument there were these words, quite free from show and *flatterie :*

" Here lyeth the body
Of Dame Elizabeth Sloane,
Wife of Sr. Hans Sloane, Baronet,
Who departed this life
The 27th of September, 1724,
Aged 67."*

[T. I. p. 390.]

---

* This Epitaph having perished with the slab on which it was written has disappeared and has been replaced by another on a substituted slab.

" Here lies interred
Elizabeth Lady Sloane,
Wife of Sir Hans Sloane, Bart.,
Who departed this life
In the year of our Lord, 1724,
And the 67th of her age." Copied April 14, 1888.

Thus not only the original Epitaph, but the date of her death, and her age, had been forgotten. [J. L.]

SIR HANS SLOANE'S MUSEUM.

Kalm visited this on the 28th April and the 26th May. The April account, pp. 376-7, is an abstract of the May account which fills 10 pp. 427-38. I shall give the April account as it stands with selections from the May. [J. L.]

[T. I. p. 376.] *The 28th April,* 1748.

Sir Hans Sloane's Natural **Samling.**

In the morning I went in company with Mr. Warner, Captain Shierman, and some other English gentlemen up to *Chelsea* where we spent some time in looking at Chelsea Garden, but afterwards went to see Sir Hans Sloane's collections, in all three Natural Kingdoms, *Antiquities, Anatomy,* and many *Curiosities.*

We saw here a great collection of all kinds of stones, **stenar,** partly polished, **slipade,** partly such as still lay in their matrix as they are found in nature. We saw all sorts of *vessels,* **karil,** *Tea-cups, Thée-*kåppar, *saucers,* skålar, *snuff-boxes,* dosor, *caskets,* askar, *spoons,* skedar, *ladles,* slefvar, and other small instruments, all manufactured out of *Agates* and Jaspis, &c.; a number of different kinds of pearls, several learned men's *Contrefaits,* among which we particularly devoted ourselves to the study and admiration of the great *Botanicus* and [T. I. p. 432] *Natural Historicus,* John Ray.

Mr. JOHN RAY'S *Contrefait,* is the only one of him that exists in England. It is very like that which is found in his "Wisdom of God in the Creation," on the title-page [T. I. p. 376.] A very large collection of insects from all parts of the world, all of which were now preserved in four-sided boxes, **lådor,** with clear glass glued on both over and under, so that one could see them quite well, but these boxes or cases were also so well stuck together and so [T. I. p. 377] tight that no worms or other injurious insect could get at them, and spoil them [T. I. p. 433.] The sides were of wood. In some both lid and bottom, **lâcket och botten,** were of a very clear glass, but in most only the lid. At the joints the glass was stuck or glued fast with paper. Where the bottom was of glass, the insect was gummed on to the middle of the bottom. [T. I. p. 377.]

Some of the East and West Indian *Butterflies,* **Fiärilar,** were far more showy than a peacock with his matchless variety of colours. A very large number of all kinds of corals and other harder sea plants, **Sjö växter,** a multitude of various sorts of crystals, several head-dresses of different races of men, musical instruments, &c. Various stuffed birds and fish, where the birds, **Foglarna,** often stood fast on small bits of board as *naturella* as if they still lived. Skeletons of various four-footed beasts, among which we particularly noticed that of a young elephant, the stuffed skin of a camel, and an African many-striped ass, **mângrandig Âsna.** Several human skeletons larger and smaller, the head and other parts of a frightfully large whale [T. I. p. 438.] This **Hvalfisk** was said to have been 90 feet long. The length of its head bone was nearly 18 feet [T. I. p. 377.] **Honungs-fogeln,** humming birds from the West Indies, which there made a show with their many colours, and sat in their nest under glass as though they had been living; the *bird's-nest,* **Fogel-bo,** which they eat in Asia as any other food; [T. I. p. 431] which they eat in the East Indies. It was white, and looked almost as if it had been made of white wax [T. I. p. 377.] A great collection of snakes, lizards, fishes, birds, caterpillars, insects, small four-footed animals [various anatomical specimens] etc. all put in *spiritu vini* in bottles, and well preserved ; dried skins of snakes from the East and West Indies, of many ells length and proportionately broad ;

very many *tomes* of an *herbarium*, among which we particularly examined those which Sir Hans Sloane himself had collected in Jamaica [T. I. p. 434]; 336 volumes of dried plants in Royal folio; on each leaf there were as many plants stuck on as there was room for.

[T. I. p. 377.] Sir Hans Sloane's *Library*, which probably has few like it among private collections gathered together by one single man, and consists of somewhat more than 48,000 volumes, all bound in superb bindings.

[T. I. p. 427.]   *The 26th May,* 1748.

To-day I accompanied some gentlemen to Sir Hans Sloane's to see once more his Natural **Samling,** and in particular to get to make more exact observations on the *Cobra di Capello,* Serpent, which has, as it were, glass eyes on the neck, **hvilken på nacken har likasom glas ögon,** [whence the French name "Le Serpent a lunettes," "Spectacle Snake"; also "Naja," *Naia Tripudians* (Merv.) M. Morin *Reptiles et Poissons,* p. 68, illustrated on p. 69 and Frontispiece], and to get to count its *scuta abdominalia* and *squamas caudales,* abdominal plates and tail scales, about which *Linnæus* asked me in a letter. . . . [T. I. p. 437]. The snake, *Cobra di Capello,* had 183 *scuta abdominalia* and *squamas Caudales.* If the small *squamæ,* which lie under the chin, parallel with the *scuta abdominalia,* are also reckoned,then there are two more. It was difficult enough to count them, because the snake lay in *spiritu vini* in a sealed glass bottle.

[T. I. p. 427.]   To describe all this great collection in detail, **omständeligen,** would fill several *Folianter :* for anyone who has not himself seen this collection would probably have very great difficulty in picturing to himself that it is so large. We had to-day the advantage that *Sir Hans Sloane*

[T. I. p. 428] honoured us with his company for a couple of hours while we were studying and examining his vast collection. What we now examined was in particular the following [many stones, *Agates*, *Jaspis* &c.] . . . *Puddingstone* is the name of a stone which we saw in abundance about *Little Gaddesden* and at other places in Hertfordshire. It is nothing else than a conglomeration, **sammangyttring,** of several small round flint-stones. In *Hertfordshire* it was used mostly for land-marks and boundary-stones, **râmärken och gränse-skilnader,** I saw there quite large pieces of it. Here, in Sir Hans Sloane's collection, it was polished, and very much resembled *Pudding* of several kinds, whence it has also acquired its name. In the lapidaries' shops there were [T. I. p. 429] snuff-box lids of it which looked very handsome. The person who showed us this collection to-day told us that a certain Englishman some years ago bought some pieces of this polished, carried them to China, and there sold them, by which he made 1,200 per cent. A good transaction! . . . [Several stones] cups, &c., some of which have often cost Sir Hans Sloane fifty guineas. [Saucers, spoons, &c.]

[T. I. p. 430.] Afterwards the most costly stones were shown us, which were arranged in a box made in a particular manner. The box was quadrilateral, a little more than 6 inches long and not quite 6 inches broad, and nearly 6 inches high. On the top it sloped from all sides together,* so that it resembled a monument on a grave, or a house with an Italian roof. It consisted of a great many small boxes, which are not drawn out as usual, but the upper box was always a lid to the under, so that the lowest box had for a lid all the boxes above it. The gems, **adla-stenarna,** were small and lay in small

---

* We should say just the opposite. [J. L.]

round holes turned or cut out in the boxes. It was said
that in this box there were 1,300 different kinds of gems.

[Various other stones [T. I. p. 431], various Foreign
curiosities, and a silly picture].

[T. I. p. 432.] Afterwards we went into a long narrow
room where the greater part of Sir Hans Sloane's rarities
are. This room is about 12 feet broad. The height
about 14 feet, the length was said to be 110 feet. Along
the sides there stood at the bottom cabinets, **skap**, of
sorts of Natural Curiosities, and other things, partly on
them partly hung on the walls; but about a fathom
from the floor above the Natural Curiosities the walls
were all covered with books.

[The rest of p. 432 and 433 descriptions of contents
of cabinets, also the greater part of 434, to same room.]

[T. I. p. 434.] In another room we saw . . . a
machine to lay books on, when one wishes to read or
requires several books at a time. I cannot so exactly
describe it. It somewhat resembles such a wheel as there
is in Stockholm at Norrbro (Northbridge), and is there
driven by the stream [T. I. p. 435] but instead of each
wing or board in that wheel there was here a long four-
sided box, which was moveable on an axle, and seems to
have had some weights in the bottom, for as this wheel
was turned round, each box always had the same side
downwards, The books were laid on the outer sloping
sides of the box, and thus stood always in the same
position, and went round with the wheel as it was
turned. The length of this wheel was about 5 feet and
its diameter about 3 or 4 feet. I do not remember, **Jag
kommer ej ihog**, how many boxes there were, but one
could have lying in front of him a very large number of
books at a time.

Here we saw twenty-four volumes of rare books, all in
costly bindings, given to Sir Hans Sloane by the King of
France.

5,300 volumes of manuscripts in Medicine and Natural History, bound in beautiful bindings.

A book of Chinese Paper with several beautiful pictures in it.

Besides the aforenamed long and narrow room there were eight other rooms, in which all the walls were full of books, from the floor to the ceiling. Each of these rooms was about 14 ft. high, the length and breadth about 15 to 18 ft., sometimes more, sometimes less.

[Other various objects of Natural History.]

[T. I. p. 436.] The shoes of several different Races **Folkslags Skor**; but the Finns' *Birch-bark* shoes, **Finnarnas Näfver-Skor**,*and the Russians'bast-shoes, **Russarnas Bast-Skor†**, made of lime-bark were conspicuous by their absence.

[Various other objects.]

In another room were several of such books as consisted of colored pictures [T. I. p. 437] of all sorts of Natural objects. Such were Mariana's, Catesby's, Sebe's, Madame Blackwell's, &c., costly works, Egyptian Mummies, Roman and other Antiquities, &c. In the garden we saw *Sir Hans Sloane's* Chair [T. I. p. 438] with three wheels under it, two in front and a little one behind, in which he was drawn about in his garden.

[T. I. p. 438.] *The 26th May*, 1748.

Thermometers **Jämförelse** *Comparison of Thermometers*.

After I was tired of seeing all this [Sir Hans Sloane's

---

* *Finnarnas Näfver-Skor*, the white birch-bark. The Lapp name for the birch is Säke, as Linnæus (*Flora Lapponica* Amst. 1737, 8vo. p. 262) remarks. " *Calceos* dum piscatum eunt, gerunt ex ramentis (p. 263) corticis betulini," &c. " when they go a fishing they wear long boots made of pieces of birch-bark," &c. [J. L.]

† *Russarnas Bast-Skor.* Ger "Bast Schuhe, Basteln, *Russ.* "**Lapshy** (*plur.*), des Souliers de cordes d'ecorce d'arbre." J. Heym. *Deutsch-Russ-Franz Wörterbuch*. 1805, obl. 8vo. [J. L.]

Collection] I went to the *Chelsea Physic Garden* as it is
called, where I compared the Thermometer of Prof.
Andrew Celsius, with that Mr. Miller used in the
orangery, and the difference was this :—

When Celsius stood at   Mr. Miller's was

23	$\begin{cases} \text{37, the graduation on the right.} \\ \text{34, the graduation on the left.} \end{cases}$
18	$\begin{cases} \text{25, the graduation on the right.} \\ \text{28}\tfrac{1}{2}\text{, the graduation on the left.*} \end{cases}$

[T. I. p. 455.]   *The 16th June*, 1748.

Botanic Garden at Chelsea.

In Chelsea lies the famous Botanic Garden, which
in London is called *Chelsea Physick Garden*, which belongs to Apothecaries Hall in London, was established
for the Education of Apothecaries in the knowledge of
herbs, and has, as regards herbs, one of the largest
collections of all rare foreign plants, so that it is said in
that respect to rival the *Botanic Gardens* of both *Paris*
and *Leyden*. At least it is believed to overgo them in North
American plants.   It is laid out at Chelsea [T. I. p. 456],
a short English mile from London, because a great
many plants cannot thrive in London for the coal-smoke.
The river Thames flows past it on one side.   On the
opposite side lies the orangery full of all such foreign
plants as cannot stand constant exposure to the open air.
Among other foreign trees which are found there are
four *Cedars of Lebanon*, which stand out in the garden
and are now as large and high as our largest firs, **Furur,**
although they were not planted there before the year
1683, and stand there in a very meagre earth.   The
ground for this garden has been presented to the

---

* Miller's was apparently a differential Thermometer.   One was
invented before 1676 by Johann Christoph Sturm, Prof. of Mathematics
at Altdorf. [J. L]

Apothecaries Hall by Sir Hans Sloane, with the condition that they shall supply it with fifty new plants every
year. In one room of the *Orange-house*, that, namely, in
which the plants are set in the winter time, which cannot
bear exposure in the open air, but still do not require
any heat, stands SIR HANS SLOANE carved in white
alabaster with a scroll of paper in his hand, on a white
marble pedestal.

On the South side of this pedestal, towards the
entrance these words are read :
" Sir Hans Sloane, Baronet,
Physician to his Majesty,
President
of the Royal College of Physicians
and Royal Society
who
That the knowledge of plants
might be preserved and improved
to the Glory of God
and Benefit of mankind
[T. I. p. 457]   Gave this ground
in the year of our Lord 1721
To the Company of Apothecaries London
To be a Physic Garden for ever."
On the East side are these words :
" They
Being sensible how necessary
that branch of science is
to the faithful discharging the Duty
of their Profession
with gratefull hearts
and general consent
Ordered this Statue to be Erected
in the year of our Lord 1733
That their successors and Posterity
may never forget
Their Common Benefactor."

On the West side stand these words :
"Placed here in the year 1737
Sir Benjamin Rawling Kn't, Master.
Mr. Joseph Miller } Wardens."
Mr. Joseph Richards }

[T. I. p. 457.] *Ray's* HERBARIUM.

In a room up in the Orangery there is preserved
as a great rarity, the collection of plants which the
great *Historicus Naturalis, Joh. Rajus* or *Ray* himself
collected and arranged, and with his own hand wrote
the names under. *Mr. Ray* presented this collection a
week before his death, which took place the 17th January,
1706, to his good friend and neighbour, *Mr. Samuel Dale,*
author of the well known *Pharmacologia.* [T. I. p. 458.]
Mr. Dale afterwards in his old age gave this as well as
his own collection of plants to the *Physic Garden* at *Chelsea,*
to be preserved for ever. The plants in *Mr. Ray's
Herbarium* were sewn with cotton on to the paper in
large paper books. The whole collection consisted of
about eight or twelve such paper books in folio. In some
places the plants had been cut out, for *Dr. Sherard* had
borrowed this collection from Mr. Dale, and when he
had found any plant, which was either rare, or he thought
much of, it was said that he had either clipped or cut it
out, so that the books had been sufficiently mutilated.*

Mr. Philip Miller, in whose charge this garden is left,
is and no mistake a great Horticulturist, **Trägårdr
mästare.** So much the better to be able to judge of
this, I will mention one thing and another, which throws

---

* This is one of the most interesting accounts in the whole of Kalm.
William Sherard was at Smyrna from 1702 to 1718, therefore the mutilation
of Ray's Herbarium must have taken place between that date and Sherard's
death in 1722, at the age of 69. Sherard bequeathed his Herbarium containing 12,000 species of plants, to the University of Oxford. [J. L.]

light on the subject, and just as they have been related
to me by trustworthy men. *Mr. Miller's father* was a
Nurseryman, who followed that occupation all his life,
and in the *Practique* of it had gone a long way. He had
begun to instruct his son, this *Philip Miller*, in the art
from his earliest years, and was in this so much the more
lucky, that his son had an uncommon liking for that
occupation. As the man throve, so he spared no expense
in also causing his son to have a sufficient education in
various languages, and other sciences, which profit and
adorn a man. *Miller* quickly assimilated all that his father
had himself taught him, both in *Theorie* and *Praxi*, of ornamental and kitchen gardening. At the same time he
went through all books which had appeared in England
on these sciences. An industrious intercourse with other
enterprising nurserymen in this [T. I. p. 459] town and in
the country round made him still more proficient. But he
did not stop with this. A change of soil, climate, &c,
often causes a plant which can, according to ordinary rules,
be transplanted at one place, not to admit of this being
accomplished with the same advantage at another place,
but a particular treatment is often required at each place.
His thoughts were therefore turned upon travelling. He
was well off, and had therefore no difficulty in accom-
plishing this. To travel out to foreign countries without
having first made himself acquainted with what remarkable things there are to be found at home, he held
neither for wisdom nor usefulness. He therefore travelled through the greater part of England, observing
everything, but was especially careful to inspect all
ornamental and kitchen gardens, and to make himself
at home and acquainted with all horticulturists, for he
was of the opinion that he could get to learn something
useful which he did not know before, at least from some
of them. He conversed with them on all matters con-

nected with their business, and had his trouble often
many times repaid with the useful wrinkles, **de nyttiga
rön,** he gained.   As agriculture has so near a connection
with horticulture, **Trägårds väsendet,** therefore he
kept at the same time an observant eye on everything
which occurred in rural economy, **landthushållningen,**
particularly in the cultivation of ploughed lands.   Thence
it comes that he is still reckoned as the greatest **theo-
reticus** in England.

After he had thus travelled through England, he
started on his foreign travels, and then explored Flanders
and Holland, because he knew that there were also great
horticulturists there, and that the science of the management of ornamental and kitchen gardens had there
reached a high pitch of excellence.   Whether he, besides
the aforenamed lands, also explored other districts, I
have not understood, but from the foregoing it can be
seen [T. I. p. 460] that no nurseryman has so much
advantaged himself in learning both the *theorie* and
practique of his business.   After his return home he
devoted much time in practising all that he had known
before, and that he learned upon his travels.   Hereupon
he afterwards published his *Gardeners' Dictionary* in *Folio,*
in which he describes in detail the cultivation of all sorts
of plants, those which belong to kitchen gardens, as well
as those which are cultivated in academical and medicinal gardens, with numerous other useful notes.   Some
time after that there also appeared the 2nd volume, in
which he completes the work by the account of the
cultivation of plants omitted in the first volume; but as
this large work was dear enough, he shortly after made
an abstract of it, in which he excluded all *philosophical*
and other *curieusa* passages, and introduced only that
which particularly belongs to a nurseryman's business,
so that nothing on that subject is omitted.   The large

book is printed in *Folio*, the latter in 8vo. His great *Gardeners' Dictionary* in *Folio* was some time back, in the summer of 1752, republished with many corrections and additions, after it had first been translated and printed in several languages.

As regards the common opinion of Miller's *Gardeners' Dictionary*, I have asked several of the greatest and best horticulturists both in England and America, what author and what book they had found and believed to be the best in Horticulture, not only as regards a number of rare plants, but in particular those which are planted for the kitchen and *Fabriquer*, both trees and plants. They have all answered with one mouth, *Miller's Gardeners' Dictionary*, either in Folio, or the abstract in 8vo., was the best of all, and that when one has it, no other book is afterwards required, because there is found in it everything that is in the others, and much more besides, and that both more clearly and better worked out than in any other, although the others often have manifold more words. The same answer I have also got from several distinguished persons who had themselves had a particular pleasure in planting trees and plants with their own hands. If any of the *Lords* and the great " Herrar " in England wished to lay out a new garden, or to remake an old one, Mr. Miller would always show them how it ought to be done. When the greatest lords drove out to their estates, he often drove out with them in the same carriage, **i samma vagn.** In a word, the principal people in the land set a particular value on this man.

AMERICAN NOTES

Made in London.

[T. I. p. 384.] **Vax af et slags Porss.**

Wax from a kind of sweet willow.

In many places where there are morasses or wet grounds in North America there grows in abundance a little bush, which is called by Botanists *Myrica foliis lanceolatis subserratis, fructu baccato.* Linn. Hort. Cliff. 455. Upsala 295. This *Myrica* or sweet willow, **Pors,** instead of other fruit has berries which have on the outside a kind of a wax, which is used as a candle, **til ljus.** They take the berries and cast them into a pot of boiling water, when the wax melts off the berries by itself and floats as a grease on the top of the water. When the water is cold, the wax hardens, and can then be taken off and kept till it is wanted. The candle is made from it in the same way as tallow or ordinary wax. They mostly mix this wax with the tallow they are going to make dip candles of, as it makes the tallow candle harder and firmer; for if the summers in Virginia are very warm then the tallow candle becomes so soft and weak from the great heat that it cannot stand straight but bends down; but if some of this wax is melted together with the tallow they never bend with the summer heat. Some of the poor people in that country are said to make [T. I. p. 385] their candles entirely from this wax.

The Duke of Argyll had some of these bushes planted in his garden, which not only thrive there incomparably well, but had also borne such a quantity of fruit that he caused wax candles to be dipped from the wax which he caused to be boiled from the berries in the above-named manner.

Villa Oxar. Wild Oxen.

When the traveller in Virginia has gone some miles from the sea shore up country, or up towards the hills, he often gets to see a multitude of the wild Oxen which are found there. When they become aware of the presence of man, they run away directly without doing any harm; but if any one shoots at them and they are only wounded by the bullet and not nearly killed, they come rushing at the one who has fired, and are dangerous enough unless one can find a means either to shoot them down directly and kill them, or to slip away. Their principal food is the great Reed (*Arundo*), which there grows everywhere in the morasses. The Indians or the wild folk there, shoot them, sometimes eat up the flesh, or throw it away and use the skin, or sell it to the Europeans, who make the same use of it as of any other ox-leather.

A certain *Gentleman of Virginia* has caught some of their calves alive and reared them at home, but he has never been able to get them so thoroughly tame that they did not at the same time retain some of their wild and buffalo nature, **yxa natur**; for as soon as they have been let loose they have run away to the woods, and no fence or hedge has been so good that they have not broken over it. Such a living calf had also been carried over to England and is the same [T. I. p. 386] which is

I

depicted in Mr. Catesby's beautiful work on *Carolina*. Some gentlemen in *Virginia* had also got these oxen tolerably tame, but they have nevertheless, mostly, in the end to shoot them dead, on account of the great damage they have caused; for when they have been let loose, they have not indeed run away but have remained at the farm, and gone in to any enclosure they chose, eaten up and trampled down the crops and other planted things; because no hedge can be so strong that they could not knock it down with their horns or at least make themselves an opening or gap through it.

[T. I. p. 405.]   *The 16th May*, 1748.

Svinens föda, Kött, &c., in North America. Dr. Mitchel said that there is hardly in any part of the world more beautiful and well-flavoured pork, **svin-kött,** than in North America. This he principally ascribed to the maize, which is there planted, and grows in abundance, and on which the swine are fed. They are also driven into the oakwoods in the autumn, where they feed on the numerous acorns, **ek-ollen,** which are there found.

[T. I. p. 409.]   *The 18th May*, 1748.

Friesland nu förloradt. Friesland now lost.

In the morning I called upon Dr. Mortimer, who was Secretary of the Royal Society. Among other subjects that we talked about, he asked me if I knew what had become of the Friesland, which in former times was named as a land which lay west of Iceland. He showed a couple of old maps, **Landt-chartor,** both of which had Friesland shown as a large island, getting on for half as large as Iceland and west of it. On Friesland there were shown the names of many havens and places.

One of these maps was engraved in the year 1666. As we at the present day do not know of any large island in the same longitude and latitude, so it is a question what to think of it. Can there have been such an island? Dr. Mortimer related that he had talked about it with several old sea captains, and one of them had told him that when he had sailed in about the same longitude and latitude as the old maps had placed Friesland, he had found there a much shallower water than elsewhere, indeed in some places so shallow that he had not ventured to proceed in that direction; for the rest, all sea captains had said that at the present time there is no land, island, or anything of the kind seen there. May there not formerly have been a large island which has since sunk?*

---

* Friesland or Frisland, one of the phantom islands of the North Atlantic, has been the subject of much speculation among geographers. The first suggestion of the island upon the map, appears on the Edrisi map, 1154, (Tabula rotunda Rogeriana) where a considerable island is shown to the north of England and Ireland marked " Resland." Next on the oval diagram known as the Imago Mundi of Ranulfus de Hyggeden, 1360, an island called " Wrislad," appears with Noravega, Islanda and Tile. Lelewel considers with some show of reason that "Resland" and "Wrislad" represent Frislanda (Geog. du Moyen Age. vol. iii. p. 101, n.). On the Genoese Pizigani map, 1367, is an island opposite to the south-west coast of Norway, called "Sialanda;" an island in a corresponding position is shown on the Catalane map, 1375, and on the map of Fredrici d'Ancone, 1497, (Wolfenbutel) named "Stillanda," and this island on both these maps bears a legend, stating that the inhabitants speak the language of Norway and are Christians. This name " Stillanda " has been read by some modern geographers as " Frislanda." There can be no doubt, however, as to the correct reading, if either the original Catalane map, preserved in the Bibliothèque Nationale in Paris, or the fine photographic facsimile published by Delisle "Documents Géographiques, 1883," (Brit. Mus. S. 35, 5, sheet 16), is referred to. The facsimile of the Catalane map in Santarem's Atlas (Brit. Mus., Tab. 1850, a. pl. xiii), gives the same reading, but is not so clear. Lelewel reads it " Scillante." The Pizigani map is given in Jomard (Brit. Mus , S. 11. 1. map. x.) and the Wolfenbutel map in Santarem's Atlas (Brit. Mus., Tab. 1850, a. page 74.) The names and positions of the Island " Sialanda " or " Stillanda," in the three

I 2

[T. I. p. 418.]   *The 22nd May,* 1748.
Silk-grass in America.

I asked Dr. Mitchel what sort of grass *silk-grass* was, which is mentioned in the description of Virginia, and is said to serve the same purpose as hemp. He answered that it is called by Morison in his *Hist.** Yucca foliis filamentosis, and grows in Virginia on the sea-shore. It was formerly used like flax and hemp to make clothes of,

maps last named show that it is the "Stillante" of the Fra Mauro map, 1459, *i.e.* Estland or Shetland. This, however, is not altogether inconsistent with its being the genesis of the Frislanda in the Zeno map, referred to below, as the name may have been then misread, as it has been in later days, and the learned ignorance of the cartographers of the XIVth and two following centuries, and their confusion as to the names and true situations of the islands in the North Atlantic, is abundantly evidenced by their maps. The first map on which the name "Frislanda" is found clearly written, is that by Juan de la Cosa, who accompanied Columbus on his second voyage (1493-1496), drawn in 1500. The name occurs also on the Portuguese "Carta da Navigar," by Alberto Cantino, 1503, but in this the position of the island is shifted farther to the east, close to the Ilhas de Fogo. "Insula de Uresland" is shown on a Map in Kunstmann, c. 1505 (Brit. Mus. Tab. 1850, *a.* Blatt. II). Neither Bordone, 1528, nor Zeigler, 1532, mentions it either in their text or on their maps. Zurla recognises Frisland in the "Ixilandia" of the Fra Mauro map, 1459.

Frislanda is mentioned by Christopher Columbus in a memorandum referring to his voyage to Iceland in 1477 (quoted in the life of the Admiral written by his son, Ferdinand Columbus, who died in 1539, in Spanish, but first published in 1571, in Italian) in which he distinguishes it from Iceland and identifies it with the Thule of Ptolemy.

But it is principally in connection with the apocryphal voyages of the Venetian brothers Nicolò and Antonio Zeno at the end of the XIVth century that the name of Frisland is known. An account of these travels was published in Venice in December, 1558, and was accompanied by a map compiled by Nicolò Zeno, a direct descendant of Antonio, and founded, as he alleges, on an old and rotten map found among the family papers of the Zeni. The narrative is given by Ramusio (3rd ed., 2nd vol., 1574), by Hakluyt (Divers Voyages 1582, and Voyages and Navigations vol. 3, 1600) and an abstract appears in Purchas hys Pilgrims (vol. 3, 1625). The Zeno map was accepted as genuine, and copied with slight alteration by Ruscelli

* *Historia plantarum Universalis*, Tomi III. Robert Morison. *Oxon* 1680, 1689, Fol. [J. L.]

but since they have been in the habit of getting clothes and other similar things from Europe, the method of preparing this has been so far forgotten that they no longer know in what way it was formerly prepared.

[T. I. p. 419.] Dr. Mitchel said that he had sown it in his garden in Virginia, where it throve well. He had attempted to treat it in the same way as hemp, when he obtained from the fibres in the leaves a sort of fibre not unlike hemp. Only a few of the wild plants grow in

---

(Ptolemy, Venice, 1561), by Moletius (Ptolemy, Venice, 1562), by Gerard Mercator, 1569, and by Ortelius (Theatrum Orbis, 1570). Frobisher thought he had actually found the Frisland of the Zeno map when he reached Greenland on his first voyage in 1576, and that he sailed along its coast four days on his second voyage in 1577, and landed there on his third voyage in 1578.

The map took a strong hold on the geographers of the day and was used by cartographers for nearly two centuries after its appearance in 1558. Since then many writers have endeavoured to reconcile its falsities with facts, while others have held that both the map and the narrative were altogether founded on fiction alone, e.g., Torfæus (1705) and Charlevoix (1744). Of the former class some have believed that Frisland did once actually exist, but that it has been submerged, or lost by some natural convulsion ; amongst these are Delisle (1720), the Duc d'Almadover, The Abbé Zurla (1806) and Amoretti (1811) ; others have tried to identify it with some land still existing, but known to us by another name. John Reinhold Forster (1786), the translator of the American portion of Kalm's travels, somewhat inconsistently adopted both these views, but he seems finally to have preferred the latter, and identifies Frisland with Fara, Fera or Ferasland, a small island off the east coast of Hoy in the Orkneys; others, e.g., Terra Rossa (1686), followed by Admiral Irminger (1879), have satisfied themselves that Frisland was Iceland, but the majority "in number and value" of writers on this subject, though differing on other points, think that it was the Faroes ; of these are Buache (1784), Eggers (1794), Maltebrun (1831), Zahrtmann (1833), Bredsdorf (1845), Lelewel (1852), and Major (1873-9).

An examination of the copy of the large map of Olaus Magnus, Venice, 1539, long missing, but a copy of which was discovered by Dr. Oscar Brenner at Munich in 1886, since any of the above mentioned authors have written on the matter, seems to make it clear that the opinion was correct that the Frislanda of the Zeno *map* has its original in the Faroes. Zahrtmann says: that the then name Faer-eyar does not appear in the Zeno narrative as it was difficult to Italianize. Frisland is probably a contraction of the adjectival form Faereysk-land. The identity of the

Virginia, but its home is farther south. Dr. Mitchel believed also that it is scarcely found in Pennsylvania because it is too cold there for this plant. I have since found this was true, and that linen is prepared from its leaves.

[T. I. p. 420.]   *23rd May,* 1748.

Nearly the whole afternoon was spent at the house of *Mr. Catesby*, a man who is very well known for his *Natural History of Carolina* in America. In this work he has in-

---

Frislanda of the Zeno *narrative* is another matter, and such is the confusion of this story, that it is not wonderful that Forster has scattered the names shown upon the Frislanda of the Zeno map, over the Orkneys, the Hebrides and the Faroes. The Frislanda of Christopher Columbus was also most probably the Faroes. The Friesland referred to by Kalm is evidently that of the Zeni. The map of 1666, which he saw at Dr. Mortimer's, was probably one of Seller's. The largest and most detailed map of Frisland is that which occurs in the Lafreri Atlas (1550–1575), of which only two perfect copies are known to exist. It contains, with three notable exceptions (viz., Monach, Ledovo, and Ilofe, which are not in the field of the Lafreri map), all the names on the Zeno map, but is much larger, and the island is shown covered with trees, fields, towns, &c. Unfortunately, the map, a later copy of which may be found in the British Museum under the name " Petri de Nobilibus formis, S. 10. 1. (156)," is not dated, so that a doubt remains which of the two maps is the older. It is usual, however, to reduce a small map from a large one and not to elaborate a large map from a small one, and this would point to the probability that the Lafreri map is earlier than the much smaller and less detailed Zeno map. However this may he, Frisland kept its place on many of the principal maps of the XVIth and XVIIth centuries.

Against the theory of submergence or destruction there is no physical impossibility, or even improbability, as the alleged site of the island lies within an area in which the land is sinking, and in the neighbourhood of extinct volcanoes. But it is incredible that a large island with many towns and ports, and having constant and considerable mercantile transactions with Flanders, Brittany, England, Scotland and Denmark, as alleged in the Zeno narrative, in the XIVth century, should have totally disappeared without some record of such a remarkable catastrophe having been preserved in the histories of those countries with which it traded. On this account alone the submergence theory must be rejected, and the identity of Frisland with the Faroes maintained. [F. W. L.]

comparably well represented with lifelike colours, the rarest trees, plants, animals, birds, fishes, snakes, frogs, lizards, painted-toads, **skildpaddor,** and insects, which are there found, so that no one can see that they are not living where they stand with their natural colours on the paper. Mr. Catesby seemed to be a man of nearly sixty years, and was somewhat short-sighted. He now devoted his time to reading, and to further elaborating the *Natural History*. His aforesaid work, which consisted of two large Volumes in Regal Folio, was very dear ; and both together now cost in England twenty-two to twenty-four guineas, therefore not for a poor man to buy.

[T. I. p. 420.]   *The 23rd May,* 1748.

Nytta och Skada af *Punch*.

Good and harm of P. I asked Mr. Catesby and Dr. Mitchel whether they thought that *Punch* was a useful or a baneful drink ? They answered that their opinion was that it is beneficial or baneful according as it is prepared. Mr. Catesby [T. I. p. 421] said that his experience in Virginia and Carolina had been as follows. They drank at one time Punch which was made of strong Brandywine or rum and water with much sugar in it, but only a little lemon-juice was added. The effect, which they gradually found, of this was, that after some time they got a kind of *Paralysis*, which was such that they could not hold anything with the fingers; for they had almost no strength in them, but were obliged to place everything they wished to take hold of between the two hands. For example, they could not hold the glass which they wished to raise to the mouth with the fingers, which they could not press together, but between the wrists, **hand-logorna.**

Afterwards they began to diminish the quantity of Brandywine and sugar but to put more lemon-juice in

it, after which they did not get such troublesome paralysis,
although commonly the sad future consequence was
that he who drank Punch generally became very palsied,
darrande, in his old age.

[T. I. p. 424.]   *The 25th May, 1748.*

Gramina perennia **nog** rara **uti** Virginien. *Perennial grasses rare enough in Virginia.*   Dr. Mitchel, who had
lived a very long time in Virginia and North America* told
me that perennial grasses are there very rare.   The
grasses that are mostly found there are generally *gramina
annua,* which sow themselves every year.   For this
reason he said he was disposed to have a large number
of seeds of *gramina perennia* collected here, and sent over
to Virginia to be sown there.   For the rest, he said that
the grass in *Virginia* has not the beautiful vivid and
green colour [T. I. p. 425] that it has here in Europe, but
the colour of the grass is there brownish, and not so
grateful to the eye.

---

* With reference to the "Dr. Mitchel" who has been so frequently
mentioned :—

John Mitchel, MD., F.R S., emigrated to America early in the 18th
century, returned to England in 1748, and died in America 1772.   He was
the author of various Botanical, Zoological, and Medical books, but is best
known for his excellent map of America, which was published in 1755.   It
has been often used in boundary negotiations, and is still regarded as an
authority.   [F. W. L.]

WOODFORD.

COUNTRY BETWEEN LONDON AND WOODFORD.

[T. I. p. 146.] *The 28th February, 1748.*

I N the morning I went out into the country to a place named *Woodford*, 10 miles from London, in Essex. The prospect of the country between *London* and *Woodford*, where we now travelled was mostly plain, or only in small hills. The whole way there is nothing else but a succession of beautiful houses, fertile arable fields and verdant meadows. At all the houses there was commonly a garden full of various beautiful trees. The walls of the houses were overdrawn either with *Syringa*, Caprifolium, [Lonicera Caprifolium] *Goatsleaf Honeysuckle*, Hedera, *Ivy* or *Mespilus pyri folio Sempervirens*, or some other kinds. In some places there were not planks but hedges round the gardens, of *Taxus*, **yew**, elm, hawthorn, or some other tree.

The whole of the land was divided into *inclosures*, or **täppor och täckter**, which were all surrounded by hedges of all kinds of planted trees, especially hawthorn, sloe, [T. I. p. 147] dog-rose, blackberry-bushes, holly, *Agrifolium*, together with a number of other trees

121

which had come to grow in the hedges.   In some places,
especially nearer to London, there were high earth-banks
cast up, about 4 feet high, instead of hedges round the
fields.   They consisted of the usual brick-colored clay of
the district, with a quantity of gravel and pebblestones,
grus och små släta flint-stenar.   These fences
gärdes-gårdar, or earth-walls, **mull-vallar,** require
repairing yearly.

The earth, **mullen,** had now slipped down in many
places and made an opening so that the cattle could go
through it.   But they are not here so difficult to maintain,
because the winters here are seldom so sharp that there
is any frost in the earth, **at det blir någon tjäla i
jorden,** which otherwise is in a position to damage an
earth-wall sooner than anything else.   The beautiful
appearance of the country must altogether be ascribed
to industry and labour.   It resembles one continuous
pleasure garden, **trä eller lustgård,** from the many
living hedges there are everywhere.

London's many towers appeared in the distance.
However clear the air may be, there seems always to be
a fog-like cloud standing over the town, which comes
from the coal-smoke which ascends in abundance from
the innumerable fireplaces, where fires are continually
burning.   The roads are full of travellers, on foot and on
horseback, in wagons and carts, who travel backwards
and forwards, so that one often has, as it were, to steer
through them.   In some places the Thames appears in
the distance with many ships and vessels sailing there
outwards and upwards.

The River Lea.   Here and there are river channels
and cuts, *Canaler,* some made expressly and artificially
from the Thames up country, for the purpose of conveniently carrying coals and other commodities. *

---

* The river Lea is rendered navigable for barges up to Hertford, by
many artificial " cuts."   [J. L.]

[T. I. p. 148.] *The 4th March*, 1748.

Bot for Brännsår.

Remedy for burns. Among remedies for burns it is reckoned an exceedingly good one to rub the burned place with ink, **bleck,** directly one has burned oneself, which not only prevents blisters from rising, but also at the same time heals, which effects are attributed to the vitriol in the ink.

The 7th March.

Epping Forest. Immediately to the North and East of Woodford there lies a beautiful forest, **löf-skog.** The soil, as in the whole district, is **en grof rödaktig eller tegel-färgad sand, som här kallas** *gravel*, a coarse reddish or brick-colored sand, which is here called *gravel*, mixed with a fine earth and a quantity of ordinary blackish flints. The forest is high-lying. Rabbits and roe-deer are said to abound in it, though we did not see any when we passed through it. Nor did we find any plants in this forest in flower, excepting the trees named below. Otherwise the ground was everywhere green. The trees had not been allowed to grow high, **ej fått växa långa,** but after they had obtained a height of 9-12 feet they had polled them for firewood, **ved,** or some other purpose. They had afterwards thrown out many branches, and thus made a crown.

The trees which we found in this forest were the following :

ILEX *foliis ovatis acutis spinosis,* Linn. *Hort. Ups.* 32, *Agrifolium,* &c., of Ray, called by the English *Holly,* was here the commonest of all trees. (I. *Aquifolium.*)

It grew mostly in bushes, but sometimes as trees of 12 feet high. The reason of its short growth was, that it was cut off by the surrounding inhabitants for firewood, **ved.** This [T. I. p. 149] bush which keeps its green and beautiful leaf the whole winter, was an ornament to these woods. It is much to be wished that it would grow in Sweden.

CARPINUS, 786, **Afvenbok**, [C. Betulus L. 1770], is called by Englishmen *Hornbeam*, and occurs in considerable abundance. It had a good many of the last year's leaves remaining, but withered enough. From some trees they were all fallen off.

CRATŒGUS, **Hagtorn,** hawthorn, in considerable abundance, though quite small bushes. The leaves were all off.

FAGUS, **Bök,** *beech*, very abundant, had nearly all its last year's leaves remaining, although completely dried up. The bark was quite smooth and resembled **Rönn,** [*Sorbus Aucuparia*] the *Rowan tree* or *Mountain Ash*.

QUERCUS, **Ek,** *oak*, here and there tolerably abundant. From the old trees the leaves had mostly fallen off, but for the most part, still remained on the young ones.

ULEX, [U. Europæus], called by the English *Furze*, grew in some places, especially on the edge of the forest, in great abundance. *Mr. Richard Warner* [author of part of a translation of Plautus, 1767, and of Plantae Woodfordienses; *Catalogue of the plants about Woodford*, London 1771, 8vo.] told me that it flowers nearly the whole year, except a couple of months in mid-winter. As this plant is very full of thorns, **taggar,** it is difficult to advance without boots where it is abundant. At a distance many might have thought that there was a group of Juniper bushes, **Enbuskar;** for its leaves, **blan**, resemble it, and it grows in exactly the same or similar places. About its great [T. I. p. 150.] usefulness for hedges, &c., an account shall be given farther on.

ROSA, *Vulg. Dog Rose*, with several other varieties of the same, grow here and there. They had now no leaves. RUBUS [*R. Fruticosus*] **Björnbärs-buskar,**

Blackberry-bushes, grew here and there especially in the hedges, **gärdesgårdar.** The stalks were often 18 feet long and more. They did not stand erect, but when they had grown about a fathom in height they curved down to the ground, and afterwards crept along it. It was not good to get along where these grew abundantly, on account of their long thorns. In the hedges they were not so uneven. The leaves were fallen off most of them, but on some few they were still remaining.

HEDERA [*H. Helix*, 190], called by the Englishmen *Ivy,* grew on a great many of the trees, up which it had clambered. In particular, it had taken up its abode in the crown which had been formed after *carpinus* (hornbeam) beech, and oak, had been polled, but the stalk went from the crown close to the tree down to the ground. It had green, fresh, and beautiful leaves.

SPARTIUM, 589 [*S. Scoparium,* now *Cytisus Scoparius*] *Broom,* grew here and there on the borders of the woods.

RUSCUS C. B. [R. Aculeatus] *Butcher's Broom,* grew in some places in the woods, but was quite small. The leaves fresh and green ; it had also remained in flower the whole winter, and flowers were now beginning to expand. The leaves ended in a spine, **en tagg.** The plant was pretty to have at the borders of garden beds, where box, **buxbom,** is now otherwise used.

DAPHNE, Linn. *Hort. Ups.* 94, [*D. Laureola*] *Spurge Laurel,* grew here and there in the wood, though in few places.

[T. I. p. 151]. *The climate of England* is quite different from that of Sweden, which the inhabitants ascribe partly to the more southerly position of the country, partly and principally to the surrounding ocean. The ground was here everywhere now quite green and bare of snow, except that some still remained near a few hedges, **gärdesgård,** which was left from the .

unusually heavy snow that had fallen a fortnight before.
All the cattle went out on the field to pasture, without
the farmers having to take thought for their food.
Indeed horses, cows, sheep, swine, geese, fowls, &c.,
often go out by themselves and seek their food in the
fields the whole winter. For the cows they have also
houses to put them in sometimes at night during bad
weather, and a haystack close by in case of need; the
sheep are not allowed any house at all, but they go
constantly under the open sky, summer and winter,
night and day. It is only on account of the small lambs, of
which they take a little care, that they are sometimes
kept under cover, **under tak.** During the last-fallen
heavy snow, which lay a long time, the sheep were kept
quartered only by a haystack, there to have their food
as long as the ground lay covered with snow. There is
also in this district no difficulty in keeping a large
number of cattle. A farmer also escapes the disadvantage of giving himself much trouble and unrest
in collecting fodder for the cattle during the winter
[as in Sweden].

In the houses where the folk dwell the fire burns on
the hearth all day, and a **spjäll** is an entirely unknown
thing, as has already been said. Therefore, when it is
cold the folk sit round the fire, when often the one side
is hot while the other side freezes.

The earth and the ground, **Jorden och Marken,**
takes here so little harm from cold and frost that one
can plough the whole winter through, and there is hardly
a month in the year in which [T. I. p. 152] some kind of
seed is not sown. Spring-rye, barley, and pease, were
already sown in the fields. Beans, pease, and other
kitchen-garden fruits, were already sown for the most
part by the close of February, and even by the middle
and the beginning of that month.

Seas, rivers, and becks were open, only some fish-pond, **fisk-dam,** and some small pool, **liten puss,** had still ice at the end of February, when it was unusually cold here, but now they were all thawed, **uptinade.** It is looked upon as a very unusual thing when the river Thames at London is over-drawn with ice. One who lives there does not have the advantage of enjoying this treat many times in his life. It is true that sometimes during the winter a little snow falls here, but it seldom lies longer than three days, and when this does happen it is looked upon as something unusual, for which reason also those who live about London do not know what a *sled,* **släda,** is.

The 8th March, 1748.

Plants standing in flower at this date included only the following, which are partly among England's wild plants, and partly planted in their gardens. I except here *Genista Spinosa* and *Ruscus,* which also now stood in flower, because I have just mentioned them. We wandered a long way round about, and made a note of those we saw standing in flower.

CROCUS *vernus* was planted in gardens at the edges of flower beds, and especially on both sides of paths, where it formed a great ornament with its yellow, **gula,** flowers at this time of year. I saw it also with white, blue, and blue-grey flowers, though seldom.

[T. I. p. 153]. GALANTHUS [G. Nivalis], *Snowdrop,* was planted in gardens in the same kind of places as the crocus. Of our wild plants in Sweden, the following were in flower, which are numbered as in Linn. *Flora Suecica :*

Alsine, 369 [Stellaria Media].
Lamium, 494 [Lamium purpureum].
Senecio, 690 [Senecio Vulgaris].
Bellis, 707 [B. perennis] *Daisy.*

Corylus, 787 [C. Avellana] Hazel.

Primula Veris, 161, *Primrose*.

Chelidonium Minus, 460 [Ranunculus Ficaria].

The 9th March, 1748.

Häckar, hedges, were planted around all ploughed fields, meadows, and pastures, gardens and kitchen-gardens, and often around the ordinary courtyards and farmyards. Instead of a plank-fence, **plank,** round the fields, meadows, and pastures, they had first of all dug a ditch and cast up the earth on the bank of the ditch. In this banked-up earth there were afterwards planted small shoots, either of hawthorn [Cratoegus Oxyacantha], blackberry-bushes, 409, or dogrose, 406, **Törne,** mixed together. The hedges especially consisted most of hawthorn with blackberries and dogroses, interspersed here and there. The hawthorn was five times as numerous as the other two put together, if not more, and the blackberry bushes quite three times as many as the dogrose. At first, as long as these shoots were still small, they had set up beside them a dead fence, **en död häck,** which was a kind of **gärdesgård,** in which the twigs of the afore-named thorny bushes were instead of a fence, **stängsel.** Before the **gärdesgård,** or dead fence, had become old, the planted trees were already so grown up, that they could afterwards fence off all cattle and completely fulfil their office.

[T. I. p. 154.] The height of these hedges was commonly 6 feet, 9 feet, and sometimes 12 feet; sometimes also only 3 or 4 feet. The thickness was from 2 feet to 6 feet or more. In these hedges accidents such as wind, birds, mice, &c., have afterwards planted several other trees, as oaks and ashes ; Hornbeams 786 [Carpinus Betulus], **Afvenbokar; Fläder,** 250 [Sambucus Nigra], Elder; Elms 219; Agrifolium (*Raj. Syn.* 466) [Holly] Ivy, 190, and other leaf-trees.

The pollard oaks spread out like a crown, and formed a good shelter for cattle in hot sunshine or storm. All the twigs in this crown were very often cut and carried home for fuel, when other shoots commonly struck out anew. Sometimes when the hedge had very much widened out at the sides, it was cut right down, and a dead hedge set up instead. After a short time the cut-off stems shot forth a multitude of twigs, which afterwards formed the most beautiful hedge one could desire. A bad habit which I noticed hawthorn, blackberries, and dogroses had, was that they commonly creep with their roots over a wide space, **vidt omkring**, out towards the arable or meadows, where they had not prevented this by a little ditch close to the hedge. When they had so crept, no one had been with the scythe to the grass which was nearest to the hedge and on its side.

Besides the manifold uses which these hedges serve, there are among cthers (1), that much wood, **skog,** which would otherwise be required for fences, **gärdsel,** is by this means saved. (2) The labour of yearly laying down **gärdesgårdar,** *dead-fences*, is avoided [T. I. p. 155] because these, once planted, last for ever. (3) When anyone wishes to cut down an old hedge he has an abundance of fuel, and a new one comes up instead in a little time. (4) The cattle have a very good shelter, **skjul och skyggd,** from them against storms and other bad weather. (5) It is a matchless protection for ploughed fields and meadows, because storms and other cold winds, which otherwise on large open fields, **öpna fält,** often thin away and destroy the plants, and cause great damage, are resisted by the hedge. (6) They are an incredible ornament to the country, because wherever one turns his eyes it seems as if the whole country were a beautiful and delightful garden.

Farther on I shall describe in detail how these hedges

K

are laid down entirely new, or renewed from old ones, and managed, with many circumstances connected with the subject.

Höet. The hay was arranged in stacks, commonly near the *cowhouse*, which in this country was mostly situated in one of the meadows or pastures.   Over the haystack was no shelter but a little straw.   It stood under the bare heavens, only that it was fenced in.   We devoted a long time to the same to ascertain exactly what kinds of plants the hay here consisted of, and found them to be the following, numbered after Linn. *Flor. Sv.*:

> Anthoxanthum 29 [A. Odoratum].
> Phleum 50 [P. pratense].
> Agrostis 62 [A. Capillaris].
> Aira 67 [Holcus Mollis].
> Poa 77 [P. Angustifolia].
> Cynosurus 81 [C. Cristatus].
>   „   83 [Dactylis Glomerata].
> Avena 96 [A. pratensis].
> Lolium 104 [L. perenne].
> Plantago 123 [P. Media].
> Rumex 292 [R. Crispus].
>   „   296 [R. Acetosella].
> Cerastium 379 [C. Viscosum].
> Ranunculus 466 [R. Acris].
> Trifolium 612 [T. Repens Sv. **Hvitväpling**].
>   „   615 [T. Pratense].
> Carduus 658 [C. Crispus].
> Chrysanthemum 700 [C. Leucanthemum].
> Achillea 705 [A. Millefolium Sv. **Rölleka**].

Nos. 62 and 67 were the most abundant, and 81 tolerably so.

[T. I. p. 156.] *The 10th March*, 1748.

Träns plantering. *The planting of trees.*

Whilst I was visiting at *Woodford* I often went about with Mr. Richard Warner, an English gentleman. He had inherited from his forelders a fine property, which he, in the English fashion, had rented out to farmers or tenants, and now lived on his rents out here on his estate, free from all unrest and oppressive cares. Few can be compared to him in a peculiar disposition to be of service in all things, both to natives and foreigners. He had travelled much, had a deep insight into nearly all sciences, but particularly *horticulture* in which his principal pleasure consisted. In his garden were nearly all the trees and bushes that could endure the climate of England, and these stood the whole year out in the fresh air, and under the open sky. They were planted in mazes, **labyrinther,** and in many other ways. One can see a list of such trees as will stand the climate of England in *Miller's Gardeners' Dictionary*, at the end. I amused myself sometimes in the daytime in standing by and seeing how he planted all sorts of different kinds of trees. He was not very tender about it. The earth in the garden consisted of a yellowish-red mould mixed with sand. A little pit was dug for the tree which was to be planted, which was sometimes only 18 inches or 2 feet, but sometimes 6, 8, or 10 feet high. The pit was then adjusted to the size of the root. He generally took care that, when the tree was taken up out of the *nursery*, **trä-scholan,** or the open country, enough earth accompanied the roots, but still it often happened that the roots were quite bare. When they were set in the hole, **gropen,** there was no manure laid under or around the roots, but the [T. I. p. 157] earth which had been cast up when the hole was dug was cast on to and around the roots, and was afterwards trampled down; but I remarked that sometimes, after the root of the tree

K 2

had been set down in the hole, a couple of spadesful were taken from the surface soil which lay under the leaf-trees, planted two or three years before, and laid close round the roots, and sometimes a little under the same before the rest of the earth was shovelled on to them.

The roots of *Agrifolium*, holly, were not cut off when they were set; but the ends of the fibres are cut off all round the roots of *Taxus*. In the case of *Acicular-leaved* trees, Coniferæ, such as *Taxus*, yew, *Pinus Abies* and *P. Sylvestris*, the *Norwegian spruce* and *Scotch fir*, **Gran och Tall,** I remarked that notwithstanding it was rainy weather the day after they had been planted, they were, nevertheless, watered plentifully enough around and on their roots. The reason was said to be this, that by that means they take root and become established sooner. In the case of some trees which had been planted the autumn before, grass or dried hay was laid over the mould or banked up earth around the plants, **mullen eller jordkupan,** which was said to be done to protect the roots the first winter from cold.

The 11th March, 1748.

Yesterday and to-day, and some of the following days, there fell a considerable quantity of snow, although it was nothing compared with the snow which falls every month through the winter with us in Sweden.

However, nearly all Englishmen said that there had not for many years been so much snow here in England as now. This snow, however, did not lie much over a week before it was entirely melted away.

[T. I. p. 158.]

Hvad förmon en Ängelsk Bonde vid sit landtbruk har framför en Svensk.

What advantages an English farmer has over a Swedish one, in his farming operations.

It is well-known that the winters in England can in

no way be compared with our Swedish ones. I here refer especially to the southern parts and around London, for farther north in England also, they are sharper. The snow seldom lies more than two or three days on the ground. Cows, horses, sheep and other animals here go out the whole winter, and feed on the grass which stands green and flourishing the whole year through. There is no month in the year in which they cannot plough and sow the fields. November, December, January, February and March are seldom so cold that any frost, **tjäla,** could prevent them from tilling the ground, for which reason also there are found set forth in English agricultural books what ploughing and duties in the fields, **åkersyslor,** they have to perform in each of these months. There is no one here who knows what a sled, **släde,** is; because the snow seldom lies so long that anyone would be able to use one. *Sledge,* which *Lexicographi* make in English the same as **släda** in Swedish, is nothing but a **släpa.** How it is farther north, I leave there.* The winter comes here very late and goes away very early, if at least I can call it winter, for the English winters are commonly such as September in Österbotten and October in Stockholm. From such a climate and so mild winters an English farmer or **Landtman** derives many advantages, which a Swedish **Bonde,** does not enjoy. An English farmer escapes the greater part of our winter charges, **Vinter-körslor.** The mild winters enable him to use sticks instead of logs for fuel, **Ris i stället för ved til bränsle,** and make it unnecessary for him to [T. I. p. 159] employ a great part of the winter in sawing up wood, **til veds körning.** His

---

* The *Sled* is used on the Pennine Chain. For a sketch of one form see Studies in Nidderdale " Glossary, *s.v.* [J. L]

fuel is from his hedges, which are commonly not far from the farm, but can be carried or carted home as it is required. He never need waste any time in hewing, sawing, and splitting wooden fences, **gärdsel,** and carrying home of staves, **samt stafvars hemförning,** because he has around his fields living fences, **lefvande gärdesgårdar,** which so far from rotting away, soon grow up where they are properly managed, and thus furnish him yearly with sufficient fuel not only for his own behoof, but also to sell to others. The houses which are built of brick, **sten,** free him from sawing timbers ; and roofs of tiles, which never rot, from cutting and carrying home rolls of birch bark, roof trees, roof boards, and shingles. The earth, bare of snow and verdant through the whole winter, which gives the cattle for the most part sufficient food, **födo,** makes it unnecessary for him to gather nearly so much hay and fodder, **foder,** as a Swedish **Bonde** must do, if he will succeed in other ways. Also there is the great advantage that he can plough and till the earth when he will, and it is convenient, without being obliged to bustle and hasten as in Sweden, where all the labours of fetching food for man and beast come, as it were, at the same time ; and to get to feed sheep on the turnip land with turnips the whole winter time ; to escape having to build houses for cattle and sheep ; to have vegetables out of the kitchen garden the greater part of the year ; most of all, never to need to fear that he will suffer harm to his cattle from wolves and bears, **Vargar och Björnar,** which do not exist there.

The 12th March, 1748.

Häckar i Trägårdar. Hedges are used in gardens of different [T. I. p. 160] kinds of trees, which partly grow wild in England, or have been imported from other places, but are now so acclimatised, that they are able to stand out the whole year, and endure the winter well. Mr. Warner did not himself know whether any American leaf trees were used anywhere in England as hedges, or whether any other American trees were so employed. I will divide the trees used in hedges into two divisons viz. :

Trän til häckar, som altid hafva gröna löf.

Trees in hedges which always have green leaves.

TAXUS (Linn. *Fl. Sv.* 825) is much used in this place, admits of being clipped, and looks very pretty. I did not see so many hedges in gardens of any tree as of this, which, besides that, was clipped in pyramids and a hundred other forms. [*Yew.* Taxus baccata.]

ILEX [I. Aquifolium] holly. A great many varieties of this are used, both with and without spines, **taggar,** also *foliis ex albo variegatis,* and several others. One could make hedges of this 12 feet high and more. A hedge of this is one of the most beautiful one could ever wish to see, and it were to be desired that this tree would stand our winters.

ULEX. [U. Europaeus] furze. As this flowers mostly the whole year, it is, with its beautiful yellow flowers, very handsome.

PADUS. [Prunus Padus], bird-cherry. This occurs in nearly all gardens. In some places it was used as a hedge, which was very beautiful.

[T. I. p. 161.] VIBURNUM, Linn. H.U. 62,2, Tinus, *Clus.* Lauro-tinus vulgo, [Laurustinus] is used in some places for hedges, but they are not particularly well adapted for that purpose. See Miller's *Gardeners' Dictionary.*

PHILLYREA. Nearly all sorts have been used for hedges, but when hard winters occur they perish; besides

other inconveniences. [There are three species, natives
of Southern Europe, Italy, Spain, *Turt.* v. 32, 1806.]
QUERCUS (Linn. *Hort. Cliff* 448, 2). *Ilex,* C.B.
[Q. *Ilex* L.], together with several varieties of it, was
used here for hedges round the "*Wildernesses,*" or "*Laby-
rinths,*" and mazes, **irrgångar,** and other "quarters."
These hedges were very thick, well admitted of being
clipped, and looked very beautiful.

MESPILUS *spinosa,* Linn. H. C. 189, 2, Pyracantha, T. B.
[Mespilus Pyracantha, L. 1770, II. 343], now *M. Ger-
manica,* was used in many places for hedges, and looked
very pretty. Especially they had planted it against the
brick walls of houses on the sides facing the roads, where
it climbed up the wall and, with its green leaves, the
whole year through, made the walls very pretty.

BUXUS *arborescens,* C. B. [B. Sempervirens, L.], was
used in different places for hedges in, as well as round,
gardens and ordinary crofts, **så uti, som omkring
trägårdar och ordinaira gårdar,** clips well, and
made one of the thickest and most beautiful hedges.

Trän til häckar som hvar Höst fälla sin löf.

Trees in hedges which shed their leaves every autumn.

ULMUS, 219. **Alm,** elm [U. Campestris], was
enough used for hedges, and grew to a considerable
height. They had two sorts of this tree, in particular,
one which grew [T. I. p. 162] very high and was used
for hedges on some sides of the gardens to ward off the
blast, and one which was less, and which was used for
smaller hedges.

TILIA, 432. **Lind,** *lime* [T. Europæa], and other
varieties of it, was used in the same kind of places as the
Elm, and grew high enough.

CARPINUS, 786 [C. Betulus], *Hornbeam,* was sometimes very much used for hedges in gardens. It was

mostly clipped off, so that it did not get to grow higher than about 4 feet high.

ROSA *Sylv. foliis odoratis*, C. B. [R. rubiginosa], "The *Sweet Briar, or Eglantine*," was enough used for hedges, looked very pretty and thick, when it was green and full of leaves.

MALUS, **Appleträd**, *Appletrees*, of different kinds. These did not form ordinary hedges, but were used in that form which is called *Espaliers*, which, however, perform the same service as a hedge.

CRATŒGUS [C. Oxyacantha], **Hagtorn**, *Hawthorn*, was used in many places for hedges in orchards and kitchen gardens, but especially around small vegetable gardens, and sometimes round the front garden, **innangården**, because it grew very thick, was thorny, and could be made very beautiful by clipping.

CORYLUS, **Hassel**, *Hazel*, was used in many places for hedges.

PRUNUS SYLVESTRIS, C.B. [P. Spinosa, L.], **Slån**, *Sloe*, was used in many places for hedges, but mostly around vegetable gardens, **Köks-krydd-gården**, and the main building, **Mangården**, in the same way as hawthorn.

RIBES, 195, Gooseberry-bushes [R. Grossularia], **Krusbärs-buskar**, were used in some [T. I. p. 163] places in gardens, as hedges, and were both beautiful and useful. [Banks MS., R. Uva Crispa.]

SAMBUCUS, 250, **Fläder**, *Elder*, was used very much for hedges round the vegetable gardens near London.

The 13th March, 1748.

Stenkols-nytta, &c.

The use of Coal, &c. The fuel which is exclusively used in *London* is coal, **Sten-kol.** In the villages which lay nearest around *London*, coal was also the principal fuel, although there also they spun it out with sticks, **risqvistar,** cut in the hedges. But a couple of Swedish miles, or about 14 English miles from London, and in places to which they had not any flowing water to carry up boats loaded with coals, for the most part bare wood was used, either from the trees they had cut down in re-pairing hedges, or from dug-up tree-roots, or fuel of some other kind, as brackens, **Ormbunkar,** furze, &c. Tin and silver-gildings soon took a black colour from the coal smoke, if they were not often scoured or cleaned. Statues of former kings, such as those of King Charles I., King Charles II., King James II., looked just as if the image of a nigger or of a crossing-sweeper, **en Morians eller Korstens-fäjares bild,** had been set up, only in royal costume.

When the snow had lain a couple of days on the roofs, it began to acquire a black colour. The houses were all either blackish or grey from the coal smoke. To a foreigner, and one unused to it, this coal-smoke was very annoying, **besvärlig,** for it affected the chest excessively, especially at night. I found in my own case that however free I was from cough when I now and again went into London from the country, I got [T. I. p. 164] one always as soon as I had been there a day, which never failed to be the case, even farther on in the summer when the air was warm, and there were not large fires in the town ; but as soon as I left London, and had been two days out in the country, I lost my cough. All who lived far out in the country, and were not accustomed to coal-smoke, even native Englishmen, had the same tale whenever they came up to London on their business. But when any-one had been for a time in London he no longer had so very manifest a sensation of it. Nevertheless, I am not altogether indisposed to believe that this great coal-smoke is even one of the reasons that cause so many in England to be troubled with lung disease and *Hectique* (consumption).

Coal-ashes mixed with clay, of which bricks, **Tegel,** are made, will make the brick or tile much stronger and firmer than the clay by itself.

The same ash carried on to ploughed clay-lands, **lergrund åkrar,** makes a matchless manure. Farmers, **Landtmän,** who live many miles from London, buy it and carry it home a long way to manure their arable with it. In gardens it is said also to be very good and of the greatest possible service.

The 14th March, 1748.

AGRIFOLIUM (*Ray Syn.* 466). *Holly* is a tree which especially occurs in the woods in England, and with its evergreen leaves makes them beautiful even in midwinter. The wood is used for toys for children, also for knife-handles, because it is hard. Coachmen's whip-handles, **Kuskarnas piske-skaft,** are made mostly of this wood; for it is at the same time flexible. The principal use which they make of this tree is for hedges, which are both thick and beautiful, and last almost for ever. *Mr. Warner* told me he knew a person whose father, [T. I. p. 165] sixty or more years ago, had had all the hedges round his property planted with this tree, which hedges are still, at the present time, so thick that a dog cannot get through them. A holly-hedge has before all others the palm in this, that it retains its green and beautiful leaves both winter and summer, and is thus a good shelter for sheep and other cattle against blasts and bad weather. *Bird-lime* is made from the bark. In woodless districts it is also used for fuel.

The 15th March, 1748.

Fåren. *Sheep* in England seem almost to be more

hardened, **härdade,** to stand bad weather than ours in
Sweden. The whole of this season there were showers
of sleet, **snöglopp,** or snow mixed with rain every day.
The thermometer of Celsius stood also sometimes in the
open air as low as 3° below 0 [26·6° Fahr.] To this I
can add that the same thermometer in the room where I
slept, **låg,** which had no fire in it, stood nearly all day
yesterday 1° below 0 [30·2° F.] and this morning at
7 o'clock, 2° below 0 [28·4° F.], from which it may be
imagined how cold it must have been out in the open
country, **på fria fältet.** None the less for that, and
although the snow now covered the ground to a depth of
nearly 4 inches, the sheep went night and day out in the inclosures or the small fenced pastures, **ute i täckterna,
eller de små instängde betesmarker,** under the
open sky without having any house or shelter, **hus eller
skjul,** to go under. I except small lambs and their
mothers, who were let under cover. The sheep had this
advantage, that the snow seldom lay the whole day over
all the ground, but one place and another soon became
bare, where they could seek their food. The quantity of
wool they now had on them seemed also to be able to
protect them tolerably well from the cold. [T. I. p. 166.]
Here they had freedom to run night and day about the
pastures, but in very many places it is also the practice
to drive the sheep in the daytime either on to the arable
fields, meadows, or pastures, to bait; but every night
they are set in folds on some arable piece, where they
not only by their droppings manure the field, but also
come to stand in the fold quite close beside each other,
because the fold was expressly made so narrow that they
thus might warm each other. After a couple of days,
just about, the fold was changed to another place, so that
all the field might be equally manured.

[Kalm was in *London* 16-20 March.]

[T. I. p. 173.] *The 20th of March.*

In the morning I went out to *Woodford.* SPARTIUM 589, [S. Scoparium] called by Englishmen *Broom*, grew in abundance on high-lying pastures, where the soil consisted of a coarse sand, **en grof-sand.** [The Bagshot Sand.] Almost all the brooms, **qvastar,** which were used, out in the country, to sweep houses with, were made of it. When it was fresh, it had a peculiar and particularly agreeable scent. According to Mr. Warner, this is used by some brewers instead of hops, when the beer, **drickat,** which is brewed with it, becomes very strong, and soon makes those who drink it drunk.

The 21st March, 1748.

Stenvältar. *Stone Rollers,* were much used here in gardens and kitchen gardens. The stone itself consisted of a kind of white limestone or coarse species of marble, **Marmor,** but the rest of the machine, by which it was drawn, was mostly of iron. There were several sizes, according to what one wished to use them for. One of those which lay in Mr. Warner's garden was 2 feet 3 inches long ; diameter 21 inches. [T. I. p. 174.] Some others in the same garden were smaller. They were used to draw along the paths in the gardens, which in this district were strown with gravel and coarse sand, **grus och grof sand,** so as by that means to press down the lumps in the gravel and make the path even and flat. This was done several times in the summer according as the earth in the paths from various causes, such as worms, burrowing, &c., puffed up. For levelling lawns, **gräs-vallens,** or grass, they did not use stone-rollers, but only wooden rollers, **trävältar.**

Rokor. *Rooks* in numbers, *injurious to arable fields,* and *how they are exterminated.* In all the villages, **byar,** in this district there was a frightful number of a kind of crow called by zoologists *Cornix frugilega*, and by the in-habitants of the island of *Öland* off the coast of Sweden, **Roka.** (*See* Linn. *Fauna Svecica*). They had built their nests up in the highests summits, **skatan,** of elms, oaks, and other lofty leaf trees, where no one could get at them. There were often seen in a single tree ten, twelve, sixteen, twenty, and more such nests, **bon,** all made this year. There was therefore constantly, but especially in the mornings early such screeching, **skrik,** in these trees that one could scarcely hear what another person said if they were standing near the trees. These birds, **Kreatur,** did the "farmers" or agriculturist, **Landt-mannen,** an incredible amount of harm, for as soon as wheat, barley, oats, pease, or, in a word, whatever kind of crop there might be was sown, they covered the fields and plucked up, **plåckade up,** as much as they could get at. When the pease were sown, which was nearly all done by the *drill*, or in rows, and began to peep up, there were the rooks collected in large numbers. They began to follow along the rows [T. I. p. 175] in which the pease were sown, and pulled up, **ryckte up,** all they could find, so that not many of the peas were left. I saw a farmer who had this spring sown a large field with pease which were so entirely destroyed by these destruc-tive birds that he was obliged to plough it up and sow it again with oats, because scarcely a single pea was left remaining. Scare-crows, **Fogel-scrämslor,** were set up in the fields, but could not frighten them, **kunde icke injaga någon räddhoga i dem.** Many might think because they always had their nests in trees near villages, that it was not difficult either to shoot them there dead, up in the trees, or to destroy their nests, or to climb up in the trees and poke down their nests with long poles, or in some other way to prevent their increasing in numbers. To this it is answered: " Certainly, sir, if one had leave to do it ; " but as the rooks have commonly been so sly, **sluga,** as to build their nests in such trees as stood in front of, **utanför,** gentlemen's and noblemen's houses, and belong to them, they were free from all attacks of enemies ; because it was very seldom that any *gentleman* allowed anyone to shoot or molest them in his trees, but seemed to consider himself entitled, as it were, to shelter them, because they had taken refuge with him, and, as it were, solicited his protection. A *gentleman* could so much the more lightly do this, because here in England they hardly ever cultivate their fields or landed estates, **landtgods,** themselves, but let them out to farmers and live on the money flowing in from their tenants. The farmers it is true destroy these rooks, **Råkor,** by shooting them, when they meet them in the fields ; or they also take *Nux Vomica,* **Räfkakor,** boiled in water, soak the seed or peas which are to be sown in it, and then sow them. When the rooks eat them they become intoxicated [T. I. p. 176], so that directly they fly up they fall down again, and either die, or are killed by the farmer's folk, without any mercy.

The seed is said not to take any harm from this steeping. In the trees near the farmers' houses no such nests are seen.

The 23rd March, 1748.

In the morning I went into London, and came back to Woodford in the afternoon, the same day.

They know how to make use of the dirt on the roads, in England.

I saw everywhere in London, as well as in the larger villages between Woodford and London, carts only made for the purpose of carrying away the dirt which from many causes, such as folk, horses, and cattle collects in the roads.

Such sweepings and other refuse as in London are

collected in the houses, are cast out into the street by
the servants, where they are afterwards shovelled together in heaps, and laid in the dung-wagons to be
carried out of the town to some particular place where
they are shot. Such a wagon or cart as is used for
cleaning the town has the advantage, that it does not
drive out of the way of anyone it may happen to meet
in the street. When farmers and others convey anything
into the town to be sold, they seldom drive with an
empty load home, but they mostly take a wagon full of
this manure out with them from the places where it is
collected together. Some of these places are such, that
the ground on which the dirt is laid belongs to one person
who lets it out to another, who does not allow anyone to
take a load from it, who does not pay a certain price
for it.

[T. I. p. 177.] Other places again are of this description, that anyone has freedom to take the dirt from them
without paying anything for it. For this reason farmers
who live not far from London, do not take the trouble to
seek after *Marle* and other manures on their own properties
because they have such a good opportunity for providing
themselves with excellent manure from *London*. Those
who sell this dirt are said to derive large incomes from it
in the course of a year, and a farmer does not think much
of paying a few pence for every load he takes on the
return journey home in an otherwise empty wagon.

The 24th March, 1748.

Genista Spinosa vulg. *Raj. Syn.* 475, is called by the
Englishmen *Furze*. It is used in some places here in
the country for hedges round the arable fields, meadows,
&c., but this is not so very common. The reason why
it is so little used for this purpose is said to be principally
that when it has stood three or four years the lowest

twigs begin to wither, dry up, and fall off, through which the hedge becomes thin at the bottom, so that small animals can creep through it. This can nevertheless, be remedied by sowing some furze seeds every year under the hedge. Also, if the twigs are cut off, or the stalks themselves down at the bottom, then it strikes out new and fresh shoots, otherwise it is much used for hedges in gardens. The use of this bush, besides this, is that in this woodless district it is much used for fuel, whence it happens that it has seldom got to grow to any height. Otherwise it thrives well, so that where it has once taken hold, **fått fäste,** it is not so easy to eradicate. The farmers, **Bönderna,** sometimes have great trouble in effecting this, where it has got to insinuate itself [T. I. p. 178.] sufficiently into the fields. The twigs are much used to light fires with, because they have the same qualities as Juniper-twigs, or straw, viz., that they flare up, and quickly take fire, and rise up in a large and bright flame.

In many places the walls of outhouses and sheds **uthus och liders-väggar,** were made of it in this way, that the roof of the shed, **lider-taket,** stood on posts; between each post there were staves, **störar,** erected, one foot or a little more apart; between these the furze was wreathed in the same way as the sprays in a **kol-skrinda,** or coal-sled, are plaited in serpentine folds. Sheep eat these shoots when they have newly run up, but they do so only from hunger, and for want of other better food. Rabbits eat it very much. It is a pity that it will not stand our climate. Who knows, however, whether it might not be able to grow down in **skåne?** [N. Lilja. *Skånes Flora,* 1869, p. 512 "**Sand Gultörne** (*Ulex. Europœus* Linn) . . . . Cultivated, very rare, Torup, Alnarp, Broby." J. L.]

[Kalm was at Little Gaddesden from March 25th to April 15th, 1748.]

L

[T. I. p. 340.] *The 15th April,* 1748.

We left Little Gaddesden in the morning and travelled this day, first to St. Alban's, and afterwards to Colney, situated three miles the other side of St. Alban's.

A couple of miles after we left *Little Gaddesden,* we came to *Great Gaddesden,* which is a *Parish,* but has not so many farms and houses as Little Gaddesden, which contradicts its name, for *Little* Gaddesden means "**Lilla** G.," and *Great* Gaddesden means " **Stora** G." Perhaps it may have been larger in former times.*

Prospecten af landet.

Between *Little Gaddesden* and St. Alban's the country was a continuous series of hills and dales. It much resembled the country between *Tveer* and *Moscow,* but still more between *Moscow* and *Toulou,* Tula, in Russia.

The hills were high, and consisted of chalk, but the highest crust of the often before-mentioned **tegel-färgade jorden eller leran,** brick-colored earth or clay. These hills, **högder,** commonly ran from N.N.W. to S.S.E., and sometimes from N. to S., although they also often had some other direction. The sides of these hills were mostly **långslutte,** long sloping, yet in some places somewhat steeper. All the country was divided into *inclosures* in the same way as has been described at *Little Gaddesden* [p. 210 *orig.*] and in many other places. These *inclosures* were surrounded with hedges of the same description.

Beautiful houses appeared here and there. **Husen bygde af sten, murade emellan korsverke af trä.** "Brick and Stud" houses, or houses built of brick,

---

* There are a large number of Roman bricks built into the east-end of Great Gaddesden Church. The area of G. Gaddesden *par.* is 4,149·29 acres, and that of L. G. *par.* only 925·497 acres. [J. L.]

walled up between crossbeams of wood, which went both *ad angulos rectos et acutos.* Some houses were roofed, **täckte**, with flat tiles, but most with straw in the way which has been described above at several places here in Hertfordshire. Some [T. I. p. 341.] outhouses had walls of oak boards. Around the farms, all sorts of fruit trees were planted, such as apple-tree, pear-tree, cherry-tree, walnut-tree, &c., of different kinds, while in some places some of them stood in the hedges round the *inclosures,* so that the houses here were mostly situated in orchards of fruit trees, **löf-lundar af frukt trän.** On the hill-sides and hills there lay either arable fields, meadows, or pastures. In a word, the country here everywhere resembled a charming and well-arranged garden.

Harvar at rifva bårt måssan på ängar med, &c.

Harrows to tear away mosses from meadows with, &c.

On a gentleman's estate, there lay a couple of such **Fåll-grindar,** or hurdles, as have been described [on p. 262 *orig.*], between whose **trän och spolar,** staves and rods, on the under side were inserted and interwoven a number of **slån-gristar,** sloe-twigs, so that they were held quite fast. With these harrows thus arranged they drove along the moss-grown meadows, when the thorns and the sharp twigs of the sloe tore up the moss in the field and swept it away with them. In like manner these harrows were used for this, that when the manure was spread over the grass-sward of the meadows they drove these harrows over the fields, by which means the dung and earth were torn asunder and reduced to pieces by the sloe-branches.

Trä rötter til bränsle. *Tree roots as fuel.*

On the same estate there lay several heaps 12 feet high and 5 or 6 fathoms long and wide at the base,

which all consisted of dug-up roots of beech, oak, ash,
&c., which were now mostly cut up to be used at the
house for fuel instead of other wood, **ved.** Thus they
knew in this district how to make use of every bit of a
tree, and to be careful of the wood.

[T. I. p. 342.] Hopgyttrade flintstenar.

Conglomerated flint-pebbles. Puddingstone.

For the most part, at all the farmhouses there were
placed here and there against the corners tolerably large
stones, such as one or two men might carry, which
stones were only a conglomeration of quite small round,
trinda, so-called *Pebblestones,* which are all a kind of small
round smooth flint-stones. They had here been bound
together by some fine clay, **lera,** which had afterwards
become as hard as flint. I do not know where they had
taken them from, for they did not occur on the open plain.
In London I afterwards got to see small pieces of it, which
were polished and made into the lids of snuff-boxes, when
they looked like the most beautiful agates, and exhibited
a variety of colours.

Hurudant vatten Här brukas til kokning, etc.

What kind of water is here used for cooking, etc.

I have said before [p. 281 *orig.*] that a spring or
any running water is very seldom found on the Chalk-
hills. Therefore those who live there are obliged to
dig large and deep ponds, **dammar,** in which the rain
water can collect, and clear itself, **sila sig tilhopa.**
In colour this pond-water exactly resembled such white
and thick water, as in Sweden usually stands in clay-pits,
lergropar, only that this, here in England, inclined a
little to yellow, which was due* to the chalk soil, **krit-
grunden,** which it stood upon. Folk avail themselves

---

* This yellow tint is caused by hydrated peroxide of iron. [J. L.]

of this water, for want of any other, for cooking food, washing dishes, linen, etc., **til mats-kokning, kärils-twättning, bykning, etc.**

We could never perceive any unpleasantness in consequence of the food we ate which was cooked with it. We also saw linen-clothes, floors, &c., become quite as clean and as white with this as with any other water. This was also the cattle's drink, who likewise did well upon it.

Sädes-stackar på stålpar. *Ricks on props.*

We saw the whole way from *Little Gaddesden* to [T. I. p. 343] *Woodford* in Essex ricks at the farms partly of round partly of oblong shape ; part of them stood on pillars, part on the bare ground. In a word, exactly the same as have been described [pp. 229 and 255 *orig.*]. Some stood on wooden posts more or less high, surrounded in the middle or at the upper ends either with polished brass or tin, others stood on stone posts, which were of the white *freestone*, which is got near *Tatternel*. They were hewn square, and quite smooth on all sides. The height of the pillar was 2 feet 6 inches. On the top of the pillar was laid a square *flagstone*, **häll,** of the same kind of stone, whose under side was quite smooth and flat, and reached on every side 6 inches beyond the square pillar, **stålpen,** so that mice and other small injurious animals could not possibly climb up these posts to the stack. On the top these square *flagstones* were so hewn that they sloped down on all sides, so that the water ran off them at once. The bottom of the stack consisted of small sticks, **stänge,** laid 3 to 6 inches apart.

On these there were first laid either brackens, **Ormbunkar,** twigs of sloe, hawthorn, or dry straw, and afterwards the sheaves of the crop, **Sädes-karfvar.**

Halm til gödsel. *Straw as manure.*

Straw of wheat, barley, oats, pease, beans, &c.,
was given to the cattle as fodder at home, and what
they did not eat was cast into the farmyard, to be
trampled down and turned into manure, in the same
way as has been described above (p. 251 *orig.*) This we
saw done at every farm, where we travelled in England.

Gödselns utförsel. *How the manure is carted.*

The manure which had been prepared in the above
manner we now saw in many places, being carted on to
the fields, and there [T. I. p. 344] laid in small loads
or heaps.

These carts, **kärror**, were very large, and made in
such a way that the body, **skråfvet,** could be turned
and sloped down backwards after a cross-board at the
back had been first taken off, when the manure slid down
by itself, after which the body of the cart fell back into
its former *horizontal situation.* Such carts are used for
the same purpose at many places in Sweden, only that
the English ones are far larger.

Huru åkrarna voro lagde, &c. *How the fields were arranged, &c.*

The fields were here everywhere divided into smaller
or larger *inclosures* surrounded with hedges, of all sorts
of different kinds of trees, as has been mentioned above
at *Little Gaddesden.* As the country here lay by turns
in hills and dales, so also the situation of the arable
fields was adjusted accordingly; yet they commonly lay
on the sides of the hills.

The soil at the top of them was the brick-colored
earth, **tegel-färgade jorden,** which has been described
above at *Little Gaddesden,* but under that, at a greater
or less depth, solid chalk came on nearly all the arable-

fields. Hereabout lay a tremendous number of ordinary
flints of the size of the closed fist and smaller, so
that one could scarcely see any of the earth or soil for
them.

They had in some places so got the upper hand,
that they were obliged to gather them, **plåcka dem
tilhopa,** and lay them in heaps. The carl who accompanied us assured us that the best and choicest wheat,
barley and oats, and even turnips, grow on such very
stony fields. These fields were now sown with wheat,
barley, oats and peas, or they were about to be sown
with turnip seed, not to mention, **at förtiga,** that a
part of them were now left fallow, **til trädes-land.**
The wheat was here nearly everywhere sown in
"stitches" or "*four thorough land.*" [T. I. p. 345.] The
breadth of such a *stitche* was just a Swedish ell, or 2
English feet. The breadth of the water furrows which
lay between the *stitches,* was, at the top 18 inches the depth
6 to 9 inches At some few places wheat was sown in
broadland, there, for instance, where the land seemed
to be very dry. Pease were here nearly everywhere
sown in the recently named *stitches,* with the exception
of some single place where they were sown in *broad-
land,* which last-named was everywhere used near *Little
Gaddesden.*

Barley, oats, turnips, clover, St. Foin, vetches, &c.,
were all sown in *broad-land.* The wheat stood beautiful,
barley and pease had already come up.

Clover, Sain Foin, Ray-grass, sown as fodder for cattle.

In some places the *inclosures* were sown with clover,
Trifolium purp. sativ, in other places with *Sain Foin,* or
also with *Sain Foin* and *clover* together. In other places with
clover and *Ray-grass* together, or also with *Ray-grass* only,
(med bara R.) "*Ray-grass*" or "Rey-grass" [rye-grass] is

Lolium radice perenni. Linn. 104 [*Lolium perenne*]. These plants now stood everywhere very beautiful. The carl who accompanied us said that when *clover* and *ray-grass* are sown together, the ray-grass prevents the cows from swelling or bursting, when they eat too much of the too satisfying clover.*

Mr. Williams at Little Gaddesden said that the same effect is produced if *clover* and *trefoil* (Medicago legumini-bus reniformibus, Linn. 621) [*M. lupulina*] are sown together.

In some places where they had last year cut clover, the 'stub' or 'haulm,' **stubben eller halmen,** which they had left remaining was now collected and laid in heaps to be carried home and laid among [T. I. p. 346] other straw in the farm yard, to rot together to manure. If this dry stub was left to stand on the ground it would hinder the growth of the new clover.

Krit-grop *Strata* in a chalk-pit. On the S.W. side of a hill in a field there was a large chalkpit where they had taken chalk, to be carried out on to the fields for manure. Here the sides were not of bare chalk, without beds of another kind of rock but the *strata* lay in the following order :—

	Ft.	ins.
1. On the top, *the brick-colored earth*, **tegel-färgade jorden,** sometimes 1 foot, sometimes 2 feet thick ; for in some places this stratum was more, in other places less thick..............	1	0
2. *Chalk*, **krita,** with which flints, **flint-stenar,** were mixed here and there ....,........	1	0
3. *The brick-colored earth*, 2 or 3 inches ....,....	0	3

---

* "They have lately sown Ray grass, *Gramen loliaceum*, to improve cold, sour, clayey weeping ground, unfit for Saint Foin." Plot. *Nat. Hist. of Oxfordshire.* 1677. *Fol.* [J. L.]

	Ft.	ins.
4. *Chalk* with a little flint, **Flinta**	1	6
5. The *brick-colored earth*	0	0¼
6. *Chalk* with a multitude of flintstones in it ...	4	0
7. The *brick-colored earth* ½ inch to 1 inch 1 inch to 2 inches	0	2
For in some places it was thicker than in others.		
8. The hard chalk which is here called "Hurlock" right down to the bottom or 1 ell, for how this was afterwards I could not see, because the fallen earth and chalk prevented that	2	0
	11	0¼

The narrow *Strata* of the *brick-colored earth* or *clay* **tegelfärgade jorden eller leran** went sometimes in long curves, **bukter,** upwards, sometimes downwards. It was remarkable that the lowest *stratum* of all, or No. 8, was *Hurlock* wherein there was scarcely a single flint, **flintsten,** which however were tolerably abundant among the chalkbeds. [T. I. p. 347.] The carl who accompanied us said that *Hurlock* is the best to burn lime of, and that such good lime does not come from pure and loose chalk. Some of the flints in the chalk resemble spigots or goats horns. Might I not have got to see freestone underneath this, such as there was at *Tatternel* if the pit had been some fathoms deeper ?*

---

* This question may be answered definitely. The bed (No. 8) here so well described by Kalm, as to make it easily recognisable, is the top of the "Chalk Rock" beds of Mr. W. Whitaker, which lie at the base of the Upper Chalk and on the top of the Middle Chalk, to which as a whole I have repeatedly heard the name of "Hurlock" applied on the area between *Tring* and Dunstable.

The thickness from the "Chalk-rock" of Whitaker to the *freestone* of *Tatternel* or Totternhoe is 310 feet.

[*continued over.*

Hedera ätes af Får och är en prydnad vid gårdar.

Ivy is eaten by sheep, and is an ornament on houses.

The carl who accompanied us told us that sheep willingly eat the leaves of ivy. I had the same story from another afterwards. At *St. Alban's*, where we dined, this had climbed up the plank fences of some gardens, and covered them, so that at a distance they looked like green-clipped hedges.

Källor.

In the dales we saw here and there *springs* of running and clear water. [Only the Gade at and below Great Gaddesden, and the Ver at St. Alban's.]

Tattare. *Gypsies.*

We encountered to-day at several places large troops of the wandering gypsies, with a number of their wives and children, and wondered highly that this useless folk could be tolerated in this country.*

"There is often a layer of flints resting at once on the 'Chalk-rock,' but there are no flints in it." *See* Mems of the Geol. Survey of Gt. Btn. vol iv., p. 46, 1872, and vol. i., 1889, pp. 67-68.

On the site of this chalk-pit I observe, pits just dug to the chalk-rock are scarce. As it was on the S.W. side of a hill it must have been west of Great Gaddesden. If Kalm rode across the fields by the path from Home Farm, Little Gaddesden, he would then pass two chalk-pits with the required aspect and depth between Little Gaddesden and St. Margaret's, and as the one on the 500 feet contour west of St. Margaret's touches the chalk-rock beds I believe it to have been this one. I am well acquainted with all the chalk-pits old and new, in the district. [J. L.]

---

* To a Romano-phil this sounds harsh, but only two years before, or in 1746, Jean Gordon was ducked to death in the Eden at Carlisle, a specimen of "toleration" that would have reduced Kalm's wonder, had he been aware of it. It is interesting to find this little notice of English gypsies, which I had not seen when I published my *Yetholm History of the Gypsies*, Kelso, 1882, in which I collected hundreds of passages relating to the gypsies of Europe, which show how fruitless were the various barbarous means used for their extermination from this and other countries. See also p. 353, *orig.*, p. 161 *below*. [J. L.]

Flinta til murar, vägars lagning, etc.

Flints for walls, road-making, &c.

In one place and another we saw walls of arable fields built of flints only, **af bara flinta.** In some places a great part of the church walls were built of them. Outside *St. Alban's* some carls were engaged in digging deep ditches by the road side. Their depth was 3 feet 6 inches. Where these ditches were on the hills, there were a great many large flints among the earth cast up from them, some of them so large that one carl was scarcely able to lift more than one of them. They were afterwards carried out on to the roads to fill up the [T. I. p. 348] deep holes made by their large and heavy cart and wagon-wheels.

In other places where the ground was more even and not in hills, small *Pebblestones* were dug up, which were **små rundaktiga kiselstenar af bara flinta,** small round pebbles of flint, which also were carried out on to the roads. Together with these *Pebblestones* there was also dug up here a quantity of brick-colored **grus** or *gravel*, which was afterwards screened, **sållades,** from the pebbles, to be used on paths in pleasure gardens and kitchen gardens. In some of these places where the ground was even, and not in hills, the soil, right down to the bottom of the ditch, consisted of the aforenamed brick-colored *gravel*, with clay amongst it, **med lera deribland,** and an abundance of *Pebblestones*. In other places also, on the hills, there was on the top the brick-colored earth, 3 or 4 feet, and chalk under it, in which was found abundance of flint.

Kyrko-torns skapnad, m. m. *Church-towers' shapes, etc.*

The church-towers here in England, especially in the country, were commonly such, that they did not taper off at the top in a spire, **spira eller spits,** but resembled

a cut-off parallelogram, so that, when the four square walls
of the tower were finished, the tower also was commonly
complete, only that the sides on the top resembled old
town walls, **gamla stads-murar**, *alias*, that on the
top of the walls there was left a row of spaces on all the
sides, the same breadth as the brickwork that was continued upwards between the openings.* In the middle,
or towards one side of this tower a thin pole was erected,
on which, on certain occasions a flag was hoisted, either
of one colour or another. To-day we saw flags hoisted
on all the church towers in *St. Alban's*, some white,
others red, some of other colours. [T. I. p. 349.] The
reason was said to be, that it was done to celebrate the
Duke of Cumberland's birthday, which was to-day.

Häst hoar. *Horse troughs.*

At *Colney* they had in one place and another *horse-
troughs*, out of which the horses drank, lined with lead. I
have also seen the same both before and since at many
other places here in England.

Örter begärlige för Svin. *Plants Enjoyed by Swine.*

Outside *Colney* there went some swine and ate of the
green plants which stood in the bank under a hedge. I
noted that *Alsine media* C.B. [Stellaria Media] *Chickweed,* was a very favorite food with them, but they did
not trouble themselves about young nettles, **Nässlor,**
of both kinds, *Urtica urens minor,* C.B. and *Urtica Urens
Maxima,* C.B. [*U. urens.* L. (*small nettle*) and *U. Dioica* L.
(*great nettle*) *Stinging Nettles,* Ger. Nessel. *Hoffm.* 1791
p. 335.]

The 16th April, 1748.

We continued our journey from *Colney,* where we lay

---

* Most of these brick *battlements* are later additions to ancient towers.
[J. L.]

the night before, through *Bell Bar, Cheshunt, Waltham Cross*, and *Waltham Abbey*, till in the evening we reached Woodford, in Essex.

Juncus til Säten i Stolar. *Rushes for Seats of Chairs.*

In several wet places and near the water we saw enough of *Juncus laevis panicula sparsa major* C.B. which grew there [*Juncus effusus* L. *Soft rush*.] The carl who accompanied us told us that chair-bottoms are made of this, when it is either plaited in three or twisted with two stems. Poor folk make their living by it.*

Åkrarnas belägenhet och läge.
The situation and condition of certain arable fields.

We saw at one place a ploughed field, which lay quite flat. The soil was a grey clay, **Jordmon var en grå lera.** No flints or very few [T. I. p. 350] appeared on it, a fact which we afterwards noticed on all the fields we saw to-day, viz.: that very few flints occur on them. The afore-named field had last year been sown with pease, when it had been laid out in *Three-bouts-land*, that is, 6 furrows in every ridge, 6 **fåror i hvar ryggning.** The breadth of such a *Three-bouts-land* was 4 feet 6 inches. The water furrows were drawn between each *ridge*, **rygg eller uphögning,** and were 2 feet wide across the top. The depth of each and every water-furrow was 9 inches. The land

---

* In the *Tarring* (Sussex) *Church Accounts*, 15 Hen. VIII., 1524, given in Cartwright's *Western Sussex* (vol. ii. of Dallaway). " It. for a lod of *versys* xvd."=" a load of *rushes*," so called probably because they were either twisted or *plaited*, Lat. Verso (freq. of Verto) to *turn often, from side to side*, or round about. The proper name as used by the straw-plaiters at Ivinghoe for the *bend* given to the straw in the operation of plaiting is "turn," *e.g.*, " We put in a *speel* at every 12th *turn*." Ivinghoe, Sept. 21st., 1886. [J. L.]

was wet.   At the ends there were water-furrows to lead
off the water.   For this summer this was left to lie
fallow, and would be sown with wheat in the following
autumn.   Farther up in the same field where the soil
was drier, the field was laid out in *Ten-bouts-land*, or so
that each ridge, **ryggning,** consisted of 20 furrows.
The breadth of such a *land* was 11 feet (5½ aln.).   They
were highest in the middle and sloped on both sides.

Svalor.   Swallows appeared to-day for the first
time this year.

Kaniner deras hemvist &c.   *Rabbits, their dwellings, &c.*

We came before dinner, **middagen,** to a plain,
slätt, which was very much overgrown with brackens
Ormbunkar.   It was nearly surrounded by ploughed
fields.   On this warren, **fält,** which was fenced round
with planks, **plankor,** we saw a great many rabbits,
of a grey colour, which had their residence here.   The
ground was quite full of the holes which they had dug,
and into which they ran down, as soon as one came
somewhat near them.   They were said all to belong to
a *gentleman*, who lived not far from thence.   In one place
and another there were traps, **fällor,** set to catch them.
These traps exactly resemble a kind of traps which are
set for large rats.   [T. I. p. 351.]   They are knocked
together of four boards, like a long box, **låda.**   At each
end hangs a perpendicular board, like a door, which by
a specially contrived arrangement above the trap,
resembled a **brunns hink,** or hatch of a stream, and
can be hoisted up so that the entrance to the trap stands
open.   In the middle of the trap, an iron pin or a little
wooden rod goes cross-wise, and as soon as the rabbit
climbs on to this and presses it down, a pin on the

outside slips loose and the boards at both ends fall down, and the rabbits are thus shut in. Branches, **Armar**, made of small sprays, **sprâtar,** go out from these traps on four sides, as in a **Ryssja,** Kipe, or "*fish-trap* "* to lead the rabbits in.

In the fence itself which separates the fields from this inclosure, there were also such traps, but only open at the end which turned towards the arable fields and nailed up at the other end towards' the plain, **slätten,** where the rabbits were. It thus seemed that the owner of the arable field was at liberty to catch all rabbits which were in his field and wished to go out of it, but had not leave to take any if one should go from the warren into the fields. We saw afterwards the same day at two other places, the one between *Bell Bar* and *Cheshunt,* the other between *Waltham Abbey* and *Woodford,* such places, on the open ground, where rabbits were kept, and where there were similar traps to catch them with. At the former place they had their dwelling in the side of a bank, where the owner had had several longitudinal and transverse ditches dug, of 3 feet deep, to lead off the water which came running down from the bank above, and prevented it from thus trickling to the place where the rabbits had their holes, but that the ground might be dry for them. We saw them run there by thousands. They had dragged brackens down into their holes. No [T. I. p. 352] other food was given them, than what they themselves could find on the ground. The owner seemed in consequence to have a considerable profit from the ground he let out as a rabbit warren.

---

* A long round tapering wicker-basket, called "fish-coop" on the Humber, "kipe" in Oxfordshire, "put," "putch," or "cype,' on the Severn, formerly "cyt," "kydel." [J. L.]

Härliga bygningar. *Beautiful houses.*

A great number of handsome large houses made a show everywhere in the woods, through which we travelled, the whole of this day.   Nature and Art seemed here to have united to make this country charming and delightful.

The 17th April, 1748.

Kall Vår. *Cold Spring.*

Our host, a man of seventy years old, told us that he could not remember a cold wind, and what is more, so much snow, lasting so far on in the spring as it has this year, for it snowed—indeed, very heavily —the greater part of this day.   All the others with whom I spoke about this had the same tale.   The leaves of the trees were now first beginning to shoot out.   Hawthorns and dog roses, **Hagtorn och Törne,** were those which were most advanced in this respect, but on the others there scarcely appeared more than the incipient buds, while, commonly, all trees are said to stand at this time with large leaves.

The 18th April, 1748.

In the morning I went into London and returned in the evening.

Asnors nytta. *The use of Asses.*

These animals are used by several people in this country.   They were commonly quite as small as year-old foals.   The principal reason why they keep them is said to be that those who have lung disease, **Lung-sot,** or *Hectique,* might have the opportunity of drinking asses' milk, because the *Medici* [T. I. p. 353] in this place prescribe it as the surest and best *medicine* for these distressing *passions.*   It is also for this reason that large troops of donkeys are seen, particularly in the district, på fälten, round about London. Besides that, donkeys are used hereabouts to carry burdens. In particular, bakers, who send round their men to sell bread, use donkeys to carry the bread-baskets, when a large basket commonly hangs, sitter, on each side of the saddle. The gypsies, Tattare, who roam about this country, use only donkeys instead of horses to carry their children and baggage. [See also p. 347, orig.]

The 19th April, 1748.

In the morning I went with Mr. Warner and some English gentlemen to the places which lay immediately to the east of *Woodford*. The hedges, *inclosures*, houses, ricks, and hay-stacks, all kinds of straw for manure in the farm-yards, in a word, all their rural economy was such as that we have described at Little Gaddesden in Hertfordshire; but the soil was a brick-coloured clay mixed very much with *Gravel* and *Pebblestones*. Chalk does not appear here. Also the land here in Essex is much more affected by wet than in Hertfordshire, where the ground was much drier.

En stor Ek. *A large Oak.*

Mr. Warner went out with us to-day, especially to show us an oak tree, which he said was one of the thickest oaks he had seen in England. We measured the periphery of the trunk, stammen, four feet above the ground, when we found that this oak was 30 feet round. At 15 feet above the roots it divided itself into twelve large branches, and each of these twelve divided itself afterwards into several smaller branches. We measured its width from the outermost twigs on the west [T. I. p. 354] to the outermost twigs on the east, in this way, that we erected at each side a perpendicular line from the ground to the outermost twigs on the W. and E. sides, when we found that there were just 116 feet between the two

M

lines.   The oak stood in Barking parish, and a fair,
Marknad, used formerly to be held under it.   Some of
these branches were now withered.*

Crambe maritima til mat.   Seakale as food.

Upon my travels in 1742 in *Bohuslän,* I found Crambe
Maritima Brassicœ folio, *Tournef* which there grew wild by
the sea shore.   I then mentioned in a Memoir (*Memorial*)
of mine at **Kongl. Sv. Vetenskaps Academien** (the
Royal Swedish Academy of Science), that this might do
for food.   To-day I saw that opinion of mine confirmed,
for Mr. Warner showed me three beds in his kitchen-
garden where this was sown only for cooking purposes.
It was used in the following way.   In the months of
April and May it begins to shoot up new shoots, nearly
like an *Asparagus.*   These are cut off and prepared in the
same way as *Spinat* in Sweden, when it is one of the
best-flavoured green vegetables which anyone can wish
for.   Our midday-meal to-day was mostly made up of it.
It is cultivated everywhere here in England by *Gentlemen*
for the above-named purpose.   When it is older it is not
good to eat ; beause the leaf becomes as tough as leather.
Its seeds are sown in April, May, June, or July, so early, that
is, as that they may come up and acquire enough strength
to resist the winter cold.   Next spring the bed is covered
over with *gravel,* **grus,** 4 inches thick, but it is most to
be preferred if sand can be got from the sea-shore.   In
this [T. I. p. 355] it thrives very well.   When it is two
or three years old, one can begin to cut it, and the
same root lasts a long time, year after year without requiring to be sown.

---

* Hainault Forest was disforested in 1851.   Here stood the celebrated
Fairlop Oak on an open space still called "Fairlop plain."   Its trunk
measured 44 feet round near the ground, and its branches covered an area of
300 feet in circumference.   *Fairlop Fair* was held under it on the first Friday
in July.   [J. T..]

Fisk-måsars nytta, etc. *Use of Seagulls in Gardens.*

Mr. Warner had four seagulls, **Fisk-måsar,** in his garden, two of which were of the common sort, and the two others a little larger and blacker, which he had got from Newfoundland, in North America, where they occur wild in abundance. He had had one wing of each clipped, so that they could not fly away. These gulls wandered everywhere about in the kitchen garden, and sought out earth-worms, **met-maskar;** *Erucas*, caterpillars; frogs, **Grodor;** snails, **Sniglar;** and many other little beasts injurious to kitchen gardens and garden plants, which they ate up. When the gardeners, **arbets-karlarna,** were digging up the earth at any place, they followed close after them, and plucked up all earth worms, and coarser insects which the carls in turning over the earth heaved up to the day. In a word, they cleared the garden industriously of many injurious things without in any way doing harm to the plants more than that they once and again trampled on them, which, however, did not matter at all. The only food which they were given was either pieces of raw meat or slices of wheat-loaves. They were so tame that even if they were at the farthest end of the garden, and Mr. Warner called "Gull, Gull," from his window, they came directly, **kommo de strax,** meaning, of course, to get something to eat. Those which had come from America were very savage, **arga.** When anyone ran after them they turned round [T. I. p. 356] to fight, **at hugga emot,** and if one then sprang away from them, they leapt or flew for some distance after him.

Orsak til tufvor på ängar.

The origin of hillocks on meadows.

In one meadow and another I saw small hillocks of about a foot high, and the same diameter. When I dug into them I found in them some of the yellow ants, **de gula etter-myror** [Formica rubra]. I asked some Englishmen what they thought was the origin of these hillocks, **tufvor.** They answered that the first cause is the mole, **mullvaden,** which casts up the heaps; but afterwards the ants, **myrorna,** take up their quarters in them and increase them.

Åkrarnas läge och häfd här vid Woodford.

The position and cultivation of the ploughed fields near Woodford.

The country here round Woodford does not lie level like a *planum*, but all slopes towards the east side so that it has full advantage of the morning sun. All the other arable and grass fields situated in this part of *Essex*, slope in the same way either to the one side or the other. The subsoil here consists of a brick-colored clay dividing into cubical masses, **Jordmon härstädes består af en tegel-färgad i tärningar fallande lera,** mingled with coarse sand and small *Pebblestones,* which *Pebblestones* are small round stones which there consist of ordinary flint, but other fragments of flint than these, such as there were on the fields in Hertfordshire do not occur here, for those which were found there were mostly broken pieces of flint, **sönder-remnade flint-stycken,** with a chalk crust round them, and with very sharp edges ; but these *Pebblestones* are mostly small, quite round, and very smooth on the surface, overdrawn with a petrified white calcareous surface, **krit-skårpa.*** Those who lived here, denied altogether that any chalk, **krit-bärg,** occurs in this district round *Woodford*, but they maintained that all

---

* These bleached flint pebbles will mostly effervesce with nitric acid.
[J. L]

the hills there consisted of the recently named brick-colored clay, coarse sand, and Pebblestones. For [T. I. p. 357] cultivating the fields there were used here the plough, harrow, roller, spade, etc. These ploughs, **plog**, were nearly like *the Essex Plough,* which in some things resembles the *Hertfordshire* [Buckinghamshire and Bedfordshire; Kalm had forgotten the county] foot plough but has a broader ploughshare, **bill**, and no foot; the mould-board, **vänd-brädet**, is also better placed. Only one person used the Hertfordshire single wheel plough. The harrows, roller, and spade, exactly resembled those we have in Sweden. They used also here, while harrowing, to fasten sometimes three or more harrows side by side, as has been before described in Hertfordshire. The wheat is mostly sown here in *Six-bout-lands* but sometimes also in the manner practised in Hertfordshire in *stitches* or *two-bout-lands* or as it is called *four-thorough-land.* The breadth of a *six-bout-land* was commonly 6 ells (12 feet) sometimes less. The water-furrows between these "lands" were 18 inches wide at top, their depth often nearly a foot. These *six-bout-lands* sloped somewhat on both sides at the ends. In the lowest part the land was designedly made sloping that the water might soon run away. The wheat on all these places stood very beautiful. In some places there were still more, in other places less, than *six bout-land,* according as the soil of the fields was wetter or drier. Barley, **Korn,** was sown here very little, and that all in *broadland. Pease* were sown in *drill,* 18 inches or 2 feet between every drill or row, and were mostly hoed, **hoades,** in between, when they drew up the mould with small hoes, **hackor,** on to their roots. *Oats* are sown here enough, and that all in *broad-land.* Potatoes were much planted here by some, and that commonly on a certain piece of the field. The manure was carried out in March on to such a ploughed plot, and spread out over the land. Afterwards the same land was dug up with a spade, when [T. I. p. 358] the manure came to lie lowest. In this the potatoes were afterwards planted in rows. To do this still more quickly they had a stick, **käpp,** of the accompanying figure, with which they made a little hole for the potato, to lay it in. D B is the part of the stick that made the hole in the earth when they trod on the pin C D. No ditches **diken**, are seen here on the ploughed fields, although the land in some places might not require them, but the furrows between the *stitches* would fulfil all requirements. The arable fields were all surrounded with hedges of hawthorn, which were set up and managed nearly in the same way as has been before described in Hertfordshire. All the land about here was divided into small *inclosures*, **täppor,** which were either arable fields, meadows, or pastures, all of which were surrounded with hawthorn hedges.

Beskrivning på Woodford. *Description of* Woodford.

Woodford is a parish or large village with a church in it, which lies in Essex, eight miles N.E. of London. The houses in this place are not built so close together as in several other parishes, but more scattered about. They are all of brick, several stories high, well built, and some of them handsome. The inhabitants are partly *Farmers*, but still more *Gentlemen*. The means of livelihood are various. The gentlemen, **Gentlemennerne,** live mostly on their money, which they get from their property. Bakers, innkeepers, butchers, have an abundant market for their wares, and thus practise a good trade, **föd-krok.** Farmers or others who are owners of some

land, make use of it in many ways: for it is partly used
for arable fields, partly for meadows, and partly for
pastures. On the fields there are sown, in particular,
wheat, oats, and pease [T. I. p. 359] which the owners
carry to London and there sell, but the most profit comes
from the meadows and pastures; for as hay in *London*
is very dear, so it is here exceedingly well worth while
to look well after the meadows, **ängarna.** By means of
the large number of horses and other animals to which
they allow freedom to go on their meadows and pastures, they make incredible profits, for several people in
London send their horses out here to bait, **at beta,** and
pay a certain sum per week for each horse. The same
thing is done with butcher-cattle, **slagt-boskap,** which
are pastured on the meadows. Besides this, the farmers
themselves buy up a quantity of sheep, calves, and
other cattle from different places, which they keep for a
time either in their *inclosures,* or in sheds, **i hus,** to fatten
them, and then sell them to butchers in *London.* The
last system returns most profit in the year to the farmers
hereabouts because no kind of provisions has such a
large consumption in England as meat.

Such farmers are called *Graziers,* for they practise
agriculture least, and devote themselves to grass and
pastures to fatten cattle and sell them. The country
round *Woodford* is charming. The houses lie on a hill.
The hills and dales in the country round form a beautiful
view in the distance. On the west and S.W. sides are
seen London's high towers, as well as the beautiful buildings which lie scattered about here and there in the
country, with a multitude of arable fields, **åker-fält,**
pleasure gardens and orchards, **lust-och trä-gårdar.**
On the east and S.E. sides, the river *Thames* appears,
where are ships going to and from *London,* to say
nothing of a diversity of beautiful villages, **vackra**

Byar, magnificent mansions, fruitful fields, meadows, orchards, plantations, **skogs-lundar,** &c., which here delight the eye. This is also the reason why some of the inhabitants of London partly have [T. I. p. 360] their own houses here, and partly hire houses here, especially in the summer time. For this reason also, rooms here in the summer are often dearer than in London itself.

Grindar. *Description of various Gates.*

The gates here were of several kinds. I will first describe those which they used very much at the entrances, **gång-vägar,** in front of, **utan för,** gentlemen's houses. These were so made that they could be opened, **tagas up,** both ways, inwards as well as outwards.

They are mostly small, made like other gates, but instead of hanging like other gates, on two **gång-järn,** "ride-hinges" or ring-hinges, and **hackar,** "driving-hooks," "gate-hooks," or pivot-hooks of similar shape, the shapes of the lower hinge and "gate-hook," **haken,** are here quite different from the upper. The upper "driving-hook," **hake,** is like our common door and gate-hooks, and is constructed as in the accompanying plate, Fig. 1. It is driven into the side of the gate-post, **grind-stålpen,** which turns towards the gate. The gate, **grinden,** hangs by a "ride-hinge" on to this **hake,** or "driving-hook," which "ride-hinge," **gång-järn,** is fastened on to the middle of the side of the gate which turns towards the gate-post.

For the lower hinge, instead of a "ride-hinge," there is driven into the bottom of the gate, 6 inches above the ground, or a little more, a double socket-iron, **et järn,** of the shape represented in Fig. 2, in which F E is the part which is driven into the side of the gate-frame,

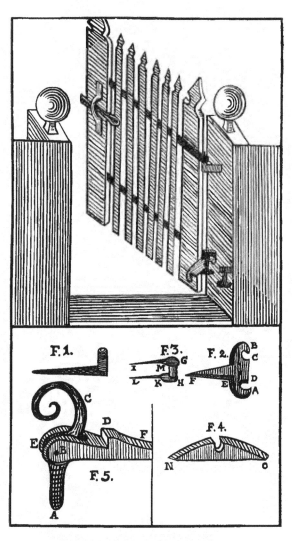

F.1.   F.3.   F.2.

F.5.   F.4.

grind-ramen, which is towards the gate-post, **grind-stålpen.** This socket-iron is driven in so that A B is horizontal. For the lower gate-hook, instead of the "driving-hook," there are two iron "knuckles," **järn,** such as are represented in Fig. 3, driven into the gate-post, side by side, and as far apart as the distance between the sockets C and D in Fig. 2. Here, in Fig. 3, M I and L R are the parts which are driven into the gate-post, and that in such a way that G H, or the knuckle-pin, comes to stand perpendicularly.

When the gate hangs on the upper "driving-hook," **kroken,** Fig. 1, then the socket or hollow, **inbögningen eller utholkningen,** in Fig. 2 [T. I. p. 362], which is between B and C fits on to the knuckle-pin, G H, of one of the "knuckles" shown in Fig. 3, and the other socket between D and A, Fig. 2, fits on to the knuckle-pin, G H, of the other knuckle, Fig. 3, so that each knuckle-pin, G H, always fits into its socket when the gate is shut, **när grinden står igen.**

When one opens the gate, it rests with one of the sockets, *e.g.,* between B and C, Fig. 2, filled by the knuckle-pin G H, of one of the knuckles, Fig. 3, while in the same case, the other socket between D and A goes away from the other knuckle, **haken eller järnet,** G H, and *vice versâ* when the gate is opened, **tages up,** the other way.

Klinkan på grinden, the latch of the gate, is like an ordinary **grind-klinka,** gate-latch, but thick, **trubbig,** at the end, and is set in the middle of the side of the gate which faces the gate-post.

Det järn hvari klinkan faller, the "hapse," "hasp," or "catch," into which the latch falls when the gate is shut, is of the shape shown in Fig. 4, from which it is seen that the gate can be opened and shut either way, because this "hapse" is fastened notch upwards, "just" on the side of the gate-post which looks towards the gate.

The "driving-hook," Fig. 1, is rather long, and the gate heavy, so that when it is opened and shut again it comes to rest by its own gravity or weight, just so that the latch falls again into the notch in the hapse for it, Fig. 4. The hapse ought to be fastened on to the gate-post, so that N O, Fig. 4, is horizontal. The latch is not made to reach farther than the *latitudo transversalis*, or breadth at top of the hapse, so that it may be able to pass backwards and forwards and not strike against the gate-post.

Another kind of **klinka**, "gate-latch," is shown in Fig. 5. **Åker-grindarna,** the gates of arable fields are for the most part exactly like our gates, and swing on similar hinges and gate-hooks. E F is an iron spike, **et järn**, driven horizontally into the side of the gate. A C is another iron, which hangs perpendicularly, but [T. I. p. 363] rides on an iron-pin, **järn-nagel**, at B, so that its under side E A can be bent in towards the latch-post of the gate, but not outwards from the gate farther than the perpendicular position. When the gate is open, and it is afterwards shut, the hapse, **klinkan,** Fig. 4 which is fixed to the gate post so that its notch faces the gate, strikes against the latch-tongue C A, Fig. 5, between E and A, when it bends its lower end A in towards the gate, and as soon as the notch in the hapse is reached, **och så snart Klinkan gått längre in,** it falls by its own weight back into the perpendicular position, and the gate cannot be opened again, before one bends either A inwards or C outwards so far that A C becomes nearly parallel with E F, Fig. 5. At D is a projection, **en hake,** as far as which this iron spike E F is driven in to the side of the latch-post of the gate, because otherwise the pin at B might be damaged while the iron-spike E F was being driven in to the gate, by striking it with a mallet at E.

In other places all this was of wood, and instead of the hapse, **klinkan,** in this case being below E F, Fig. 5, it lies above it, so that when the gate closes, B C which is not then curved but straight, bends in towards the gate, and A then goes out from it, and also from its weight at A it shuts by itself, when the fixed hapse comes opposite the latch-post of the gate.*

Sädes-lador ; Sädens-tröskning, etc. *Barns, thrashing corn, etc.* The barns in this district were sometimes built of brick with cross beams of wood between ; sometimes the walls were of oak boards, **Ek-bräder,** nailed fast horizontally. On the top they were mostly covered with tiles. A few were thatched with straw.

Logen, the "lodge" where the corn was thrashed was in the middle, and a "bay" or "lathe," **lada,** on either side. **Golfvet,** the floor of the lodge was not higher above the ground than in the bays on each side of it nor was there any wall between them. They [T. I. p. 364] continued the thrashing far into the summer. **Slagorne,** the flails, were the same kind as ours.

Some people used to clear the corn of chaff, **agner,** by means of fans, **Kast-skåfvel,** others had a particular machine for the purpose, which was made of wood in shape like a **Rännträ** or loom in which one weaves cloth, but instead of standing perpendicularly like a loom, this winnower is laid horizontally, as it has to be

---

* From the indiscriminate use by Kalm of the same word for different objects, and of different words for the same parts, the translation of this passage would have been impossible without the figures and a knowledge of the English technical names and uses of the various parts of the hinges and latches described. [J. L.]

turned round. It lies also with each end of its axle-tree in a post with a hole cut in the top of it, **en uti ändan upgräfven stålpe.** To each of the outer longitudinal outer-bars of the frame, **långträn,** which lie parallel with the axis, there is fastened a foursided cloth, either of coarse linen or wool, which hangs downwards. When the machine is turned round, these cloths, which are four in number, produce a strong wind. The thrashed corn, together with the chaff, **agnarne,** lies in a coarse sieve or "riddle," **rissel,** which either stands upon a trestle, **trä-ställning,** or hangs by ropes. This riddle is placed between the winnowing-machine and the barn-door, **logdören.** Thereupon one carl begins to turn the machine round, and another to jog, **stöta,** the sieve backwards and forwards, when the strong wind which comes from the cloths drives the chaff, which together with the grain falls from the sieve, out to and through the lodge-door ; but the grain falls down, the more so the heavier it is, in a perpendicular line.

Afterwards the grain is sifted and winnowed or fanned once more till it is clean. The faster the machine is turned round the stronger is the wind it produces.

Anmärkningar vid några delar af hushållningen uti Essex. *Notes on some branches of Rural Economy in Essex.*

Several of the farmers here kept a large number of cows, from which they got very much milk. I have before [T. I. p. 365.] mentioned that the women never went out to milk, but that this office was always performed by the carls, who went out into the pastures where the cattle were kept, morning and evening, and milked, and after-wards carried home the milk from thence, when it was taken from them by the girls, **pigan,** who siled it in winter in wooden vessels, **träbunkar,** but in summer in large square boxes, **lådor,** of lead, 4 or 6 inches deep, in which the milk curdles, **skal löpna,** in the summer very well, and becomes most delicious. The sweet milk was sold to the neighbouring inhabitants, who did not themselves keep cows; but that which was over was siled in the above-named manner and made into butter. The butter was churned or "Kerned," [*Nidderdale*], in tub-shaped kerns, **kärnades i tunnor,** which were turned round by a handle. The kern-milk, **kärn-mjölken,** was sold to the poor, or swine were fattened with it.

Drängarne. The farm servants were sufficiently occupied during the day with various outdoor duties such as the care of cattle, ploughing, **plöjning,** sowing, carting, **körning,** repairing hedges, &c., but as soon as they entered the cottage, **stugan,** in the evening, they did not apply themselves to the least work, more than that they ate, sat, and talked till eleven o'clock in the evening. They never troubled themselves to make wagons, or agricultural implements, for all such things were bought of certain people in the country, whose special business it was to make them.

For fuel, coal was partly used, which was bought in London and carted here, partly and mostly wood, **ved,** which their hedges so richly provided them with, especially their oaks, **Ekar,** and other trees, which they poll, **topphuga,** and leave to strike out new shoots, as has been mentioned before.

Stekvändare, meat-jacks, or *spits*, they have in every house in England. They are turned by a weight, which is drawn up as often as it has run down. The spits themselves are of iron, simply made, a very [T. I. p. 366] useful invention, which lightens labour amongst a people who eat so much meat.

[Kalm was in London from April 21, to May 7, 1748.]

[T. I. p. 390.]   *The 7th May,* 1748.

In the morning I went from London out to *Woodford* in Essex, to Mr. Warner.

Gräs, ogräs, &c., til dref-bänkar.
Grass, weeds, &c., in forcing beds.

Mr. Warner had had the grass cut in several places in his garden, and laid it in a heap, to be carried down to the bottom of a hot-bed, **dref-bänk,** and afterwards mould, **mull,** over it, to use instead of unfermented horse-dung; for when moist hay, **rått hö,** comes to lie tight together it begins to ferment, and thus generates as much heat as unrotted horse-dung causes, when it is laid and trampled down in a hotbed.   At several places in *Chelsea,* near London, I saw that the market gardeners had all the weeds collected together, which they had come across in their market gardens, and had laid them in large heaps to use for the same purpose.

Måssans hastiga växt.   *Rapid Growth of Moss.*

The earth seemed in many places here in England, especially if it was meagre, to favour the growth of mosses almost more than I have seen in other places.   When they had laid earth in pots, and had sown some plants therein, it often happened that the moss began to come up in the pot some few days afterwards.   The more meagre the earth, so much the quicker was the moss said to come up.   This moss was all of the genus *Bryum.*   Pots, **krukor eller påttor,** in which they had laid mould, and sown plants six months [T. I. p. 391] or so before, were on the top so covered over with moss that the mould in the pot could with difficulty be seen.   Some of these pots stood in hot-beds under glass, others under the open sky.   I saw the rapid growth of this moss in pots in many places.

Kalm's England]   Extract from Rocque's Survey 174

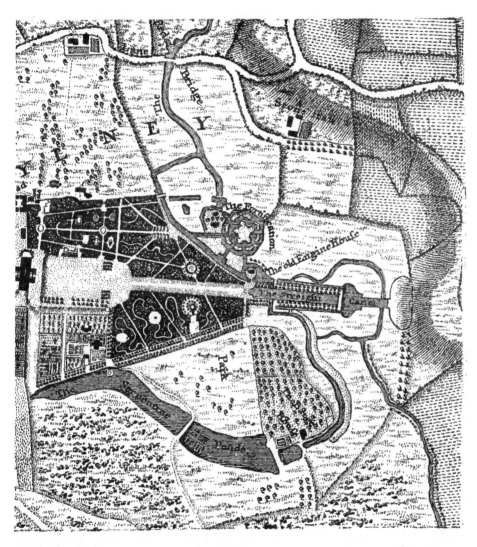

ng Wanstead Manor and surroundings

[To face p. 175.

The 8th May, 1748.

My Lord Tilney's Magnificent House.

In the afternoon Mr. Warner took me and several of his Swedish friends with him to show us My Lord Tilney's magnificent *Palais*, which lies between Woodford and London, about six miles from the last-named place. We had here a clear example of how disadvantageous it is not to observe moderation in what one is about to undertake. The following was narrated to me about this house:—It was about twenty years ago, or a little more, that *My Lord Tilney*, an Irish earl, was pleased to erect here a new and magnificent house with a large and beautiful garden round it, because the site lay uncommonly well, and the view from it was very delightful on all sides. *My Lord Tilney* was then a lord possessed of much money, which he had inherited from his forefathers. The difficulty met him at the place where the house should be built, that there was no water; but money could cure all such things. Where, previous to that time there was scarcely anything but a ditch with a little water in it, we now saw a large flowing river, all made with art and human labour. He had had dug about the whole place many ponds, **dammar,** of which one and another resembled a little lake, so that the one which lies in front of the windows of the mansion, and is all artificially made, is so large that they can sail to and fro [T. I. p. 392] on it with large boats. Around the house there is on one side a large and beautiful garden with manifold *allées*, **Alleer,** promenades, trees clipped and hewn in all sorts of ways, several summer-houses, orangeries, forcing-houses, **dref-hus,** ruins, and arches of bent trees. In a word, all that can be required and produced by art in a garden. For a long distance, towards all sides, there were planted in *allées*, rows, and other forms, all sorts of trees, but that which principally excites the admiration of the spectator is the magnificent large building, which is all of hewn stone, and more resembles a royal palace than a private man's property, without as well as within.

In it there were very many rooms furnished in the most costly way, and this so that one room was not like another. Magnificent paintings, extensive tapestries, **Tapeter**, costly tables of many kinds of marble, large crystal *lustres*, **ljus-kronor**, gilded chairs, tables, ceilings, **tak**, &c., various kinds of statuary, **Bildhuggeri**, and what varieties the East and West Indies can supply, were here displayed before the eyes. We saw tapestries, **Tapeter**, or more correctly, a kind of screen, **skärm**, of crosswise-laid glass threads, **glaströ**, of several colours, and picture-scenes, which resembled fine cloths, **tyger**, and were said to have come from the East Indies. It was affirmed that My Lord Tilney had laid out so much on all this that he has barely as much left that he can in some sort support his state, or maintain, **hålla vid magt**, what he has here erected.

This was evident both with the house and garden, which had not been fully completed, because the owner's resources did not allow him to incur further expense.*

---

* The house was Wanstead Manor.

In *Magna Britannia*, &c., Lond., 1720, 4to, Vol. I., p. 653. twenty-eight years before Kalm's visit, legitur : " Sir Richard Child, the son of Sir Josiah, now enjoys it, and has by his great expense so much improved it, though a princely habitation before, that the world itself cannot parallel it for buildings and fine gardens." *The Beauties of England and Wales*, 1803, 8vo., E. Brayley and J. Britton, Vol. V., p. 466, adds : " Sir Richard, afterwards created Earl Tylney, erected the present Wanstead House in the year 1715." "The principal front is 260 feet in length. The whole building is cased in Portland stone; its depth is between 70 and 80 feet." "Colin Campbell was the architect." There is a view of the house opposite p. 466 (P. 467.)" The river Roding, which is formed into canals," &c. *A Topographical*

Dict. of England &c. S. Lewis, 7th Ed., 1849, 4to., Vol. IV., p. 459, adds : " Sir Richard, created Earl of Tylney, 1731."

"From Lord Tilney it (Wanstead Manor) passed to Sir James Tilney Long, whose only daughter inherited this magnificent estate early in the present century."

THE REST OF THE STORY.

Annual Register, 1812. Chronicle p. 157.

MARRIAGES. March. "William Wellesley Pole, Esq., to Miss Long, eldest daughter of the late Sir T. Long, Bart."

ANN. REGIST., 1823. Chron., p. 65. May.

"Wanstead House was sold by auction on the premises on Monday last for £10,000. One of the conditions of sale binds the purchaser to clear everything away, even to the foundation, by Lady Day, 1825. The biddings commenced at £1,000," &c., &c.

"Thus is sacrificed to extravagance and gambling a mansion which cost in its erection more than £360,000, and which has no equal in the county of Essex."

ANN. REG., 1825, p. 280. DEATHS.

"Sept. 12th. At Richmond, aged 35, Mrs. Wellesley-Pole-Long-Wellesley. On the 19th, the remains of this amiable unfortunate lady were removed from Richmond on their way to Draycot in Wiltshire, the seat of Lady Tilney, there to be deposited in the family vault," &c.

Tourist's *Essex.* E. Walford, 12mo., Lond., 1882.

"The house was pulled down, to pay his debts, in 1822-23, and his wife died soon after from a broken heart."

William Pole-Tylney-Long-Wellesley, the husband of Mrs. Wellesley-Pole-Long-Wellesley, succeeded to the Earldom of Mornington in 1845, and died 1st July, 1857. (Burke's Peerage.) [J. L.]

SIC TRANSIT GLORIA MUNDI.

LITTLE GADDESDEN.

COUNTRY BETWEEN WOODFORD IN ESSEX AND
LITTLE GADDESDEN, HERTFORDSHIRE.

[T. I. p. 178].   *The 25th March*, 1748.

IN the morning I undertook at the cost and at the request of Herr Vice-President Baron Bjelke, a journey to see Mr. Ellis, who lived at Little Gaddesden in Hertfordshire. Mr. Ellis was a man who had a great reputation for his *Practique* in **Landthushållningen,** or Rural Economy, but still more for his many writings on the same Art, which latterly he had published yearly.

I started at 9 o'clock together with **Jungström,** and a man who was our guide.

The principal villages and places we passed through this day were the following.

WALTHAM ABBEY, situated six miles from Woodford, is now a little town, but has formerly been much larger.

178

The houses are tolerably [T. I. p. 179] good, and the church built in an antiquated style. Close to it was an old monastery, **Kloster.** At this town we saw in a gentleman's garden the largest *Tulip-tree* in England, which rivalled the largest elms in height. The fruit however does not ripen sufficiently to be available for seed.

WALTHAM CROSS, a beautiful village an English mile from the last named place, and on the borders of *Hertfordshire*, for hitherto we had been in Essex. Here we saw one of England's antiquities, a specially carved pillar, **pelare,** erected in former times in memory of a Queen. [Eleanor, wife of Ed. I.]

CHESHUNT, a small but pretty village situated an English mile from Waltham Cross. Here we saw several beautiful and costly orchards. A river, **en bäck,*** which was artificially dug, getting on for sixty miles through the country, flowed through this village down to London. It is partly from this river that the water is led through subterranean channels and pipes, into houses, kitchens and cellars in London.

ST. ALBANS, a tolerably large and pretty town, is 12 miles from Cheshunt, and 20 from London. It has in former times been very large and is reckoned one of the oldest towns in England, and is remarkable for its many antiquities. One of the existing churches, remarkable for its size and architecture, **särdeles byggnad,** looks as if it must be very old.

Close to the same church there still stands a gateway, **en port,** which was built by the Romans during their occupation of this country. The gateway is, however, built round about, and the same house is used as a

---

* The New River. From an exact measurement made in 1723 by Mr. H. Mill, the engineer and surveyor of the N. R. Co., its extent was ascertained to be 38¾ miles, 16 poles. Matthews "*Hydraulia*" 1835 [J. L.]

prison. [T. I. p. 180.] In the town there are four churches, but one of them is used as a market-place.

HEMPSTEAD (Hemel Hemsted) is situated 5 miles from St. Alban's, and 25 from London. The town is small but tolerably pretty, lies down in a dale, **däld**, and has a church with a high tower.

Little Gaddesden is a long village situated 30 English miles from London. We arrived there at six o'clock in the evening. I shall have farther on a better opportunity of describing this place. Now, I will give several notes which I made to-day on *the journey* between *Woodford* and *Little Gaddesden*.

The appearance of the country which we passed through to-day was simply beautiful. There was not the smallest sign either of rock or granite, **bärg eller gråsten.** It was not entirely even and flat, but went in a continuous succession of undulations so that it was like a collection of hills and dales; yet the hills were for the most part very long-sloping down into the dales. Between these ridges there sometimes flowed a little beck.

Jordmon, the soil, was here the same as in Essex and Hertfordshire, viz.: on the top, *soil,* **svartmylla,** but immediately under that a reddish-yellow or *Ochre*-colored clay, **lera,** mixed with a number of pieces of flint, and, in the neighbourhood of Essex, of a similar colored gravel or coarse sand, **groft grus.** Around Hempstead in Hertfordshire, the hills consisted partly of chalk.

All these hills and dales were divided into arable fields, meadows, and pastures, the spaces near the towns or villages being occupied by gardens and kitchen-gardens side by side, and here and there beautiful parks of all sorts of different kinds of trees, which were for the most part fenced round with living hedges of various leaf-trees which [T. I. p. 181] commonly consisted of hawthorn blended with blackberry-bushes, sloe, ash, oak, ivy (*Agrifolium*), elm, etc.

These last-named had mostly been brought there by different chances, such as birds, &c.

I saw not the smallest sign of such a farm fence, **gärdesgård,** as is used in Sweden, unless the dead fences which are erected in places where an old quickset hedge has been cut down to get a new one to grow in its place, can be called a kind of **gärdesgård.** Gentlemen's estates and farms were scattered here and there. The houses of the former were handsomely built, and of the latter very beautiful, all of brick, **sten.** In a word, the whole country in *Essex* as well as in *Hertfordshire*, through which we progressed, everywhere resembled a garden, **trädgård,** so that neither nature nor art and diligence had here spared anything which contributes to the adornment of a country.

Husen, the houses which we saw in this journey were nearly all of brick, **sten,** yet not everywhere only and solely of brick, but in some places were **korssverks-väggar,** ' cross-work walls,' *i.e.*, brick and stud walls. In most places the houses were two or three stories high.

Of the English house-building I note, that the houses are commonly so built, that even the upper stories, which with us in Sweden are usually only a granary, **en vind,** consist here of chambers and a room, in which the servants commonly lie, so that the roof slopes just close on to this room, without any granary, **Skulle eller Vind,** above.

The walls in the upper stories consist often of thin boards and laths, daubed on the outside as well as the inside with clay and lime, so that it seems as though they were of stone.

Such thin boarded walls are possible in this country

where the winters are so mild. The roofs [T. I. p. 182) of the houses are mostly of tiles, which, however, are not concave or trough-shaped, as with us in Sweden, but commonly quite flat and plain, quadrilateral and oblong. They are fastened in this way, that on the under framework of the roof, which consists of *rafters*, are nailed horizontal laths of wood in rows, along the length of the roof, the one a little above the other, or about three fingers' breadth between the laths. On these laths are hung the tiles, which begin down at the eves, **takfoten,** and so go upwards *imbricatim.*

In these tiles there are at the upper end two holes side by side in which are set wooden pegs, which, on the lower or inner side are 3 or 4 inches long; but on the upper side they are cut off even with the upper surface or outside of the tile. There are always two holes in each tile, although they often do not set more than one peg in either of the holes, because one such a peg seems to suffice. The rain water cannot rot away these pegs, because they are always covered by the projecting end of the tile that lies next above.

The roofs in these places on that account look exactly like church and other roofs with us in Sweden, covered with square shingles, **spån,** only that the colour is somewhat different. On a great many outhouses and a great many cottages, **stugor,** (which, however, were of brick), the roof, **taken,** consisted only of straw.

Tak-resningen, the roof, was here mostly high, and very steep, so as to run off the rainwater more quickly, by which means the roof is rotted less. In some places there were seen some wooden outhouses, whose walls consisted of oak boards.

Gålfven, the floors of the houses, were mostly of fir or pine boards, which they had bought in London. In the lowest story, tiles or some other [T. I. p. 183] stone were used as a floor.

Korss-stenarna, the chimneys, were often built, as has been before remarked, in the gable, **gafveln,** of the house itself, and this sometimes so that nearly all the chimney stood outside the house-gable, while the gable formed one side of the chimney. In so mild a climate as England has, this was good, in case the fire ever fastened on the chimney soot; but otherwise it seems to be of little use that the back of the fire-place, towards which the fire mostly plays, stands outside the building.

Âkrarna, the ploughed fields, were everywhere where we travelled, very well cultivated. I have said before that the country consists of hills which slope on all sides. The fields, therefore, lie so that they have particular advantage from the morning, midday, or evening sun, towards which they lie. Sometimes also arable fields are found on the north side of the hills, yet it was mostly the practice to leave this side either for pasture, meadow, or other parks,* **Parker.**

Jordmon, the soil was here everywhere the sandy brick-colored fat clay which around London is common enough, **den med sand utblandade tegelfärgade feta leran som omkring London är nog allmänn.** [The London clay.]

On the ploughed fields lay a multitude of ordinary flint fragments, in some places so thick that many would wonder how the crops could there get any room to take root. I never saw any ditches on the ploughed fields, besides those which at times were found close to the hedges which were planted round about the fields. But the manifold *water-furrows,* **vattu-fåror,** here served for

---

* Park in the Coverdale district means an enclosure *for horses,* its original sense (see "*Studies in Nidderdale,*" p. 34 and glossary). T. Rothe's "*Nord Staets forfatning for Lehnstiden* I., 291," showed that the word in its sense of *deer-park* was of English origin. [J. L.]

ditches, for most of the arable fields were so laid out that there was not more than 2 feet between the water-furrows. The breadth of such a water-furrow was (as occasionally measured) 9 inches to 1 foot, and the depth 6 to 9 inches. They were nearly always drawn from the hills down the ploughed fields, that the water might have [T. I. p. 184] free escape, but where the fields sloped too much they were drawn parallel with the dales, and not right down to the same for this reason, that a great water-flood might not scour away the soil and crops.

No *acre-reins* in the middle of the fields, but only round about at the sides, near the hedges, but these reins were nearly always overwhelmed with mosses, like the worst of our moss-choked meadows.

In some places the water-furrows were not so close together, but the ploughed fields were laid out in broad-land,* that is, in even and wide plots about 20 feet between each *furrow*, or *grip*. The space between the *water-furrows* was laid out in small *ridges*, or *riggs*, **ryggar**, which are here called 'stitches,' which were highest in the middle and sloped on both sides towards the water furrow.

Thus *no balks* of earth, **inga balkar af jord**, appeared here, which would hinder the water from flowing down into the furrows.

Magra orter.

Arid and sterile places also occur in England.

We saw to-day between *Cheshunt* and *Bell Bar* a great plain, yet not even, but having ridges and hollows, which

---

* *Broadland.* On the chalk these broadlands run now, 1886, generally 20 yards, but sometimes 18 yards wide. Two I measured at Albury, Herts., ran 56 feet and 58 feet. The "yards" are only stepped. On Grove Farm, Ivinghoe Aston, two adjoining old curved ridges were 62 and 48 feet wide. Sep. 21. 1886. [J. L.]

was little better than our barren ling heaths, **Ljung-hedar,** in Sweden. This plain extended nearly four English miles across, with a proportionate area.* The subsoil was brick-coloured clay.

An abundance of the common ling grew upon it. Otherwise the plain was overgrown with ling-tufts, **Liung-tufvor,** between which were found a great quantity both of brackens, **Ormbunkar,** and mosses, but only some isolated blades of grass. Sheep were now pasturing here. In some places grew hornbeam enough, six feet high, and tolerably thick. The tops were cut off for fuel, otherwise it was of no particular use. This was a *common land* or **allmänning,** and may have been left in [T. I. p. 185] such a neglected state, without any improvement having been effected there, for that reason. [Northaw Common.]

Kaniner, rabbits, occur wild in many places in this country. We saw on the afore-named heath some of them on a bank, of a grey colour. Now, in the middle of the day, there were only a few up, but the great multitude of holes which were seen everywhere in the bank, together with the information of our guide, that they are especially to be seen in the evenings, assured us that there were probably a very great number of them, although they were now down in the ground. They were said to belong to a lord [the Earl of Salisbury] who lived not far off, and that no one without his permission had leave to disturb them.

Fàr, sheep, were feeding almost everywhere on the hills where there are pastures. In some places, where the hills were long-sloping, the *water-furrows* appeared drawn with the plough in a direction straight down the field, and sometimes obliquely down the sides. The

---

* From Gough's Oak to Bell Bar (4 miles) the road runs most of the way on gravel-capped ridges of London clay. [J. L.]

reason is said to be to give the water by that means a free escape, so that it might not stand and become acid, **sura,** and by that means make the grass unwholesome for the sheep.

Krita, chalk, is seen in many places between *St. Alban's* and *Hempstead* spread out on the field as a manure. The arable pieces were nearly as white as chalk with it, since it was in some places laid on in tolerable abundance. They intended now at the first opportunity to plough it down. The soil on which it was laid was the frequently-mentioned coarse, reddish-yellow sand, mingled with a reddish-yellow clay and fragments of flint. Near to Hempstead we saw an entire hill, which consisted only of chalk. [T. I. p. 186.]

Kodynga, cowdung lay in some places carried out into the fields lying in heaps side by side, but not yet spread out.

Mâssa, *Moss*, both *Bryum* and *Hypnum,* grew in distressing quantities on all the **utmarker,** ' out fields ' heaths or commons, and meadows, and acre-reins, which lay near the hedges. It had in these places for the most part strongly taken root ; indeed, many of these meadows and commons resembled in that respect the most mossy of our meadows.

[Here follows a short notice of a fire in London given above under " London."]

The 26th March.

[At Little Gaddesden.]

In the morning I went to call upon Mr. Ellis but he had already gone out on to his fields. I therefore took, in company with **Jungström,** a walk out on to the arable fields around Little Gaddesden to inspect the same, the rather because it is commonly [T. I. p. 187] held that in Hertfordshire and on this side, there are the best Agriculturists, **åkermän,** in England. We now found here part of the arable fields very well husbanded, so that they lay almost like beds in a kitchen garden, others again sufficiently carelessly managed. The same description mostly applied to the inclosures, or **täppor,** which were laid out as meadows that one part was very well cared for, **skött,** the grass-growth very thick, and not a sign of moss in them.

Others stood beautiful with clover, *Sain Foin,* and such like kinds of hay, but there were some also, which deserved our pity. The moss had there so got the upper hand, that it had almost entirely extirpated the beautiful hay which had formerly been sown there. It resembled, in a word, our most moss-choked meadows. After a time we met an old farmer, and enquired of him " to whom the field belonged which was cultivated with so much care ? " *Ans.* " It is mine, if I may make so bold as to say it."

Q. "Who is the cultivator of this *inclosure,* which stands so green and luxuriant with clover, and on which there is not one blade of moss ? "

Ans. " This is mine, that is Mr. Williams'," etc.

Q. " Who is the owner of this field, which to a great extent stands under water, and is so ill cultivated?" *Ans.* " A Mr. Ellis as he is called." " Mr. Ellis?" I asked, "you must have forgotten yourself, or is there here more than one Mr. Ellis ? " " No," replied the man, there is not more than one Mr. Ellis here, and to him the field belongs."

Q. "Who works on the inclosure away there where the moss has so excessively got the upper hand ? "

Ans. " The same Mr. Ellis." I had from such paradoxical answers soon forgotten all my *Latin,* and asked therefore " if it is the same Mr. Ellis who is so celebrated for the many beautiful works he has published on [T. I. p. 188] Rural Economy ?" The man answered that it

is the very same, and as for Mr. Ellis's beautiful books on
Rural Economy, he let them be for what they were worth,
dem länmade han i sit värde, but this he said he
was sure of, that if Mr. Ellis did not make more profit
out of sitting and scribbling books, and selling the Manuscripts to the Publishers, than he realised from his
farming, he would soon have to go and beg —for Mr. Ellis
mostly sits at home in his room and writes books, and
goes sometimes a whole week without going out into his
ploughed lands or meadows to look after the work, but
trusts mostly to his servant, **dräng,** and young son, who
is still a boy.

I feared that the farmer said this from envy, and therefore left such a heretic! after he had constrained me
to confess at least to myself that he had a very large
experience in farming.

We had now walked through a great many of their
arable fields, meadows and inclosures, and had at
last entered the churchyard to view the church, when
Mr. Ellis himself came to meet us. He had got to hear
from someone that strangers from foreign parts were
come to visit him. We then, at his request accompanied
him home to see the *inventions* he had discovered for
the improvement of agriculture. He showed us a
mixture of a particular manure which he had under a
thatch-roof. He said that this manure had not its like,
to produce the growth of a manifold crop, but we could
not get out of him what this manure was composed of.
He next showed us his *four wheeled drill plough*, **fyrhjulta
drill-plog,** which he considered to be worth its weight
in gold.

This is now to be seen drawn on the title page of
Mr. Ellis's *Farmer's Instructor.*

[T. I. p. 189]. Afterwards he showed us the double
Hertfordshire plough, of which there are both an illustration

and description in Mr. Ellis's *Agriculture improv'd. Item*, a sieve with steel wires, **et Såll med ståltrå**, to separate the small wheat and barley-corns from the large, by that means to obtain a choice and much-sought-after seed-corn; *item*, three small treatises which lay ready and fair-copied for the press. They treated of the management of sheep and the duties of the shepherd. These treatises waited for the printer who would pay most for them. They have since been printed under the name of "The Shepherd's Sure Guide," together with a lot of letters to him, and several which he himself had written.

I asked Mr. Ellis whether he had at his own house all the kinds of ploughs which he describes in his writings, and particularly those which he praised so highly for their usefulness. He answered "No," and gave as a reason that if he had them at home he could not have them in peace, partly because gentlemen took them away, partly that they were stolen by others.

I then asked if he had not at home the useful ploughs and other kinds of machinery which he himself had invented. He answered "No," and gave the same reason for not having them. I asked, supposing anyone wanted them how one could get them made, and if there was any-one in the village who constructed them? He answered that none can make them here, for it requires a singu-larly intelligent head for the purpose, but he had a man who lived 30 or 40 English miles from Little Gaddesden at whose place he had all such things made for one and all of the eminent persons and others, who ordered them. It is, therefore, obligatory on those who wish to have [T. I. p. 190] such a plough or implement to pay the cost of its carriage from the maker to Mr. Ellis, as well as thence to London, or to any place one might wish.

During my visit to Little Gaddesden I enquired on

different occasions—not one, but very many—of those
who lived here—farmers and other men—where and at
whose establishment they believed Mr. Ellis had his
implements and ploughs, &c., made.   They answered
that all implements that gentlemen, and others who had
read his writings, order of him, are made by the plough-
maker, **Plog-makaren,** who lived close beside the
house where I lodged, for Mr. Ellis gives him the
model and describes it to him, and contracts with
him what he shall have for the woodwork, but the
smith who lived close to the park (Ashridge Park),
constructs the iron, according to the model and
description Mr. Ellis has given him, and that he receives
from Mr. Ellis the payment they have agreed upon, **som
de kommit öfverens om.**   Afterwards, Mr. Ellis sets
whatever price he likes on the ploughs or implements
which have been ordered of him.   These farmers denied
entirely that Mr. Ellis had his implements made at the
establishment of any other man at a distance from here,
as he himself told me.

Still, I put to those who lived here, not once, but
many times, the following questions :—Q. Whether Mr.
Ellis uses, or has used, on his arable land any other kinds
of implements than the other Farmers in this parish or
village ?   All answered unanimously that he had never
used other or more than they, and that the ploughs
which he uses are the same as they had used from time
immemorial [T. I. p. 191], only they said that he on
some single occasion, for his amusement, may have used
some others, perhaps, for an hour.   They unanimously
bore testimony to the fact that he sells a number of the
same implements as he has described in his books, to
different gentlemen.

Q. Whether Mr. Ellis uses on his arable any other kind
of manure than the other farmers in Little Gaddesden ?

Ans. Absolutely no other.

Q. Whether Mr. Ellis gets annually from his arable a more abundant harvest, **skörd,** than the other farmers ?

Ans. Never more than others ; for if he gets more one time, they get more another.

Q. Whether Mr. Ellis uses to plough, **köra,** and treat his arable in any other way than the other farmers in the place ?

Ans. Never; but entirely in the same way.

Q. Has he a large number of sheep ?

Ans. No more than the other farmers, but rather less.

Q. Has he a large number of cows?

Ans. Two individuals ; for in the whole of Little Gaddesden there are hardly twenty cows in all.

Q. Has he a large number of work-people, **tjenste-folk** ?

Ans. One girl and a boy, besides his son and daughter; for in this place it is the custom that a farmer does not keep many servants, but always employs day-labourers, **dagsverks-folk,** for which reason in every village there live a great many poor, who hire themselves out to work for pence.

They gave here eight to ten pence a day to one carl, who for that is obliged to work from 6 o'clock in the morning till 6 in the evening. This character they said they were obliged [T. I. p. 192] to give Ellis: that he never let any of the labouring folk wait for their money, as is otherwise very common, but he gives them each evening their day's money, **sin dags-penning.** In the same way he pays down, **straxt,** those who make any·thing for him.

The farmers maintained that Mr. Ellis's principal occupation consists in writing books, and selling to gentle·

men the ploughs and implements which he has lauded therein, although he had seldom tried them himself.

He has also been for a time a Custom House officer, or Exciseman, **Tull-betjent,** also for a long time with a brewer in London.

The Treatise he has written on Brewing, **om Brygg-ning,** is considered by several in England as the best of all his writings, because he relates therein his own experiences. When he first came to Little Gaddesden he was quite ignorant of Rural Economy. He had learnt most of it there, but his neighbours will not yet recognise him for so good a Farmer, **Landtman,** as many of them, but said that he does not cultivate his arable and meadows so well as the others. With his present and second wife he had made a rich marriage, and with her money bought the farm he now lives upon. At first he undertook several experiments in husbandry, but he had not been particularly lucky with them, for the most part of what he had left of the money he got with his second wife had in this way taken its departure, so that he was poor enough. His spouse had grieved so much over it, that she had not been able to recover herself, **komma sig före.**

After a time, when he had made several tours in England to note all sorts of things in Rural Economy, he sat down to write books, and to have various [T. I. p. 193] agricultural implements made to sell to others, in which he had found his reckoning better, so that he has now tolerably recovered himself, although he is not just so particularly rich. Through this assiduous book-writing it happens that his arable and meadows are worse cared for than his neighbours'. Meantime his writings proved their good and great worth, and gained especial renown; because he gave in them what he had with much trouble and great industry collected during many journeys through

England in all departments of Rural Economy, very much of which it is useless to seek for in other books, and has never before been mentioned, far less described. He seems, however, to be too diffuse, and to bring much in that does not belong to the subject, and sometimes a thing is found inserted in ten, twenty, and more places in his writings. The worst is, that one cannot build upon what is said in them; for he has been too credulous, and has taken as true what false and made-up stories his mischievous neighbours often amused themselves by telling him—of which several persons assured me.*

Harfningen. The *harrowing* which we saw to-day in a field near LITTLE GADDESDEN, where pease were being harrowed down was somewhat peculiar. They had taken six harrows. Each harrow, which was square, con-sisted of four wooden bars, and on each bar, **trä,** five iron tines, **järn-pinnar,** so that the whole harrow had twenty tines. They had bound all these six harrows side by side, by laying a long pole or 'stang,' **stång,** across them, and binding them fast to the stang. In front of the harrows were six horses harnessed abreast, one horse for each harrow, **harf.** With these harrows thus arranged the field was harrowed. A young boy went and led one of the side horses and [T. I. p. 194] another went behind and drove them. They had by that plan the ad-vantage that the field was sooner harrowed, and that they did not require to employ more than two persons for six harrows and horses.

Jordmon, the soil, was here very loose and fine, so

---

* Although Ellis was a charlatan, and did not help to solve the great problem of how to make farming pay, it is probable that, had he been able to read Swedish, he could have recovered substantial damages in an action for libel. [J. L.]

O

that the harrow-tine, **harf-pinnan**, could easily tear it
to pieces.*

The 27th March.

Mr. Ellis did me the honour to spend a great part of
the day with me. He esteemed it a great pleasure to
talk with me on various things in Rural Economy; yet
he seemed more to ask than to be asked. When I enquired of him about one thing and another, I seldom got
any other answer than that he referred me to some of
his writings, where I should find the subject exhaustively
treated.

He said he had travelled nearly all over England, to
see and write up their Rural Economy, **hushållning.**
Often when he had got to hear that anyone experienced
in Rural *Œconomy* lived at any place, and whose name
was known for his particular insight into some special
branch of Rural Economy, **Landthushållningen,** he
had travelled expressly to him, although he lived 20, 30,
or more miles out of the way. When he observed that this
other was interested in his conversation, and did not wish
to lose any of it, Mr. Ellis always had something pleasant
and delightful to relate in some branch of Rural Economy
which the other was fond of, after which the other to pay
him back again, began to tell something to Mr. Ellis,
and so by turns, till Mr. Ellis got to know all that the
other professed or was noted for. Often has he posed as
if his object had not been to learn something, merely
[T. I. p. 195] to get a better insight into what he
wanted, because the other did not then take him for
what he was.

---

* This seems to have been a species of *co-operation*, in which several
farmers lend horses and implements for the day to one, especially when he
takes a new farm, as still practised at Kelso. It is unlikely that one of these
small farmers would have had six harrows. [J. L.]

After some of his books had been printed, he travelled about himself and had with him some *examples* to sell to gentlemen. He then travelled *incognito*, and let no one know who he was, but gave himself another name, and said he was sent by the publisher to sell books. This he did, partly to collect many observations, and partly to hear the opinions of others upon his writings.

I asked what he thought of Mr. Bradley's writings. He said that Bradley had written very well about Horticulture, but in Agriculture and Rural Economy he was no use, because he was entirely inexperienced in Agriculture, **Landtbruk**. Mr. Ellis said also that he had never thought of writing anything on Rural Economy; but when he got to read Bradley's writings, and saw how inconsistent they were, he had taken up his pen to write something better.

Mortimer's books on Rural Economy he said he had not seen, or at least read.

Switzer's writings he considered in many things to be very good.

He also said he was now a man of somewhat over 60 years of age, for he said he was born in the 80's in the last century. Nearly all his life he had been and was still quite fresh, only that he had now and then been troubled with gout. He said he had been related to Mr. Sherard. [James Sherard the botanist.]

When I said that he by his writings had caused Little Gaddesden to get an undying name, and that no one before his time knew that a Little Gaddesden existed, he answered " No prophet is accepted in his own country " *Luke* iv. 24.

The tobacco which he had by him, and which he smoked, was strongly mixed with aniseed by which it was agreeably scented. He thought such a tobacco very wholesome.

Bot mot Ormbett. *Remedy for Snake bite.*

Mr. Ellis said he knew a sovereign remedy for snake
bite, which consisted in this, that when anyone had been
bitten by a snake, **blifvit huggen af en orm**, he must
at once kill the snake, take its fat or lard, **fett eller
ister**, and lay it on the wounded place.   This, he
assured us, supersedes everything hitherto discovered.
I have since on my foreign travels heard from very
many this given as one of the surest remedies against
snakebite.

Bot mot Såra ögon. *Cure for Sore Eyes.*

Mr. Ellis assured us that sore eyes are cured by
nothing so well as fat and lard of snakes and swine,
which Sir Hans Sloane first discovered, and has since
made generally known through the press.

As Mr. Ellis wished to hear something of the mode
of life among the Lapps, I mentioned to him as a
peculiarity that one scarcely ever finds a Lapp afflicted
with scurvy, and added that Linnæus ascribes as a
reason the Lapps' *diet,* which is never to use salt, or eat
salt meat ; also that one from that seems to have reason
to believe that salt might possibly be the principal cause
of this sickness.   Also I told him that few of the Lapps
use bread, and many of them, perhaps, have never seen
it, but that they avail themselves of dried flesh, and fish
instead.   But I note that Mr. Ellis [T. I. p. 197] did
not rightly understand my meaning, for in a book which
he has since published, and which he calls *The Country
Housewife's Family Companion,* he says, pp. 22 and 23, that
he gathered from me " that the Lapps are never plagued
with scurvy, for the reason that their bread is dried fish,
&c." whereas I not only ascribed to the salt, the first and
greatest, if not the only principal cause of this sickness,
and *vice versa* that when salt is not used one does not

hear of it, but also told him the question which the great
Boerhave put to our learned Linnæus, whether all the
Lapps were not full of scurvy because they dwelt in so
cold a climate? and Linnæus' answer thereto. I have
thought it necessary to insert this here, so that nothing
should stand as my opinion that I do not own.

The 28th March, 1748.

In the morning we walked out on several grass-lands
and arable fields, **fält och åkrar,** which lay around
Little Gaddesden. In the whole of the latter half of this
month the ground here was entirely bare of snow, **bar,**
and green, and the weather sometimes tolerably fair; but
for all that there is up to this date hardly a sign of the
trees putting forth their leaves, much less flowers; so
that to all appearance they do not seem to see the trees
in leaf here so very much earlier in the spring than in the
southern provinces of Sweden. Hazel and some species
of willow were in flower now, but almost no other trees.

Et stort fält. *A large Common* [Ivinghoe Com-
mon] lay on the N.W. side of Little Gaddesden, where
a number of sheep were pasturing. It was a down or
summit of the country, **en högd af landet,** long-sloping
on all sides. [T. I. p. 198.] The soil was the same gravel
and sand of reddish-yellow or brick-colour as has been
described above. Here and there appeared **tufvor,** mole,
or anthills, enough. The whole table-land was overgrown
with furze and brackens, and a little grass in some places.
The ground, on the places free from furze and brackens
was very much choked with mosses. The districts
around Sköfde in Väster-Göthland, when Billingen is excepted, is very like England in appearance, although
there are granites, **gråstenar,** instead of which in these
parts in England, flints lie on the arable and commons,
or 'outlands,' **utmarker.**

Örter. Plants which stood in flower at this time of year, were noted, that thereby the difference between England and Sweden in this respect may be somewhat judged of. They were the following :—

VERONICA, 17. [V. Agrestis] was here an evil weed on the arable fields.

PRIMULA VERIS Vulgaris, *Raj. Syn.* 284, *Primrose.*

NARCISSUS, H. U. 74 sp. 2, **Pâsk-liljer,** "*Lent Lilies,*" *Daffodils* [Nar. Pseudo-Nar.]

Smultron. [Fragaria Vesca.] *Wild Strawberry.*

RANUNCULUS, 460. [R. Ficaria.] *Lesser Celandine.*

LAMIUM, 494. [Lam. purpureum.] *Purple Dead Nettle.*

DRABA, 523 [D. Verna.]

ULEX, H. U. 212. [U. Europæus] *Furze.*

LEONTODON, 627. [L. Taraxacum. L.] *Dandelion.*

TUSSILAGO, 680. [T. Farfara.] *Coltsfoot.*

BELLIS, 707. [B. perennis.] *Daisy.*

HASSEL, *Hazel.*

[T. I. p. 199.] SALICES. Willows.

DAPHNE, 94. [D. Laureola.] *Spurge Laurel.*

FURZE was, of all plants, the one which grew most plentifully on the aforenamed common. From being constantly cut down for fuel by the people, it was now scarcely 4 inches high. Two boys went on one place, and with a "bill," a particular kind of scythe or axe, **lia eller yxa,** cut it off close to the ground. The length of the blade of this bill was 1 foot, the breadth 3 inches, the thickness at the back about ¼ inch. It was sharp on one side so that it could only be used by one who was right-handed, or who, while holding the shaft with both hands, has the right hand foremost or nearest the scythe, **lian.**

The bill-blade itself made with the shaft which was of wood, and the part of the iron which the shaft was fastened to, a very obtuse angle, so that the carl escaped having to stoop while he was striking the cutting stroke.

The boys thus cut down with this scythe *Furze*,
Brackens, old grass, and whatever came in their way, all
of which they then raked together into heaps, bound
them into bundles, and used the thin shoots of black-
-berry-bushes, Rubus, 409 [*R. Fruticosus*] as a band
to bind them with. It was, therefore, highly necessary for one who would bind these into bundles that he
should have good gloves, because both furze and the
blackberry bushes are among the most thorny kinds of
trees or bushes. We saw several heaps of such bundles,
which lay here upon the plain, and which were to be
carried home for fuel. This [T. I. p. 200] furze with its
thorns, had the effect that, when one walked where it
grew, it tore great scratches on the shoes, and where it
encountered the stockings, they were not respected. It
pricked the legs savagely. We afterwards saw boys in
many places in this district cut down the same in the
above-described way for fuel.

Flinta. Flint of the ordinary and common kind,
which is used to strike fire with, and in fire-arms, lay
plentifully on the arable fields. On some fields there
was such an abundance of them, that one had difficulty
in seeing a bit of earth for them. It was found here
both of the lighter and darker sort, and sometimes in
larger sometimes in smaller pieces. The largest as large
as a common clod, **klot,** but mostly they were quite as
small as the closed fist and less. Since there is not the
least sign of granite, **grâsten,** in this district, it is often
the practice to take flints for the foundations of houses.
In one place and another the outhouses are for the most
part built of them. Bricks also are commonly used both
for foundations and walls.

The 29th March, 1748.

Fâr. Sheep are found everywhere in this country

in great numbers, which originated partly in this, that
they get to sell all the more wool, partly also because
there is no nation which eats so much meat as the
Englishmen, and among the same, their mutton or **Får
stek** is not to be despised, and therefore the farmer has
a considerable profit, who is the owner of a large number
of sheep, not to mention their other uses.   Nearly all
their sheep were white.   There was scarcely one in a
hundred that was black or brown or any other colour.
They commonly had either [T. I. p. 201] on the back,
the nape of the neck, the head, or elsewhere, wool
coloured red in one pattern or another, with ruddle,
röd-krita, and water mixed, by which colouring every
owner knew his own again.   The greater number of them
had two horns.   Every farmer had commonly one sheep
which carried a little bell, **skälla.**   The little lambs had
a very long tail which reached nearly to the ground, but
as soon as they were nearly six months old half the tail
was cut off, which was said to be done partly because
the sheep looked better, partly and principally because a
great deal of dirt fastens on to the long tail.   The
English sheep were far from shy, at least nowhere near so
much so as our Swedish.   They went day and night
out on the pastures under the open sky, without having
any house or roof to go under.

In one single place I saw that a boy went with them
to pasture, but commonly and almost everywhere they
were left without a shepherd, **vall-hjon,** entirely by
themselves.   At home at the farms they had in some
places small *Skeelings*, **skjul,** built of short posts and
the roof of the skeel of straw, under which the sheep
could go when it rained, or was bad weather.   Some had
also another outhouse, into which the shepherd, **Fåra
herden,** in such a case, and in some places every evening,
drove in the sheep.   Some farmers had in the middle of

the farm-yard under the open sky erected as it were a
crib or rack, **krubba eller häck,** of two narrow hurdles,
grindar, which were fastened together at the bottom, and
between which fine hay was laid of which the sheep went
to eat in the night when they stood at home in the farm-
yard.

The sheep are clipped here not more than once a
year, and that in the summer. They are folded from
Michaelmas in the autumn till this time [T. I. p. 202] in
the spring, and later, on turnip-lands, a better description
of which shall be given farther on.

The hurdles, **grindarna,** wherewith, and within
which, they are folded, are about 8 feet long, and 3 feet
6 inches high, which hurdles are 'keyed' or looped,
klafvas, close together in a row, a post being driven
down into the ground between each ; and thus, according to the number of sheep, they made a larger or
smaller fold, **fålla.** From the fold there commonly
runs a narrow passage made of similar hurdles, to some
one of the living hedges, by which the field is surrounded, that the sheep in bad weather may be able
to go to such hedge and shelter there. In the sheep-fold
there is mostly a " sheep-crib " or " sheep-trough," **ho,**
knocked together of two boards *ad angulum acutum*, or a
little less than an *angulus rectus*, and a board-lap at each
end, so that the fodder may not run out. When it is bad
weather barley is laid in this trough, or oats, or pease,
for the sheep to eat.

Halm-tak. Straw-thatch was much used in this
district, on outhouses as well as on cottages, **stugor
hvari folket bodde.** It was also hereabout not uncommon to see beautiful brick houses, **stenhus,** with
straw-thatch over. A great many outhouses were, however of wood, the walls, for instance, being made of thick
oak-boards. The roofs of the houses, whether they were

of tiles or thatch, were very steep and high-pitched, so
that it was quite impossible to go upon them, as with us
in Sweden, where straw-thatch is used, but for all such
one was obliged to have a ladder to stand upon when
there was anything to do to the roof. The rain-water
could also not remain so long on such a steep-sloping
thatch roof.

Halmtaken, the thatch roofs, were here made in
this way, that one first erected a framework of wooden
beams upon which the thatch roof [T. I. p. 203] is to
rest, by erecting wooden rafters from both the 'long-
walls,' which rafters at their lower ends stood on the
roofplate, **tak foten;** but at their upper ends leant
against each other at the roof-tree of the house and
formed there an *angulum acutum.* Across and above
these rafters were nailed horizontal laths all the way
up the rafters up to the ridge, **Krâpp-âsen,** one
row of laths above the other, about a foot between
each row. They had afterwards begun to lay thatch
down at the eaves, **takfoten,** so that the thatch might
be a foot thick, sometimes more, sometimes less. The
straw was then laid so that the large ends of the straw
were turned downwards, and the small ends upwards ;
but at the ends of the sides of the ridge-shaped roof, it
was turned so that it did not there lie parallel with the
other straw on the roof but obliquely, that is to say, the
lower ends obliquely outwards from the ridge and the
upper more on to the inner part of the thatch, as is seen
in the accompanying Figure. [Fig. omitted. J. L.]

The straw is fastened thus : when it had been arranged
as one would have it, it was then bound round at the
upper end with a withe of willow, **en vidja af Vide,**
or hazel, and so [T. I. p. 204] fast to some of the
above named horizontal laths. That is to say, the lowest
row of straw was first bound in that way fast to the roof-

plate, **takbandet,** afterwards, other straw was laid on that, but a little higher up, **ofvanföre,** so that the latter comes to cover the upper parts of the first laid straw, together with the withe or band, **banden,** with which it was bound. In this way it was continued in layers right up to the ridge, **kråpp-åsen,** till the whole roof had thus been thatched, **täckt.** Across the ridge was laid long straw, **lång-halm,** as much and as thick as one wanted, when it was bent and turned in that position, **sålunda,** down on both sides of the ridge, and was afterwards bound fast in the above described manner on both sides of the ridge. On this thatch there were not laid any sticks, **Riskor,** or anything else to press down or retain the straw against storm and wind, because the straw was so well fastened that it was not necessary. Besides that, such weights on the straw have the disadvantage that the rain-water easily comes to stand against them, and in these places causes the thatch to rot more quickly. It was wheat straw which the roofs here were thatched with, and in this district it grows very long.

The 30th March, 1748.

Svartmyllan, eller den jorden, som på åkrarna lång öfverst, the soil which lay on the surface of the ploughed fields was not here of so black a colour as I saw in Russia, about Moscow, and between Moscow and Tulou, where it often looks as black as gunpowder; but it strikes here for the most part somewhat of a reddish-yellow or ochre-colour, which without doubt proceeds from the gravel and clay immediately under it, which have the same colour. The soil under [T. I. p. 205] the grass sward on the hill sides, and such like places was also commonly of the same colour.

Väpling ; Trifolium purpureum...pratensi simile —*Raj. Syn.* 328 [T. pratense L.] which is called

Clover by Englishmen, was sown here on a great many
of the arable fields and *inclosures* or small **täppor,** and
that always, where I saw it, on 'broad-cast land,' or on
nearly flat-ploughed land, and not on that which lay in
high ridges. After this is sown, it seldom lasts more
than two years before it dies and must be sown again *de
novo*. Some have it for three years, but never more.
Here it is usual to sow it with some kind of crop. The
second summer after it is sown it is cropped once and
often twice. After that, the land is ploughed up and
sown with wheat, till, after a few years, it is laid down
as meadow again.

Åkrarna. The arable fields in this district, which
stood sown with wheat, were for the most part laid out
in *Stitches* or *Four-thorough-land** : that is, that the whole
field was laid out in small ridges, **ryggar,** each of the
ridges only of *four furrows*, **fyra fåror,** with water
furrows between all the ridges, **med täta wättu-fåror
emellan ryggarna.** The breadth of the ridge between
the water furrows was a Swedish ell, or 2 English feet.
The ridges, or *Stitches*, were so made that they lay highest
in the middle, and sloped after that on both sides
towards the water furrows. The *Water furrows* were
drawn from the highest lying part of the field, to that
part of it which lay deepest down towards the dales,
all in *lineâ rectâ*. The depth of the water-furrows was
6 inches, sometimes more, sometimes less, the breadth
1 foot, just about. At both ends of the water-furrows,
both upper and lower, were drawn four such stitches, or
ridges [T. I. p. 206], with water-furrows between, all of
the same breadth as the others across the field, or so
that the stitches and water-furrows, which went from the

---

* Four-furrow-land. " Furrows are here called 'thoroughs.'" (Colloq)
1886. [J. L.]

highest to the lowest part of the field, made with these
['headlands' or 'butts'] *angulos rectos*, or abutted perpendicularly against them.

These cross-ridges may have come to be made for
this reason, that when ploughed up and down according
to the field, there is always left at both ends a bit
unploughed ; that is to say, the ['headland,' or] piece on
which the horses, **dragarne,** are turned round, which
must afterwards be ploughed up crosswise just as it
lies, **på detta sättes.**

Humla. Hops we saw planted in no place by the
farms and villages here in Hertfordshire where we
travelled. I asked the farmers whether they had no hops
here ? They answered that they do not plant any hops
in this district, but they buy all that they have need of
for their requirements from Kent and the districts in
England where they specially lay themselves out for hop-
planting. In England the wholesome custom is much in
use, that nearly every district lays itself out for something
particular in Rural Economy, to cultivate, viz., that which
will thrive and develop there best, and leaves the rest to
other places. They believe they win more by this means
than if they cultivated all departments of Rural Economy ;
for, besides that he who has many irons in the fire must
necessarily burn some, they also think it is not worth while
to force nature. Thus their principal occupation in
Hertfordshire is *Agriculture; Hop-growing* and *Cherry-tree*
cultivation in Kent, sheep-farming in another place,
cattle-breeding in another, &c.

They thus sell their own ware, and buy what they
themselves have not, or they also exchange ware for ware.

Tjenste-folk, *Farm servants.* A farmer in this
district does not himself keep many servants. When he
has a **dräng**, manservant, and a **piga**, girl, he has
enough. There are also many farmers who have no

manservant. I was assured that in all Little Gaddesden
there were not twelve menservants who serve as such for
annual wages. For here it is the custom that every
farmer mostly employs **dagsverks - karlar, som
arbeta för dags-penning,** day-labourers who work
for daily wages, to perform all their affairs with, both in
the arable field, in the meadow, in the lathe, thrashing, &c., by which arrangement they believe, for many
reasons, that they come out much better than if they
themselves kept and fed many agricultural labourers.
It is also for this reason that in every town, parish, and
village, **Stad, Socken, och By,** there live a great many
labouring men and poor folk, who only feed themselves
and their families by going to work for farmers, gentlemen, and other wealthy persons for daily or weekly
wages. Here in Little Gaddesden a labouring man gets
from 8 or 10 pence to a shilling a day. At Woodford,
in Essex, my host gave 9 shillings a week to each
labourer whom he had at his farm to thrash, and kept
them in **svag-dricka,** small beer, besides. When
a labourer here in Little Gaddesden gets a shilling a day
or a little less, he is bound to provide his own food, and
he is given by the farmer, or the one who hired him,
nothing further except small beer, **Svag-dricka eller
Spis-öl,** as it is everywhere the practice not to let the day
labourer have anything further. Carpenters who had set
up a new plank-fence received from our landlord eighteen
pence a day and kept themselves in food and all.

Kor. *Cows.*

[T. I. p. 208]. They had not a particularly large
number of *cows* here in Little Gaddesden. One farmer
had seldom over 3 or 4, often less. I was assured that
in the whole of Little Gaddesden there were not more
than twenty cows. The whole winter up to the month of

May they are kept at home at the farm in a cow-shed, **hemma vid gården i hus,** and fed with dry hay, but afterwards they have freedom to go out in the pastures, **beteshagarna,** during the summer, and there seek their food. The reason why they have so few cows in this village and the other villages lying round about, is said to be this, that they have so little pasture and meadow land; because it is mostly arable; but in other places some distance from here where they have large pastures, **betes-marker,** there are said to be plenty of cows.

Getter brukades ej här. *Goats are not used here.*

One farmer only, Mr. Williams, had two goats, viz., a buck and a goat, which were shown to me, as something rare, that they believed I had never seen before. He said he kept them mostly in the stable because he was of the opinion that the horses did well with them.

Ormbunkar, Pteris, 843. [Pt. Aquilina] *Brackens* grew in very great abundance on the hills, near and in the hedges, and elsewhere. At a farm I saw the same dried, carried home, and there laid in two heaps, each of them as large as a small house, and nicely thatched with straw. I asked for what purpose they would use this large quantity of brackens. They answered "for fuel for all purposes for which otherwise wood or furze, &c., is used." In particular they said they used this in the pre-paration and drying of malt, [T. I. p. 209] brewing, and such like. In my walks afterwards on different sides around Little Gaddesden, I always found this growing in great abundance on all common pastures or hills. From the good soil, it had commonly grown here to a greater height and luxuriance than with us in Sweden. We also saw several places where they cut the same and collected it for fuel. In the Duke of Bridgwater's Park [Ashridge] which lay close to Little Gaddesden, there

was a large brickyard, **Tegel-bruk,** where a multitude
of bricks, **Tegel,** were made. The fuel which was then
used to lay in the brick-kilns, **Tegel-ugnarna,** and to
burn the bricks with, was small bundles and twigs of
beech, but especially these brackens. We saw large
heaps of it lying in the brickyard, thatched with straw.
The folk said that these ferns give in the burning a much
stronger heat than many kinds of wood.

Furze is said not to come up to this, in that respect,
by a long way. A worthy old farmer assured me that
brackens ought to be reckoned amongst the best fuel, as
he could testify from a long experience. He used it for
baking and much else. In many places it was also seen
collected, and thrown amongst the straw under the cattle
in the farm yard, there to lie and rot, and by that means
form manure. It is also used to lay on the ground under
wheat, pease, and barley stacks.

The 31st March, 1748.

In the morning we went over several arable fields,
meadows, and pastures, to view the condition of the
district and the country.

[T. I. p. 210]. **Ärter,** pease were sown here in very
many places, and that always in ' broad-cast-land ' or
on flat-ploughed plots, **jämna åker-stycken.** Each
' cast,' or space between the water-furrows, was about 20
feet broad. A cross furrow went down at the end, but I
saw not for what use, for it lay like an earth bank down
there, and held back, **qvarhölt,** the water which had
flowed down there from above when it was raining, for
the bank of the water-furrow was so large and broad
that it dammed back the down-flowing water and
hindered its running off. The pease were here either
sown in the same way as we sow our crops, or also
in rows.

Belägenheten af Byarna.

The arrangement of the villages, or a *Parish,* was commonly thus. The houses, **Gårdarna,** were built all in one row, sometimes quite close together, sometimes farther apart. On one side, about and alongside of the village always lay the common pastures and heath or outlands, **betes och utmarker,** and on the other their gardens, ploughed fields, meadows and inclosed pastures, **beteshagar.** On the side where the out-land was, there always went a road, **gata,** or way close to and along the village [the Back Lane].

Sometimes there were seen cherry-trees, walnut-trees, beeches and such like trees planted outside the gates, yet not thickly.

On the other side of the village where the arable fields, &c., lay, there was nearest to the house their kitchen-garden or flower-garden. After that came the ploughed fields, commonly, but not always, for they alternated with meadows and pastures. All these were fenced and inclosed with hedges, which consisted mostly of hawthorn, but mixed with that were sloe-bushes, **Stärkebärs-buskar,** blackberry-bushes, **Björnbärs-buskar,** Dog-rose, **Törne,** ivy, holly, *Agrifolium,* [Ilex Aquifolium], ash, **Ask,** lime, **Lind,** willows, *Salices,* oaks, **Ekar,** bird-cherry trees, **Fogel-kirsbärs-trän,** [*not* Prunus Padus the bird-cherry, but *Prunus Avium,* the *Gean*] and often a number of large beeches, **Bökar,** etc. In some places the [T. I. p. 211] farms lay on the hills, in other places in the dales, so that on that point there was no certainty. Some villages, however did not lie in this fashion, in particular those which were in *Vale Land,** but the houses were there built, for the

---

* Vale Land, low-lying plains on the Gault clay outside the chalk range, as the Vale of Aylesbury, and that which lies spread to the view from Dunstable Downs and Ivinghoe Beacon. [J. L.]

most part scattered, as in a town, but much farther apart. Ploughed fields and fenced inclosures appeared there on all sides. A number of different kinds of trees were planted both in the villages in front of the houses and along the streets, and round about outside the villages, which all served as an ornament for the village or the parish, which lay as in a garden, and as a shelter, **skygd**, against blasts or cold winds, which in *Vale Land* played over the large open fields.*

Höstackar. Haystacks are used here in England everywhere, in Essex as well as in Hertfordshire and elsewhere, where I have been. I hardly ever saw any **hölada,** 'hay-lathe,' on the meadows. Thus, they had the hay also at home at the farms almost more in stacks than in hay-sheds. The shapes of the English hay-stacks was in all places the same, that is to say, they had the shape of a house standing by itself, or of a hay-lathe on the meadows with us in Sweden, yet the thatch is a little steeper ; and the lower half which resembles walls, is ordinarily made so that it slopes more and more inwards the nearer it gets to the ground, so that the eaves of the thatch on the sides, and the higher gable at the gable ends (which as I have before compared it to a house, I may now call them) project, which is done entirely that the wet and rain may injure the hay less. On the top these stacks are commonly well thatched with wheat straw.

A hay stack is made here (Little Gaddesden) in the following manner :—

When the hay is quite dry, it is carried to [T. I. p. 212] the place where the stack is to be made, after which the hay is laid in the aforenamed four-sided house-like form, and is well trampled.

When the hay-stack has quite got its right shape,

---

* Alas ! these are nearly all inclosed. [J. L.]

like a house with a span-roof, they begin to thatch it with wheat-straw, which is effected thus: A little above the thatch-foot of the hay-stack, a hole is stuck here and there horizontally all the way along the roof of the stack with a **käpp** or "*rick-peg;*" thereupon long wheat-straw is taken, at one end of which is made a fold or twist, **et veck,** and the straw is twisted tightly together by the twist. The highest part of the straw, or the twist, is then stuffed into the holes which have been made in the hay, with the rick-peg, by which means it is fastened. [Here is a figure.] When the straw has thus been stuffed into the hay, a whole row along the *roof,* **hela raden långs öfver taket,** they begin a foot or more higher up, to do likewise along the whole roof, taking care that this row is parallel [T. I. p. 213] with the former or lower, when this stuffed-in straw covers over the upper ends of the lower rows. They continue thus to stuff in the straw into the hay as far up as the ridge or the highest top of the *roof,* when in every case the upper straw covers the ends of the lower. Along the ridge, which resembles a roof-ridge, **kroppås,** there are first laid brackens, **Ormbunkar,** and then straw on those, which is fastened at the summit, thus: Two long split-sticks or "rods," **långa spjälkor eller språtor,** are laid over the straw along and on opposite sides of the roof or thatch, which are fastened with many rick-pegs, as the accompanying Figure shows. The rick-pegs are knocked down into the hay, so that the crook at the top presses down the "rods," **spjälken,** and holds the straw fast. [It is not necessary to reproduce the figure. J. L.]

On both sides, at the *gables* from the highest ridge down the edge of the thatch there are laid long rods which are in the same way fastened with similar "rick-pegs" which hold fast the straw and prevent the wind from carrying it away at the edges.

I have asked several old farmers and labourers why
they do not use lathes, **lador,** here to keep the hay in?
They have answered that they considered haystacks,
when they are well thatched with straw far better than
lathes (haysheds). The reason they gave was that when
the hay is laid in lathes, the part of it which lies nearest
to the walls, 6 inches or a foot from the wall commonly
becomes spoilt, musty and mouldy, **skämt, unkigt och
mögligt,** loses its beautiful scent, so that the cattle
will not eat it at all willingly, but on the other hand in
the stack it retains its sweet and fragrant scent, is eaten
by the cattle very greedily, and it is only the outer surface
of the uncovered part which takes a little harm from
rain, but is for all that not so bad as that which is laid
next the wall in the lathe. All the hay, which was set in
stacks in the parts [T. I. p. 214] of England where I
travelled, is not taken out of the stack in the same
manner as is usual with us in Sweden, viz.: that one
tears off the highest first and so continues downwards,
but all this hay is cut out of the stack with a 'hay
knife' specially made for the purpose, which is done in
this way: When they require any hay out of the stack
for the cattle, they begin to cut at one of the gable ends
of the stack first, that is to say, they begin at the highest
ridge or top to cut loose slices, **flingor,** of about 2 feet
broad or more, just as they please. Thus it is continued
with the cutting, across the whole gable end from above
downwards, as it is required. On this cutting, **skärning,**
it was noted, that it is not cut perpendicularly down, but
the lower one gets, so much the more it is cut sloping
into the stack, so that the upper part of the stack where
one is cutting overhangs the under, that the hay in the
stack may not take any harm from wet. In this way the
stack is cut to pieces until there is hardly any more hay
left.

The English haystacks have also the advantage that they do not take harm from rain, whether they are touched or not. Against which the Swedish way compels one either to take in the whole stack at once, or runs the risk that bad weather will injure it, after it has once been robbed on the top, not to mention that the structure of the English haystacks in every way obviates the wet, which the Swedish on the other hand seems rather to assist. Moreover, the English farmers also think that the hay thus cut in little *billets doux* from the stack, **skurit litet i Sänder från stacket,** smacks much better to the cattle, and is more readily eaten by them; and retains its fragrant scent longer, than if they were to tear the stack to pieces all at once; when at least a great if not the greater part of the hay's delightful fragrance would disappear and be lost.

[T. I. p. 215.] *Sain Foin* was sown in one or another enclosure; we saw sometimes whole fields sown with it, and that always in broad-land. No sheep or other animal had pasture on it this year, for which reason it was now standing beautiful enough, grew mostly in clusters, **klasar,** and was now a couple of inches high. The place where it grew lay towards the morning sun, but a great quanity of mosses had rooted in it in the vacant spaces between this *Sain Foin.* The soil was the same as everywhere about here. When this has once been sown, it can remain for fifteen, eighteen or twenty years' time, if it is only manured every third year, on the ground where it grows.

Clover was sown in one and another inclosure, **täppa,** and that always in *broad-cast-land.* On the places which seemed to have been sown the past year, it stood very green, thick and beautiful, an inch or two high. On older places it was somewhat thinner, but nevertheless, of the same height.

Lucerne is not sown at all in this district because they think that it is not worth while.

Skogs-lundar. Woods appeared here and there. They consisted of all kinds of trees growing wild here in England; for of *Scotch Fir*, **barr-trä**, I have not seen any where I travelled in Essex and Hertfordshire, except those which had been expressly planted out near houses, and in some places on the fields, **på fälten.** *Beeches* were, however, the principal trees in the woods, and in this district grew in considerable quantities. **Fogel Kirsbär** (*Prunus avium*), the *Gean*, lime, **Lind**, Ash, hazel, oaks, willows, poplars, hawthorn, dog-rose, **Törne**, sloe, ivy, blackberry bushes, maple, **Lönn,** and many others, often vied with each other in numbers. The hornbeam, **Afvenbok,** was here [T. I. p. 216] very rare.

On all sides of these woods lay either arable fields, meadows, pastures, orchards, commons or outlands, **utmarker,** or villages. Holly and *Laureola Semper-virens* [Daphne Laureola], also ivy, which clambered up the trees, adorned these woods with their beautiful green leaves.

I saw one and another group of blackberry bushes which retained its green leaf the whole winter, although some of them had become brown and as if burnt, **bruna och lika som brända.** Furze showed itself among them, and might at a distance lead one to believe that it was a Juniper, so like is it. Its natural soil is high-lying, dry, and sterile sandy plains and hills.

Mullvadar. *Moles* are found in great number in Essex, as well as in Hertfordshire, and often cause the farmers great damage. I saw in several places in Essex one mole hill, **Mullvadshögen,** beside another, and that in great abundance, and mostly on the arable fields. Here in Hertfordshire also, a multitude of their upcast hills appeared. They do not avoid any earth which is dry. In Essex they had their abode under the soil, **Svartmyllan,** even so in Hertfordshire; but then I also saw here in Little Gaddesden that they cast up their hills in bare chalk in a ploughed field on a chalk hillside. They are commonly caught here with a particular kind of trap, **fållor,** which is set out for them in their hole. The farm servants frequently amuse themselves by setting these traps, **giller,** for them, because the farmers, or their employers, pay them a certain price when they deliver to them so and so many moles, **så och så många Mullvadar,** at a time. Therefore they collect them diligently, and hang them up in bundles, till they can reach the [T. I. p. 217] desired quantity, when they show the same to their master and get the promised reward. Farther on, these mole-traps shall be described and illustrated.

[This promise was never fulfilled].

Åker-renar. 'Acre-reins,' *Balks,* were found in some arable fields, but very seldom. The breadth of them was a Swedish ell, two English feet. These were only on the larger [open] fields, and served as boundaries between the farmers' strips, **tegar.**

Åkrarna. *The arable fields* were almost everywhere divided into small inclosures, **täppor,** always with living hedges around them instead of fences, **gärdesgård;** but where the hedges were cut down, a dead-fence, or **gärdesgård,** was set up till a new hedge grew up. Commonly, nearly all these inclosures were quadrilateral, only they sometimes resembled squares, **quadrater,** sometimes oblongs; yet they had also sometimes some other figure, as, one somewhat circular, trapeziform, &c., but these were, nevertheless, scarce enough.

Ängarna och beteshagarna. *The meadows and*

pastures were divided in the same manner, mostly of similar size and figure. The greatest part, if not all of them, have formerly been ploughed fields, and become *per ordinem successionis* ploughed fields again, because the English custom, for the most part, is by turns, to lay down ploughed fields to meadows, and meadows to ploughed fields.

The greater number of these were so overgrown with mosses, *Bryum, Hypnum,* that our most moss-grown meadows in Sweden could scarcely be worse. What the reason of this may be I know not. Sheep pasture, **gå i bet,** on a great part of these the whole year, day and night, in dry and wet. May not their trampling, and baiting, as the ground is often wet enough, cause the grass to be damaged [T. I. p. 218] as well as destroyed at the root, and worn away, **förtynat?** or is the land very favourable for mosses? I believe so; for a ground does not lie here long after it has ceased to be worked with the plough before it becomes overgrown with mosses. May not the leaf-trees planted round about contribute somewhat to this? It seems very likely, for one commonly sees that the moss keeps to places near and under leaf-trees, and rather in their shade, especially on the north side of them, whence it extends farther and farther out on the land. I saw, however, here and there one and another inclosure, **täppa,** which was almost entirely free from them, and in these the grass growth was thick and very beautiful, and when I looked more closely, dung or manure was spread out over the grass-sward on these places.

Ärter. *Pease* were thrashed in some places even at this season. In a large barn, **sädes-lada,** which was built of itself, far from other houses, in the fields, **åkrar,** we saw a large stack of pease-straw, **ärthalm,** still unthrashed. It consisted of the kind of peas here called *Maple*

*Pea,** and was used as food for swine. The pease-straw stack had the same shape as the haystacks hereabouts, that is to say, it resembled a **hölada,** *hay-lathe.* Its length was 20 feet, breadth 16, height at the sides 4 feet 6 inches, but in the middle of the gable-end, or up to the ridge, as it were, 10 feet. On the top it was thatched with wheat straw. Round about it was fenced in with sloe, **omgärdad med Slån,** which was set close beside it, and prevented the cattle from coming near it.

Rof-kåls eller Rof-blads nytta til Sallad eller Grön-kål.

Turnip-tops used for Salad or as Greens.

It is well known that here in England [T. I. P. 219] it is the custom to sow turnips on the ploughed fields as fodder for sheep; on which they go and bait—of which more further on. The turnips consequently stand in the fields at this time of year. The women are in the habit of cutting off the young delicate leaves, **klena bladen,** which shoot out at this season, and prepare them in the same way as we prepare spinach, **Spinat,** in Sweden, with a little butter, and eat it so with their roast meats, **Stekar.** One who has not eaten it would have difficulty in imagining what an agreeable and well-flavoured dish, **rätt,** this is. They said that the turnip leaves are no use at any other time of year but this, for that purpose.

Igelkottar. *Hedgehogs* are found in this district wild. The carls brought me one, which they had taken on the ground, and which afterwards quietly decamped, **practicerade sig ut,** through the door at night. An old farmer told me that they suck the milk from cows,

---

* Still called "Maple Pea," 1886. [J. L.]

when they lie down on the ground, and otherwise do them harm. *

Ko-dynga. *Cowdung* was carried and arranged in small heaps close beside each other on the arable fields, but still unspread. It consisted mostly of straw-litter, **halm-byssja;** for here it was the practice to spread a quantity of straw out on the farm-yard under the cattle, where they lie; which straw is afterwards shovelled together, **skåttas tilhopa,** into heaps, left to lie and rot a little, and is afterwards carried out on to the fields. This dung thus carted out, will, after a few days, be spread out, ploughed down, and the land sown with barley or turnips, **Korn eller Rofvor.**

Grindar. *Gates* are used in nearly all inclosures, **täppor,** through which one may drive a horse, **köra med häst,** or drive sheep, **eller drifva Fåren.** The height of the gate was seldom over 3 or 4 feet, often it was in a deplorable state. Every inclosure had commonly one such gate. One [T. I. p. 220] was obliged to lift it up and back again. Otherwise, where a footpath ran through any inclosure, there was commonly in the hedge a stile, **klif-stätta,** in some place, over which one could go; for the hedges which consisted of prickly hawthorn, deprived one of the pleasure of climbing or forcing his way over or through them, but one must go through the gate or over the stile.

---

* "'*Hertfordshire Hedgehogs.*' This proverb seems to have no other meaning than that of pointing out the number of hedgehogs found in this county. Hedgehogs are harmless animals who, from the vulgar error of their sucking cows, have, time out of mind been proscribed, and threepence, or a groat, paid for every one of them brought dead or alive to the churchwardens, by whose order they are commonly gibbeted on one of the yew trees in the churchyard," &c. Fras. Grose, *Local Proverbs*, app. of *Prov. Gloss.* Lond., 2nd Ed., 1790, 8vo. [J. L.]

The 1st April, 1748.

Agrifolium *Raj. Syn.* 466. [Ilex Aquifolium.] *Holly* had grown by itself in some places here at Little Gaddesden, close in front of the houses, on the green, **på betesmarken.** Those living near had constantly clipped off the same expressly, so that this tree did not get to grow high, but spread out with its branches to a considerable width. The reason why they thus clipped it was that the women might get to lay their linen, which they had washed, on it to dry, for which purpose these trees were now very useful.

Såg-ställen. *Saw-pits,* where they sawed asunder trunks of trees and logs, **ståckar och klabbar,** into boards and other things, they had here in England at most farms, and made in a very handy way. Instead of having **Såg-båckar,** sawyers' trestles, as we have in Sweden, on to which we must with much difficulty lift the stocks or trunks we wish to saw to pieces, they have here dug a pit down in the earth of a fathom's depth more or less. The length of the pit is commonly 6 to 8 feet, the breadth 3 to 4 feet. Internally it is commonly lined with boards, so that the earth may not fall down into it from the sides.

De Sågar. *The Saws,* which are commonly used here consist of a broad saw-blade, **såg-blad** [T. I. p. 221], with handles, **handtag,** at both ends. One carl stands therefore down in the pit, and the other [the top sawyer] above, each of whom holds his end of the saw. They have the stocks rolled *across* the pit, when they wish to saw it *across,* or *along* the pit, when they wish to saw it into boards. They thus avoid having to lift the stocks up into the **Såg-båckar,** or high frames. When any carpenters or others buy a whole beech in the woods or in any of the fields, they first saw it off close to the

ground, and when they have thus got the tree down they
do not incur the cost of carrying the tree home whole, as
it had fallen, but they saw it into smaller pieces on the
spot where it grew, dig there a pit 6 feet deep, or of the
shape which has just been described, where they saw the
tree to pieces, or to boards, or whatever they wish.

Sniglar. *Snails* can often cause great damage on
arable fields and meadows. Mr. Ellis showed me yesterday a letter which he had received from a learned and
experienced gentleman, who has a great taste for Rural
Economy, in which letter this gentleman relates that
when he succeeded to his estate after his father's death,
there was found on a brick wall, **sten-vall,** on his estate
a dreadful lot of snails.

In the morning before sunrise they were out on the
grass and ploughed fields, where they did great damage.
On one occasion he remarked that when the swine were
turned out in the morning, and came to pass close to this
wall, they left all other food and began only to seek for
and eat these snails. From this, he concluded to send
out boys in the morning, while the dew still lay heavily
on the ground [T. I. p. 222], and collect them in baskets,
and attempt to give them to the swine at home, when he
had the pleasure of seeing how greedily the pigs ate them
as if they had been their choicest food. He did not
afterwards regret that he caused them to be collected
every day, and fed the swine with them, for they not only
became astonishingly fat, so that the hair fell off them, but
when a pig, **gris,** which was fed on the snails, was killed,
his flesh was found to be of the best possible flavour.

Tegel-sten. *Brick* brayed into fine dust or meal is
used here to scour or polish all kinds of iron or brass
implements, &c., in a household, such as candlesticks,
ljus-stakar, snuffers, **ljus-saxar,** knife-handles, **knif-
skaft,** tongs, **eld tänger,** &c. Some of this dust was

laid quite dry in a cloth, with which the iron or brass utensils were polished. If this dust is wet, the utensils which are rubbed therewith become æruginous, **ârgig,** in consequence.

The 2nd April, 1748.

In the morning we walked about in [Ashridge] Park, which lay S.W. of and close to Little Gaddesden, and belonged to the Duke of Bridgwater, who lately died in early youth and left his estates to his sisters and young brother, who was only eleven years old. [" John, 2nd " Duke of Bridgwater, was born in April 1726, and died " in February 1748, unmarried. *Francis, third and present* " *Duke of Bridgwater,* and only surviving brother of the " last was born in 1736. His grace is not married (1775), " and, if he dies without legitimate issue, will be succeeded " by his cousin. . . . But he is best known by that " noble canal in Lancashire which takes its name from " him, and will effectually transmit it to future ages, " being by all accounts a work worthy of the ancient " Romans." *The Complete English Peerage,* Rev. F. Barlow, 2nd Ed. 1775, vol. I. pp. 225-6.]

The Stone House itself, which was very handsome* lay in the midst of the park, from which there were prospects on four sides through the midst of the park, cut in straight lines.† The park consisted especially of lofty, thick and dense beeches, with some oaks mingled amongst them, **blandad deribland,** hawthorn, ash,‡ hazel, also appeared in it in some places.

---

* The frontispiece of Todd's *Bonhommes* shows the north front, as it was in 1768.

† These still exist, 1886. The Prince's Riding runs N.W. straight for 1½ miles to Money Bury Hill. At its summit is the obelisk erected to the memory of *Francis,* 3rd Duke, whose likeness will be found on page 56 of Todd's *Bonhommes.* He died 8th March, 1803, unmarried.

‡ Skelton in his *Crown of Laurel* has the distich :
" Fraxinus in clivo frondet que viret sine rivo
Non est sub divo similis sine flumine vivo."

[T. I. p. 223.] **Hjortars föda och nytta, &c.**
Deer's food and use, &c.

We saw a very large number of deer, **Hjortar**, both large and small, which were kept in this park. Some few of them were snow-white, but the greater number of them were for the most part of a brownish grey or fawn colour similar to hares, **Harar.** A man who accompanied us, assured us that there were over 1,000 head, **stycken,** now kept here, and which we had no difficulty in believing, in view of this, that we saw large herds, **hopar,** of them whenever we went in the park. In several places there lay cut down and laid for the deer, fresh young beeches, ashes, and hawthorn, from which they had gnawed, **gnagit,** the bark, so that these trees were now quite without bark. It was the ash, however, which of all trees was most laid for them, **mâst lagd för dem,** and from which they gnawed most bark. These barked, **afskalade**, trees, after they had become dry, were an excellent fuel.

In one place and another in the park there was a shed, **hus,** erected, which commonly consisted of a roof on posts under the middle of which there ran a long rack, **häck,** made of two hurdles which were tied together by their lower sides, so that the hay could be laid between them. Here the deer had their refuge in bad weather and got their fodder, **föda,** from the hay which was there spread for them in the racks, **uti häckar.** In the summer they got their fodder from the grass in the park, but in the winter from the hay which had with this object been carried in the summer into lathes, **lador,** of which there were several here in the park. It is well known that the male deer, **hjort-hanarna,** or stags, have horns, but the hinds, **honarna,** have not, and that the stags shed their horns once a year, when new ones grow instead.

It was also at this time of year that they began to shed their horns, **fålla sina horn.** We saw some which now had only one, the other had already fallen off.

The use which was made of these deer, **djur,** besides the pleasure the owner had of them, is that the flesh [T. I. p. 224] is esteemed a delicacy, while the skins are excellent for breeches, &c., the horns are in great request among various mechanics for knife-handles, and such like, together with this, that they are sold to apothecaries for their medicinal purposes.

At förekomma höets hopbrinnade.
To prevent the spontaneous combustion of the hay.

In one of the lathes, **lador,** when the hay was collected for the deer, a plan was shown to us, how they prevent hay which had been newly carried in, from taking any harm from spontaneous combustion, which was managed thus ; they knocked together square tubes, **trummor,** of four boards about 6 feet long more or less, and 1 foot square. These were set here and there, perpendicularly in the hay when it was laid in the lathe, **i ladan,** and were arranged so that the wind, by means of the hole they left came to play through the hay, by which means the warm vapour which causes the hay to take fire, finds an escape. These pipes are placed in the hay when it is laid in the lathe, and when it has been packed in they are drawn up, and leave a hole behind them through which the vapour ascends. Some use tubs, **tunnor,** or " well-frames " or " curbs " (?) **fjälingar,** for this purpose. In a similar manner these are used when it is necessary to place grain crops that are not thoroughly dry in barns or lathes, **lador.**

Hölada med tak, at lyfta up och ned.
A Hay-lathe with a roof to lift up and down.

Among other lathes, **lador,** in which the hay was

kept for the deer, we got to see one here, which was
made in a particular manner, that is, that when some of
the hay which lay in it was taken away, the roof could
be lowered after it, so that it nearly always lay close
on to the hay when it was so desired. The plan was
this ; they had driven down four posts, **stålpar,** in a
square, one at each corner, **hörn.** The length of the
posts was 30 feet, the distance between two posts was
14 feet. At the bottom, [T. I. p. 225 is occupied by an
illustration] [T. I. p. 226] between these posts, there
were made walls of oak boards which were nailed fast
to the posts.

The height of the walls from the ground was 8 feet.
Above the board-walls there was a thatch-roof between
the posts, which thatch suspended above the house was
convex, and formed absolutely a half, **octahedron,**
octagon, which, however, at the border had slightly
oblong sides.

The ' thatch-band ' or roof-plate, **tak-banden,** consisted of wooden bars, dovetailed into each other at
the ends. They all went close outside the posts, so
that the posts stood right in the angle which two
sides of the roof-plate, **tak-foten,** made with each other.
A crooked stick was afterwards nailed fast by one end
to the one side of the roof-plate, and by the other end to
the second side, which formed a right angle with the
first ; yet in this way, that this crook came, as it were,
to form at the corner a little triangle, of which the crook
made one side, and the other two were formed of the
two sides of the roof-plate, and the post ran right through
the middle of this triangle.

On others which I saw, the thatch-band or roof-plate
went inside the posts, and the crook outside, just as they
wished. In the posts were several holes, right through
them, the one a little above the other.

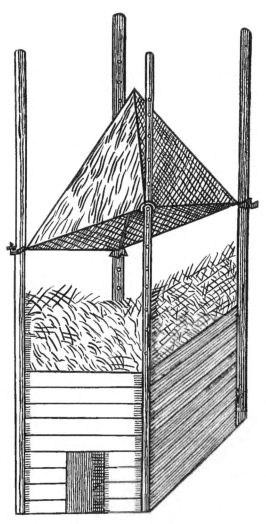

Hay-lathe with moveable roof

To face p. 224.

When the thatch-roof is to be lifted higher up, a carl climbs up at each corner and lifts it up with his shoulders, when a thick iron pin is set in one of the holes, as high as one wishes to have it, on which pin the roof is then rested. When the roof was lifted up, the corners of the roof-plate went up close by the posts. If they wished to lower it further down, the pins were taken out, so that it gently descended as far as was desired. The thickness of the straw on the thatch-roof was 9 inches. The stack was now full of hay, loaded up to 4 feet below the roof.

[T. I. p. 257.] **Af hvad växter höet härstädes bestod.**

What plants the hay in this place consisted of.

As the grass-growth on the meadows and pastures at this time of year was so short and cropped by the cattle that I could not possibly distinguish the plants and herbs, **de växter och örter,** of which the grass sward here consisted, we devoted a couple of hours to ransacking the hay here in the lathes, and in seeking out and register-ing all kinds of plants which were found therein, that we might from that be able to judge of the goodness of the hay. I will, as far as practicable, place them in the order of their abundance, so that the plants, which were found here in the greatest numbers, have the honour to stand first, while those of which there were found the least of all, come to be left to the last.

They were the following :—

[1.] Lotus. Loti-corniculatœ major species J[ohann] B[auhin]. *Raj. Syn.* 334. I could not find in what this differed from Lotus s. Melilotus pentaphyllos minor glabra C[aspar] B[auhin], which especially occurs with us in Sweden. A boy who was with us called it *Lady-finger grass.* [Anthyllis vulneraria, *Kidney Vetch.*] I afterwards carried a plant of it home to Mr. Ellis, and asked if it was not his *Lady-finger grass* which he praises

Q

so beyond comparison, and sets before all other kinds of grass in his *Modern Husbandman* as, **fôr**, "in the highest perfection the most proper hay for feeding saddle-horses, deer, sheep, and rabbits," as well as for "cattle," with many exalting words? He answered that it was just the right and the same one, which he in the above-cited, and many other places, so highly praised. This is found among the hay in great abundance, and most of all its constituents.

[2.] **Röd Väpling**, *Red Clover*, 615, in great abundance. [Trifolium pratense.]

[T. I. p. 228.]   [3.] **Hvit Väpling**, *White clover* 612, much, yet not so much as the foregoing. [T repens.]

[4.] **Kambexing**, 81, *Crested Dog's-tail grass*, most of all the grasses. [Cynosurus Cristatus. Linn. writes Kamb-Exing].

[5.] Gramen lanatum, Dalech, Linn. *Fl. Sv.* 67, tolerably abundant. [Holcus Mollis.]

[6.] **Hundäxing**, *Rough Cock's-foot grass*, 83, [Dactylis Glomerata], rivalled in numbers the preceding.

[7.] CENTAUREA, 709, Jacea C.B. [Pin. 271] tolerably common. [Centaurea Jacea.]

[8.] LATHYRUS, 599. Sylv. C. B. [*Pin.* 344] some. [Lathyrus Sylvestris.]

[9.] PHLEUM. **Äng-Kämpe,** *Cat's-tail grass*, 50, tolerably abundant. [P. pratense.]

[10.] **Äng-hafre,** 96, a little. [Avena pratensis.]

[11.] HIERACIUM, *Hawkweed*, a sort thereof, with fol. lin. hirsut. some [probably H. umbellatum.]

[12.] FESTUCA, 93. Some plants. [F. Rubra L. now F. ovina, *var.* rubra.] *Fescue-grass.*

[13.] CHRYSANTHEMUM. Bellis Major, J. B., *Ox-eye.* Some plants. [C. Leucanthemum Linn. Syst. Nat., 1770, T. II., page 562.]

[14.] BRIZA [B. Media], *Quaking grass*, some plants.

[15.] AGROSTIS Arist. maj. prat., some plants.
[? A. Vulgaris, *var.* Aristata.] *Bent grass.*

[16.] SERRATULA C.B. [Pin. 235. Linn. Fl. Sv. 660.]
Some plants. [S. Tinctoria] *Saw-wort.*

[17.] LINUM CATHARTICUM, 255. Some plants.
Purging Flax.

[18.] VICIA, **Mus-ärter,** 605. [V.Cracca] some plants.

[19.] FILIPENDULA vulg. [C. B. Pin. 163. Linn. Fl.
Sv., 404 Spiroea Filipendula] some plants.

[20.] PLANTAGO, 123, do. [P. Media.]

[21.] MILLEFOLIUM *vulg.* alb. C.B. [Pin. 140] one
single plant. [Achillea Millefolium.]

There were many we could not find here, although
we searched long for them. The *Papilionaceæ* alone made
almost double as much as the others. A part of the hay
had become slighly musty, but much of it was uninjured,
and smelt very good.

At befria Sädes-stackar för Möss.

To prevent Mice from getting into ricks.

In the Duke of Bridgewater's park we got to see a
particular way in which to build stacks, so that mice
shall not approach them, in that the *bottom*, **botten,** on
which the rick stood, or "rick-staddle," was not down on
the ground, but stood on pillars, **pelare,** 3 feet from the
earth. The "rick-staddle," which was of wood, was
either four-sided or round. It rested on eight or ten
pillars, besides another *ditto*, which stood under the
middle of the bottom, **midt under botten.** The
pillars were square, built of bricks, each side 1 foot wide.
The length of the pillars was 2 feet 6 inches. Upon each
pillar in every case was laid a thick flag-stone or stone,
hälla eller sten, the "flat-stone" or the "resting-
stone," which extended 6 inches on all sides beyond the
pillar, and thus prevented mice from possibly reaching

the stack.   Upon these pillars the bottom was then laid.
On some posts there was no such "resting-stone" on the
top, but the upper part of the pillar was for the height
of one foot covered on all sides with a thin polished
sheet of brass, which also prevented the mice from climbing up, because they could not possibly get a foothold on
this polished brass.   These ricks had beyond that the
advantage, that the wind got to play under them.   On
the top they were well thatched with straw.

Vattu-Konst, at draga up vatten med.

Hydraulic machine to draw up the water with.

The above-mentioned duke's house was situated on
one of the chalk ridges of this place, where there was no
spring to get good water out of. Therefore they had caused
a well, **en brunn**, to be dug down through the chalk ridge
to a depth of very many fathoms [275 feet.]   To get up
the water out of the same, a large wheel was built, which
had a thick axletree, around which there went a long rope,
which had a large bucket, **balja,** fastened to each end,
yet in [T. I. p. 230] this way, that when the one pail
went up with the water, the other went empty down.
Inside the great wheel a horse was led, who by his walking inside the wheel drove it round, and thus the buckets
were lifted up and down.   The water was poured out of
the bucket into great troughs, **hoar,** made of lead, from
which it was afterwards led through leaden pipes and
gutters to the places where it was wanted.

---

* This is a very old well. It appears in an Inquisition made 20th
October, 17 Eliz. [1575], before Sir Edmund Asshefyld and Richard Young,
supervisors of Her Majesty's possessions.

"*Item.*—Presentant insuper juratores. . . . Domus vocata the Well-
House, cum appendicibus. Valet vendi vij£." Todd's *Bonhommes,* p. 63.
Lond. 1823, Fol.

"When the Earl of Bridgewater came into possession of the estate
[1803] . . . there were remaining . . . the Engine House, which
covered a well 275 feet deep." *ib.* p. 70. [J. L.]

Spånors förvarande. *The saving of Chips.*

Just outside the Duke's house a number of labourers were engaged in wood-cutting of different kinds, **at slögda åtskilligt.** The chips, **Spånorna,** which resulted, were not left to lie strewn around on the hill, but it was the duty of one of the carls to gather them together and lay them up in heaps, which were mostly conical in shape, **liknade coner,** so to be left to dry, after which they were carried under cover, **tak,** to be afterwards used as fuel, **til bränsle.**

Trärötters och qvistars aktsamma samlande til bränsle. *The careful collecting of tree-roots and sticks for fuel.*

I have said before that this extensive park mostly consisted of large and lofty beeches, and many other trees. Here and there they had cut down some of them, and sold the smooth part, **den släta delen,** or sawn it up into boards, but those of which the stem had been knotty and uneven was cut up for firewood and piled up in cords, **trafvat up i famnar,** * either to be used for the duke's own requirements, or, principally, to be sold to those who lived round about the park, but had themselves no access to fuel.

When the beeches and trees were cut down and felled to the ground, they were cut off close to the earth. Two or three years after that, the stub that had been left, **den qvarlåmnade stubben,** together with all the roots proceeding from it, large and small, which one could find, was dug up, cut up into small pieces, and arranged†

---

* *Fathoms,* "FAMN VED, *corde de bois.*" Veste. Lex. [J. L.]

† "CORD OF WOOD, a parcel of firewood 4 foot broad, 4 foot high, and eight foot long." Bailey *Eng. Dic.*, 15th ed., 1753—the date of Kalm's present, or 1st Vol. [J. L.]

[T. I. p. 231] in four-sided oblong heaps, to dry. Their height was 6 quarters, or 3 English feet, and the breadth the same, but some of them were 3½ ells long, 7 English feet, others double as long, or 7 ells, 14 English feet. In digging up the roots they had been so careful **så noga**, that among these heaps there lay a great many fibres of the roots, whose length was not over 6 inches, and thickness not greater than a quill pen. These roots thus arranged were sold as fuel to those who lived some English miles round about. The twigs of the trees were carefully collected, cut into lengths of 6 inches and less, and bound in bundles, to sell in the same way to those who had not themselves any access to fuel. The Swedish wood vendors ought to consider this.

Råg, hvartil den sås och brukas.

RYE, what it is sown and used for.

An old farmer told me that they did not sow Rye here as food for people, but that it is sown in the autumn to be used the following spring, in April, as food for sheep, after they have first eaten up the turnips on the turnip-land, **Roflanden.** The sheep are then turned on to the rye-gratten, **på Råg-brådden,** to gratten on it, till it becomes so short that they can find no more to eat. Some farmers afterwards leave the rye to stand and grow, and when it has become ripe, cut it, but most plough up the earth on which it has grown, and prepare it for wheat seed, when the sheep's dung, together with the rye-gratten, **råg-brodden,** becomes an excellent manure.

Rofvors rätta ans. *The right way to treat Turnips.*

Turnips are much sown here in England, as food for people as well as for all kinds of cattle, such as cows,

swine, sheep, &c. To make them large, clever husbandmen have the *finesse*, **bruka kloke hushållare det
grepet**, to employ " Hoeing " about the turnips when
they have come up after the sowing, and have attained
some size, [T. I. p. 232] that is, they cut away a part
of the sown turnips so as to leave 9 inches between those
that are left, for this purpose they employ a hoe, **en
gräfta eller hacka**, whose blade is quite blunt and
nearly straight at the end and nearly 6 inches broad.
This space between the turnips, is so hacked up with
this *instrument* that the soil becomes quite loose.   In this
loose earth the turnips increase so considerably, that
they grow to a larger size than a man's head.   They are
afterwards used for different purposes, **til åtskilligt.**
The sheep are either turned on to the turnip-land, yet
on to a small part, a little at a time, **i sänder**, by
means of a fold, where they not only have an abundant
fodder from the turnips, but also manure the same field
considerably by their dung; or the turnips are taken up
as fodder for the sheep or other animals at home in the
shed, **i huset**, or sold to such as have sheep or other animals
to fatten, and so forth, so that they turn them to account
in many ways.   An old farmer told me that from a single
" acre land," when the turnips grew somewhat quickly,
he could commonly gain £14, £16 to £18 sterling profit,
inkomst, only, however, if he had taken in this " acre
land " at a certain time of year. *Obs.* The " hoeing
instruments " which they used here in all places, exactly
resembled the **hackar**, which they use in Sweden, *e.g.*
at *Ultuna*, for hoeing tobacco, which may perhaps have
originally taken their pattern from here in England.

Mr. Ellis's *Four-wheel drill plough.*

In the afternoon I was at Mr. Ellis's, who then
showed me the use of his newly invented four-wheel drill

plough.   He to-day sowed a little wheat with the same.
The land was first well ploughed, harrowed, and laid out
in *broad-land*.   One carl went and drew the plough, and
[T. I. p. 233] another went after and steered.   The use
of this plough was that in front was set a little ploughshare, **plogbill,** which ploughed up the furrow into
which the seed which is sown will fall.   Immediately
above this ploughshare, but farther back, was a little
funnel, **tratt,** from whence the seed fell down behind
the ploughshare into the furrow.   Out of the funnel
behind this fell the fine compressed manure on to the
seed just sown, and last of all was set the harrow, which
either had tines or iron blades, **tinnar eller järn
skällor,** to harrow the seed again.   In a word it was
nearly of the same construction as that which Herr
Probsten VESTBÄCK invented, and described in *Kongl
Vetensk. Acad. Handlingar.*   Mr. Ellis and I were not of
the same opinion on this point.   He flattered himself so
much on his invention, that he also said that since Adam
was made there has never been invented so useful an
Instrument and *Machine* as this Drill-plough.   I should
too much weep for human-kind if this were true, for after
Mr. Ellis had, with two carls, devoted the whole afternoon to using this plough, he had not succeeded in sowing
a pint, **en kanna,** of seed.   Scarcely was a half-furrow
sowed before one was obliged to stand and attend to the
plough.   Now, the seed would not run; now, the mould
stuck fast in the hole at the bottom of the funnel; .now,
the corn was not harrowed well down, so that there
were here *frictiones frictionum.*   Had man for all time
past not been able to sow in a better manner than was
done here to-day, mankind would long before this have
died of hunger.   I do not deny that if this plough is rightly
worked and used, it may for some kinds of seed have its
great service, as with pease, &c.

Järn-broddar. *Iron Crampoons for climbing up trees with.* *

At the house of a labourer I to-day got to see a particular kind [T. I. p. 234] of iron crampoons, which they
use when they wish to climb up in any tree, either to take
young squirrels, **Ikorn-ungar,** rooks'-nests, **Kråkbon,**
or anything else; for as the trees here, for example the
beeches, are for many fathoms in their lower part entirely without branches, and quite smooth, they can get
up in no other way than by ladders, or with these crampoons. The former were too costly, and difficult to
carry everywhere with them, but the latter
not so. Their shape can best be seen from
the accompanying Figure, where C B A
D shows the whole crampoon, which is
of iron, and D E the strap or band by
which it is bound fast to the leg. A B is
the part of the crampoon which comes
to be under the shoes, and on which one
stands when one climbs up. The length
of the space between A and B is just fitted
to the breadth of the shoes. C is the
very point of the crampoon, **sjelfva uden
på brådden,** which is always on the
inner side of the foot towards the tree.
The length from F to C is just two fingers
wide. It is whetted as sharp as the
sharpest and keenest knife's point that
one may so much the better be able to
strike into the tree with it. This point,
udd, does not slope off in an *acumen*, like

---

* "Crampoons (*Crampons* F.), pieces of iron hooked at the ends, for
the drawing or pulling up of timber, stones, &c." Bailey, *Eng Dic.*, 15th
Ed. 1753.

the point of a knife, but is more obtuse, and more nearly
resembles a small punch, **hugg-bårr,** yet the point is
not quite so obtuse, **trubbig,** but more oval. If it were
as narrow-pointed as a knife, it could not then possibly
be so strong, but would more easily break off.

[T. I. p. 235.] **Järn-spik funnen midt i en trä.**

An iron nail found in the middle of a tree.

Some carls were engaged to-day in sawing up some
stocks into boards. As they were sawing a thick log,
klabb, of ash in half they could not for a time get the
sawblade to advance much, but several teeth therein broke
off. In the end, after they had with much trouble got
the log sawn in two, and would look what the reason was
that the saw stuck so, they found a large iron nail in the
middle of the tree. It was on all sides so grown round
by the tree, that we could scarcely see otherwise than that
it had grown there, for there was no rottenness visible in
the tree round it. It was probably knocked into the tree
when it was young, and afterwards became thus surrounded and enclosed by the tree.

The 3rd April, 1748.

Kaniners slagt och gällning. *The slaughtering and
gelding of rabbits.*

Mr. Ellis told me that they here used to slaughter
rabbits in the same way as a pig or other animal is
slaughtered, viz., that they stick it in the throat and so
tap out the blood, when the flesh will be much more
agreeable than when they are killed in the usual way,
with a blow on the nape of the neck, or as hares, **Harar,**
are killed. He believed he was the first who had begun
thus to take their lives by drawing off the blood. He
also told me that he always caused some of the bucks to

be castrated, because their flesh has a much better flavour than when they are left ungelt.

Spisars skapnad. *The shape of the hearth.*

There is almost more wood burnt by one farmer and labourer, **Landtman,** in England than by one **Bonde,** &c., in Sweden. England lies some degrees more to the south, which diminishes [T. I. p. 236] the cold in the winter time. Therefore it is not extra-ordinary that there is so great a difference between the winters in England and Sweden, so that while the cattle in Sweden, must be fed for seven or eight months in the stable, they here go out almost the whole year, winter and summer. Many would therefore not be able to imagine that the English cottages, **stugorna,** in which the folk reside during the winter, were colder than the Swedish, and still less will anyone be able to believe that an English farmer, labourer, peasant, **Bonde, Landtman, Torpare,** or other, would burn as much if not more wood in the year than a Swede, especially because the winters here are so mild and short; and moreover, that the districts in most places near London are very woodless, **skoglös,** but for all that this is in most cases, and in a certain way, true. I will name the reason. The fireplaces, **spisarna,** are here mostly built, in all the ways in which we build them in Sweden, only with this difference, that here they never use a **spjäll,** or anything else in its place to retain the warmth; but a **spjäll** is to an Englishman who has never been out of England a thing so unknown, that it is difficult so to describe to him what a **spjäll** is that he shall understand it. No, here all the warmth goes freely up the chimney; windows, doors, roof, floor, &c., are not stopped or made tight, but the wind and cold get freely to play through them. There is no moss on the inner side or in the middle of the roof. Therefore it is not wonderful, if in the winter time it is as cold in as it is out. In this country in the farm cottages, **bond-stugorna,** the fire-hearth, **elds-härden,** is commonly so low that it is a *planum* with the floor itself. The chimney places, **spisarna,** in these are also so large, that three or four stools can be accommodáted within the chimney-place, **spisen,** on which they sit to warm themselves. As soon as the wind begins to be somewhat fresh, as it commonly is from and in [T. I. p. 237] a great part of October, till and in a great part of April, wood is for the most part burnt on the hearth from morning till evening. Round it the folk sit and warm themselves and when the cold is somewhat more severe, the women are seen sitting near the fire, without doing the least thing, more ·than prate, **utan at göra det ringaste mer, an prata.** Therefore, also it is not wonderful that an English farmer, &c., burns in the course of the year, as much if not more wood than a Swedish **Bonde.** The same can also be said about an English townsman, **Borgare,** priest, *Gentleman,* &c.

The 4th April, 1748.

In the morning we walked about over very many arable fields to make our notes on their mode of Agriculture, &c.

Jordmon härstädes. *The soil hereabouts.*

I have said above that the whole of this district consists of bare hills. These hills are nothing else than solid chalk, for commonly when they dig 6 feet down into the earth, and often less, the chalk itself occurs, **tager sjelfra kritbärget emot.** The earth, **den jord,** which lies at the surface, is here everywhere of a brown colour, which inclines a little to yellow.

Åkers-gödning, såning med Rofvor, upkör-
ning, etc.

The manuring, sowing with turnips, and ploughing of the arable fields.

In one place a farmer was engaged in ploughing up his field, **at köra up sin åker,** which had before been manured and grown with turnips, &c. I asked him how he had treated this field? He answered: Last year, in May, chalk was carried into it, together with a large quantity of dung, which is here mostly bare straw, and which was all spread out and ploughed down. In June the whole of this enclosure was sown with turnip seed. In September, at Michaelmas, the sheep were turned on to it, where they had since been, and baited, **betat,** till [T. I. p. 238] this day. When it was sown with turnip-seed, **Rof-frö,** the field was laid out in *broadland,* and to-day, when it was being ploughed up anew, it was similarly laid out in *broadland,* in which they intended to sow barley this morning if the weather is fair. The sheep by their droppings, together with part of the half-rotted turnips, which have just been ploughed down, helped considerably to make the soil fertile. They first ploughed four to six furrows at both ends of the field, and across, **tvärs för,** the same, and afterwards ploughed the whole field lengthwise, **långs efter,** so that all the other furrows stood perpendicular to the furrows at the ends, which the horses always trampled down in the turning. I asked the reason why he did not plough the furrows, which had been ploughed at the ends, last, as we do? The farmer answered that if he should have so dealt this morning with, **som han i morgon torde vela så,** only a part of the field, for instance, as much as he will plough up to-day, then he would have been obliged to plough the *long-furrows,*

lång-fårorna, at the ends first ;* for it should be noted that in private enclosures, **enskildta täppor,** there are never any **åker-renar,** "*acre-reins,*" or balks, in the midst of the field. Ditches, also, are never seen in these districts in the fields. The *Inclosure* looks inside as if it were only an **åker-stycke,** "field-plot" or "land," which may be large or small, therefore when he ploughs the furrows at both ends, he ploughs them at once from the one end of the field to the other, by which means the labour is lessened. Also, if he had to-day ploughed in our way, viz.: laid out the field first in furrows, and afterwards drawn the *Cross-furrows,* **tvär-fåror,** at both ends, so as to plough up the land on which he turned the plough, or the "headlands," he would then only have been able to plough up a piece of the *cross-furrows* at the ends (*i.e.* of the headlands) ; that is to say, so much as answered to the part of the field he had ploughed up to-day; through which he would have had more trouble than if he had driven the plough from one [T. I. p. 239] end to the other.

The fields were ploughed deep enough (as is said to be the case) to extirpate the weeds. It was the *Two-wheel single Hertfordshire plough* that was used for all this work.

For some purposes two horses were used; for others, three; again, for others, four; but if the ground was hard, as many as six horses were harnessed to the plough. Here the horses are always set in pairs before the plough, that is to say, two abreast, and not *tandem,* as is practised in some places. Several experienced farmers said that the fields are not manured with chalk oftener than every sixteen, eighteen, or twenty years. The reason given is that where it is manured oftener, the earth becomes too

---

* And would therefore have had to plough the ends twice over. [J. L.]

dry, loose, and friable, **lucker,** but the field is always manured with other manure every third year, industrious farmers even manure it thus every year.

Trä-verket i Plogarna.

The wood-work in the ploughs.

All the wood-work in the ploughs hereabouts was of ash, which is a very hard and tough wood, except the "*mould-board,*" **vänd-brädet,** which was mostly made of beech, because the ash is not always found of the thickness.

Huru gamla Bök och Ek-stubbar, &c., upgräfdes, etc.

How old beech and oak-stubs, &c., were dug up, &c.

In one of the arable fields there was beside a hedge a long acre-rein, **åker-ren,** of 5 or 6 fathoms broad. Here and there, stood thick beech-stubs, **Bök-stubbar,** and now and then an oak-stub, **Ek-stubbe.** The trees which had grown on these stubs were for the most part cut down two years back. Here a carl was now engaged in digging and hewing them up, which he did thus :—He first hacked up the mould on one side of the stub, together with all the small roots and fibres, which proceeded from the same, with a mattock, **yxa,** of the shape shown in *Fig. A.* It was sharp and somewhat broad, [T. I. p. 240] at both ends, but with this difference, that the edge at one end was turned in the same way as the edge of an ordinary cutting axe, **hugg-yxa,** and at the other end as in a hoe or adze, **hacka eller skarf-yxa,** though the shape of this mattock neither resembled a cutting axe nor hoe. All these loose cut roots were collected together, and laid in small heaps to dry. After that he began to cut the stub to pieces, which he did thus:—He had a lot of iron-wedges, **järn-viggor**, some of which he set in a row right across the middle of the stub, knocked in one after another, and by that means split the stump.

Afterwards the carl continued to set one iron wedge beside another, according as the rift in the stub increased in size, up to as many as four or more wedges, side by side, by which the stub was more and more split, and the half of the stub, which began to widen out from the other, always went towards the side on which the carl had previously dug away the earth, and hacked up the roots, because there was not the same resistance as on the other side.

As soon as he had thus got the stub tolerably broken to pieces, he used the iron hook, **järn-hackan,** (see *Fig.* B.) which he called ' Dog,' so as further entirely to sever and break off the half stub. In doing this he hung the kook, **haken,** D B A, fast on to the cloven stub, the point A being in the rift itself. Next, a strong pole, **stång,** also called ' Dog,' was set through the iron ring C D E, which pole was shod with iron at the end which is passed through the iron ring. At the end of this iron shoeing, **järn-skoningen,** were two iron teeth, **järn-tänder,** by which the dog, pole, or stang * could be fastened into the stub. He then set this iron-shod end down in the ground, or near the roots of the stub, and began to bend the other end of the dog-pole, **stången,** down, when the point A of the hook drew and split off the half which had been loosened by the wedges from the other half of the stub. In the above described way they

---

* **Stang,** *Hop-dog*, S. An instrument "consisting of a long piece of " wood, to act as a lever, with a piece of iron at the end, standing out a few " inches, grooved, so as to make teeth to clasp the hop-poles and draw them " readily from the ground. S[ussex.] Also used in Kent." W. D. Cooper, *Suss. Gloss.* 2nd Ed., 1853.

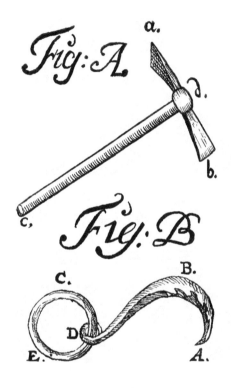

Fig: A.

a.

d.

b.

c,

Fig: B

C.

B.

D.

E.

A.

[*To face p. 240.*

split the whole stub loose and to pieces. This dog was entirely, ring and hook, of iron. The diameter of the ring was 7 inches; the length of the hook, **kroken,** 1 foot; the breadth of the hook at B, where it was thickest, was 2 inches, and at the same part of the hook measured across, 1 inch, **derstädes på hakan en tum.** Inside the hook between A and B, were several scores, **in-huggna skåror,** so that it might get a better hold. After he had got up the whole stub, it was hewn and cloven to pieces for firewood. The reason, why the carl took up this stub was partly thereby to get firewood, partly and principally because he wished to take in this broad 'rein,' **ren,** to the ploughed field. He told me also that many acres of land, **många,** Acre-land, in many places hereabouts had been cleared and made into arable fields or meadows in the same way.

He drove down the iron wedges with a wooden beetle, **trä-klubba,** [T. I. p. 242] and when he went home, he had two boards of the length of the beetle nailed together at the sides *ad angulum rectum,* which he laid like a roof over the mallet, so that it might not take any harm from the rain.

Måss nog på krit-jord. *Moss enough on the Chalk-soil.*

I have said before (p. 237 *orig.*) that all the soil, **jordmon,** on this tract was nothing else than chalk-ground, **krit-grund,** none the less for that mosses will thrive incredibly on the same; for nearly all meadows, acre-reins by the hedges, pastures, commons, **utmarker,** in a word, all grass land, which is not often remade, **omlagad,** and manured was so overgrown with mosses, *Bryum and Hypnum,* that our most moss-choked meadows in Sweden can scarcely be worse. We remarked that in some of these moss-grown places there were here and there green plats, **plättar,** of a luxuriant green grass,

R

which is ascribed to the sheep-dung which they may have
dropped on these places, or to some other manuring
thing.

Huru Bökar fällas omkull. *How Beeches are felled to the ground.*

In this district the beech is 'the most plentiful of all
trees. It is seldom cut down with an axe, but is sawn
down with a long saw. The saw-cut is made quite close
to the ground, or scarcely a hand's-breadth above the
same. When somewhat more than half the tree has been
thus sawn through, and it begins by its weight to press
down on the sawblade so that it cannot be drawn forwards or backwards, they drive in iron wedges into the
kerf or rift, **hålet eller rännan,** which the sawblade has
made, and thus lift up the tree on one side, so that it
cannot hinder the saw-blade by its weight.

Bökars sönder-sågning och såg-spåns nytta.

The sawing up of beeches and the use of the sawdust.

In one of the fields a carl was engaged in sawing up
beeches into small boards [T. I. p. 243] to be used for
shovels, **sköfflar.** They had dug a pit, **et hål,** down in the
ground, in the way which has been described on p. 220
(*orig.*), over which they laid the stocks, **ståckarnar;** when
they were sawing, one carl always stood down in the pit,
gropen. The tree was sawed first into logs, **klabbar,**
of 3 feet long, these again into such small and thin boards
as were required. The logs which had been sawn across
were stood up on end, so that the one end stood down on
the earth and the other up in the air. The upper end
was covered for nearly an inch thick with the sawdust,
såg-spån, which fell during the sawing. This was done
with the object of preventing the log from forming any
cracks or fissures from the sun. I asked whether this

sawdust was used for any other purpose ? Several whom I asked about this gave me the answer that when it is dry, it is used as fuel, **til bränsle,** and that it is sold in woodless districts 'per bushels' or by the ton, **tunntals,** to be used for that purpose.

Bökars ålder. *The age of the Beeches.*

In one of the largest beeches which was here cut down we counted the sap-rings, **saf-ringarna,** to get to know the age of the tree, as well as to see how good the soil was to drive the tree quickly to size. Some four inches above the ground the diameter was 3 feet 6 inches exactly. We counted here eighty-six sap-rings, which showed that the age of the tree was eighty-six years. The innermost and outermost sap-rings were narrow enough, viz., from one-sixth to one-eighth inch thick, but at the time when the tree was about thirty years old it had made the strongest growth annually in thickness, for a single sap-ring was then often as much as half an inch thick. Seldom was there one under a quarter-inch thick, **Föga var någon under, &c.,** but they were commonly between a quarter and half-inch.

[T. I. p. 244.] It was very easy to measure the diameter of the stock, **stocken,** for it was cut down with the saw, **med såg kullsågad.** The length of this stock, from the large end to the little end, was 29 feet 6 inches. The sap-rings were afterwards counted at the small end, when the age of the tree showed sixty-five years. The diameter was here 19 inches; 2 feet 6 inches above where the tree was cut off near the root its diameter was 2 feet 8 inches. The periphery at the same place was 8 good feet.

En eks ålder. *An oak's age.*

An oak stub was measured to see how old it was, when we found from the sap-rings that its age was forty

R 2

years. Its diameter was 1 foot 5 inches. The sap-rings
were very thick. The oak, according to the account of
an old man, **en gubbe,** who owned the field, had been cut
down for two years and carried away, so that we could
not for that reason get to see its length. The soil of this
tree was the same as has often been described above.

Flinta jämn på en sida. *A flint even on one side.*

We found here a large piece of flint, which on one
side was as even and flat as a board.* The breadth and
length of this flat side was just a little more than, **vid-
pass litet mera än,** 6 inches. . [2½ lines omitted.]
. . The surface of this flat side was blended with a half-
petrified chalk. That it may not be relegated to oblivion,
I will now remind you that in this district round about
Little Gaddesden there is not found any other kind of stone
than ordinary flint and "Puddingstone," or conglomerated
masses thereof, **sammangyttringar deraf.†**

Arbets-karlars skor. *Labouring men's shoes.‡*

The shoes which the labouring men [T. I. p. 245]
commonly used were strongly armed with iron. Under
the heel was set an iron which followed the shape of the
heel, and somewhat resembled a horseshoe.§ Round

---

* These beds of tabular flint occur in the lower part of the upper
chalk. [J. L.]

† A man sinking a well in gravel near Bedale, Yorkshire, told me he
came upon a "samman" at the depth of 25 feet, and on his showing it to
me, it proved to be a mass of conglomerated gravel. Near London these are
often called "Rock." [J. L.]

‡ Grose gives a proverb, "Hertfordshire clubs and clouted shoon,"
which latter, as Fuller observes, being worn by the tenants, enables their
landlords to wear Spanish-leather boots and pumps. Grose. *Local Proverbs,*
1790, 8vo. [J. L.]

§ Clouted Shoon. "CLUTA. *Clouted-shoes,* or horse-shoes, also *strakes*
of iron with which cart-wheels are shod." Bailey, *Eng. Dic.,* 1736, 15th Ed.,
1753, 8vo. "CLOUT. *v.* to piece or mend with cloth or *iron.*" F. Grose,
Prov Glos., 2nd Ed., 1790, 8vo. [J. L.]

about the soles were nails knocked in quite close beside each other. It was also knocked full of nails under the middle of the sole, far more than under our dalesmen's shoes, **Dalcarlars skor,*** so that they can go with these a long time before they are worn out. They had sometimes gaiters, **lösa stöfvel-skaft,** which were not fastened to the shoes, but were used in the same way as *damascor* with us in Sweden, only that these are strapped together on the outer side of the leg.

Tegel af den gula jorden. From the reddish-brown earth inclining to yellow, which everywhere here lies immediately upon the chalk, they make and burn their bricks, **Tegel,** here. Some are said to make bricks of it without adding any sand. This yellow earth looks like a yellowish-red clay, **gulrod lera,** and is very tenacious and binding.

In the afternoon we walked a long time about the arable fields and pastures with Mr. Williams, a farmer here in Little Gaddesden, who of all who lived here was indisputably the greatest *Practicus* in Rural Economy. He counted it a special pleasure to relate to me his different contrivances in farming economy, **sina hvarjehanda hushålds grep.** When we got to see his arable fields and meadows, with their state and manner of cultivation we could not sufficiently admire them, for they excelled many fold both Mr. Ellis's and the other farmers' arable fields. Indeed, all that belonged to Mr. Williams out of doors and at home in all departments of Rural Economy was such that the others could not come near it.

[T. I. p. 246.] Âkrens gödning.
Manuring the ploughed fields.

If practicable, and the season permits, he causes his

---

* Dalecarlia is in Swedish, " Dalarna," *the dales.* [J. L.]

labourers to manure his arable every year with the manure, which results from the cows, sheep, and horses, in the manner which shall be described further on. The time of year when he has this manure carried out is in the winter, on the days when the weather is such that he cannot use the horses for any other field work, **åker-bruk.** As regards manuring with chalk, he had the same story as has been mentioned above (p. 239 orig.).

Nedhuggna häckar til bränsle.

Cut-down hedges as fuel.

When Mr. Williams cuts down an old hedge to make a new grow in its place, he employs, as is usual, part of the cut-down hedge for the erection of a dead fence; but the other part, which is over, and is the most, be it twigs or thicker timber, **qvistar eller tjockare virke,** he has cut shorter, to 3 feet or 4 feet long, binds it into small bundles, and sells as fuel to the surrounding inhabitants who have need of such, or it is left for payment of the day labourers and such like folk who work for him,* **til betalning åt dagsverks-karlar, som arbeta hos honom.** For two or three logs of the larger timber, each of which is little thicker than an arm, he gets as much as for a bundle of twigs, **en knippa af qvistar.**

Ärt-land. *Pease land.*

We accompanied Mr. Williams over one of his arable fields, which was entirely sown with different kinds of pease. The field consisted of 10 acres of land, **Åkern bestod af** 10 acre land. The pease were now getting on for 3 inches high. When the pease stalk is 3 or 4 inches long, a

---

* Payment in kind is not even yet wholly extinct, as in the neighbourhood of Kelso. [J. L.]

roller is driven over the field to make it flat. He said that the pease take no harm at all from it, but it is useful to them. Part of these had been sown for eight weeks. *Maple Pea* for about three ditto.

[T. I. p. 247.] Viciœ, *Tares*, &c., sown for horses. On several arable plots, **åker stycken,** they had some *Viciœ* or **Vicker,** *Vetches*, of different kinds. One of these sorts was much praised. They were sown there last autumn on *broadland*, and had the peculiarity that they endured the winter cold, and were already nearly three inches high. In the month of May he has them cut, and gives the green stalks, **halmen,** to the horses, for which they are very wholesome. This purges them and makes them fat and in good condition. After they have thus been cut in May, they stand and grow, either to be again cut once more towards autumn, or to be left for seed.

One and another large arable plot was also sown with clover, which now stood very beautiful and green.

Gropar der de fordom tagit Krita.
Pits, where they formerly have taken Chalk.

We saw in several places in the fields, and also on the pastures, large deep pits, where in former days they have taken chalk, either for manuring the fields or for something else. In most of such old pits, not only was the bottom overdrawn with thick grass sward, but in some stood high and thick beeches. On all the hill slopes, **backar**, round about this tract such old pits appear.

Bökar skadeliga för häckar.
Beeches injurious to hedges.

Everywhere here in the hedges round about the arable fields there grew large and high beeches. Many inclosures were so surrounded by them, as if by a hedge. Mr. Williams said that these did the arable field little service, partly because with their widely outspread roots they drew the nourishment, **födan,** both from the crops sown on the arable, and from the other trees in the hedge, partly and principally that by their shade, and the dropping of the water from their branches [T. I. p. 248] and leaves, they, as it were, killed the hedges and trees which grew under them, of which, **hvarpå,** plain proofs were everywhere visible, for under all these trees the hedges were very poor and thin, **usle och glese,** not to mention that these, by their shade, incredibly furthered the growth and increase of the mosses, especially in the meadows and pastures lying on the north side of them, where it was always found that the moss under their shade throve best of all, and thence afterwards extended along the surface of the ground. But the farmers must endure this, for they had not liberty to hew down so useful, and for the country so ornamental a tree, more than was absolutely necessary ; because few of the farmers owned the farms they lived upon themselves, but rented, **arrenderade,** them from others.

Sot til gödsel. *Soot as Manure.*

Several arable fields were shown us just sown with wheat, on which Mr. Williams had soot strown as manure. He had bought it in London, and conveyed it from thence hither, so that it had cost him tenpence a bushel before he got it here, which cost however he did not grudge, for he reckoned soot as one of the choicest manures on the field. He had also strown some of it over the grass-sward, **gräsvallen,** on some of the small enclosed meadows, which he said was partly because it was very manuring, and partly because the mosses were destroyed by it.

Ek-bark åt Garfvare. *Oak bark for Tanners.*

About three or four weeks after this, they begin to fell

oaks, and strip, **flå**, the bark off them to sell to tanners. They now get commonly a shilling for a yard of it, that is of the bark, 'stapled,' **upstaplad**, or piled up in the cubic yard.

Bök och Ek-ollon til föda för Svin.

Beech and Oak mast as food for Swine.

From the Beeches which here grew in abundance, were collected [T. I. p. 249] annually a great number of beechnuts with which the swine are fed, who flourish and grow very fat on them. In the same way, acorns are gathered as food for pigs; yet they do not willingly eat acorns as their food as against beech-nuts, **dock spisa de samma i godhet til deras föda ej up emot Bök-ollon.** Some lost a great many swine last year, which happened through this, that they gave them acorns to eat before they had lain any time, and had, as it were, been prepared for food, through which the swine died. This could never happen with beech-nuts, which they can eat without harm as soon as they fall down from the tree.

Genista Spinosa **at bränna tegel med.** *Furze* [Ulex Europaeus] *to burn bricks with.*

I have said before (p. 199 *orig.*) that they almost everywhere in these woodless districts use *Genista Spinosa Vulgaris, Raj. Syn.* 475, as fuel in fireplaces, **i spisar.** Mr. Williams now told me that it is also used in this district to burn bricks with, when they collect it in small bundles, dry them, and during the brick-burning stuff these bundles into the brick-kiln, instead of other wood. I also saw afterwards at the brickyard, which belonged to the Duke of Bridgewater, that this, like the brackens, was collected and arranged there in heaps by the bundle, **lagd der i högar knipptals,** so as to use it as fuel during the brick-burning.

Aska til gödsel på ängar. *Ashes as manure on meadows.*

Mr. Williams had strown ashes over the grass-sward in one and another of his meadows, partly to destroy the moss, partly by this means to increase the growth **gräsväxten,** for he counted ashes as a beautiful manure on meadows.

Dikes-jord til gödsel. *Ditch earth as manure.*

Down in a dale a ditch had newly been thrown out. The earth, **jorden,** which had been taken out of it, was arranged in heaps alongside of the ditch, to [T. I. p. 250] lie some time, but afterwards it would be carried out on to the ploughed field, spread out, and blended with the other soil of the ploughed field, **åker-mullen,** as a manure. This earth which was dug up out of the ditch, **diket,** was mostly a beautiful soil, **en skön svart-mylla.**

Nyttan af the two-wheel double Hertfordshire Plough, **eller den tvåhjulade dubbla** Hertfordshire **plogen.**

We afterwards accompanied Mr. Williams home to his farm, where he showed us the two-wheel double Hertfordshire Plough which no one else besides himself in the whole of *Little Gaddesden* had. It is well-known that this plough consists only of one plough-beam, **plog-ås,** but on this beam there are two ploughs, the one before and the other behind, **den ena framföre, den andra bakefter.** Plog-åsen, the *plough-beam* makes a bend, **en krok,** between the two ploughs, through which it happens that each plough ploughs a separate and new furrow, so that the latter plough turns over its furrow on to the furrow which the first plough has made. Thus this plough casts up two furrows at one time, and, as all *wheat* fields hereabouts are mostly laid out in *two-bout-*

lands or what they here call *four-thorough-stitches,** *i.e.*,
ridges, **ryggar** or "*rigs*" consisting of four furrows, so
this double plough effects the saving of labour, that
while others must plough twice forwards and twice
backwards, to make such *four-thorough-stitches* or *riggs*,
consisting of four furrows, it is not necessary with this
plough to plough more than once forwards and once
backwards, when the field similarly becomes so arranged.

Mr. Williams showed me quite large ploughed plots
åker-stycken, which he had laid out with this plough
in *two-bout-lands*. When this plough is used, three pair
of horses must always be set before it, whereas before
other ploughs no more than two pairs or less, are required.
[T. I. p. 251.] The field ought also to be very loose
and dry, where this plough is to be used; for if the field
is not loose and dry, Mr. Williams said he never uses it,
because it then becomes so heavy that no horses can
draw it, **årka draga den.** The plough-beam and wood-
work should also be very strong, if it is otherwise to stand
the work, **om den annars skal hålla.** In a word, in
loose soil and sandy earth, **uti lös-mylla och sandjord,**
this is of great service, but not so in clay, **lera,** and
hard fields.

Halm af Korn, Hvete, Ärter, Bönor, etc., til gödsel,
Straw of barley, wheat, pease, beans, &c., as manure.

Here and there in his farm yard, **fä-gård,** there stood
racks, **häckar**, under the open sky to lay fodder, **foder,**
in for the cattle. The racks were made of two long
hurdles, **grindar**, such as are used in Sweden in the
stalls for horses, to lay their hay in. Two such long
hurdles were fastened together at their lower ends, and

---

* "One bout" is once up the field and back. "Four thorough stitches,"
="four-furrow stitches." [J. L.]

the upper ends widened out from each other so that
they thus formed a *rack*, **en häck,** in which the fodder
could be laid.   This *rack* stood upon two trestles,
bâckar, of wood, viz. : one under each end, of such a
height as was most suitable for the cattle to be able to
reach up to the fodder.   In these racks was laid straw
of wheat, barley, oats, pease, or beans, as well as hay,
of which the cows and sheep got to eat at nights.   The
cows stood at home the whole winter, day and night,
and ate of the fodder in these racks when they would ;
for they went loose in the farmyard, but the sheep were
only at home in the yard when it was rainy and bad
weather, for otherwise they were folded, **fâllades**, at
nights out on the arable fields or went in the *inclosures.*
Of this straw in the rack the cattle, **Kreaturen,** ate
part, and part they drew down under-foot, which was
afterwards spread out over the whole farmyard, and
was left for them to lie and trample upon.

[T. I. p. 252].   It goes on like that the whole year,
whence the thickness of the straw that lies spread about
all over the farmyard is considerably increased.   The
cattle continually let fall their droppings thereupon,
besides any refuse which is cast there.   When this
collection has risen to some considerable quantity, it
is then shovelled, **skâttas,** together into great heaps,
which commonly happens in the spring season, and
is left so to lie and ferment, **brinna tilhopa,** for
a time, viz., for three or four weeks, not more, because
it takes harm.   By this means a farmer can obtain a
quantity of beautiful and choice manure for his arable.
This mode of providing himself with manure **at skaffa
sig gödsel,** is practised by one and all of the farmers
here in Little Gaddesden, as well as in the parishes round
about.   I saw not only the farmyards full of trampled
straw or "haulm," **halm,** of all the above named kinds

of crops, but in many places *Brackens,* **Ormbunkar,** mingled with them, to increase the manure. In or outside the farmyards I saw everywhere large haulm heaps, **halm högar,** piled up, which are left to lie and ferment. This manure so prepared is afterwards carried at a convenient opportunity out on to the ploughed fields in carts, **kärror,** where it is laid in small heaps close beside each other, spread out and ploughed down. It is especially carted out at a time when wet weather hinders them from using the horses for ploughing. When this farmyard manure, **halmen,** is thrown out, **måkas,** or shovelled, **skåttas,** in heaps, there is nearly always some mould, **mull,** cast over the haulm-manure, **halmen,** or it is covered with it, that the sun may not get to dry it too much, and draw the " nature," **kraften,** out of it. These dunghills always lie under the open sky, although a shelter, **skjul,** might be better.

Åtskilligt slags foder åt hästar.

Different kinds of fodder for horses.

Mr. Williams took us out to his stable, to see in what way [T. I. p. 253] he uses to feed and fodder, **föda och fodra,** his horses. Here he had with a steel-mill, **stålqvarn,** caused to be chopped up, **låtit sönderkrossa,** the kinds of peas which were called *Maple Pea* and *Grey Pea**, into large pieces, mixed with it ' malt-dust ' or **malt-fän,** together with white and black oats, which he gave several times a day to his farm horses, which throve upon it incomparably well. This fodder was given them morning noon and night, and

---

* These are still so-called, 1886. I find also in Ray's " *Synops s,* ' 318 :—

(2) Pisum arvense flore roseo fructu ex cinereo nigricante, &c. *Gray pease.* . . .

(3) Pisum arvense flore roseo fructu variegato. . . . *Maple pease.*

[J. L.]

just as it was required, but their ordinary food was the
following chaff, **hackelse** : He had the haulm of barley
and pease, wheat-awns and ears chopped up, and with
this was put a little of the straw about 4 inches long,
more or less, together with hay. This was all cut up so
small, that it was little larger than coarse cut tobacco.
After that they had blended all these together, and laid
it dry in the crib for the horses, who ate it willingly and
flourished well on it.

Strata uti **Kritgropar,** *in chalk pits.*

In the hill, **backen,** on which Little · Gaddesden
was built, there was a chalk pit from which they had in
former times taken chalk.   Here the strata were in this
order :—

	Ft.	Ins.
1. The top soil, **svartmyllan,** or the brick-colored earth, consisted of decayed plants and the brick-colored clay and chalk, in some places ½ ell, in other places 1 ell	2	0
2. Chalk of the ordinary loose kind [shrave], 6 ells	12	0
3. A stratum of the brick-colored clay, 3 inches ...	0	3
Total	14	3

Mält-hus. Besides that Mr. Williams was a great
farmer, he had also large profits from malting, **at han
mältade malt,** and sold it to [T. I. p. 254] all the
surrounding inhabitants.   He showed us the malthouse,
which was large enough. The floor was made of the stone
called *Freestone* which is dug six English miles from
hence, and which is brayed to dust, **bokas sönder til
stoft,** mixed with water, and prepared as clay, **ler,** and
after that the floor of the malthouse is made of it. The
floor was somewhat sloping, so that the water could run

off from the malt. This *Freestone*, together with the pit or mine, **grufvan,** from which it is taken shall be described farther on. [Totternhoe Stone.]

Stål-qvarnars bruk, at mala Malt och Ärter.
The use of steel mills to grind Malt and Pease.

Here were shown to us two steel mills, one of which Mr. Williams used to grind malt in, and the other to crush to pieces the pease which he mixed with oats as food for the horses. They both had a large fly-wheel, **svänghjul,** which made the labour lighter for those who had to work them.

The 5th April.

In the morning we took one of the smaller farmers or **Landtmän,** who was known for Agriculture and Rural Economy, with us, and started on the way to *Ivinghoe,* which lay in Buckinghamshire, four miles N.W. from Little Gaddesden, which lay in Hertfordshire, on the borders of Buckinghamshire. The object of this walk was to see the district around Ivinghoe because Mr. Ellis told us that the appearance of the country and the soil, **jordmon,** was entirely different from what there was at Little Gaddesden; for at Little Gaddesden is "Chilturn Land," but around Ivinghoe "Vale Land." That land which consists of high hills and the chalk formation is called 'Chilturn Land.' 'Vale Land' consists of large plains and flats, **stora fält och slättar,** and lies mostly in valleys.

[T. I. p. 255.] *Agrifolium,* Holly, *of a considerable size.* In a hedge, a little away from a farm, we saw a tree of *Agrifolium, Raj. Syn.* 466, [Ilex Aquifolium] which was one of the largest I had hitherto seen in England. We estimated that the height of this *Agrifolium* was 36 feet, and it would certainly have been higher if it had not been cut off at the top. We measured the periphery 2 feet above the ground, where it was 4 feet 6 inches. The stem was, for a length of 16 feet from the roots, quite straight and smooth, only that here and there on the bark grew small protuberances, **knylor,** in size and figure like hazelnuts. These were hard and woody, but seemed not to have any communication with the tree itself inside the bark. We had previously found on beeches just similar protuberances and of the same description. The carl who accompanied us knew no other use of this tree than that it is used for fuel.

Sädes-stack på stålpar. *Ricks upon posts.*

In one place and another we saw ricks built in the same way as has been described before (p. 229 orig.), viz., standing on posts, **stålpar.** The posts were at the middle surrounded by polished brass, to hinder the ascent of mice into the rick, which here consisted of wheat, and was called by our guide a ' wheat frame.'

Skått-kärra. A boy came along pushing a very large *wheel-barrow*, loaded with furze for fuel, which he had cut on the large dry common, **fält,** which lay close by. The body of the barrow, **kärran,** was built like a *sled*, **skrinda,** only that at the back or towards the handles, **skalmare,** there was no *frame*, **grind,** but it there stood open. In short, there were high frames, **grindar,** where in ordinary wheel-barrows there are boards in front and at the sides.

[T. I. p. 256.] Stort fält. *A large Common.* [Ivinghoe Common.]

We had the whole way, almost as far as Ivinghoe, on the right hand *inclosures*, or **täppor,** of arable fields, meadows and pastures, fenced in by living hedges, and sometimes a farm ;* but on the left hand was a very large

---

* The farm of Ward's Hurst. [J. L.]

down and common, * **mycket stort fält och utmark,**
which to the view seemed somewhat to resemble our
arid, sterile **Ljung-hedar,** Lingheaths, in Sweden, only
that no ling was found on this one, and that the land did
not here lie flat, but rose by degrees, and by degrees fell
off again, or sloped downwards.   It was nearly all overgrown with *Genista Spinosa,* furze, which here was not
much over 4 inches high, because it is altogether cut
down by poor folk close to the ground, and is carried home
for fuel.   The whole plain, with much more, belonged to
the Duke of Bridgewater.   [This is the same elevated
plateau described at T. I. pp. 197-8, and p. 197, above.]

Jordmon i dälderna, en flint-sand och des nytta.
The soil in the dales a flint-sand, and its use.

It was curious, that for the most part down in all the
dales between the hills, the soil consisted mostly of pure
flint gravel, or a coarse sand, **bara flint-grus, eller en
grof sand,** which was not such as our most common
sand in Sweden, viz., of quartz, but it consisted of bare
flint, such as is found everywhere about here, which
had been reduced to a coarser or finer sand.   From some
little mixture of chalk soil, **krit-jord,** amongst it, the
colour of this deposit was a rust-colour.   We sought
diligently a long time to see whether we could not find
any grains of quartz, **sand-korn af** Q., but in vain.
Nor was there found here any other kind of stone, large
or small, but flint.   Those who live in this district, mix
this sand with clay [T. I. p. 257] of which they make
and burn bricks, and when they build a house it is mixed
with lime.

Kalk af Krita. *Lime from Chalk.*

I enquired of the carl who accompanied us what kind of

---

* Ivinghoe Common.   [J. L.]

S

lime they use here for their houses, and where they get the same ? He answered, that they dig up ordinary chalk out of the chalk hills, lay it together in heaps, and burn it in the same way as is usual in burning lime from lime-stone, **kalk-sten,** when the chalk, after it has been burnt, is reduced to a fine powder or meal, which is an ordinary lime. With this lime blended with flint-sand, they build all their brick or stone houses. All those who lived round about this place, told me as a very well known and common thing, that the chalk is burnt by them everywhere to lime, by being laid in lime kilns, **kalk-ugnar,** and after burning is slaked, of which more further on.

Näslor til grönkål. *Nettles as Green-meat.*

When the nettles first come up in the spring, they are plucked by the women, and prepared as green-meat, **grönkål,** in the same way and method as we in Sweden prepare *Spinat.* They here maintain that nettles prepared thus or in any other way, and eaten, are very wholesome, and purify the blood.*

Dagg-maskar, en begärlig mat för Anckor.
Earth-worms a favorite food of Ducks.

Everywhere on the range, at *Little Gaddesden,* as well as the villages round about, the whole of the ground appears to be full of worm-holes. Close to all these holes are found small heaps of fine mould, **mull,** which the worm had heaved up when it made the hole [worm-

---

* NETTLE SALAD. I enquired at Ivinghoe whether this is still made. The negative answer is inconclusive, as it is still prepared in Surrey, 1886, where they only call them *boiled* nettles.   Sir W. Hooker (Flora, 5th Ed. 1842) says : " In Scotland the young tops of nettles are boiled and eaten by the common people." (*U dioica,* p. 296.)   Sir W. Scott also : "Nae doubt I suld understand my ain trade of horticulture, seeing I was bred in the parish of Dreepdaily, near Glasco', where they raise lang-kail under glass, *and force the early nettles for their spring kail."* Andrew Fairservice in *Rob Roy.* [J. L.]

casts]. Around *Woodford*, in Essex, the ground is in the same way full of worms and their holes. I saw to-day that a troop of ducks waddled about and, as it were, sought for something. I asked the carl who accompanied us if he knew what they were seeking for? He answered that in the evenings and very early in the morning the worms creep out of their holes on to the ground, for which reason the ducks go very early in the morning afield to seek for them, and eat them very greedily, **ganska snålt**. When it advances a little farther into the day, so that the sun mounts higher up in the heavens, the worms creep down into their holes under the earth, when the ducks also, as they can no longer reach them, return back from the plain, and wander home to the farms. We got afterwards several times to see that the carl spoke truth.

At *Woodford* Mr. Warner had four *Sea Gulls*, **Fiskmåsar,** who went in his garden, and diligently followed the gardeners, when they were digging in the garden. These gulls were very clever at swallowing the worms which were cast up in turning over the earth.

Jordens tjocklek på Kritan i dälderna.

The thickness of the soil over the chalk in the dales.

The carl who accompanied us told us that when a well, **grop,** is dug in the dales between the chalk hills, one often may have to dig 14 or 20, and more feet deep before reaching the place where the chalk is met with, **tager emot**: but on the other hand, it is often not necessary to dig on the chalk hills or ridges, **kritbärgen eller högderna,** more than 1 or 2 feet, before the chalk rock itself occurs, **tager vid.** The soil was here everywhere in the dales, for a great part, the before-described [p. 256 orig.] flint-sand which nearly always had a reddish or rust colour.

S 2

Genista Spinosa [Ulex Europaeus]. *Furze* as fuel.

We saw in many places in the before-mentioned great arid common, **betesmarken,** considerable heaps of *Genista Spinosa*, furze, which had been here cut and afterwards laid together to be thence [T. I. p. 259] carried home for fuel. This fuel was a collection of furze, brackens, **Ormbunkar,** and dry loads of grass, amongst which, however, *Genista Spinosa*, furze, formed the greater part.

Buxbom planterad på torra backar.

Box bushes planted on dry hills.

On one of the high chalk hills that exist here the Duke of Bridgewater had caused to be planted, partly in rows as hedges, partly in the form of small woods, a quantity of box-tree, *Buxus arborescens*, C[aspar] B[aauhin] The height of these trees was 4, 5, or 6 feet. They throve here very well. The place on which they grew was one of the highest-lying and driest of all that can be imagined, where grass and other plants from the dryness, and perhaps from the sterility of the soil, had entirely perished and died out, for these lay just facing the greatest heat of the sun **starkaste Solbaddet,** a little below the highest ridge on the south side of a high hill.* In appearance, dryness and sterility, the hill sufficiently resembled Polaks-backarna near *Upsala* ; but the soil was here quite another kind, viz., the yellow chalk soil, besides that this hill was getting on for two or three times higher than the Polaks-backe. The Duke of Bridgewater sold much of this boxwood in London to turners.

---

* Buxbom. These bushes still exist, 1886 ; the highest about 15 feet. The height of the ground is 760 feet on the east side of *Steps hill*, just below the highest ridge, which here runs N. and S. where I saw them. Sep. 22nd. [J. L.]

Åkrarnas belägenhet, Jordmon, &c., omkring, Ivinghoe.

The situation of the arable fields, soil, &c., around Ivinghoe.

On the south side of the hills, about an English mile before one arrives at Ivinghoe, there lie some frightfully high chalk hills, which on almost all sides are steep, **branta,** but most of all on that which faces the N.W. [Steps Hill.]

At the foot of these chalk hills, to the N.W., N., and N.E. [Ward's Coombe] sides lie very large arable fields, which for the most part are quite smooth, **jämna,** and to the view sufficiently resemble the arable plain of Upland. The arable [T. I. p. 260] hereabouts, on which wheat was sown were laid out partly in *broadlands,* or mostly flat-ploughed plots, partly in *two-bout-lands,* or in small *riggs,* **ryggar,** with water furrows between : still *broadland* was most used. The *broadlands* were also, for the most part, quite flat, or just the least thing higher in the middle, **så godt som föga ting högre midt på.** Here appear no ditches, no acre-reins, not even fences, **gärdesgård,** or hedges around the arable fields, **åkrarna.** They lay in *Common-Field,* or in **teg-skiften,** though there was no *rein* between the ' *lands,*'* **tegarna,** but they were separated only by a narrow water-furrow, **vattu-får.** The colour and the soil, **Färgen och Jordmon,** here were now quite another sort, and different from what we had seen before, for the colour of the arable was here mostly white, or very light grey, which caused anyone who saw these ploughed fields from a distance before he had taken a good view of them to think they had been spread over with chalk. The soil here also was quite another sort, for it consisted of a

---

* ' Lands.' So-called, 1886. Ivinghoe, Ward's Hurst, &c. [J. L.]

harder kind of chalk which is here called *Hurlock*,* and
has ordinarily the quality that it will with difficulty fall
to pieces for use on the fields.   Sometimes, when there
is a great drought, it is said to fissure, **rämna,** very
much.   Otherwise they call this soil *loam,* or *loamy ground,*
and it is just, as I may say, a medium between chalk
and a stiff clay.   It is a species of chalk, **kritaktigart,**
in a certain way ; but the chalk is so hard that it cannot
easily be loosened or turned to any use on the fields.   I
speak of the soil which is dug up in the chalk-banks, or
slopes, **Kritbackarna,** for that which is found in the
ploughed fields was, through the folks industry and
manuring, more loose, yet it seems almost to have the
qualities of a potclay, **spiklera,** namely, to hold moisture.
On the north side of the great hills [that is the range of
Ivinghoe Beacon, Steps Hill, and Clipper Down] the
ploughed fields were still, at midday, quite [T. I. p. 261]
wet, which came from the sharp frost there was the night
before, whose remaining moisture the sun had not yet
been able to dry up.   But when we went home in the
evening the mould on the ploughed fields was quite dry.
On the wet roads where the soil was much trodden it
everywhere looked like a lime-mortar which is used for
walling.   The wheels of the carts with which they drove
on the roads were so coloured by it as if they had driven
them into a heap of mortar.   It was a special feature
that there were no flints on the ploughed fields, unless it
were some single bit, of which it is quite uncertain how
it had come there ; while, on the other hand, the fields
around Little Gaddesden and in all *Chiltern Land* were
quite full of them ; but, instead of these, there here lie
pieces of this hard chalk.   In the same way, in all the

---

* *Hurlock,* the name for the Lower Chalk, near Tring and Dunstable,
1886. [J. L.]

banks, **backarna,** where they had taken chalk the whole quarry, **brott,** seems to consist of such hard chalk lumps, **kritstycken,** but not a single *flint-bit* among them, except at one single place. Wheat is said to grow very well in this earth, barley tolerably, black oats somewhat better. In wetter places beans thrive very well, but pease are said not to flourish.

Får i fållor på nyss sådda Korn-åkra.

Sheep in folds on newly-sown Barley-fields.

They were now busily engaged here in sowing *Barley,* **Korn,** which was done in *broadland,* and the seed was harrowed down directly after the sowing. The plough which was here everywhere used was only and exclusively the so-called *Foot-plough.** Many may think, because *the two-wheel single Hertfordshire plough* † has such great advantages over other ploughs, that they also would use it, because it is generally and almost exclusively used in Hertfordshire, which lies [T. I. p. 262] only 3 or 4 miles from here. But they said that their *foot-plough* is better, because the before-named Hertfordshire plough with its wheel could not advance in this soil, which at certain times of year is very soft and miry, **blöt och sank,** but the wheel would sink deep into it, and become stuck fast, **full-klibbade.** On these newly-sown barley-fields stood several folds in which they keep the sheep at night, which by their droppings manure the field con-

---

* *Foot-plough.* A few years ago these had almost disappeared, but within the last 7 or 8 years they have come into use again on the *Gault,* as at Slapton, where they are used in wet weather. They are now made by the blacksmith at Eaton Bray, 1886. The iron plough is used in dry weather, 1886. [J. L.]

† The Hertfordshire plough has apparently disappeared. I have not succeeded in seeing one, though I have been sent on more than one wild goose chase to remote farms to see one, 1886. [J. L.]

siderably where the barley is sown. When the sheep
have stood one night on a place, the fold is changed next
morning to the space immediately adjoining, and thus it
is continued over the whole barley-field for a whole fortnight after it has been sown, until it is an inch or more
high. They have always a bundle of good hay, which
is strown out in the rack,* i häcken, for the sheep, when
they come there in the evening. The folds, fållorna,
consisted here as everywhere of such *hurdles*, grindar;
which are made exactly the same shape as our common
åker-grindar in Sweden, although all the timber, verket,
in those which were used for folds, was much smaller,
klenare, so that they might be so much lighter to change
and carry from one place to another. The breadth or
length, as I will call it, of these hurdles was for the most
part 8 feet†, the height 3 feet 6 inches. They had as many
such hurdles in readiness, as their number of sheep was.
When they are set up into a fold, one hurdle is fastened to
another in this way that a stake, stör, is knocked down
with a mallet, klubba, between the side posts, sid-träden,
of two hurdles, to which pole, påle, one end of the
hurdle is bound fast, and the fold thus consists of a lot
of hurdles set in a four-sided figure, and a pole driven
down between each hurdle, to which they are bound
fast, so that they may stand firm. In these folds the
sheep stand at [T. I. p. 263] nights under the open sky,
and seem not to have it particularly warm on the wide
plain, when a strong north wind blows; because the
fields here are very large and lie open to that wind. But
as the sheep are clipped here only once a year, and that
in the middle of the summer, they can well make shift,
bärga sig.

---

* I saw one of these, Sep. 21, 1886. [J. L.]

† Some I measured, Ivinghoe, Sep. 21, 1886, were 7 feet 8 inches long.
[J. L.]

Klädes-klutar til gödsel på åkern.

Rags as manure on arable fields.

On the fields which were sown with wheat, we saw here and there rags, **klutar,** or small *laps,* **lappar,** of old clothes, which were ploughed down in the field. Those who dwell here about *Ivinghoe,* and are 34 miles from *London,* do not fail to take the trouble to buy from tailors and others in London, all sorts of old rags which they carry from thence home, cut them into small bits, strow them over the field which they wish to sow with wheat, plough them down, and sow wheat therein. They said they scarcely knew of anything, which so manures the fields, and forwards the growth of crops in such a soil as they have there; for these laps hold back the moisture a long time and are a good manure, with several advantages.

Åkrar utan häckar eller stängsel.

Arable fields without hedges or fences.

All these large flat fields which were situated down in the valleys around *Ivinghoe,* lay quite open, without any fence or barrier, **hägnad eller stängsel,** either of hedges or deadwood fences of any kind, **häckar eller gärdsel.** I asked why they had not planted hedges around the field as a barrier, **til stängsel,** as in all the other places in the neighbourhood? Some answered that hedges will not grow quickly in this soil. Others said that the fields all lie here in **teg-skifte,** exchangeable slips, intermixed, **om hvart annat,** so that it is thus not commonly done; for if one will go forward another wishes to go back, and if one wishes to plant, the other [T. I. p. 264] does not, and thus it is left undone. Hence it comes that no one had liberty to do it without a special Act of Parliament. I was tolerably satisfied with the latter reason, but the former I had difficulty in believing ; for I saw old hedges in one place and another by the'fields where the trees seemed to flourish as well as up in *Chilturn Land* about Little Gaddesden, &c., for the hawthorn, sloe, blackberry bushes, and other leaf trees formed here as beautiful and thick hedges as in Hertfordshire. I enquired further, how the cattle can then be restrained from springing into the arable fields and there doing harm ? To this they answered that each farmer keeps a *cow-herd*, **fä-herde,** who accompanies the cattle and sheep, and drives them on to the places which it is allowed for them to bait upon, and keeps them from running into the ploughed fields or meadows to do har m there.

Huru åtskillig slags halm, ormbunkar, etc, beredes til gödsel.

How different kinds of straw, Brackens, &c., are prepared as manure.

At a place just outside *Ivinghoe* there lay by the roadside a large dunghill of dung, straw, &c., shovelled together to ferment. Its length was 48 feet, breadth 24, and height about 1 fathom. It consisted of the fodder which they had given to the cattle and spread out under them in the farm-yard, **i fä-gården,** namely, wheat, barley, beans, pease, and oat-straw, together with a multitude of brackens. They dispose of it, as has been mentioned above (p. 251, *orig.* p. 251 *above.*)

Huru de göra sig nytta af orenligheten på vägar vid byar.

How they use the dirt on the roads near the villages.

Everywhere I have travelled in this country I have remarked that straw and other litter has been strown on the parts of the roads in the villages which were wet and dirty. The object of this was [T. I. p. 265] partly to get the roads through the villages into a fitter and dryer state to go upon, partly and principally to procure by that means an increase of manure for the fields, for this straw or litter is trampled down by folk, horses, and other animals, mixed with the droppings of the animals, and the mud or soil the roads consist of, &c.

When it has lain thus for some time it is shovelled together into larger or smaller heaps by the wayside, which mostly have the shape of a cube, or oblong. Their height is seldom under 3 feet, but indeed more, up to a fathom. Commonly a little mould is cast on the top that the sun may not dry it too much. Here it gets to lie thus the whole summer in the heaps to rot and ferment, **brinna tilhopa,** after which it is carried out on to the fields as a beautiful manure.

Sädes-stackar på stålpar. *Ricks on posts.*

At Ivinghoe we saw a great collection of ricks at their farms, which all stood on posts, just 3 feet from the ground. The posts were mostly of *Freestone,** hewn square. On the top of each stone-pillar, **sten-stålpen,** was laid a '*flat stone,*' or '*resting stone,*' † **hälla,** of the same kind of stone, which reached far beyond the pillar on all sides, to prevent mice from slipping up into the stack. Some had the pillars either in the middle or towards the upper ends, clad with a thin very smooth brass or tin plate, **mässings eller bläck-skifva,** which likewise hindered the mice from climbing up into the stack, because they could not possibly get fast hold of the brass or tin. Yet it was equally necessary that no sticks, timber, or other things should come to rest against the stack, of which they could easily avail themselves to get

---

* Totternhoe Stone.
† Called Flatstone or ' Resting Stone,' 1886. [J. L.]

up. These stacks were sometimes four-sided [T. I. p. 266], sometimes round, and their shapes can best be seen from the accompanying figures; for they did not have them in many varieties. On the top, these, as well as all ricks in these places, were very well thatched with straw, **ganska väl täckte med halm,** which was done in the same way as has been previously treated in detail in respect of hay-stacks [p. 211 *orig.*] In such stacks were built up not only wheat, barley, and oats, (for rye is not sown in this place), but also pease and beans. Besides, the feet or pillars, **pelare,** which stood round about the sides, there was always a foot or pillar set under the middle of the stack for the sake of greater strength. The number of the pillars was commonly nine—viz., one under the middle and eight round about. These ricks always stood at home at the farms, and never out on the fields. The crop, **säden,** can be kept for a long time good and uninjured in such a stack, without turning musty, or taking any harm; for manifold experience has shown that all kinds of seeds are kept [T. I. p. 267] best and longest in their own *seedhouse,* or husk. Down on the bottom, **botten,** ' *Rick-staddle,*' or ' *Rick-frame,*' * is spread out preferably, furze, hawthorn, and sloe, and sometimes brackens. These thorny trees are especially used for the bottom of the rick, so that if any chance has brought mice into the stack, their thorns should deprive them of the pleasure of staying there long, and also hinder the ascent of others. Down at the ground the stacks were always narrower, and broadest in the middle, where their thatch ended, so that the sides might not take harm from rain which drips down from the thatchfoot on to the stack. The pease and bean stalks were thatched with straw in the same way as the corn-ricks.

---

* So called, 1886. [J. L.]

Vält. *The Roller.*

On a pasture at Ivinghoe lay a large roller, which was made in this way, that above the roller was as it were a roof, on which stones could be laid when one wished to make the roller heavier, and taken off again when one wished to roll anything which did not require such a great weight. The diameter of the roller or the stock was 18 inches.

Bladen på *Hedera, &c. Ivy leaves as food for Sheep.*

The leaves of *Hedera Arborea,* C.B. are said to be gathered here by good economists, **hushållare,** who give them green to their sheep, which eat them very greedily. The carl who accompanied us related as a fact, that small pills, **ärter,** are made from this tree, which pills are laid in sores to keep them open.

Beskrifning på *Ivinghoe. Description of Ivinghoe.*

Ivinghoe is a parish or large village, whose inhabitants, for the most part, live by agriculture. Yet there were here also a few shopkeepers, as is usual in all parishes or large villages in England. The houses [T. I. p. 268] or farms are not built all in a row, as in Little Gaddesden, but more in a round form, as in a town. In the middle of the parish there stands a beautiful stone church,* with a tower to it, **med torn på,** yet not built in the manner usual in England, viz., cut off at the top, but with a spire, **spir-torn,** in which was set a timepiece without a hand.†

---

* Principally flint with irregular lumps of *Freestone* (Totternoe Stone). [J. L.]

† There are now two clocks, both with two hands. Such a one-handed clock may still [1886] be seen on one of the west towers of Westminster Abbey. [J. L.]

All houses in this parish, besides some outhouses, which were of oak-boards, were built of stone or brick, **tegel,** yet the brickwork was entirely between cross-work or cross-timbers, **korsverke,** which went both *ad angulos rectos et acutos.** The roofs nearly all of straw, **halm,** well-thatched, and very steep. Everywhere by the streets and round about the houses there were trees planted, so that the place lay almost in a garden. The village lies mostly in a hollow. On the east side are high chalk hills, on which arable fields go right up to the highest point.†

Såg-spån af Bök til bränsle.
Saw-dust from Beech for fuel.

In some places we saw that they had in their sheds, **lider,** among other fuel, also heaps of beech-dust, **Bök-spån.** Their use, when they are dry, was said only to be this—that by them the fire can be kept alive on the hearth, but that they are no good to cook food with. Some sticks were always laid at the bottom on the hearth, **nederst i Spisen,** upon which these were afterwards cast.

Flinta til gålf och grundval pä hus.
Flints for floors and foundations of houses.

In some places the floor of the entrance, **Förstugu-gålfven,** consisted only of flints, which were there laid in clay, **ler,** so the flat side came to be turned up. In many places, also, the foundations of the houses, often for a height of 4 feet above the ground, were built only of flints.

---

* Many of these old houses are still to be seen at Ivinghoe. At Eaton Bray, called ' brick and stud ' work, 1886. [J. L.]

† On a conical eminence seen from Ivinghoe village on the northern end of Pitstone Hill, over 600 feet. It is one mile S.E. of Ivinghoe. [J. L.]

Allehanda slags halm til gödsel.

All kinds of straw for manure.

In each and every farmyard there was wheat, barley, oats, beans [T. I. p. 269], pease, and other straw in abundance strown under cows, by that means to increase the manure in the manner which has been described above [p. 251 *orig.* 251 above].

Åkrarnas belägenhet, etc.

The situation of the ploughed fields, &c.

North of Ivinghoe, those fields which lay nearest the village were situated on the north side of a chalk hill,* so that they slope considerably. On them appeared neither *reins* nor ditches, but only poor broken hedges around them. All were laid out in *broadlands*. The breadth of each broadland was commonly 20 feet. The soil was white and of the same character as has been described [p. 259 *orig.*], viz., of a very hard chalk without any mixture of flint among it. It is said to have the property that in severe drought it cracks all to pieces in deep and wide fissures, **vid stark torka spricker alt sönder i djupa och breda rämnor,** often 2 or 3 inches broad. But the lower parts of the fields north of Ivinghoe, those, namely, which lay at the bottom lowest down on the flat plain in the valley were laid out in an entirely different manner, namely, in *ridge half-acre land*, and *ridge acre land*, that is, the whole field, **åkern,**† lay in great ridges, **ryggar eller uphöghingar,** highest in the middle, **hälst midt på,** and sloping on both sides, just in the

---

* The escarpment of the Lower Chalk or Hurlock. [J. L.]

† There is one particular field from which Kalm evidently took his description—the third from Ivinghoe, through which the footpath to Ivinghoe Aston passes, before it crosses the beck. [J. L.]

same way as the fields are laid out in Westmanland and
Nerike in Sweden. Each 'rigg' was here so large that
it contained a *whole* or a *half* **tunnelands land,**
'*Townland's land.*' The breadth of each ridge or **rygg**
was 20, 24, 28, 32, or more feet.* The perpendicular
height of these ridges in the middle above the plane of
the bottom of the water-furrows, **midt på, mot det de
voro i botten af vattu-fären,** was 18 inches, 2 feet,
or 2 feet 6 inches ; for some ridges were higher than the
others. They were obliged to lay out their fields in this
way, because they lie so low and are very favourably
placed for wet, **och äro mycket benägne för väta,**
and because there are not here used any [T. I. p. 270]
other ditches than water-furrows, **vattu-färar,** between
these broad ridges. Thence also it comes that the land
which stands nearest the water-furrow has been entirely
drowned and ruined by the water. These low places were
last year sown with beans.† All the ryggs and water-
furrows were drawn from the highest part of the fields
down to the hollows so that the water might run off so
much faster. Down at the bottom of the valley, there
flowed a little beck, scarcely larger than an ordinary ditch.‡
Flints seldom appeared on these fields, much less any
other kind of stone. The fields this summer lay fallow,

---

* *The breadth of each ridge.* On Sept. 21, 1886, I measured five of these.
They are very high, and there is a furrow along the summit of each—not
for water, but for the reason that the plough started at the bottom on both
sides and finished at the top of each ridge last time it was ploughed—which
must have been very many years ago. The field is now old pasture. The
following are the breadths in feet :—
    Furrow to Ridge, and Ridge to Furrow : 25, 24, 23, 19, 25, 21, 23, 25,
       17, 26.
    Furrow to Furrow : 49, 42, 46, 48, 43.
This kind of ploughing is still called "Ridges." [J. L.]

    † Grassland, 1886. [J. L.]

    ‡ That running from Ivinghoe N.E. to Ivinghoe Aston. [J. L.]

and will in autumn be sown with wheat, but still they had not begun to plough them up, but they were in the same state as when the beans were cut.

Âkrar och annan jordmon, etc.

Arable fields, and another soil, etc.

We afterwards crossed over the afore-named beck on the other side of which arable fields occurred which were of an entirely different colour from those we have just described, although they were only separated from the others by a little beck ; for the soil here was white no more, but of a *dark grey* colour*, **af en mörkaktig färg,** and had flint stones enough. It seems also not to be so stiff as the white earth, but more loose, and resembled **mylla** mould. On account of their low situation, it was similarly laid out in broad *ridge lands* or ryggs, still the ryggs here were not quite so high as the former ones, or those on the other side of the beck, which were exactly like the ploughed fields of *Westmanland;* but these were more like our fields in *Nerike,* where the ridges are not so high. It was wonderful that a little beck of 2 or 3 feet wide should make so great a difference, especially as the same beck was not over 2 feet deeper than [T. I. p. 271] the water furrows themselves in the fields on both sides. The reason might be this. The beck runs from west to east. On the south side lie high chalk hills of the hard kind of chalk, which slope gradually towards the beck. On the north side of the same beck there lie for 2 or 3 miles small hills of another, or a little darker earth,† which also slope towards the beck, but their slope is so slight,

---

* The Gault. [J. L.]   † The Gault. [J. L.]

T

that it scarcely departs from a horizontal plane, **streket.**
The white earth, **jorden,** which occurs in the valleys
on the south side of the beck, has doubtless been washed
down from the neighbouring chalk hills, because the soil,
jordmon, is identical; but that it has not gone on to
the other side of the beck, may probably have been
caused in this way, that the water in the beck, which
runs tolerably swiftly, always carries the same away with
it.*

I also imagine that in the first instance the earth on
the south side of the brook has been down in the valleys
of the same black, **svarta,** colour as it is immediately
on the other and north side; but has afterwards been
covered, **öfver hölgd,** by the white earth which has
been washed down from the chalk hill: for the black soil
on the north side of the beck seems to have to thank the
beck for it, that it has got to retain its colour. Here on
the north side of the beck, the land was again divided
into small inclosures or **täppor,** of arable fields, meadows
or pastures, surrounded with living hedges, though here
also we were met by large arable or Common Fields†
which there lay in **teg-skifte,** *exchangeable slips*, or
'lands,' and were ridged like the ploughed fields in
Nerike. When we came two miles north of *Ivinghoe,* the
fields acquired a still blacker colour, so that the soil there
was almost like a **svart-mylla,** 'black-earth.' They
were all laid out in 20-feet broad ridges, tolerably high,
exactly like the arable in Westmanland, only that a great
part of these *ridge-* [T. I. p. 272] *lands* were so, that along

---

* The true reason is that the base of the chalk is reached near the brook,
which here flows from S.W. to N.E., and that the Gault passes under the
chalk, dipping S.E. [J. L.]

† Alas, by a mistaken political economy, these and other open fields
have been enclosed. [J. L.]

the middle of the highest ridge was drawn a little water-furrow 6 or 9 inches deep. The water-furrows between the ridges were now nearly full of water. A great part of these ploughed fields had been last year sown with beans, and were now left this summer fallow. Most part of the fields lay low, and in watery places. Some of them were now sown with beans, and that in *broad cast*, and afterwards ploughed down. This land where the beans had just been sown had the summer before been sown with wheat. That this land was low-lying and wet could also be seen from several plants of *Juncus Aquatilis, rushes*, which grew on the very ploughed fields themselves.

Dikes-jord til gödsel på äng.

Ditch-earth for manure on the meadows.

There was at a place close to the road a ditch,[*] through which a great deal of water had its escape, **lopp,** which came from the arable fields just described, which there consisted of a black earth, **svart jord,** This ditch, which had been filled up again by the black earth which the water had carried with it from the arable fields, had just been cleaned out. All the mould, **mullen,** which had been taken out of it was arranged in a high long bank on the ground alongside of the ditch, where it would now be left to lie for a time in the open air, to be, as it were, tempered. After that it would be carried home to the farm, cast on the dunghill, where it would lie for a time, to draw to itself more juice from the dung, and, after that, would be carried out on to the arable or meadows, and spread out over the grass-sward, where it will incredibly increase the grass growth, especially if rain conveniently happens to fall directly after it has been outspread.

---

[*] *Vidi*, Sep. 21, 1886, Ivinghoe Aston. [J. L.]

T 2

[T. I. p. 273.]

Âkrarnas belägenhet, etc., vid Carrington.

Situation of the ploughed fields, etc., near Carrington.

At *Carrington*,* which lay a couple of miles north of
Ivinghoe, the arable fields consisted of an earth which
was almost as black as gunpowder, very fine and loose,
and looked nearly like the black earth, **den svarta
jorden,** which we dig out of our **kärr,** bogs, in Sweden.
There seldom appeared any flint-stone in it. The whole
field was laid out in broad *ridge-lands* or **ryggar,** in the
same way as in Nerike. A part of them was now sown
with wheat, which now stood green and very beautiful.
Along the middle of the highest ridge there went a little
water-furrow,† 6 inches deep, or sometimes a little more.
The breadth of each and every *ridge-land,* or rygg, was
nearly always 20 feet. The wheat had always been sown
in the ordinary manner, and ploughed down.

Halm til bränsle. *Straw as fuel.*

We saw on a ploughed field large heaps of wheat-
straw, **hvete-halm,** and also in one place and another
by the farms this straw arranged in heaps, partly under
shelter, **skul,** partly not. They told us that they would
use the aforenamed straw in this woodless district as fuel
for boiling water, washing dishes, &c.

Korn såddes. *Barley was being sown.*

Everywhere we wandered about to-day they were
engaged in sowing barley, both on flat-ploughed plots
and on broad *ridges.* When the barley is sown they

---

* I have failed to identify this place, unless it be Cheddington. [J. L.]

† "Water-furrow." I am told these are not water-furrows, but simply
the result of the last ploughing having been started at the bottom on each
side of the ridge and turning downwards, so that the last bout on each side
leaves a furrow at the top. [J. L.]

harrow it under. There were commonly three or four harrows bound together abreast in the manner before described [p. 193 *orig.*], and a horse for every harrow, so that they all drew abreast. One single little boy drove all three horses and harrows, so that for three or more harrows bound together, and the same number of horses, there was only required a little boy.

[T. I. p. 274.] **Stora åker-stycken sådda med Bönor.** *Large ploughed plots sown with beans.*

The arable fields which lay immediately north of *Ivinghoe*, which were very low-lying and wet, were almost entirely sown with such kinds of beans as they here call *horse-beans.** It is with them that horses and swine are fed the greater part of the year, but to sheep and cows they are not commonly given.

Tjenlig mark til Får-bete.
Land suitable for sheep-pasture.

One and all whom I asked about it truly told me that the fields and arable, **fälten och åkrarna,** here about *Ivinghoe* are not good for sheep-pasture, because they are wet and low-lying, for when rainy summers happen the sheep here commonly get the rot, **Röt-sjukan,** and dropsy, and often die off in large numbers. On the contrary, they consider all *Chiltum land,* that is the districts lying on the hills, or the chalk-formation, as the most suitable of all and most wholesome for sheep, and there they thrive the best of all, all of which a long experience has shown to be true.

Kalk af ordinair **flinta.** *Lime from ordinary flint.*

Several people in *Ivinghoe* related that those who dwell 20 miles from thence† burn their lime from the

---

* They are still called so, 1886. [J. L.]
† The folk say that this was probably near Leighton Buzzard. [J. L.]

ordinary flint, which in Hertfordshire occurs everywhere
on the fields. I made the suggestion that it might
be some kind of limestone that resembled flint.
They answered 'No,' but that it was the same
ordinary flint as occurs here on the fields, and that
which is used to strike fire with, but the manner in
which it is burned to lime they were unable to describe.
The smith at *Little Gaddesden* and another old man also
confirmed the same—viz., that in some places they burn
lime from flint, and added that [T. I. p. 275] this lime is
very good and strong, and better than other lime; also
that it is a special way how they burn flints to lime, which
these men, however, had not themselves understood. Mr.
Ellis also told me that he heard told as a fact that lime
is in some places burnt from flint, but that he himself
had never seen it done.   The truth, however, seems to
result in this, that it is some particular kind of limestone
which in colour, shape and hardness tolerably resembles
flint, and it is of this the lime is burnt, but strangers
mistake it for flint; for it is somewhat difficult to believe
that '*ordinair* **Flinta skal så lätt gå til kalk,**'
ordinary flint will so easily change to lime!

Petrifications in Chalk.

At Ivinghoe, also, several related that everywhere
here lime is burnt from ordinary chalk, but as I made the
suggestion that it might be some kind of limestone which
resembled chalk, the landlord, **Husbonden,** went into
the house, **i gården,** and produced, **tog fram,** a piece
of ordinary chalk and showed that it was of this that
lime is here burnt.   When we began to examine the piece
of chalk we found several *mussel-shells* imbedded in it.
We broke the piece of chalk asunder, when shells like
mussel-shells, **likalødes mussel-skalen,** were found
inside it, which were all of the kind which are called

Pectinites. They were all very small. This was an unfailing sign that the chalk-formation, **Krit-bärgen,** had in former times been sea, as well as that the chalk is a child of later times, unless these so-called mussel-shells are *lusus naturæ.*

Nyttan af den hårda kritjorden vid Ivinghoe.

Use of the hard chalk at Ivinghoe.

The white earth, **jorden,** which was dug up in wet places at or near Ivinghoe below the chalk of the hard kind or *Hurlok,* looked just like [T. I. p. 276] a lime mortar.

The carl who accompanied us, told us that they here use to build walls with it because it is very binding. The pieces which had become very hard, and as it were half petrified, were carried out on to the roads, to repair them with. Otherwise, ordinary flint was also very much used for carrying on to the roads to fill up the deep ruts, **spåren,** with, which the wheels of the large and heavy carts and wagons which are used in England had made, often getting on for 2 feet deep in the ground.

Häckar af bök. *Hedges of beech.**

In one place and another between *Ivinghoe* and *Little Gaddesden,* the hedges around the inclosures consist principally of small beeches, which had been industriously planted there. And as the beech in this district retains its old leaves the whole winter right up to the spring when the new begin to shoot forth, such a beech-hedge is of especial use and advantage, as it is a very good shelter for sheep in the winter time in bad weather and cold blasts, while on the other hand the other hedges stand leafless.

---

* As on north side of Edgeborough churchyard, 1886. [J. L.]

Ändring på jordmon. *Change of soil.*

As soon as we had gone $1\frac{1}{2}$ miles south* of *Ivinghoe* the soil acquired quite another colour and appearance. The white disappeared, **tog af,** and the yellowish-red of which all the fields round about *Little Gaddesden* consist, again appeared. The fields were full of flints, the hills clad with an abundance of leaf-trees, and luxuriant hedges around all the fields. What the reason was of such a change we could not discover, for the *facies* and appearance of the chalk hills near *Ivinghoe*, and here where this change of soil began, was the same as around [T. I. p. 277] *Little Gaddesden*, only that the dales between were here many times larger and planer.

, May not the dales in former times have stood under water, while the hills on the other hand, which were above it, were cultivated and inhabited, and the soil, **svartmyllan eller myllan,** resulting from decayed plants and animals have had many times many centuries to increase, and by mixing with the chalk, to have acquired the yellowish-red colour? But then it seems that rain and water-floods wash down the mould or soil, from the hills down into the dales? May not the white earth around Ivinghoe, perhaps after some centuries, acquire the same reddish-yellow colour as the soil around Little Gaddesden and thereabouts. May not the difference in the ripeness or hardness of the chalk be due to that difference of the time and the ages since the chalk formation has come to stand above water or under the same?

Fläckar af särskild jordmon.
Patches of different soils.

In some parts of the commons, **utmarken,** which

---

* $1\frac{1}{2}$ miles S. of Ivinghoe. Kalm here seems to have ascended Albany Nower. The only "dales" are Albury Dale and the far larger and planer pass of the Bulbourne. [J. L.]

consisted of the reddish-yellow earth, there occurred *plats*, **plätter**, of a totally different colour, viz : almost as black as pitch. Such a spot might be about 6 feet diameter. The carl who accompanied us, told us that they call these spots *land springs*, that they are sometimes very wet and boggy, **sura ;** if they dig quite deep down in such a place, no other colour is met with than this black, which is, as it were, a *pipe* or *vein* of quite differently coloured earth among the other. May not a long continued pollution, **syrande,** of the water have produced this colour ? May it not be that there is under the chalk formation a black earth, and that a water-vein or pipe ascends from it up to the day,* or may some mineral cause this ?

[T. I. p. 278.] **Skillnad på hvete-broddens grönska och längd.**

Difference in the greenness and length of wheat stalks.

It is well known that here in England they do not sow all their wheat at one time, but some earlier, some later. Some in September, other in October, November, December, January, February, &c. Therefore the sprouts must also be different from one another. We saw to-day some of all sorts. Some was quite green, long, thick, and very beautiful, others less and less, according to the time it had been sown, so that some was only just coming up.

Skada af Teg-skifte. *Evils of the common fields.*

To-day we had manifold proofs of this, what harm and hindrance it is for a farmer to have all his property in **teg-skifte,** *common fields*, with his neighbours, and on the other hand what an advantage to have an *isolated*

---

* No. [J. L.]

farm and possessions all to himself, when he gets to manage and cultivate them according to his own discretion. Around *Little Gaddesden* and on all *Chilturn-land* every farmer more or less had his own severalties which he afterwards divided into small inclosures by hedges. There was one inclosure sown with wheat, another with barley, turnips, pease, oats, *sainfoin,* clover, trifolium, tares, potatoes, or whatever he wished.

While the fields were lying fallow, he could sow it with turnips, feed sheep on it, and afterwards plough down the remaining bitten turnips, and have thereby a much greater advantage than if he had left it fallow. In short, he could in a thousand ways improve his property and earn money. On the other hand, here about Ivinghoe, where the common fields are everywhere in use, no hedges are seen. Nor are there here any pease or kinds of grass sown as fodder for sheep, cows, horses and [T. I. p. 279] swine. When wheat, barley, some oats, beans, and turnips at anyone's farm are excepted, they had nothing more.

Nor had they any turnip land to feed sheep upon. Therefore they were deprived of the advantage of getting to sell any fat sheep or other cattle, &c. The reason they gave for all this was that their arable was *common field,* **allmäninge,** which lay in **teg-skifte,** and thus came to lie every other year fallow, when one commoner always had to accommodate his crops to the others; but the principal reason of all was said to be that on a *common land* no one has freedom to inclose his strips, without a special *permission* and *Act of Parliament.*

The 6th April, 1748.

In the morning we set out again, with the same man who accompanied us the day before, on a walk to a place where they dig the white, hard, chalky stone of which churches, houses, &c., in this district are built. This kind of stone is here called *Freestone*, and shall be described immediately below!

Åkrarnas belägenhet, &c.

The fields between *Little Gaddesden* and *Dagnal* lay for the most part on long sloping sides of the chalk hill. A great part of them were laid out in *broad-lands*, especially those on which barley was now sown. These *broad-lands*, **breda åker-stycken**, lay almost entirely flat, so that they were not higher in the middle. Between each *broad-land* there always went a water-furrow drawn from the highest part of the field down to the dale. Down at the bottom, where the water-furrows and *broad-lands* ended, was a water-furrow drawn across the others, but commonly this defect was remarked, that this [T. I. p. 280] furrow had laid an earth-bank at the end of every water-furrow running down to it, without the owner having taken the trouble to shovel up the mould out of the water-furrows running down the field so as to leave the water free escape into the cross-furrow. Mr. Ellis's fields were in this respect nothing better than the others. It seems also difficult to avoid the result that the water, if a wet summer should happen, would here come to be dammed up and injure the plants.

Halm-tak. *Straw thatch.*

On most of the houses, where we went to-day, in Dagnal as elsewhere, the roofs were mostly of thatch, **voro taken merendels af halm,** built in the usual manner, previously described, very steep, and 1 foot in thickness. Sometimes also the highest part of the gable-wall, getting on for half of the gable from the top, **upifrån,** was clad with straw, or made like a thatch

roof, so that some of these roofs somewhat resembled the
so-called *Italian* roofs. The carl who accompanied us
said that these roofs are subject to great risk of fire and
sparks, whence it happens that they are now beginning
to provide themselves with tile roofs, **tegel-tak,** as fast
as they can afford to. The roof-tile, **taktegel,** which
they use here for their roofs is almost always of the
square kind,* and flat like shingles, **tak-spån.** They
are made and burnt from the yellow earth, which is found
everywhere about here. In many places they had at least
tiles on the cottage, or the part of the cottage, in which
the fire was, still there were a great many cottages
thatched with straw thatch.

Tre-hjulad vagn, at köra säd, &c., med.

Three-wheeled wagon to carry seed, &c., with.

At *Dagnal* we saw a little *vagn* with three wheels to
carry seed, harrows, ploughs, etc. in, on to the fields, and
for other purposes. The diameter of the wheels, which
were all the same size, was 2 feet. Above the cart,
kärran, was an awning, **skrinda,** of 6 good [T. I. p.
281] feet long and 3 feet broad. The wheels were set so
that one stood in front and two behind, side by side, as in
a cart, **kärra.** The front wheel was fastened to and ran
in the shafts, exactly like the wheel on a wheel-barrow,
where it would nevertheless have been better if it had
been so arranged that in turning it could have been able
to turn itself about in the same way as the front wheels
under a wagon.†

Rariteten af källor, bäckor, och åar här på orten.

The rarity of springs, becks, and rivers in this district.

It was remarkable that in the whole of this district

---

* And still is, 1886. I have seen no pantiles in this district. [J. L.]

† Similar wagons are now used by railway contractors. [J. L.]

it was a very rare thing to get to see a spring. The
parishes or the villages lay partly on the chalk hills,
partly in the dales in the same, yet commonly without
having access to any spring. This was so at *Little
Gaddesden*, and at other villages. All the water they
had was taken out of wells or ponds, **brunnar eller
dammar.** Thus there were at nearly every village, one
or more large ponds expressly dug to be collecting places
for the water. Here the people took their water, and
here the cattle slaked their thirst. In some places in the
pastures there were also similar ponds for the sake of the
cattle. The country is here little else than a collection
of chalk hills, as it were, set beside each other, long-sloping nearly on all sides. Between these chalk-hills are
deep dales. When the land in other parts of the world
goes in such undulations up and down, or consists of a
chain of hills and dales, there nearly always runs a small
if not a larger beck down in the dales between the hills.
So have I seen it in Russia, so it is in Sweden, so have
I since found it in America, but not so here. The
bottoms of the dales consist either of arable fields,
meadows, pastures [T. I. p. 282] or *commons*, **utmarker,**
without any running water being seen. It is very seldom
that any beck is met with here. The conclusion, therefore, seems to be that a land which consists of chalk-
hills has indeed its springs, becks, and rivers; but still
not nearly in the same abundance as a land which consists of granite and clay soil, **gråbärg och lergrund.**
After we had to-day walked over very large arable fields,
which lay smooth and even, and closely resembled the
fields in Upland in Sweden, only that on these English
ones no acre-reins are found, but the plots lay all in flat
broad land, we met with a spring,* **råkade vi på en**

---

* This was Buckshead or Boxstead Spring. [J. L.]

källa, as a great rarity in these districts. It took its rise in the middle of a large arable field, where it, with its beck, formed a valley 60 or 70 feet below the surface of the fields. In this deep dale the water streamed from under the earth in several places just as if small becks had come rushing out, and formed at once a tolerably large beck. The banks of the spring-beck, **Käll-bäcks-backarna,** consisted entirely of chalk, although they were now mostly overgrown with grass.

Watercress. Down in the beck grew an abundance of *Nasturtium aquaticum supinum,*[*] C.B. A common complaint was that high-lying districts had great want of water.

Allehanda slags Halm til gödsel.
All kinds of straw for manure.

At all the farms which we passed by to-day, we saw all kinds of straw laid out in the farm-yards, to be changed into manure in the way which has been described in detail above [p. 251, *orig.*].

Sädes-stackar på pålar eller stålpar.
Ricks on poles or pillars.

At Edgeborough,[†] Eaton,[‡] and all the villages and farms we passed by to-day we saw a number of ricks of wheat, barley, oats, pease [T. I. p. 283], and beans, which there stood on pillars, **stålpar,** hewn out of the white so-called *Freestone.* The height of the pillars was 2 feet 6 inches to 3 feet. Their shape, and the build of the stack in other respects the same exactly as has been described above [p. 265, *orig.* 267 *above*]. But, besides these kinds of

---

[*] Nasturtium Officinale. *Watercress* is still largely cultivated at all the chalk springs, of which there are six within a mile, and eight within the two miles between Coombe Hole and Well Head inclusive. [J. L.]

[†] Still so called (1886), though spelt *Eddlesborough.* [J. L.]

[‡] Eaton Bray. [J. L.]

stacks or *ricks*, we also got to see at *Eaton* and *Edgeborough*, and at other farms, another build of ricks, which was as follows:—The rick, or the crop itself, was set on a staddle, **botten,** of twigs, which staddle stood on six posts of wood. The height of each post was 8 feet. In the middle of the same, or 4 feet from the ground, was a tin-plate of 6 inches broad, bent round the post to hinder the ascent of mice to the rick. At the upper ends the posts were cut in tenons, fitted into mortises in the horizontal beams which lay on them, and formed the bottom of the stack, or rick-staddle. Down at the ground these posts stood on logs, so that they might not be rotted away at the ends from the moistness of the ground. On the top the stack was very well thatched with straw. Commonly, these stacks were of the four-sided shape (as in Fig. p. 266 *orig.*). A dead rook was mostly hung thereupon to frighten others of the same kind. In these stacks there was the advantage that they could also be used as a *skeel* and shed, **skjul och lider,** to keep all different kinds of implements under for rain, for carts, ploughs, harrows, &c., were commonly placed under them; but then it was necessary to look carefully to it that none of these implements were so arranged that they could serve the mice as a ladder up to the stack. These and many kinds of ricks were used only by those who had large farms, or **gårdar,** may be of very many acres, for those who were small farmers or **Landtmän,** had no need of such, because they soon arrived at the stage of thrashing out their crops.

[T. I. p. 284.] **Säten, at sitta på vid spisar.**
Settles, to sit on by the fire-places.

At the taverns or inns, **krogarna,** it was the custom that the carls sat by and around the hearth and either smoked tobacco or drank. It has been said before, that no **spjäll** is used here, and that the door of the room is seldom shut, especially in taverns and inns, so that the wind has free entrance nearly from all sides. On the hearth the fire always lies and burns. Therefore, when it is cold, one can often warm oneself on one side and freeze on the other. To prevent this, there was used here in many places a kind of settle or bench, **säten eller bänkar,** made of boards, in shape like a sofa with very high back, so that when one was sitting therein, the head could not be seen from behind. These settles, **såffor,** did not go in a straight line, but were *curved* like the arc of a circle, because those who sat in this settle thus had better advantage of the warmth of the fire, which came, as it were, from the centre.

According to their size, six or more persons could find room to sit in them. When one sat in such, in front of the fire, he was never exposed to a draught on his back, because the high frame of close boards prevented that.

Vinter föda för Bi. *Winter food for Bees.*

The carl who accompanied us told us that the best food which can be given to bees in winter time is salt, which is finely powdered and set for them. He said further that the bees in this district are commonly fed in the winter with sugar and honey, which, however, is not nearly so good as this, viz., salt, however absurd it may seem to one who has never tried it. He assures me that out of 100 who keep bees there are not ten who know this [T. I. p. 285], not Mr. Ellis himself. The carl himself, however, had many times tried feeding bees with it. He believed that I should one day have occasion to thank him for it.

Fåren bette på Hvete-brodd.
Sheep pastured on Wheat-sprouts.

The wheat fields now stood here in many places

beautiful and green with luxuriant shoots, on to which flocks of sheep, **Fâre-hopar,** were always driven to pasture there. As this was a *Vale Land,* or land consisting of large open fields in the vale, so there were not here used many inclosures bounded by living hedges, but mostly *common fields,* or lands, which lay in **teg-skifte,** *lit. exchangeable slips,* or 'lands,' for which reason, also, we saw here no inclosures sown with turnips or grass seed as food for sheep.

Korn sâddes. *Barley was being sown.*

The folk were this day occupied everywhere in the fields in sowing barley, which was done on smooth or flat ploughed land, when it was sown out in the same way as with us in Sweden, and was harrowed down.

Âkrarnas belägenhet.

On the north side of Eaton [Bray] there were very large arable fields which lay* between the chalk hills in the *vale,* **dalar,** in sufficiently low-lying and wet places. They much resembled the fields, **âkrarna,** in *Upland,* in this, that these were large, and lay quite flat and not on hills.

Since they lay so low and were so very wet, they were all laid out in *Ridge Acre lands,* or in the *Westmanland* manner. They differed only from them in this respect, that along the middle of the highest part of each ridge there went a little water-furrow 6 to 9 inches deep, and the same breadth on the top. In the water-furrows between the ridges there now stood a large quantity of water. No other ditches were seen. Wheat was sown on a part of these fields, and [T. I. p. 286] they were now very busy sowing barley on the other.

---

* On the Gault. [J. L.]

U

Snäckor uti ymnoghet. *Abundance of Snails.*

We went through an inclosure, **täppa,** where was a little wood of leaf-trees. In it there lay on the ground under the trees a very large number of snails.

Breda åker-renar vid häckar och hvar-före.

Broad acre-reins by the hedges, and why.

In nearly all small inclosures and tofts, **täppor,** of arable in this district at *Little Gaddesden,* as well as in other places, the 'reins,' **renarna,** by the hedges were commonly of considerable breadth—12 feet wide or more. I asked the reason of this. The answer was that, as in all these places there is very little meadow-land, **äng,** they carefully cultivated the reins to increase their supply of hay. Besides that, it is not convenient to have the ploughed fields too near to the hedges, for as the trees of which the hedges consist, run out into the soil of the ploughed portion, so no crop can grow near the hedge, because the roots of the trees then draw all the nourishment out of the soil, for which reason it is also found that the seed which is sown too near the hedge, as it were, dwindles away and dies out.

Beskrifning på Tatternels* Stengrufva.

Description of the Totternhoe stone-mine [called the " Quarry-pit," 1886.]

We went afterwards to the place where the white stone is hewn, which is here called *Freestone,* and of which churches and other houses, &c., are built. The place where it is taken out is one of the highest chalk hills in this district, situated in *Bedfordshire,* just 6 miles north of *Little Gaddesden.* The nearest village to it is called

---

* Tatternel. Still so called (1886), though spelt Totternhoe. [J. L.]

Tatternel, after which the mine or stone-pit, **grufvan eller Sten-brottet,** likewise got its [T. I. p. 287] name.

In some places these chalk hills were long-sloping, in other places steeper. In some places the ploughed fields were on the top of all, where the chalk seems white enough, yet not quite so white as chalk, doubtless because it has from time to time been mixed with all sorts of different manures which have been carried on to the fields. Here there were ploughed fields in many places on the top of these chalk hills, when just under the same, many fathoms into the hill there were large ' drifts ' or ' adits,' **gånger,** where they hewed and dug up this stone.

When the hill was observed, on a side where it was steep and all the grass sward was off, so that the clear white chalk showed itself to the open day, it then lay mostly in this order :

Ft.

On the top was the grass sward, **gräs-skårpan,** with the soil, **svartmyllen,** immediately under it about 1 foot thick, or sometimes a little less   1   0

After that the ordinary chalk came on, which however was blended with the harder kind of chalk which is here called *Hurlok,* and is so hard that one cannot write with it. The deeper one gets the more he meets with this *Hurlok,* and less and less of ordinary loose chalk, till after 3 or 4 fathoms perpendicular depth there is nothing else than bare *Hurlok* 24   0

Among the chalk and *Hurlok,* flints next to never appear, so that flint is here very rare. When one comes still farther down, this *Hurlok* begins to be mingled with *Freestone,* when the Hurlok, as one gets deeper, diminishes more and more, while the *Freestone* on the other hand

U 2

increases, **tager til,** until very low down one sees
nothing else but bare *Freestone.*

[T. I. p. 288.] This freestone is dug deep under the
hills. Here were three places, where they had formerly
hewn the same, and where adits down at the foot of the
hill went far under the earth, or the chalk hill. I was as
far in as the ends of two of them, one of which was
longer than the other. The former went as far as 40
poles—660 feet under ground.

At the entrance into the hill the same was walled
round for about 12 feet, as a door to this *Freestone*, to
prevent the *Hurlok* on the steep side of the hill from
slipping down and closing up the entrance again. But
after one gets farther in, it was not any longer walled,
but the roof and walls consisted entirely of *Freestone*,
just as nature had set it there. When anyone wished to
enter, a light, which was carried in the hand to light oneself with, was lighted at the entrance of the adit. For
after one had come 6 or 7 fathoms into the mine, there
was no more daylight, but it was coal-black darkness as
of night. The breadth of these adits under ground was
for the most part 6 feet, the height 7 feet. Still the
breadth and height were sometimes a little greater,
sometimes again somewhat less. The water now trickled
down everywhere through the roof, or vault of the adits,
gångarna, from the hill above, **ofvan ifrån backen,**
which was said to come from the snow and rain which
had collected on the hill in the winter-time, but in the
summer, according to the unanimous account of the
workmen, this is everywhere as dry as it is on a dry
highway road. The carls avail themselves of this water
which is thus filtered down, **silas ned,** when they would
sharpen their tools with which they perform their work,
but for nothing else. Both roof and walls were very
uneven, for sometimes the sides projected, &c., some-

times went in hollows, according as [T. I. p. 289] it occurred to them to hew the stone, and its natural divisions. The adits into the chalk hill went mostly horizontally, yet they sloped a little down in some places. On both sides of the main adits there were other adits, both *ad angulos acutos, rectos, et obtusos*, so that if the entrances of all these cross-galleries had been open, this would have been to one unacquainted with them the worst *Labyrinth* and maze, **irrgång,** there could possibly be, but these adits were now mostly filled up with the loose bits of *Freestone* which had been broken off in the process of hewing.

The stone divided itself here in the mine all in cracks or fissures which all went from above downwards, **ofvan ifrån nedåt,** more or less perpendicularly, but no fissures ever ran horizontally or very obliquely, which was the unanimous account of the workmen. These fissures were sometimes broader, 6 inches wide or more, sometimes quite narrow, but nearly all very deep, so that a stick 4 feet long could be stuck into them without reaching the end of them. These stones clear each other somewhat perpendicularly *ad angulos rectos*, or as though the whole of the lower part of the chalk hill inside, as it were, consisted of four-sided pillars, placed perpendicularly, yet of unequal thickness, that is to say, that some of these square pillars were larger, some less. Similarly the sides also are not of the same breadth, so that when on one pillar all four sides are of equal breadth, on another only the two opposite sides may be of the same breadth—*e.g.*, two of the opposite sides may be 6 feet broad, but again the two other sides standing opposite to one another [T. I. p. 290] are not more than 4 feet, 2 feet, or 18 inches broad, and so forth. One does not here expect an absolute mathematical equality in breadth of the four, or of the two sides which stand opposite to each other, but one is content if only they are somewhat about the same breadth. Thus these stones naturally clear each other perpendicularly on all sides, and form as it were perpendicular sides of cubes and oblongs, but they are never naturally divided horizontally, but all horizontal division must be effected artificially. When the carls wish to have a stone broken horizontally of any perpendicular height or thickness, they hew with their picks, **hackor**, a horizontal line where they wish it to be divided, and then knock wedges of iron into it, by which they spring it loose horizontally to any thickness they please.

The loosened pieces are afterwards carried out on a low wagon or truck, **vagn**, which instead of four wheels has two rollers, **kaflar**, of ash, one at each end. The diameter of each roller is nearly 1 foot. The body of the wagon is made of solid oak timbers. This wagon, with the stone which lies upon it, is drawn by the carls along the adit till they get it out to the day, and if they afterwards wish to have it up the hill at the entrance of the mine, it is wound up along the road with a windlass, and is so drawn to the place where they intend to hew and work at it.

The stone, down in the mine, and when it was first hewn, was of a grey or clay colour, and so soft that it could be cut with a knife as easily as a hardened or dry pot-clay, **spik-lera**. Similarly one could then [T. I. p. 291] with the hands and fingers break it in pieces, provided the pieces were not too thick ; but when it had come up to the day, and lain for a time in the open air, it became very white, although not quite so white as chalk : for it could be seen that there was a considerable difference, if one wrote with a piece of chalk on a wall built of this stone; which I tried, and the man who had the direction of the mine, also showed me. Similarly it has also the property that after it has come into the open air it always hardens more and more as it gets older and comes to lie longer in the open day. Hence it is, that as soon as it comes out of the mine or stone-pit, it is worked by the carls, while it is still soft, for any purpose they please and which it can be used for.

That these chalk hills where this stone is quarried have not been as they are from the world's beginning, the various *heterogenea* seem to testify, which are often found in hewing in the same, and of which we noted the following :—

1. Kesbâllar. *Balls of iron pyrites.* For the most part round and spherical, uneven on the surface, sometimes externally ochre-colored, sometimes shining like a ball of iron pyrites, **Svafvel-kes.** When they were broken asunder, it was seen that a centre existed nearly in the middle of the stone from which *radii* proceeded to all sides of the periphery. The carls called them *Crow's Gold*, that is, **Krâke-guld,** and did not know that they were of any use. When laid in the fire they burned, and emitted strong fumes of sulphur. These lay here and there in the stone. They had a considerable weight, nearly as great as that of a piece of iron of a similar size.

[T. I. p. 292.] **2. Trä-rötter,** *roots* of trees. The labourers said they sometimes find pieces in this stone of the thickness of a carl's arm, on which not only can the bark be seen and separated from the tree within, but also it is plainly seen that they are small pieces of oaks. Such fragments seldom occur here of more than 1 foot long. I was so lucky as to get here a stone in which such a twig or root lay, which the carls hewed loose, together with a piece of the stone, and gave it me as a rarity. The twig in this stone is about the thickness of a little finger.

3. *Concha, Pectinites dicta.* The shell called P. occurred in great numbers in these stones. Seldom was any side of a stone hewn flat on which was not found one, if not more of its shells. The number of cockles, **strimmorna,** was also not equal upon all the shells. The small ones, the thickness of a nail, here formed the greatest number.

4. *Concha, Oftrea dicta. Oyster shells.* We saw two of these which lay in the side of a large stone which we had not liberty to hew asunder. They were so *naturella* that it seemed as if some one had taken an oyster shell and crammed it into the stone. The man who had the supervision of the mine said that such natural oyster shells are very often found in this stone when it was hewn asunder. These *oyster shells,* as well as the aforenamed *Pectinites,* always lay, according to the supervisor's account, horizontal in the stone as it stands in the mine, or so that they turn the convex side down and the concave up.

[T. I. p. 293.] We could not see many *heterogenea* here, nor did the supervisor of the miners know of many kinds, however much we questioned him about them.

The use of this freestone, and the purposes it is used for, are various. The principal is to build houses of it, when it has first been hewn here at the mine into a four sided oblong form. Likewise it is used for window-frames and door-posts, and arches over fireplaces, windows, and doors, for several kinds of pedestals and pillars, the bottoms of baking-ovens, and other such things. Most of the churches in this district are entirely built of this stone, which indicates the great age of this stone-mine. A quantity of it is carried to various gentlemen's estates round to build houses and other things. The small pieces which are struck off and chipped in the mine, when the stone is

broken loose, are used, partly to be carried on to the roads
to fill up the deep wagon and cart-ruts; partly they are
carried home by some farmers, brayed into fine dust
mixed with water, and worked into a cement, **bruk,** of
which the floors of malt houses and 'lodges,' or the part
of the barns where they thrash corn, are made, because
this, thus prepared, binds very strongly together. I asked
the carls whether lime can be burned from this stone?
They all answered no, and added that one may burn it
as long as he likes, but he will never make lime of it—
which I leave there. Likewise they said that it is no
good for laying as a floor, because it softens and is reduced to a sediment by water which comes to stand upon
it [T. I. p. 294]. The tools and other things which the
miners use here at their work are the following :—Inside
the mine, where the stone is hewn loose, there are used
only a pick, iron-wedges, and a mallet, **hacka, järn-
viggar, och klubba.** The picks or pickaxes, **hac-
korna eller yxorna,** exactly resemble the picks which
we use in Sweden to hack mill-stones with, only that
these English ones are very sharp, and are often
sharpened. The iron-wedges and mallets are of the
ordinary kinds. They avail themselves of the before
described (p. 290, *orig.* 294 *above*) wagon to carry the larger
stones out of the mine; but small bits are carried out
with a wheel-barrow. All the labour in the mine is performed with a light, because not the least daylight can
get to the places where they work, but when the light is
put out or taken away, it is pitch dark. After they have
got the stone to the place they wish, they hew it with the
aforenamed picks, of which some are larger, some smaller,
some are broader, others narrower. With these the
stone is hewn tolerably even and flat on the sides. If
anyone wishes to have a very broad stone, or any other
narrower stone in half, a long saw is used, with which

one or two carls saw it asunder, just as they please. To make the sides even, and the corners square, a ruler or straight-edge and set square are used, **brukas** *lineal* **och vinkel-hake.** To finally make all quite plane and smooth, they use an iron scraper or rimer, **skaf-eller slät-järn,** with which they scrape or shave, **skafva,** it flat.

Down in the mine which went under ground, were set here and there on the walls of the adits fast-stuck shoots of *Wild Thyme,* **Timjan,** sweet briar, **Törn-rosor,** &c., about which the carls related that if these are set there fresh in the summer time, they will remain there green and as fresh, and smelling as sweet in a couple of months' time.

Some whom curiosity had driven [T. I. p. 295] down or into this mine had written their names with the date on the walls.

I asked the carls whether those who continually labour in these mines are affected by any particular illness above others? They answered that they for the most part get to enjoy good health, and are not aware that they are exposed to more illnesses or cramps than others. It is also very seldom that any stone falls down by itself from the roof into the adits. They remembered only one unlucky accident, which had been timed in such a manner that a carl had been killed by a stone which fell from the roof and crushed him to death. This may doubtless have been the god-forgotten man of whom Mr. Ellis tells in his "Shepherd's Sure Guide," pp. 231-2.

The carls also said that they had not remarked any sign of approaching weather from this mine.

When this stone is hewn, sawn, or scraped with an iron, it smells and stinks like a *Stink-stein,* **Orsten.**

The place and entrance to the mine was well on for 20 fathoms (120 feet) perpendicular depth below the highest summit of the chalk hill, if not more.

In several places appeared unsightly large pits, **gropar,** which now on the bottom were overgrown with grass, where they in former times had hewn up this stone. The workmen told us that in one and each of the same pits there is a hole or *adit* in under ground, but that the entrances to them were now fallen in. The deepest hole which was 40 poles into the hill where they were now working, and in which I was, was said to be over 500 years old. The whole mine was said to have been worked for 1,000 years. There was a house or two [T. I. p. 296] here built of this stone thatched with straw, in which the workmen took their meals, kept their tools, and worked in bad weather.

Åkrarna. The ploughed fields which lay on the chalk hills over or upon the mine were sown either with wheat or black oats, which were both said to grow on this soil very luxuriantly. But other kinds of crops do not flourish there so well, because the earth is too dry.

[Here omit 16 lines. The art. ' **Krita förvandlad til flinta,**' in which Kalm records a superstition that chalk lying on fields exposed for some time to the sun and open air is changed to flint.]

Rinnande vatten genom Källare håller drickat svalt.

Running water through cellars keeps the beer fresh.

In Eaton [Bray] where we dined, the landlord showed us his cellar in which he had his ale, **öl,** and beer, **dricka,** which was situated close to a little running beck, and so arranged that the water came to run in the cellar right under the middle of the beer-barrels. On either side of the cellar was a row of beer-barrels, and the water ran [T. I. p. 297] under each row, for which purpose it was also at the entrance to the cellar divided into two branches. He assured us that the beer never turns sour in this cellar

in summer, but is kept quite fresh by this water running
below. When he wished, he could always exclude the
water from the cellar, if only the hole was closed again,
through which it ran in ; when it flowed its course in the
beck itself which ran close by the cellar.

At stiga til hästar från en trappa.

To mount horses from a step.

Everywhere here at the farms in the country and in the
small places, there was a little **trappa** or ‘mounting-
step,’ built 3 feet or 4 feet high, with steps up to the
highest part of it, on which the men, but especially the
women, went up when they wished to set themselves in
the saddle upon the horse. This mounting-step was
sometimes built against the wall of the house ; but at
times also it stood by itself alone out in the yard or out
on the hill.

Qvarnar. *Mills.*

On the tract where we went to-day we saw two or
three windmills, built in the same way as is most usual
with us in Sweden. We also saw a water-mill at one
place,* which differed in nothing from óurs more than
that here there were quartered a frightful number of
large rats, which they called *Hanoverian* rats.

Âkrars belägenhet, &c.

On the south side of *Edgeborough* there were very
large fields. They were all laid out in *broadland* and **teg-
skifte,** but not the smallest acre-rein, **åker-ren,** or
ditch was found on them. These last, however, were
not required, because they lay sloping enough. They were
now devoted to crops for this summer. We remarked

---

* There are now three water-mills at Eddlesborough, and one at
Totternhoe. [J. L.]

here what we [T. I. p. 298] had also found before on all much-sloping fields in the whole of this district, that the water-furrows between the '*lands*' were not drawn from the highest parts of the fields to the lowest, but across, and almost parallel with the beds of the valleys, which was done that the water in heavy rain might not wash away the mould and the sown crop, as it would otherwise do to some extent if the water-furrows ran right down from the hill to the valley, which is prevented by drawing out the ploughed fields and furrows in the aforesaid way.

Fâra-fâlla på åkrar, och dessa Kreaturs mångfaldiga nytta.

Sheep-folds on the arable fields, and the manifold uses of these animals.

Sheep dung and urine are here considered as the choicest manure for arable land, and the folding of sheep on fallow land is reckoned such a useful thing that it cannot be paid for in money. It is also only through sheep that many a poor man has all his food and the necessaries of life. The thing goes on thus:—A poor man lays by something by labour, or how he can, so that he is just able to buy a few sheep—the more the better. Thereupon he goes to a farmer and offers to fold his sheep at night on his fallow fields, if the farmer will give him a reasonable payment therefor. The farmer is quite satisfied with an offer which is so good for his fields, and agrees with the owner of the sheep to pay him a certain sum for every acre of land of his on which he folds his sheep. If now the sheep-man sees that the farmer will not give him so much as he thinks he has a right to ask, he tells another farmer about it, and always strikes a bargain with the highest bidder, or where he gets the largest [T. I. p. 299] profits. When the agreement is

entered upon, the sheep-man drives his sheep in the daytime to pasture on the *Common-lands,* or **Almänningar,**
and [common] ' arable-field-pastures,' **betes-åkrar,*** or
also on the farmer's own land, where he always has
freedom to pasture them, because they by the droppings
which they leave after them always pay for what they
eat. The abundance of all kinds of *weeds,* which grow
upon the fields, gives them also an abundant feed. The
sheep-man goes himself to pasture with them, **Fåre-
mannen går sjelf vall med dem,** and in the evening
he drives them out on to the fallow-fields of the one whom
he has made an agreement with, where they are folded
at night in the same way as has been described above
[p. 262 *orig.* 263 above]. The more the sheep-man's sheep
are increased, the more acres of land can he manure in
the year, and, consequently, the larger is his profit.
When it is very bad weather, he feeds them at home at
night with all kinds of straw and hay, which he afterwards
converts into manure, in the manner which has been
described above, and sells the same. The mild nature
of the air here in England which allows the sheep to go
out to pasture the whole year, summer and winter (and
in consequence nearly all the time they are folded on the
arable), causes the profit on a small flock of sheep to be
considerable, especially when the advantage of England
is added to that, that they have here no need to fear
wolves, **vargar,** which are not found in this country.

The sheep's wool, and the manure collected at home
in bad weather, from the straw, together with the sheeps'
droppings, all of which the sheep-man can sell, in
addition to his being able now and then to sell some
sheep to the butcher, richly repay the few pence he had

---

* Of course these, which are only pastures after the crops are carried,
disappear with the enclosures. [J. L.]

laid out on hay and straw for the sheep at times when bad weather had compelled him to keep them at home. Some assured us that when a man is owner of thirty or forty sheep he can [T. I. p. 300], by only folding them on another man's arable, gain for himself in the year from £10 to £12 sterling. Others said that if a man has 150 sheep, he can in two weeks' time just manure an acre of land with them, and receives commonly from the farmer 16s. in payment for each acre of land he so manures.

The sheep are kept no more than one night on each place in the field, but they stand tolerably thick. The farmer leaves the man entire freedom to bait his sheep in his own way, and pays him, nevertheless, the above-named *summa* for each acre of land. Some of these sheep-men, **Fåra-män,** sell their sheep in the winter, and buy others in the spring instead, from the districts where they keep many sheep. They do this for the reason that in mid-winter they cannot so easily fold sheep on the arable, but are then often obliged to keep them at home and feed them with all kinds of straw and hay.

Late in the evening we returned to *Little Gaddesden.*

The 8th April, 1748.

Kyrko-tak af halm eller Ljung.

Church-roofs of straw or ling.

Mr. Ellis told us that he had seen, on his travels in Suffolk, churches with stone walls, but for want of something else, thatched with straw in the same way as houses are here thatched with it. Such a straw thatch he said may last 100 years. A gentleman from *Cumberland* told us the same, that in one place and another there are churches in *Cumberland* thatched with ling.

[T. I. p. 301.] **Löf til bränsle.** *Leaves as fuel.*

Mr. Ellis told us that poor folk use to collect the leaves which fall down from the trees, dry the same, and use it for fuel.

Huru kalk brännes af Krita.

How lime is burnt from chalk.

When I to-day questioned Mr. Ellis about the process how lime is burned from chalk, he bade me accompany him to a place where they burn it, which I did, and found it done as follows :—

Here was an ordinary walled kiln, **ugn,** in which bricks are burned. In it lime and bricks are burned together and at the same time. The chalk is first dug up in large or smaller pieces out of the chalk hills and is carried to the brick-kiln. Then, when one wishes to burn bricks, the kilns are walled over nearest to the fire with bare chalk, and that in the quantity which one wishes to have of lime, or has of chalk, but not more than that the bricks also may be burned through.

The largest pieces of chalk are laid nearest the fire and the smaller ones on the top, **ofvanpå.** Above, **ofvanför,** the chalk are laid the bricks, **tegelstenar,** which are burned in the usual way. After that a fire is made in the kiln pipes, **ugns-piporna,** of which there were two. First of all large wood is laid in, with which the kiln is made hot. Afterwards only small bundles of twigs, **ris-qvistar,** are used. *Genista spinosa, furze,* with *grass* and *moss,* or also *Brackens.* With these the burning is continued for three or four days and nights, **dygnen,** when both the bricks and the chalk are full-burnt. After the bricks and chalk have somewhat cooled, they are covered over on the top with moss and furze blended together, such as they had cut and bound together on the common.* At the same time all the kiln-mouths are also stopped, so that no moisture may draw in. Thereupon the bricks are first taken out and afterwards [T. I. p. 302] the chalk, which chalk is now, after burning, much lighter than before. It is then slaked with water, like another unslaked lime, when it falls asunder into a fine white meal or powder, which is the lime with which they here build houses, manure arable fields and meadows, etc.

Får-bete, som är godt. *Sheep-pasture which is good.*

I asked Mr. Ellis what the nature and quality of the sheep-pastures was here in England in the Provinces, where they had the best sheep and the choicest wool. He answered, all the sheep pastures in the said Provinces consist of bare high chalk hills or escarpments, **kritbärg eller backar,** yet differing from these districts here in *Hertfordshire*, in that there are no hedges, but all common land and open plains. He said further that the sheep will not thrive so well in this district, where there are too many inclosures surrounded with living hedges, although the pasture itself is good enough ; but least of all will they flourish on wet places and *Vale lands* where they always fare ill. He added that the place the sheep should thrive best upon, ought to be dry hills, where the wind has free access on all sides, and is not hindered by hedges, &c. There should be no sumpy places. The higher the place lies up in the air the better for the sheep. If the meadows lie low, but consist of salt-grass, the sheep also thrive tolerably well, although they do not make such fine wool.

---

* På fältet. Ivinghoe Common. *See* T. I. pp. 197-8 and p. 256 *orig.* and pp. 197 and 256 above. [J. L.]

Hushållningen *in Cumberland.*

From a man from Cumberland I learned the following. There are no chalk hills, but only high granite mountains, **gråberg.** The sheep are much smaller than those in other parts of England, and the wool considerably inferior, but the flesh good. The horses not of so large a kind as here. [T. I. p. 303.] The sheep go out and bait the whole winter. A great number of cows are kept there. The cheese, **osten,** which is there made is not so good as in other parts of England; but the butter, **smöret,** is beautiful, and is bought there for many places. The swine there are beautiful and fat, and every year a multitude of them are driven from thence to London. Very little wheat is sown there, but rye largely, and still more barley and oats, of which two last most of their bread consists. Earth-walls, **jord-vallar,** are used mostly as fences, **til stängsel,** around their arable fields. In ploughing, **åker-körsel,** they mostly use horses. In the river which divides *Cumberland* from *Skottland* are found the best salmon which occur in England. The farmers are mostly them-selves the owners of their farms, or the home, **hemma,** they live at. It is rare to find any beeches there, but oakwoods enough. No goats are kept there. The houses are in some places built of clay and straw mixed together, but in some places in Skottland the walls of the houses are made only of grass turfs, **grästorf,** and thatched with straw or ling. The fire-places and fuel are used in the same way as in England, viz: without, **spjäll,** coal is what they mostly burn. Carts are mostly used to drive in. The district is very cold in winter-time. Most of their manure for the fields is cattle dung.

The 9th April.

In the afternoon we walked about several arable-fields

and meadows, as well as *inclosures* to make notes on one thing and another.

Af hvad växter höet bestar.

Of what plants the hay consists.

On p. 227 *orig.* 225 above, are enumerated of what plants the hay consists in one of the Duke of Bridgewater's hay lathes, **hölador.** [T. I. p. 304.]

To-day we amused ourselves by seeking out and describing the plants which occurred in a haystack at *Hudnall.* The hay smelt incomparably sweet, so that there could hardly be a more agreeable scent from hay. The owner said they had no other art with it than to take care that it is dry weather when the hay is cut, and the same dry weather will require it frequently to happen that it is cut the one day and before the evening of the next day it stands in the haystack; only that it has necessarily been turned and dried before it is set in the stack. He ascribed the good scent that the hay had only to the goodness of the soil. How it is with this, I leave there, but this I know, that I have seen not only here where the soil, **jordmon,** was blended with chalk, and on the chalk hills, but elsewhere in England where the soil consisted of *Gravel,* **grus,** and where no chalk was found for several miles—I have seen hay, which in colour was somewhat red, **til färgen ronnat något,** and which at a distance many might have taken for spoilt, but which had nevertheless, the loveliest scent that hay can ever have, so that it was a pleasure to smell it, and which besides that was eaten more than greedily by horses and cattle. The art, **konsten,** by which this was prepared, shall be discussed a little farther on. As this hay which we saw to-day was grown here on high banks or hills, **höga backar,** we sought diligently to see whether we could not find Linnæus' **fär-**

gräs or får-svingel in it, but it was labour in vain.
We saw not a sign of it. For the use of those who know
how to apply the principles to the care of meadows, I
will give a list of the plants of which the hay consisted.
In the same way as I have done before I will set down
the plants in the order of their abundance. They were
the following :—

[T. I. p. 305.] 1. CYNOSURUS, **Kambexing**, Linn.
Fl. Sv. 31 was commonest of all [C. cristatus.]

2. **Fälthven**, (Linn. *Fl. Sv.* 62) very common.
The fine blades of this made here the best grass-growth
and the most hay. [Agrostis capillaris.]

3. ANTHOXANTHUM (Linn. *Fl. Sv.* 29), enough. [A.
odoratum.]

4. **Hvit Väpling**, White Clover, much. [Trifolium
repens.]

5. **Hundexing**, (Linn. *Fl. Sv.* 83) tolerably common.
[Dactylis Glomerata.]

6. LOLIUM PERENNE, some. [Rye grass.]

7. **Röd Väpling**, red clover.

8. **Ängs-svingel**, 91. [Festuca Elatior.]

9. **Ängs-grön**, 77. [Poa angustifolia.]

10. *Plantago*, 123. [P. Media.]

11. *Lotus pentaphyllos* flore majore luteo splendente,
C. B.

12. *Dens Leonis*, Linn. 627. [Leontodon taraxacum,
Dandelion.]

13. JACEA nigra 709, [Centaurea Jacea.]

14. **Mjölk-tistel**, Hieracium, 639. [H. umbellatum.]

15. **Ängs-syra** (Linn. *Fl. Sv.* 295). [**Äng-syra**.
Rumex acetosa *Linn.* Lilja *Sk. Fl.* 239, *Sorrel.*] Each of the
foregoing group was found here in tolerable abundance.

16. GRAMEN LANATUM Dalech 67. [Holcus Mollis.]

17. **Äng-hafre**, 96. [Avena pratensis.]

18. **Ängs-Kämpe**, 50. [Phleum pratense.]

19. LATHYRUS Sylvestris lutea, 599. [L. pratensis.]

20. **Darr-gräs, 80.** [Briza Media, *Quaking grass.*]

21. **Röd-svingel, 93.** [Festuca rubra, subsp. of F. ovina, Hooker, Stud. Fl., 1870, p. 448. *Fescue-grass.*]

22. TUSSILAGO VULG. *Coltsfoot.* [T. farfara.]

23. EQUISETUM pratense.

24. BRUNELLA. [*Prunella vulgaris, self-heal.*]

25. Millefolium vulg. alb., Bauh. Pin., 140. [Achillea Millefolium.] *Yarrow, Milfoil.*

26. CERASTIUM Villoso-viscosum 379. [C. Triviale *Link*, is the C. *Viscosum* Linn. of W. Hooker and Arnott, see J. Hooker, *St. Fl.* 1870, p. 55. *Mouse-ear Chickweed.*]

27. BELLIS Sylvestris minor C[aspar] B[auhin]. [B. perennis L. *Daisy.*]

28. LINUM Catharticum [Linn. *Purging flax.*]

Of each of this last group there was found only a single example.

Klädes-lappar til gödsel på åkern.
Rags for manure on the arable.

We afterwards went over small *inclosures* which were sown with wheat, partly in *broadland* and partly in *four-thorough-stitches.* Everywhere on these fields lay small pieces of clothes or *clothes-laps* and *clouts*, or rags of all sorts of different colours, some of which lay down in the ground, others on the surface. They were bought from a tailor in London, and carried here from thence, and laid out on the fields as an excellent manure to increase [T. I. p. 306] the growth of crops. The soil, **jordmon,** was here the same brick-coloured earth as is found everywhere on *Chilturn Land*, but in addition these fields were very full of flints.

Bökars växt och ålder. *Beeches' growth and age.*

On the north side of a hill there were several beeches

cut down, where we passed the time for an hour to see their age. All these stood in the open air not close together, but far away from each other.

A beech trunk was measured which had at the large end fifty-four sap-rings. The diameter was just 2 feet. The sap-rings which were found nearest the heart, **kärnan,** were narrowest and smallest, **smalast och smärst,** from which they grew larger, *gradatim;* the further they lay from the heart out towards the surface, the larger they were. The length of the log was 9 feet. At the small end there were forty-four sap-rings, and the diameter was 19 inches. The distance between the heart and the surface which had turned towards the east, was 7 inches, the other 12 inches was all on the west side.

Another beech trunk had at the large end seventy sap-rings. The diameter could not be measured where it was cut off at the roots, because the stem toward the roots branched out so much on all sides; but 2 feet 6 inches above the place where the large end was cut off, the diameter was found to be 19½ inches. The length of the trunk was 17 feet. At the small end there were 59 sap-rings; the diameter 14½ inches.

Another beech-trunk had at the large end 51 sap-rings. The diameter was there 2 feet. The length of the log 10 feet 3 inches. At the small end there were 41 sap-rings; the diameter there 16½ inches. [T. I. p. 307.] Always when the diameter of a tree was measured, the bark was not included.

Hedera ganska lång. Dess växt och ålder.

Ivy very long. Its growth and age.

In a wood, **en Skogs-park,** we saw 3 or 4 bushes of *Hedera Arborea* C.B., which were the highest and longest I ever yet saw.

They had twined themselves around beeches, and climbed up them right to the top. Their green leaves covered the beeches so as to make them look at a distance as if they were covered with verdure, and with full fresh leaves close to the stem. The height of these ivy-bushes, to the best of our judgment, a good 60 feet if not more. We cut off one of the thickest, 4 feet from the ground, to see how old it was, and measured its thickness. The diameter was $1\frac{3}{4}$ inches, and it had here thirty sap-rings, which showed its age in years. As it had climbed up the tree it had everywhere driven in a number of fibres and roots into the same, from its stem, to hold fast by. It had branched itself in many branches, which all ran upwards. Some went right up to the top, others wound themselves somewhat spirally round the tree. This is not particularly liked by wood-wards or gardeners, because it injures the trees, draws the nourishment from them, and causes decay.

The 10th April, 1748.

At förvara rötter om Vintern.

To keep roots in the Winter.

Our host told us that among the best ways that are practised in England for keeping carrots, parsnips, **Mor-rötter, Palsternackor,** and other roots in the winter uninjured by the cold, etc., is to lay them in dry wheat-straw. Mr. Ellis said that some keep them in dry sand [T. I. p. 308] in cellars. Others let them stand out on the land the whole winter, only that the land is covered well over with straw, or something else, so that the cold cannot get at them.

Tecken till väderlek af Bellis.

Sign of the weather from Daisies.

It was pleasant to see how *Bellis sylvestris minor,* C.B.,

which here grew in multitudes on all pastures and grass ground, and was now in full flower, drew together its petals when the air was cold, or when it was like rain or bad weather. A great many flowers of *Syngenesia* or *floribus compositis* [*Compositæ*] had this quality.

Kes-bållar här och där på åkrar.

Balls of iron-pyrites here and there on the fields.

I have before (p. 291, *orig.* 295 above) given a description of the **Kes-bållar** which lay embedded in the *Freestone* at **Tatternel,** and were found in abundance in the same stone mine. In our walks hither and thither in the fields and in other places in this district we often found these **Kes-bållar,** *Crows' gold, Iron pyrites,* either in pits where they had dug up the chalk to carry on to the fields for manure, or also out on the ploughed lands, in many places round *Edgeborough,* as well as here round *Little Gaddesden.* Those which are found on the fields have doubtless been carried there with the chalk from the chalk pits. When these had lain for a time on the fields, the air, rain, and sun had considerably altered their colour and appearance. They exactly resembled a piece of the iron ore which is dug up in bogs and morasses, and were of the same irony rust and ochre colour. The interior looked very much like *Ochra,* although it was harder, but the surface itself retained its radiated sulphurous colour and structure. They had still their former considerable weight. [As these are found here in all chalk hills among the ordinary chalk [T. I. p. 309] so I ask, "May not the bottom of all chalk hills, although it be low down, consist of *Freestone ?* May not the *chalk* and *Freestone* differ, if only in the degree of hardness or development, according as they lie nearer the surface or deeper down ? May not this which is now *Freestone,* in former times have been chalk, or *vice versâ* ? May not the chalk sometimes, perhaps, change first to *Hurlock* and afterwards to *Freestone* or *vice versâ* ?"*]

The 11th April, 1748.

Huru en ny häck anlägges.

How a new fence is laid down.

When anyone wishes to erect an entirely new hedge of living trees, either round arable fields, meadows, or other property, it is done here in *Hertfordshire,* where folk are held to be most expert in the art, in the following manner :—

The hedge is planted generally *in lineâ rectâ.* If the ground is free from trees and stubs, a pair of furrows are ploughed straight on, where the new hedge is to be planted. These furrows are turned towards each other, but if the ground is full of tree-roots, so that the plough cannot advance, the earth is commonly dug up with the spade. Some use not to dig up anything on the place they wish to plant, but are content with the mould they cast up out of the ditch. When the earth has thus been ploughed or dug up where the hedge is to be planted, a ditch is dug along and close beside the same, which ditch, after all the earth has been cast up out of it, is commonly 2 or 3 feet deep below the surface of the ground. This mould, which is taken out of the ditch, is cast on to the ploughed-up, or dug-up, earth, at first as much as to make a bank of 1 foot high or a little more. Thereupon, young shoots of hawthorn or sloe

---

* In answer to the questions which I have enclosed in brackets:—

The Totternhoe Stone, a marly sandstone, might be called a development of the Grey chalk, but that it lies at its base, above which the sandy element disappears. The answer to the latter questions is negative. They are separate beds. [J. L.]

are taken, and cut [T. I. p. 310] off obliquely a good 4
or 6 inches above the root, and afterwards planted in the
cast-up bank all in a row, or *in lineâ rectâ*. The thickness
of these shoots is about the size of a finger, sometimes a
little less. They are set so close together that there is
commonly not more than 3 inches between each. When
they are planted there is made, as it were, a water-
furrow right along the whole bank about 4 inches deep,
in which these shoots are set by their roots, but are so
placed that they do not come to stand perpendicular, but
very much leaning towards the ditch, so that they might
later on so much the better keep off the cattle. Upon
that the furrow in which they are planted, is turned over
again, by which mould is cast on to their roots, so that
the newly-planted shoots often do not come to stand
with their ends over an inch above the ground. The
shoots which are commonly used for this purpose
are either hawthorn or sloe, which are intermixed, but,
besides these, there are set here and there, either at a
certain distance or length from each other, or just as
they please, small shoots of willows, **Vilar,** *Salices;*
beeches, **Bök;** ash, **Ask;** maple, **Lönn;** lime, **Lind;**
elm, **Alm;** and other leaf-trees; which are cut off, so
that they are as short as the others. When this has
been arranged they begin to make the bank, **vallen,**
higher, in that more mould is cast up out of the ditch on
to the roots of the newly-planted shoots, till the wall or
bank, **vallen eller banken,** has been raised 1 foot
higher than when they were first planted, and of such a
slope that when a stick is laid on the side or slope of the
bank there is commonly 18 inches between the row the
first shoots were set in, and the summit of this added
earth. Herein is now planted, in exactly the same
way, a row of hawthorn or sloe, and several of the above-
named leaf-trees, whose [T. I. p. 311] roots are

afterwards well covered over with the earth which has been cast out of the ditch. When a perpendicular line is erected from the row the lower planted shoots stand in, it is seen that they stand 1 foot nearer the ditch than the upper row, whence the slope of the bank towards the ditch can be judged.

The earth which is here cast out of the ditch, and in which the hedge was planted, consisted of the brick-colored earth which is found everywhere about here, with some flint-sand and small flint stones among it. On one side the ditch hindered the cattle from getting at the newly-planted shoots to do them any injury, and on the other there were set up, as it were, **ledstängar,** *railings,* or also a dead fence, which somewhat resembled a **gärdes-gård,** similarly to prevent the cattle on that side also from approaching the young trees. It is commonly in the month of October or February that this work is carried out in England. At a place between *Little Gaddesden* and St. Albans there was a new hedge planted in the above-named way, but to hinder the cattle from injuring the young shoots, there were on the summit and along the bank set what I may call **ledstänger,** *railings.*

Down below the shoots there was a deep ditch dug, partly for the same object, partly and principally to get earth in which the shoots could be planted. On the other side of the ditch opposite the hedge, close to the edge of the ditch, there was a dead fence erected to hinder the cattle and sheep from getting down into the ditch to bite off the newly-planted shoots.

In another place there were, with the same object, erected hurdles exactly the same as are here used as folds on the arable, and have been before described (p. 262 *orig.* 264 *above*). These were placed just at the edge of the earth-bank [T. I. p. 312] in which the shoots were planted, to hinder the cattle from climbing up on to the earth-bank.

Obs. In England there is the advantage that nearly in every town and large village there is one or more nurseryman, **Trägårds-mästare,** whose principal occupation is, to sow and plant the seeds of a number of different kinds of trees, and to keep ' tree-schools,' so that they can sell a number of all kinds of different young shoots for a reasonable price to one who requires them. When, then, a farmer, **en Landtman,** wishes to lay down, for example, a new hedge, he goes to such a nurseryman and buys of him as many 1,000 shoots as he requires, which he can at once plant out as a hedge without waiting from the time they are sown till they have grown so large that they can be planted out, which would be too longsome, **för långsamt,** because the hawthorn-berries lie, for the most part, two years in the earth before they come up.

Sometimes a new hedge is made with a ditch on its outer side, as in the afore-named manner, sometimes also, without a ditch, when the mould to plant the shoots in is taken from both sides of the place where the hedge is going to stand. In planting the shoots, it is especially necessary that the soil should be arranged close into and around their roots. If the hedge is laid down without any ditch, a dead fence must first of all be erected on both sides of the planted shoots, to keep the cattle off them, till they are somewhat large.

Huru en gammal häck förnyas, och en död upresas, &c.

How an old hedge is renewed, and a dead fence erected.

It has been mentioned above several times that no other fences, **stängsel,** are here used around the arable fields, meadows, pastures, orchards, flower gardens, and

kitchen gardens, &c., than [T. I. p. 313] hedges of all
sorts of prickly trees, sometimes also of trees without
thorns, and when these are somewhat old they are cut
down that new scions may shoot up from the cut-off
stubs. A dead fence is in the meantime erected for as
long a time as the upshooting scions take to acquire a
sufficient height, so that they can themselves fence off
the cattle. Now, I have just above described how an
entirely new hedge is used to be laid down in England,
therefore I will here give in detail the latter, or how to
renew an old hedge, and erect a so-called *dead-fence*, **död
häck**, &c. I will describe it in the manner in which this
work is performed here in Hertfordshire, where it is
commonly held that the folk understand this work best
of all in the whole of England.

When a new-planted hedge is nine years old, it is
commonly cut down, partly that the owner may get fuel
from it, both for himself and to sell to others, partly that
he may get a new and better hedge from the upshooting
new scions; for when a hedge has stood for nine years,
a part of the trees in it begin to grow old and to go off,
so that it is no more so thick as before. In performing
this job all the trees are cut down quite close to the
ground, which do not grow in a straight line in the
middle of the hedge where the dead fence is to be
erected; but a part of the trees which thus stand in the
middle of the hedge, as many, namely, as one considers
on the spot will be necessary, are left to stand till one
has entirely cut down the others.

After that, *staves*, **stafrar,** are taken from the leaf-
trees which had stood in the hedge, the twigs, **qvist-
arna,** cut off, and the staves made quite smooth. The
length of every *staff* is made 4 feet 6 inches. The thickness is from ½ [T. I. p. 314] to 2 inches diameter, and
sometimes more. These 4 feet 6 inch *staves*, are set all

in a row, where the fence is to be, the one staff after the
other, never two staves abreast, so that just 2 feet length
is left between every staff, sometimes a little more, and
sometimes a little less. These staves are driven a good
4 inches, if not 6 inches down into the ground, and, that
this may be done more easily, the carl has a little mallet
with which he drives them down. Hereupon be it noted
that, if any of the trees which grow along where the
fence is to be erected, are found not to be particularly
long and thick, they are cut off 4 feet above the ground.
The remaining 4 feet stub, is made quite smooth from
twigs, and left to stand to be used as a staff or ' hedge-
pole,' **stafver.** The more one can get of these the better
it is, because they, as root-fast trees, make the dead fence
stand steady and fast. After that, the carl takes the
longer trees left remaining in the hedge, cuts them more
than half through, about 4 inches above the roots, and
bends them so, gently and cautiously down along the
hedge. This down-bending is begun at one end of the
hedge thus :—Let the hedge, for example, go in a straight
line from north to south. If the carl intends to begin to
tress, **at fläta,** the dead hedge at the south end, he cuts
the tree standing there a little more than half through,
4 inches or more above the ground, which cutting is done
on the north side of the tree. After that he takes hold
of the tree, bends it softly and carefully down towards
the south ; and as the lower parts of these trees are thick,
so that after they have been thus bent down they will
not further admit of being bent somewhat *serpentiformiter*,
if I [T. I. p. 315] may so call it (by which I mean when
it is first on one side of the one staff and immediately
after on the other side of the next), he causes the thick
stem to lie close against one side of the *staves*, and that
commonly on the twiggy side—of which more anon. Yet
he regulates this according to the situation of the tree, on

whichever side of the hedge it stands most; but the upper ends of these trees thus half cut through near the roots, which admit of being bent, he bends right and left *serpentiformiter* about the staves, that is, if in this hedge which stands north and south he makes the narrow end of this tree to go on the east side of the one staff he causes it afterwards to go on the west side of the next staff, still he mostly arranges it so that the ends of these are turned to the twiggy side. I will at once describe what I understand by the twiggy side, **den qvistiga sidan.** Now, as these turned-down and half cut through trees, are here to perform the same service as **gärdsel** or **gärdsel-trädor** with us, they are commonly laid at the inclination, or in the same sloping manner as some of the **gärdesgårds-trädor,** 'fence-trees' with us, viz., not horizontally but obliquely and sloping, yet so that the inclination is nearer a horizontal than a perpendicular line.

In this way the carl continues from the south end northwards, so that he successively bends the trees which follow in the hedge over those which have previously been bent down, and that nearly in the same way as we in Sweden make a sloping **gärdes-gård,** only that he here leaves the larger ends, as said before, to stand on one side close to the staves, and bends the little end now to one side of the one staff, and then to the other side of the next staff, and so arranges that all the outer ends of these [T. I. p. 316] trees are left on one and the same side of the *dead fence* or **gärdes-gård,** viz., in the foregoing example, if he has turned the end of the first down-bent tree to the east side of the fence, **häcken,** so he ought also as far as possible to turn all the other outermost ends of the down-bent trees towards that side also. The height of the hedge is equal to that of the staves, viz., 4 feet. When the tree is cut near the roots

somewhat more than half through, especial care is taken
that the cut or incision in the part of the tree which
is to be bent down is made very long, so that rain water
and other wet may be all the less able to damage it, as
well as that it may so much the better be able to be
bent ; but the stub which remains down in the ground,
one does not trouble himself about how the end of that
is cut. And as it is seldom that so many trees grow in
the middle of the hedge, that they alone, when they are
bent, will be sufficient to fill up the fence with, but
there are openings all the same here and there, long sprays
and stems, **språtar och stånd,** of hawthorn are taken,
which are bent or laid in the hedge in the same way as
the little ends of the former trees, viz., that they go
somewhat *in formam serpentinam horizontaliter,* or, now on
the right hand side of the one staff, and afterwards on
the left of the next following, and so by turns always so
that the outermost ends are ultimately turned to one
and the same side of the hedge, as here, in the example
given, to the east. They are especially particular, to
in this way wreath or set in hawthorn or sloe down to
the ground, to thereby hinder the swine from going
through the hedge in their explorations, because both
these trees with their long thorns usually deprive them
of all pleasure in such a research. [T. I. p. 317.] But
that this dead fence may have still more strength, they
procure for themselves long sprays either of hazel,
willow, blackberry-bushes, or some other tree of which
they take two sticks of about the same length, which are
twisted, or wreathed spirally about each other on the
top of the fence over the others, always so that the ends
of the staves, **störarna,** come to be wreathed in between
those two sprays, and thus fastened. They begin with
this, thus :—

The large end of a spray is set on the one side of a staff

en stör, and the large end of another spray on the other side of the same staff. Next, the sprays are bent across each other, so that the spray, whose large end was now for example, on the west side of a staff comes in the next place to lie on the east side of the next staff. So it is commonly done with the sprays at their large ends, where they are thick and stiff, but afterwards they are wreathed spirally, so that they had commonly got in one, if not two spirals between every staff. When these sprays are complete two new ones are taken, and it is continued in the same way along the top of the whole length of the gärdes-gård. But hereupon be it noted, that if the trees a little more than half cut through near the roots and afterwards bent down, turn the root ends or the thicker ends, for example, towards the north, and the point or the smaller end towards the south, as they lie in the hedge, these spirally-wreathed sprays ought to turn the large ends, on the contrary, to the south and the little ends to the north, also the work of wreathing them is begun at the north end, because it is believed that the dead hedge is by this means steadier and bound faster, than if they are turned with the ends in the same direction as the large trees, which lie obliquely and sloping.

In respect of this also [T. I. p. 318] care is taken that these spirally-wreathed sprays, all come to lie horizontally.

In most cases the *sprays* were only wreathed once *spiraliter* between each staff so that one and the same spray by this arrangement always came to lie on the same side of the staves. It was also commonly arranged that the small end of these came eventually to be turned to the twiggy side, and if it at any time came to be turned out to the other side, it was always cut off. I have in this description often mentioned the twiggy side, den qvistiga sidan. Now, I will say what it is   After the

Y

dead hedge has thus been erected as has been described, all
the twigs on one side, by preference on that which looks
inward, are cut off, so that it is quite smooth and even,
but on the outer sides of this dead hedge to which the
carls had turned all the points of the so bent down and
inset trees, the twigs are cut off in this way, that the
twigs near the ground are allowed to go out 2 feet or
2 feet 6 inches from the hedge, but are afterwards cut
off shorter and shorter the higher they are up, so that
the highest are scarcely 4 inches long.

If one stands on the flat side, and looks over the
hedge, and along it on the twiggy side, then it looks like
a sloping earth wall. The reason why the twigs on the
one side are left so long is that the young shoots and
scions which come to run up just between these twigs
may in their tender age be shielded from the approach
of the cattle by these dry twigs, which are mostly
hawthorn.

In several places it was the practice that when they
cut down an old hedge near the roots and erected a
[T. I. p. 319] dead, in the manner just described, in
the same place, they dug close alongside of the hedge
on one side a little ditch of 1 foot deep, and the same
breadth, which was done for two reasons.

1. The mould which was taken out of the ditch was
cast up on, and over the roots of the hedge, which is
accounted a choice manure to force the cut-down hedge,
both to shoot faster, and to form a larger number of shoots.

2. The ditch on one side hindered the cattle from
coming to the young shoots and injuring them. On
the other side they were protected by the thorny twigs
left remaining, but in many places, in short, in most
places, this was neglected, nevertheless, it seemed to be
a very wise provision.

All the trees and twigs cut down in the hedge were

collected together, cut into different lengths and bound up in bundles. The stems of the thicker trees, which were of an arm's thickness, more and less, were set out and bound separately together. The twigs and the smaller sticks were also bound together in bundles. Scarcely any twig was left, however small it was, which did not find its place with the others in the bundle, an unfailing sign that the folk here knew to set a right value on the wood, and to be careful of such a precious treasure. It is incredible, however, what use and profit a 'farmer' and **Landtman,** in these woodless districts had from these hedges, which gave him not only sufficient fuel for his own requirements, but put him also in the position to sell a quantity of it to others who had not such themselves.

The larger a tree was, the dearer it was sold. I noted also that more prudent [T. I. p. 320] economists always carried the smallest bundles of twigs home for their own use, and were content with them; but spared all the thicker timber to be sold to others. I even saw one who himself burned brackens the greatest part of the year, and sold all the wood which he yearly got from the hedges he cut down, which was a considerable quantity. Wherever we wandered about we saw large fagots and bundles of larger and smaller timbers, which they had bound together from the cut-down hedges, and left for a time near the hedges to dry, from whence they were either carried home, or sold for ready money. They were also sometimes left for poor folk, who in return did day-work for the farmer.

When a hedge had thus been cut down and arranged, it commonly made such strong shoots, that in two or three years' time it could do service as a barrier, and be in a position to keep out the cattle. The dead fence was then taken away, and carried home for fuel.

Y 2

The cutting down of these living hedges and the erection of the dead hedges in their place was commonly effected in October and November, in the autumn, and in January, February and March, and at the beginning of April, in the spring, only with this difference that the young hedges were cut down in the autumn, but the old in the spring, which experienced economists had found to be best.

In the hedges there stood here and there large trees, such as beeches, ashes, elms, limes, &c., which were an ornament around the arable fields; but the large leaf-trees are said, however, to have the disadvantage that they by their dripping when rainy weather set in, as it were [T. I. p. 321] killed the hedges which stood under them, besides drawing considerable nourishment from the arable fields close beside them.

The height of these dead fences was, as has been said, commonly 4 feet; but it was also lower in some places, where they had only sheep and no large cattle.

The reason why the trees were cut little more than half through, near the roots, and afterwards bent down, was in addition to what has been given above, partly that the dead hedge might be steadier, partly that young shoots should shoot up where a long-sloping incision was made in the tree so bent.

The hedges here consisted of different trees, such as hawthorn, sloe, dogrose, blackberry-bushes, willow, ash, elm, maple, beech, holly, oak, etc., among which the hawthorn formed the most part, and next to that the sloe. This last was an arrant rogue at creeping under the earth with its roots, so that it was not long among the others in the hedge before it came creeping from them forward out into the fields. Here it so pulled the wool from the backs of the sheep, which sought for the fine grass under it, that large locks of wool remained everywhere on its thorns. Jungström called it **Ull-rjuf,** 'wool-stealer,' in consequence, for which name this bush here gave very good reasons. A little ditch drawn along-side the hedge could easily have stopped its bad habit of creeping far from the hedge. In cutting down a hedge, as soon as the trees which were not wanted for erecting a dead hedge were cut down to the ground, there was commonly dug up a narrow ditch close to the hedge, out of which the mould was cast up on the stubs which [T. I. p. 322] were covered with it that the sun might not injure the stubs, but that they might be forced to make stronger shoots, and strike out many scions.

Helge-dagars firande i Ängland.

The celebration of Holy Days in England.

England has nearly the same high-days as we in Sweden, and the Gospels and Epistles for them are also nearly the same; but the Church ceremonies are **ganska skilljaktige,** very different. The sermon itself (in the English Church) which is all read from a paper writing, does not last over half-an-hour. The priest does not interpret in it the Gospel or Epistles, but he takes some Bible text which he explains and moralises over, and it sometimes happens that in the whole of his sermon no more Scripture Texts are cited and expounded than the single one he has taken for a *Text*. Sunday is esteemed outwardly in some things very holy, so that no ordinary work is carried on on this day. To dance, play cards, play on an instrument, to hum or sing dances on Sunday is esteemed a very great sin and scandal, and the man who was so indiscreet and transgressed in these respects, might at least in any town, soon place himself in great danger and risk. But to sit all day at the beer-shop, **krogen,** drink himself drunk, to visit **mindre tuk-tiga hus,** and pass the day with dissolute scum is not so rigorously guarded against. On the other holy days, **Helgedagar,** except Sunday, such as the second and third days in great high-feasts, **stora hogtider,** the Feast of the Annunciation, Midsummer-day, &c., a service it is true is observed in the church, but all work is carried on exactly the same as on any week day. In a word, they are observed here in the same way as Apostle days in Sweden.

Ängelska Qvinfolkens kläder-drägt, maner, &c.

English women's costumes, habits, &c.

When the English women in the country are going out to pay their compliments to each other, they commonly wear a red cloak, **klädes-kâpa.** They also wear their *pattens,* **järn-skor,** under their ordinary shoes when they go out, to prevent the dirt on the roads and streets from soiling their ordinary shoes. All go laced, and use for everyday a sort of *Manteau,* made commonly of brownish *Camlot.* The same head-dress as in London. Here it is not unusual to see a farmer's or another small personage's wife clad on Sundays like a lady of ' quality ' at other places in the world, and her every-day attire in proportion. ' Paniers,' **Styf-Kjortlar,** are seldom used in the country. When they go out they always wear straw hats, **halm-hattar,** which they have made themselves from wheat-straw, and are pretty enough. On high days they have on ruffles, **manchetter.** One hardly ever sees a woman here trouble herself in the least about outdoor duties, such as *tending,* **at vara med,** in the arable and meadows, &c. The duty of the women in this district scarcely consists in anything else but preparing food, which they commonly do very well, though roast beef and *Pudding* forms nearly all an Englishman's eatables.

Besides that, they wash and scour dishes and floors,

etc., for about cleanliness they are very careful, and especially in these things, to wash clothes, and to hem one thing and another minutely.

They never take the trouble to bake, because there is a baker in every parish or village, from whom they can always have new bread. Nearly the same can be said about brewing. Weaving and spinning is also in most houses a more than rare thing, because their many *manufacturers* save them from the necessity of such. For [T. I. p. 324] the rest, it belongs to the men to tend the cattle, milk the cows, and to perform all the work in the arable fields and meadows, and in the 'lodge' and 'lathe,' &c. I confess that I at first rubbed my eyes several times to make them clear, because I could not believe I saw aright, when I first came here, out in the country, and saw the farmers' houses full of young women, while the men, on the contrary, went out both morning and evening to where the cattle were, milk-pail in hand, sat down to milk, and afterwards carried the milk home. I had found, then, that every land has its customs. In short, when one enters a house and has seen the women cooking, washing floors, plates and dishes, darning a stocking or sewing a chemise, washing and starching linen clothes, he has, in fact, seen all their household economy and all that they do the whole of God's long day, year out and year in, when to these are added some *visitors*. Nearly all the evening occupations which our women in Sweden perform are neglected by them, but, instead, here they sit round the fire without attempting in the very least degree what we call **hushålls-syslor,** household duties. But they can never be deprived of the credit of being very handsome and very lively in society. In pleasant conversation, agreeable *repartie*, polite sallies, in a word, in all that the public calls **belefvenhet,** *politesse* and *savoir vivre*, they are never wanting.

They are lucky in having turned the greater part of
the burden of responsible management on to the men, so
that it is very true what both Englishmen and others
write, that England is a paradise for ladies and women.
It is true that common servant-girls have to have somewhat more work in them, **hålla något mera uti,** but
still this also is moderate, and seldom goes beyond what
has been reckoned up above. But [T. I. p. 325] the
mistresses and their daughters are in particular those
who enjoy perfect freedom from work.

To us in Sweden, where the wife, no less than the
husband, is obliged in every way to bestir herself and
keep her wits about her, **fika och vara om sig,** to
help to win the bare necessaries of life, an English wife
would not seem to be particularly well-suited. I have,
however, with my own eyes, seen some proof of this, that
when constrained by necessity to exert themselves, they
have been as clever managers as anywhere in the world,
for they are not wanting in sagacity to carry them through
the most difficult cases.

The 13th April, 1748.

Ängars gödning. *Manuring meadows.*

This work of manuring meadows is mostly performed
here in the autumn, after they have carried the hay,
when soot and other kinds of manure are spread over the
inclosures, **täckter,** sown with *Clover, St. Foin,* and
other kinds of hay.

Huru mycket de få efter en bushels utsäde.

How much they get in return for each bushel sown.

Several farmers said here that two bushels of wheat
are commonly sown out on an acre of land, **acreland,**
and in return, when the field is well-managed and the
year's growth is good, twenty-five bushels are reaped. At

Ivinghoe it was related that they get ten bushels of barley, **korn,** for every bushel sown.

At så laga, det höet blifver grönt och välluktande.

How to arrange that the hay may be green and fragrant.

Of the many good kinds of hay here in England I have in particular seen two; the one is quite green and as if it were newly mown, though it may be one or more years old ; the other has a brownish appearance, but smells incomparably well, so that no more delightful scent could attach to hay. I asked that clever farmer, Mr. Williams, in what way both these kinds of hay were prepared. He answered [T. I. p. 325] that the hay retains its green colour if it is treated in the following manner :—As soon as it has been mown, and has lain a little time, it is turned over, in which way, if it is sunshine, it is continued the whole day, so that it is turned over nearly once in each hour ; because with hay there is the peculiarity, that if the sun gets to shine long on one side and dries it, it loses its green colour and becomes pale. This turning is continued until the hay is dry, when it is carried home and laid in the lathe, **lada,** or rather in the stack. An hay thus managed has a very fragrant scent, although not quite so strong as the following brownish sort, which is prepared thus :—After the hay has been mown it is turned as usual from time to time, and when it is nearly dry, but has still some moisture left in it, which however should necessarily be a certain degree, for which an exact knowledge is required, it is carried home, laid in the lathe, **lada,** but by preference in the stack, when from the still remaining moisture in it, it comes to have as it were a kind of sweating, which far from injuring the hay, or giving it any unpleasant taste or smell, causes it to have the loveliest and most delightful scent which can

ever be in any hay.   Mr. Williams doubted, however, very
much whether anyone, after a mere account of the process, would be in a position to do this, unless he were
present when the hay was so prepared and got to learn
to know then how far it ought to be dried before it is laid
together to undergo this sweating.

This is the hay which is so agreeable to cows and horses,
that they nearly forsake everything else, when they can
enjoy this.   The farmers also consider this very wholesome [T. I. p. 327] and good for cows, because they
become very thirsty and drink much when they have
eaten it, and afterwards give an abundance of milk.

Here I will now add, that all the farmers I talked
with in this place, unanimously affirmed that it is far
better to lay the hay in stacks made and thatched as
above described (p. 211 *orig.* 210 *above*) than to lay it in
lathes, **lador.**   The reason they gave was, that after the
stack has been well thatched, the hay can be kept far
better in it, because the air has free access on all sides to
weather and dry it, while on the other hand that which
is arranged in lathes has not this advantage, but is in part,
especially that which lies nearest the walls, musty and
mouldy.   Nor can the hay which is laid in lathes ever
acquire the delightful fragrance, which well managed hay,
laid in the stack, commonly has, although the kind of
grass itself often does not seem to be so choice.

Aske-trädets ålder.   *The Ash tree's age.*

An ash which grew in a hedge, and was newly cut
down, had at the large end 104 sap-rings, which gave its
age in years.   The diameter was here 22 inches.   From
the 14th to the 30th year the tree had made the thickest
sap-rings, but the outermost were very thin.   The length
was 12 feet.   This tree had not had freedom to grow in
height, but after it had attained 6 feet in height, it had

been cut off at the top, that it might strike out many shoots, which were cut off after they had grown to some thickness, and carried home for fuel, after which the stub was again left freedom to strike out others, which twigs again, after some time were cut off for the same object. This mode of providing fuel, I have seen very much used [T. I. p. 328] in the districts where I travelled in England. On the stub left remaining in the hedge there was a shoot left, which had run up from the roots, and could at some future time be used in the same way.

Another ash had 92 sap-rings at the large end, which denoted the age. The diameter at that place was 19 inches. Up to the 19th year it had made quite small sap-rings, but in the 19th year it had made one large enough, and in the 20th the largest of all. After that it had had, **Sedan hade hon framgent hade,** large sap-rings, until it reached 38 years, after which they began to be narrower and narrower. The length of this log was 19 feet 6 inches. At the little end there were 80 sap-rings. The diameter was there 13 inches. It was cut and managed in the same way as the former one.

Ek-trädets ålder och växt.

The Oak tree's age and growth.

We afterwards came across a felled oak, which we also examined, to get to know its age. At the large end were 48 sap-rings. The diameter was 22 inches. After it had attained a height of 9 feet from the roots it had been cut off, that it might strike out many shoots, which could be used for fuel. It had considerably thick sap-rings. On one side of the hedge in which it had stood, was a road, on the other ploughed fields, only small trees with it in the hedge. The soil the same as everywhere here at *Little Gaddesden.* At the little end the sap-rings could not be distinctly seen, for it was cut several times.

[T. I. p. 329.] Harfvarnas beskrifning, som här brukas.

Description of the harrows which are used here.

The harrows in use here are made in the same way as with us in Sweden. Their length is commonly 4 feet 3 inches, breadth 3 feet 2 inches. Some consisted of five bars, **trän,** and some of four, with always five tines, **tinnar,** in each bar, **trä.** The distance between the tines was commonly 9 inches, the length of the tines 6 or 7 inches. The breadth of each of their sides ¾ inch. They were not fastened, **fast häftade,** as is commonly done with us by being thrust in from below, and then clinched on the top, **nådas ofvantil,** when the part which is thrust into the bar is narrower than that below, but they were here thrust through from above, when the upper end of them was beaten thin, bent *ad angulum rectum,* with a nail-hole in the same crookt and thin beaten part of the iron, through which a nail was knocked down into the harrow-bar, **harf-träden,** which held the tine, **pinnan,** fast. But as the hole for the *tine* or harrow-tine, **harf-pinnan,** was as large as the thickness of the tine, the tine was often shot up, and became loose, in this flint-full earth.

Jordens tjocklek somligstäds på kritan.

The thickness of the soil in some places on the chalk.

In a thick wood of leaf-trees was a pit, where they had taken chalk, in which we measured the thickness of the soil, which we found to be 4 feet 3 inches. This earth which lay upon the chalk was of the same brick-coloured kind as is found everywhere about here.

Such was the thickness at this place, but in other places it was sometimes more, sometimes less.

Åldren och växten på Agrifolium. *The age and growth of holly.*

In a newly felled hedge there lay among other trees a somewhat thick holly, Agrifolium *Raj. Syn.* 466, which at the large end had thirty sap-rings, which [T. I. p. 330] showed that it was thirty years old. The diameter was 4½ inches.

The 14th April, 1748.

Manfolkens syslor och plägsed här på orten.

Men's duties and habits in this place.

Men have here to take thought for the heaviest part of the cares of husbandry. They have to do all the work in the arable fields, meadows, in the wood, the lodge, and the lathe, **på åker, äng, i skog, loga, lada.**

The women have also bishop'd the care of the cattle on to them, even to the extent that the carls commonly milk the cows, as has been said before. In short, all out-door work belongs to the men. They have to collect together the wherewithal to feed, nourish, and clothe both themselves and the women, for here the women do not get sore fingers by much spinning, **spånad,** or arm-ache or back-ache from weaving. It is the part of the *Manufacturers* to make up for this, and the men's purses are punished in this matter. The men consequently think it no more than reasonable that they should some-times take a little rest. [The Village Inn.] We staid here at the *Inn*, where the host kept ale and brandy for sale, and into which the men of this village very often came, to pass some hours over some *Pint beers* (pints of beer). There were seen, sometimes both before and after dinner, a number of labouring men and others killing time in this way. Still, the evenings after six o'clock were especially devoted to this, after the carls had finished their regular labour and day's-work. I often wondered how some of them could have their means of subsistence in such a way, the more so because ale and brandy were here very dear; but most of all I wondered over this, that folk who could only provide food for themselves, their wives, and children, out of daily wages, **dags-penning,** could spend time and money in this way. It was, however, not unusual [T. I. p. 331] to see many sit the whole day at the inn. But the custom, **maner,** of the country that friends and neighbours come together, sit and converse, the abundance of money in this country, the ease with which a man could in every case have his food, if only he was somewhat industrious, seem to have conduced to this result. However, I more than seldom saw anyone imbibe so much that he became drunk from it.

Ale, **öl,** was the drink that was most used here. Brandy was seldom asked for. It only occurred to me, a foreigner, how folk, who commonly are so self-seeking, **fikande om sig,** could spend often a great part of the day in this way. This manner of life was customary at all the places I travelled through in this country. It is not to be wondered at then, if a great many labourers and others, however large the daily wages and profits they can make, can, for all that, scarcely collect more than what goes from hand to mouth.

Tussilago **på åkrar.** *Colts foot on arable fields.*

On the greater parts of the arable fields, which were somewhat damp, *Tussilago vulg.* [*Coltsfoot,* T. Farfara] grew in great abundance, and that mostly on the ploughed plots which had been sown the year before.

Göken, the *Cuckoo,* I heard to-day the first time this year, though some said they had heard it a week before.

Mullvads-högar upkastade. *Mole-hills cast up.*

I have often before said that in this place are found a very great number of moles. The earth and mole-hills which they had cast up on the meadows, the farmers caused to be spread out over the meadow, that they, in any case, should not originate any hillocks, **tufvor,** on them.

[T. I. p. 332.] **Bökars ålder och växt.**

Beeches' age and growth.

Below the house where we had our lodgings was a wood of high and thick beeches. Among them were some cut down, on two of which we counted the sap-rings, to see their age and growth, and to gain from that some idea of the fertility of the soil. One of the beeches which lay here had at the large end 162 sap-rings. The diameter there was 2 feet 10 inches. The length of this beech-stock was 20 feet. At the little end there were 142 sap-rings, and the diameter was 2 feet 4 inches. Another beech in the same park had at the large end 168 sap-rings, or years old. The diameter at this end was 3 feet 5 inches. The length was 18 feet 6 inches. At the little end there were 156 sap-rings, and the diameter was 2 feet 1 inch.

At this point I make only this remark: This wood or park consisted of high and thick beeches. The soil was here the same as is found everywhere about Little Gaddesden, viz., the often described brick-coloured earth, **tegelfärgade jorden,** but the reason why these trees had not come to increase in their thickness in proportion to their age is, that those previously described had grown in hedges, where they had had open air on all sides, a long way between each tree, and the roots had the use of the neighbouring ploughed fields, &c.; but these had stood crowded together where the air was prevented from getting to them by those standing round. In that position they could only hasten to run up in height. Perhaps, also, it might somewhat have contributed to this, that the ground had always been overgrown with grass, which had not given the tree-roots so much nourishment as where they ran under the cultivated fields.

[T. I. p. 333.] Huru frukt-trän planteras vid murar och deras nytta.

How fruit trees are planted against walls and their use.

Everywhere I have travelled here in England in the country as well as in and near London and other towns, I saw a particularly profitable custom with the planting of certain fruit trees, which consisted in this :—Around most of the gardens here in England there were built brick-walls of various heights. When anyone had a fruit tree which he wished to be able to bear either early or ripe fruit, the same was planted, if the wall ran from west to east, on the south side of, and close against the wall. Afterwards its branches, **qvistar,** were carefully spread out along the wall, on both sides of the tree, after which a little bit of cloth was taken and bent round the twig, **qvisten.** This bit of cloth was afterwards nailed fast to the wall, by which means the twig or branch of the tree came to be stretched out along the wall. According as the twig grew longer it was nailed fast to the wall with more laps in the aforenamed manner. They began in this way when the tree was little, and afterwards went on so continuously, according as the tree grew. No twig or branch got to grow on the outer side away from the wall, but the tree was obliged only to extend itself on both sides. By reason of the tree thus coming to stand right in the heat of the sun, it could not be otherwise than that its fruit should be very early ripe and very beautiful. The trees whose fruit otherwise could never be ripened in England ripened quickly in this way as well as if they had been indigenous in England. Apricots, **Apricoser,** Pistachios, **Pistacier,** Peaches, **Persiker,** in their manifold varieties, with other beautiful fruits, were managed in the same way.

They were planted in the same manner against walls, or the walls of houses, which in summer time looked very pretty in consequence, when a choice [T. I. p. 334] fruit tree often overclad the whole wall. No side of the garden-walls or of the house-walls, for the houses were here nearly always built of brick, was left bare and void of them, whether it was that which faced the south, east, west, or north ; for they chose out for those aspects such trees as either preferred the morning, noon, or evening sun, or loved to stand in the shade. Thus it is often seen that cherry-trees which bear *Morels,* **Moreller,** were spread out on the north side of the garden-walls or house-walls. In the same way were red and white currant bushes, **Vinbärs-buskar,** planted on the last-named or north side.

Halm-hattar. *Straw-hats.*

I have mentioned before (p. 323 *orig.* 327 *above*) that the greater number of the English women in this district trouble themselves very little about such domestic duties as in other countries form a great part of the occupations of women, but that they had laid most of the burden of that on to the men. I saw, however, in some places some part of the women afford proof that they are not wanting in ability for various things, if only the custom of the country had not freed this sex from such. Here were several women who were very busy in making straw hats which they afterwards sent hither and thither to be sold. The straw which was used for this purpose was only

z

wheat straw, nothing else. Of this, long straws were taken, which were cut off into pieces 9 inches long, which were bound into small bundles after the tubes had been first cleaned out. Such a straw as has been speckled black by the rain, ought on no account to be taken. To make the straw still whiter they did this: One of the bundles was dipped in water; afterwards sulphur was laid in a round iron ladle, **stöpslev,*** which had no handle, [T. I. p. 335] and it was set fire to, after which this lighted sulphur, together with the **stöp-slev** was set on the bottom of a can, pint-pot, or similar vessel of the same width above and below. Round about the sides of this vessel these straws, **halm-strån,** are set up, so that the sulphur is in the middle of the bottom. The pint-pot is covered over with a cloth, when the vapour and smoke from the sulphur makes the straw in these bundles much whiter than it naturally was before. When they wish to plait, **flåta,** with it, such a bundle is first dipped in water, so that the straw may be softer, and not break off. The particular manner in which this plaiting is afterwards done cannot so clearly be described in words.†

Anmärkningar vid Krita och Flinta.
Notes on Chalk and Flint.

It has often been mentioned before in this description of my travels, that the hills in the whole of this district in *Hertfordshire*, consisted only of chalk, **af bara krita,**

---

* **Stöp-slev.** In Ivinghoe village, Sept. 1886, sulphur about the size of a walnut is laid in a shallow circular iron pan, shaped like a scale-pan, nearly 6 inches diameter and about ¼ inch deep. This is set on to live coals which are contained in a circular iron pan 6 inches diameter at top, and 2 inches deep, narrowing towards the bottom. The whole apparatus is called the "Steam-pan," and is bodily put into a box or can with the straw round it, and covered over as described by Kalm. [J. L.]

† Straw plaiting is still to be seen, as described, at every cottage between Hitchin and Tring. The women earn 2d. a day for all they can plait. [J. L.]

and that the surface soil, **öfversta skårpan,** was full of flints, often in such multitudes that the ground, **marken,** could scarcely be seen for them. Here we noted that the most flints lay on the surface, but commonly the deeper they were in a chalk pit the less the number of fragments that occurred. I saw many chalk-pits, on whose sides there scarcely appeared a single flint, while notwithstanding that, the ploughed fields and the soil above were quite full of them.

[Here omit 7½ lines to bottom of page 335, and 6½ lines on page 336, recording the superstition of Mr. Ellis and other farmers, that lumps of chalk exposed to the sun and rain hardened into flint.] I made the suggestion that the flint might lie in the middle of the lumps of chalk, and that no one had seen it before it came out on the field, when the air, rain and sun, reduced the chalk itself to a fine meal [which is clearly the true explanation of the appearance of angular flints ' in places where they knew that no flints had been before and which afterwards, when the chalk had lain some time were found full of flints.'] But they answered that then they would meet with a large number of flints in those chalk pits where the chalk is dug or hewn loose for manuring the fields, but they had not found such, or only very few. It is not every kind of chalk that undergoes this change, but it must be a particular sort, because when chalk is carried on to the fields for manure the greatest part of it goes to pieces to a fine meal or mould after it has lain some time on the field in the open air; but only certain pieces of it are left to lie and harden, without thus going to dust, but what kind of chalk this is I cannot say.*

---

* There is no foundation whatever for this story of the farmers beyond that on clayey parts of the fields on to which they therefore carried chalk, flints afterwards appeared in the manner suggested above by Kalm. [J. L.]

It cannot be the harder kind of chalk which is here called *Hurlock,* because we observed near *Ivinghoe* that there occur scarcely any flint fragments where an abundance of the *Hurlock* lay on the fields . . . . . [Omit nearly 2 lines] . . . Fields situated on the north side of a hill were commonly less full of flints than those on the south side [Omit 3½ lines to bottom of p. 336, and 9 lines on p. 337, where Kalm adverts to the possibility of flints being carried on to the fields with the chalk manure, and to the practice of picking flints off the fields and laying them in heaps.]

[T. I. p. 337.] When ordinary chalk comes to lie exposed to the weather or becomes wet, it sometimes hardens so that no one can write with it. Besides what has just been advanced, it seems to be tolerably clear that both the chalk and flints behaved so, for we found in some places on the fields large pieces of chalk, which were quite hard, and when we broke them to pieces, they consisted of chalk all through. Others of them had at the centre a flint the size of a pea, or of a bean, others as large as a hazel-nut, and others still larger; but all that which was outside this flint was a hard and half-petrified chalk. This went by degrees, so that from a flint the size of a pea at the centre, and all the rest a hard chalk around it, it went to a flint the size of a closed fist, and still larger, in the middle, so that at last there was only an outer crust of this hard chalk of some ¼ inch thick. . . . [Omit 2 lines.] We saw and collected several pieces in which we could plainly perceive, to all appearance, the whole process from a black fully developed flint at the centre to a loose chalk at the outer surface, and all grades of hardness between these two points, ripe flint and [T. I. p. 338] loose chalk. A great number of flints on the fields had a white chalk-crust, **Krit-skârpa,** round them. Several flints were entire and of the same

quality throughout. Sometimes flints were found of all
kinds of curious shapes, which resembled goats'-horns,
spigots, etc. In some pieces appeared traces of bivalve-
shells, **musselskal,** especially of the kind called
Pectinites.

When a flint has lain a long time in the sun it acquires a white colour on the surface like a burnt flint,
Kisel-sten, and in some places among the white it has
a bluish colour. In chalk-pits there are often seen *strata*
of an entirely different colour, viz., of **tegel-färgade
jorden eller svartmyllan ôfverst,** the brick-coloured
earth or soil on the top, which is a sign that these districts in former times stood under water; for in deep
chalk-pits, **Krit-gropar,** there sometimes occur two or
more *strata* of such brick-coloured earth with several ells
pure chalk above and between them.*

The 15th April, 1748.

In the morning we set out on the journey back from
Little Gaddesden to Woodford, in Essex.

The whole of the time we stayed at *Little Gaddesden*
we got to learn a great deal more of English rural
economy from the farmers than from Mr. Ellis, who was
very *jaloux* and 'close' about the little he knew of the
subject. When we first came to Little Gaddesden he
had his *four-wheel-drill-plough* which stood out on the
farm; but directly afterwards it was locked up, so that I
did not get to see it any more than when Mr. Ellis, with
two carls, devoted a whole afternoon to sowing out with
it about a pint of seed. When we took our leave, he
gave me a leaf written full of various of his so-called

---

* These latter earth beds are 'pipes' in the chalk. The explanation of
the flints on the surface, and their absence in the pits is that the latter are dug
in the middle chalk which has very few flints, and that the hills are capped
by upper chalk which has many. [J. L.]

receipts.　For example, 'How to prepare an excellent
manure for arable fields.'　'How several [T. I. p. 339]
cattle diseases may be cured,' &c. ; but he did not disclose the method how all this is to be set going with so
much advantage, but set forth only at what price he sold
one and all of these *Receipts*.　Most of them cost 100
dollars (copper pieces); but then the purchaser was
obliged to swear never to disclose the same to anyone
else.　It is a pity that the man had so short a memory
that he himself forgot to practise these receipts on his
own farm and land, for his arable fields and meadows did
not look as if they answered to that which was promised
in these surpassing receipts.　He offered to make with
me a tour through several counties in England of fourteen
days' duration, to instruct me in English Rural Economy,
and for all this inconvenience to him, he demanded no
more than that I should only keep him a horse, pay his
expenses, and find him in everything he required on this
tour, together with twelve or fourteen guineas into the
bargain.　I thanked him for his attention, and asked him
to defer this tour till another time.　Nevertheless, I asked
after all, that he who had travelled so much about in
England in the places where the best English sheep and
choicest English wool were found, and now also had three
tracts on the management of sheep ready for the press,
would let me know what districts and kinds of grass they
are in particular, which the sheep eat and flourish so well
upon ? and again what the plants are which are so baneful or injurious to sheep ? because this is one of the principles of the management of sheep.　Mr. Ellis stood for
a little time at this, and remained silent ; but in the end
said that he had never given it a thought.

GRAVESEND.

[T. I. p. 475.]

N the 30th June, 1748, we left London at 3 p.m. in the so-called ' Gravesend Tilt-boat ' for Gravesend, where we arrived at half-past seven in the evening. It is a great convenience for travellers to go by this boat. A single person only pays 9d. for the passage down to Gravesend, or for the up voyage from Gravesend to London, but if he has anything more to convey, it is increased to a shilling for one person, or more according to what he may have to take with him.

The moment the water at London Bridge is at its highest, and begins to turn to go back with the fall, this boat sets out, after giving notice for an hour previously by ringing a little bell, that those who wish to accompany her shall go on board. In this boat there is a most comfortable seat. A tilt or shelter is put up over it [T. I. p. 476] so that one has no fear of rain. If the wind is

343

with the boat, it goes all the faster for the tilt; if it is against her, they avoid it as far as regards the tilt, by lowering the same. We now went on before down to Gravesend, there to wait for the ship, which was soon to follow, and in the interval we had the opportunity of seeing the country round Gravesend.

The 1st July.

The country round Gravesend is at once the prettiest and the most delightful that can be imagined. It goes here in hills up and down, all divided into small ploughed fields, meadows, pastures, gardens, **trägârdar,** &c., by quickset hedges, **lefvande häckar.** The hills are mostly of chalk, **krita.** The whole south side of the Thames consists of bare chalk, and here there is one chalk pit beside another, where chalk and flint are taken.

Papaver erraticum, 428 [P. Phœas, *Red Poppy*] was here among the wheat and beans the rankest weed. I have never seen it in such abundance as here in the arable fields, for its beautiful red flowers seemed absolutely to cover the fields, but for small pleasure or profit to the owners, because it both smothered the crop, and was, for its untold multitudes of seeds, next to impossible to eradicate.

The 2nd July.

Jord-vallar vid brädden af Thames.

Earth-walls on the banks of the Thames.

In the afternoon we walked along the *earth-walls* which were cast up on the banks or sides of the river Thames to prevent the water at high tide from overflowing the adjacent meadows on both sides of the river. It is well known that at this place there is ebb and flood, **ebb och flod,** *fluxus et refluxus maris,* so that the water in the Thames stream for six hours falls rapidly [T. I. p. 477] outwards and goes lower, and for the next six hours the river rises and becomes very high, in some places often 12 feet and more perpendicularly higher than it was six hours before. The land which lies on both sides of the river is for the most part flat, **flakt,** level, **slätt,** and low, **lâgländt,** so that if there were no obstacle, **hinder,** when the river is high, the water would go over all the land round about, for an English mile on both sides, and sometimes more. They * had, therefore, when

---

* ' They.' ' De hade derföre.' Kalm, in using the word ' De,' has no suspicion of the difficulty in proving who ' De' were. Camden, Dugdale, and others of the Old Antiquaries, regarded the embankments of the Thames as Roman work. There is one positive statement, to which Lambarde drew attention (*Peramb. of Kent,* written 1570, Pubd. 1576). It is in the Folio Vellum MS. *Augustin[i] Ecclesiæ Cantuar. Annales,* Corpus Christi Coll., Cambridge, 301, 1. Fol. 96, *bottom line.* ' A° Mcclxxix.°,' after other entries, ' Eodem anno inclusus erat primo mariscus de Plumstede per Abbatem de Lessnes mari,' the last word being at the top of Fol. 97. Again, on Fol. 103, *line* 6, ' Anno Mcclxxxxiij,' occurs the entry, ' Eodem anno inclusus est mariscus de Plumstede.' The entries are in abbreviated Latin, and the *Annales* end at the year 1316. I copied the extracts by the kindness of the Rev. S. S. Lewis, [Alas! I must now add 'the late' 1891], Fellow and Librarian, C.C.C. Cant., on May 20th, 1886. The words, ' primo' and ' mari,' under the year 1279, are positive. The marshes referred to extend from Plumsted to Earith. The Manor of Plumsted was given by William the Conqueror to S. Augustin's Monastery, Canterbury (see ' Carta Willelmi Conqs. de Manerio de Plumstede,' in Thos. of Elmham, *Hist. Monast. S. Augustini Cantuar,* Chron. and Memor., 1858, p. 350). The Lands of Lessness Abbey were given, on its foundation, by S. Augustin's Monast. to the Abbot of L. out of the Manor of Plumstede. Wm. Thorn, who had been a monk of S. Augustin's, and who wrote his ' Chronica' of Canterbury some fifty or sixty years after the events recorded, and whose *Chronica* was printed by Roger Twysden (*Hist. Ang. Scriptores X.,* Lond. MDCLII., p. 1930, b.), tells us, Cap. XXVII., that " In the year 1281 a final agreement was made " between the Abbots of S. Aug. and Lesnes concerning an advowson claimed by both. " At length these contentions were settled as follows : The Abbot of S. Aug. ceded, and gave up all right to the advowson " . . " and for this recognition the Abbott of Lesnes conceded for himself and his successors that they at their own expense after the year next to come ' *intrabunt mariscum* de Plumstede et Lesnes will *inclose from the sea* the marsh of Plumstede and Lesnes,' that is to say, the whole tract which lies towards the east, ' inter gutteram de Borstall, et novam Wallam,'

the water was low and it was ebb, cast up on the Thames banks high and strong earth-walls which prevent the water overflowing the country inside the walls, which is mostly bare meadow land and pastures.

The breadth of these walls or banks down at their base was 4, 5, or 6 fathoms, the height above the plain 1½ fathoms, the width at the top about 1 fathom, sometimes barely 4 to 6 feet, so that they on both sides diminished gradually in width from their base to their top. Outside, against the river at the base of the wall, pile-work, **pålverke,** which they took from old ships, was driven down compactly together, everywhere one row thereof. But in some places were two rows of such pile-work, one a little within the other. Immediately within the piles were laid a large number of lumps of chalk,* together with large flints, to bind the wall against

---

* "Tiers of piles driven close to each other, in rows about 18 inches apart, row from row, the foot of one tier being nearly even with the middle of the piles of the tier below, and the space between the tiers filled with chalk or stone, and these *rooms*, as they are called, succeeding each other, from the bottom or foot of the bank to its top." Wiggins' *Embanking Lands from the Sea* [p. 215, Ed. 1867], Weale's Series, 1852, 12mo. [J. L.]

---

between the gutter of Borstall and the *new* wall which Johannes Renger made in Heyflete, *which wall* they will for one month following maintain, 'contra mare,' *against the sea* at their own cost," &c., &c. It seems as though Joh. Renger had finished his portion of the wall necessary to complete the *inning* of this large tract of marsh before the Abbots had done quarrelling, and that the original inning took place in 1279 according to the *Annales*, and 1281 according to Thorn. These marshes lay drowned again, through the breaches formed in 1522 (probably from the rotting of the wood of the 'water-gangs' under the walls) for seventy-five years, or till 1606. Lambarde, writing in 1570, says : 'The Great Breach is not yet made up' (*Peram* Ed., 1826, 8vo., p. 396). As many other breaches from the same cause occurred for two centuries or more up to the beginning of the 18th century on both sides of the Thames, it is probable that all of the Thames walls so breached within that period are of the same epoch. As far as I know there is no other record of the first making of a wall hut this. [J. L.]

the attacks of the water. In some places these walls
were 3 good fathoms higher than the meadows, ploughed
fields, and pastures, lying within and behind them ; and
1½ fathoms higher than the water at ordinary high tides
in the river. Sometimes there was double and sometimes treble pile-work outside the wall against the river.
The rest of the wall itself was made of the earth which
they had dug on the spot. Here and there [T. I. p. 478]
was some opening under the walls to the meadows,
through which the water could be made to go either to
or from the meadows. These small *water-gangs*,* **vatten-
gång,** which on both sides were built in with boards
had a *sluice*, **damluka,** which could be taken up and let
fall again. These *sluice gates* were fastened with locks, that
wanton people could not take them up, and lay the whole
country near the river under water. The *flat land* which
lay inside the earth walls was laid out either as meadows
or pasture, or also in some places where it was a little
higher, as ploughed fields. Here and there it was inter-
sected with *runnels* and *dikes* to lead off the water, and
drain the sour and low land. It was pleasant to go on
this wall and see, that when the water in the river stood
at its highest, the land and meadows, together with the
ploughed fields immediately inside the wall, were much
lower than the surface of the water in the river. It was
also at high water a pleasure to see how great ships in
the river were moving at a much higher level than the

---

* **Vattengang,** 'Watergang' is the word used in the old Ordinances.
Thus, in the suit of Godfrey le Fauconer, *re* Romney Marsh, 43 Hen. III.,
1259, Defdts. plead "that distress taken for repair of those banks and
Watergangs was justly made." (Dugdale *Embanking and Draining*, 1652,
c. xi., p. 21, Ed. 1772.) So also in *Ordinances* of John de Lovetot (p. 24),
1288 ; and, of the Thames, the *Ords.* of Henry de Apeldrefeld, 1290, respecting *inter alia* 'banks and *watergangs*' (*ib.* p. 27); and many other Ordinances
in Dugdale. [J. L.]

land itself, which at a little distance made a pretty appearance. On the meadows inside the wall grew a
beautiful grass. It sometimes happens that when there
is an unusually high tide the water in some places breaks
through these earth-walls, overflows the whole ' level,'
fälten, or plain around, drowns cattle and other animals
which go on the meadows, sweeps away the hay, and
beyond this, does much other damage. There are, therefore, certain persons appointed, whose duty it is not only
annually to examine whether the dam or earth-wall,
dammen eller mullvallen, is in all places strong and
properly maintained, and where it in any place needs
repair, to cause that to be effected without delay, but
they have also their assistants, who in short, daily walk
along the wall, and look whether the water [T. I. p. 479]
is beginning to damage the earth-wall in any place, so
that the damage may be able to be prevented and cured
in time.

The sides of the walls were almost everywhere covered
with. **qvickrot,** *Triticum,* 105 [T. repens] *Couch-grass,*
Quickens, Twitch, or *Stroil,* which grew here very luxuriantly to 30, 36, or 42 inches high, and thick enough.
In some places it was cut, in others left. Where it was
cut, which was done by those who owned the meadows
adjoining, it had begun to grow again very luxuriantly,
and stood thick and green, so that this grass seems to be
an excellent thing to fasten the sides of the earth-walls
with, as I said before. No trees were planted on these
walls except a few privets, **Ligustrer,** which had established themselves on the inner side. On top of the walls
grew plenty of *Gramen Murinum* J. B. [Hordeum murinum, wild barley, wall-barley], but it was now mostly
withered away. If these earth-walls did not exist, the
river Thames would always look like a very large lake
when the water in the river flooded the whole tract. In

one place and another a piece of land [called ' Salting ' or ' Saltings '] has grown up outside the wall, which, when it is large, is often taken in within the walls by this means. A new wall is built outside it, and the old one inside is torn down ; but this must be with the consent of those who have the direction of the walls.*

Nyttan af Flint-sten. *The use of Flints.*

The whole country at this border, mostly consists of bare chalk, in amongst which is found a great number of flint-stones, both large and small. In the *Chalk pits,* **krit-groparna,** these flint stones are collected together from the chalk, laid in great heaps, and sold to strangers, who on the voyage from London often take a large quantity of them in passing. Here, in Gravesend, the streets were paved entirely with flints.

On the S.E. side, about an English mile from Gravesend, was a very ancient church,† which [T. I. p. 480] in short, was entirely built of bare flints, except that they had used *Portland* stone for the frames and arches around doors and windows,‡ and in some places § covered the tops of the walls with it. Some *Portland stone* was also here and there built into the walls.

Tegel-bränneri. The *brick-kiln* thus seems to have

---

* The Commissioners of Sewers. [J. L.]

† St. Peter and St. Paul's Church (Rectory), Milton Parish. [J. L.]

‡ The tower has buttresses—nearly as much Portland stone as flint. At E. end P. S. predominates. Porch on S. side alternate regular courses. E. window, now perpendicular, 8 feet 6 inches wide—an insertion—has been originally 14 feet wide. There are two original two-light windows on N. side. Cruden gives (*Hist. of Gravesend*, p. 70) a view of one, and says there were six in 1843, and that the church was built between 1307 and 1377. [J. L.]

§ Somligstads cannot refer to the *stone battlements* which then existed. Irregular patches of stone are still seen along the top of the church wall (Aug. 4th, 1887). The battlements are shown in the Frontispiece to Pocock's *Hist. of Gravesend*, 1797, which gives a view of Milton Church from the S. West. [J. L.]

been little used in this country in ancient times, for in the whole of this church, from the very bottom at the ground to the top of the tower, not one single brick, **tegel-sten,** was seen. The roof of the church was of lead.* The wall around the churchyard was built of flints for at least 6 feet, and only on the top covered with brick, which was laid so that it resembled a span-roof, **röst,** or roof of a house or church, in order that the water might run off quickly. A little S.E. of this church was an old church,† **et gammalt klöster,** of which the walls only were now standing. It was also similarly built mostly of bare flint, only that the frames and arches of the doors and windows were of Portland stone. Great trees now grew in the midst of this church.

So Time changes all things!
Så ändrar tiden alt!

In the same way a church at *Northfleet* ‡ (Northfleth) an English mile west of Gravesend in Kent, *Chadwell* church in Essex, and several other churches, were built from the ground up to the top of the tower of bare flint, except that the corners of the churches and towers together with the frames of the windows and doors were of Portland stone, and if there was any brick in these churches it could be very clearly seen that it had been inserted in later times to repair some dilapidation.

When they built a haystack in any of the chalk-pits, and the stacks here mostly consisted of *Sain Foin,*§ they first laid at the bottom on the ground, one or two beds of thick flints, afterwards dry sticks thereupon

---

* The old lead roof and the battlements were taken off in 1790, and the hideous new roof with dropping eaves erected. Pocock, *Hist.*, 1797, pp. 134 to 150. Cruden, *Hist. of Gravesend*, 1843. [J. L.]

† St. Mary's, Denton, 13th century. [J. L.]

‡ St. Botolph's Vicarage. [J. L.]

§ SAINFOIN. Kalm always always spells it St. Foin. [J. L.]

[T. I. p. 481] and then on the top the hay or Sain Foin, which was thereby prevented from taking harm from the moisture from the ground.

Near the chalk-pits several outhouse walls and garden walls were built entirely of flints, which were nearly always so placed in the wall, that after a large flint had been struck in half, the perfectly black and even, or fractured face was turned outwards ; but the round and white side, which before was the outer surface of the stone was set inwards in the wall. In many places flints were carried out on to the roads for their repair.

The 3rd July, 1748.

Âkrar. *Ploughed Fields.*

The whole country around *Gravesend* was like a chain of hills on whose sides the *ploughed fields* lay.

They were middling large enclosures, **täppor,** mostly surrounded with a *hawthorn hedge,* or also sometimes with a fence of wattled twigs or small branches. I did not notice any *ditches,* **diken,** in the arable fields, and what is more, *no water-furrows,* **vattu-fårar.** The reasons may be that there are here no winters which cause the water to accumulate, the sloping position of the fields, and the soil, **jordmon,** which does not seem to retain the water long.

Wheat, **Hvete ;** Barley, **Korn ;** Oats, **Hafre ;** Peas, **Ärter ;** and Tares, **Viciæ,** were the plants which we found sown on those ploughed fields, which were not lying fallow, **som ej lågo i träde.**

The soil was a clay of a very pale brick-colour blended with a fine sand. Some *pieces of flint* lay here and there ; no other stones were found either on the ploughed fields, or in the whole of this district. The soil was so loose that it could be ploughed in the greatest drought, when-ever they wished, without waiting for the moisture of the

second ploughing, **utan at vänta efter Snedmust.**
When the ground was ploughed up the earth fell to pieces
tolerably small, and was still further crushed to pieces
with a large and heavy *oak-roller,* of 6 feet 6 inches long,
and 18 inches or 2 feet diameter, and was harrowed,
harfvades, still smaller, first with a large harrow, and
afterwards with two smaller *harrows,* **harfvor.**

After this it was rolled [T. I. p. 482] again so that
the earth on the ploughed fields, **trädes-åkrarna,**
lay now as fine and loose as a fine mould on a bed in
a newly sown kitchen-garden. There were no **åker-
renar,** ' acre-reins,'* *i.e., strips left unploughed,* except
only an ells-breadth close to the hedges. The ploughed
fields did not lie in **teg-skifte,** or 'lands,' originally
exchangeable strips,† but entirely in severalty, **ensta-
kade.** The same was the case with the meadows and
pastures, each of which was separate from its neighbours.

Hvetet. The crop that was mostly sown here was
wheat, which by itself made three or four times as much
as barley and oats together. I saw no rye here.

Among the crops were found a great many weeds,
among which *Papaver,* 428 [P. Rheas] *Cucubalus,* 360,
[Silene inflata, *Bladder Campion*] and *Ranunculus,* 468,
[R. bulbosus] were the most plentiful.

The luxuriance of the *Wheat,* the length of the straw,
and of the ear, and the number of grains in each ear

---

* REINS. *Studies in Nidderdale,* 1872, 8vo. (p. 60). "In N. a *Reean* is
the strip that was formerly left unploughed around a ploughed field." For
other " Reins," *ib.* p. 61. [J. L.]

† For the land-division in the common fields, *see* Col. A. H. Ouvry's
transl. from the German of E. Nasse, "Agricultural Community of the
Middle Ages," 1871, 8vo. ; "Primitive Property," the Eng. *transl.* of
Laveleye, 1878, 8vo. ; and "The English Village Community," F. Seebohm,
1883, 8vo.; also "Studies in Nidderdale," 1872, 8vo. viii. "The
Reins." [J. L.]

were nowhere greater than in well-cultivated fields here in Sweden. The same can also be said about *the Barley*.

Ärtland. *Pease-land* is found in many places. *The Peas* were sown in rows. The distance between two rows was sometimes 18 inches, sometimes 21 inches, sometimes 2 ft.

In the same manner, beans were also sown in rows. This was done partly because the weeds, which both smother and draw food from the peas, could then more easily be cleared away between the rows with a hoe, **hacka;** partly because one could then conveniently go and pluck the peas without trampling them down; for it is to be remarked that the Englishmen are very much given to eating green peas in the summer ; besides that, those who live near *London,* or have the opportunity of sending green peas in the shell thither, sow a great quantity of peas for that purpose only, that they may turn an honest penny by selling them.

They had here cleaned away the weeds between the rows with a hoe, and drawn the loose mould up against the roots and stalks of the *pease plants*. The peas grow all the better for the soil being so friable and loose. No cut sticks, twigs, or anything else, were laid on the ground for the peas to creep upon and cling to, but they lay stretched out upon the bare earth.

[T. I. p. 483.] Here and there were hung up dead crows, **Kråkor,** of that sort which in the island are called *Rooks,* **Rokor** [Corvus frugilegus] thereby to strike terror into those of their relations who are left behind, more especially because this kind of bird is in England the greatest pest for the pease fields.*

---

* Montagu says Rooks are "content with feeding on the insect tribe, particularly what is called the grub-worm, which is the *larvæ* of the chaffer [? cockchafer]. But in rendering the husbandman this piece of service, it pays itself by taking some of his corn also." (*Ornith. Dict.*, 1802, 8vo. [J. L.]

Sain Foin was the kind of hay with which they here mostly fed their horses, who eat it very willingly. It was given to them either whole with all the grasses and plants which were among it, or cut up very small, like fine chopped straw, and afterwards laid in the crib for the horses.

The 4th July, 1748.

Tistels utrotande. *The eradication of Thistles.*

Here we found that the farmers were more thoughtful than in Sweden ; for in the last named place they allow the thistles, **Tistlarna,** to stand and ripen, when the wind afterwards carries about their fine seed on to all the near and distant fields, orchards, etc. Yes, who has not sometimes found them so thoughtless that when they cut rye or barley they cut away the crop round about the thistle but leave it standing,* as though they were afraid that it would otherwise have no chance of sufficiently propagating itself ! Here, in England, the farmers had entirely different ways of thinking and acting. We saw large tracts of ploughed fields, meadows or pastures where *Onopordum,* 653 [O. Acanthium, the *Cotton Thistle*] and other kinds of thistle which grew thereon had been mown with the scythe before they had well begun to expand their flowers, and left to lie and wither on the plain.

Bohvete. *Buckwheat* was sown in one and another of the enclosed arable fields.

The 5th July, 1748.

Gödning. *Manuring.*

In one place and another the manure, **gödselen,** was carried out and laid in great heaps on the ploughed fields, about 2 or 3 fathoms between two heaps. The manure consisted mostly of pieces of straw and such like stuff as

---

* " And lingering thistles the rough fields deformed." *Georgics.* Bk. 1, l. 151, *orig.*—173, Tr. J. Mason, 1801. [J. L.]

is spread under the cattle in *the farm yard*. It lay still unspread. The field was [T. I. p. 484] quite fine-ploughed. In other places they had already carried out the manure on to the ploughed fields, spread it out, and ploughed it in. We afterwards remarked that these lands now manured were made into *Turnip land*, for on the 21st July following they were sown with *Turnip seed*, after the manure had previously been spread out, ploughed in, the land rolled, and the mould worked fine.

Vicia Sativa. TARES. Several places round Gravesend were sown with *Vicia Sativa Vulgaris, semine nigro*, C.B. which stood thick, luxuriant, and very beautiful. Its length was commonly 2 feet to 2 feet 3 inches. In some places a part of this was already cut and carried away for food for the farm-horses. It seems to be a plant which it is worth while to sow and cultivate.

Fœniculum Vulgare Germanicum, C.B. [Fennel], grew as well around London as here about *Gravesend*, and also in Essex, on the hills and chalk slopes.

Bränsle. *Fuel.*

The fuel which they mostly used here in Gravesend was *Coal*, **Sten-kol,** which they could easily obtain from the *Colliers*, which daily passed close by the town when bound for London.

The Farmers, **Farmarne,** who dwelt in the country round Gravesend, and also on the other side of Essex, availed themselves most of such timber, **verke,** as they obtained annually when they cut down an old hedge and laid down a new, as before described (T. I. p. 319, *orig.*). I saw great heaps of such sticks and timber lying by the farmers' houses without reckoning what they sold, so it is worth while to have hedges.

In Essex I saw that poor people even collected a quantity of *Genista spinosa vulgaris*, Raj. Syn. 475 [Ulex Europæus, *Furze*] which they used instead of other wood.

En
Resa

Til

Norra AMERICA,

På
Kongl. Swenska Wetenskaps
Academiens befallning,
Och
Publici kostnad,
Förrättad
Af

PEHR KALM,

Oeconomiæ Professor i Åbo, samt Ledamot af
Kongl. Swenska Wetenskaps=Academien.

Tom. II.

Med Kongl. Maj:ts Allernådigste Privilegio.

STOCKHOLM,
Tryckt på LARS SALVII kostnad, 1756.

ESSEX OPPOSITE GRAVESEND.

[T. II. p. 1.] *The year* 1748.

The 6th July.

In the morning, in company with the then Pastor of
the Swedish Congregation in London, Master *Tobias
Biörck*, and an English gentleman, I crossed over the
river Thames to *Essex*, to see the country there. Directly
we were across the river there was about an English
mile of quite lowland to walk over before we came up to
where it began to be hilly.

This low-lying land has, in former times, been part of
the river Thames, but is now, through the earth-walls
and banks which are cast up on the banks of the river,
separated from the same, and turned to account, and
divided into arable fields, meadows, and pastures.

When it is *High Water* in the river, which happens
twice in the twenty-four hours, the surface of the water
commonly stands much higher than these lowland plains,
so that if the aforesaid earth-walls did not exist, the water
would then overflow the whole of them, and cause these
great plains to resemble a vast lake.

The whole of this low-lying land was [T. II. p. 2]
divided into different portions by deep *ditches* about
a fathom wide, which was done to lead off the water and
drain the land. Besides that, these *dikes* here performed

357

the same service as *hedges* or fences to hinder the cattle from coming out of the pasture-lands into the ploughed fields and meadows.

In most places these ditches were full-grown with *Reeds, Arundo Vulgaris Palustris*, C. B., which the cattle bit off as far as they could reach.

Barley was most properly sown on these lowland arable fields, and now stood very beautiful. The soil was clay, **Jordmon var lera.** A part of these arable fields was lying fallow.

They were now very busily engaged in mowing hay on the places which were laid down as meadows or grassland.

Gödning. *Manuring.*

We found here in Essex, as well as all around Gravesend in Kent, that the cattle's dung was carried out and laid either by some ploughed field or some meadow where it was thrown together in great quadrangular heaps, yet not entirely by itself, but mixed in alternate layers with turf, thus to lie and ferment into a compact mass before it came to be used on the arable fields, meadows, or gardens.

At home at the farms we saw both in *Essex* and *Kent* the manure collected and treated in the same way as we have described before at Little Gaddesden (T. I. p. 251. *et seq. orig.*)

Krita. *Chalk.*

Here and there on this side in Essex are also chalk hills of the same kind and shape as in Kent. We saw in one and another place that the chalk was carried out on to the fields, where it lay partly in, and partly spread out over, the ploughed portions of land to manure them with.

Hus. *Houses.*

The husbandmen's houses, **Böndernas hus,** here in

Essex, were built partly of bare bricks, **tegel,** partly
with cross-beams, **Korss-verke,** and bricks between,
and partly they were of cross-beams with boards nailed
over them, partly of cross-beams with laths thereon,
which were plastered and daubed over with clay and
lime. These last were only those which were inhabited
by *peasants*, **torpare,** and other poor labouring people.

The houses of the farmers, **Farmernas eller
Böndernas,** themselves were so well built that they
might well be taken for beautiful gentlemen's houses,
Herregârdar.

Taken. *The Roofs* were partly covered with tiles,
partly with straw.

Uthusen. *The outhouses,* such as **lada,*** the *lathe,*
loga,† the *lodge,* &c., also the poor people's **stugor,**‡
cottages, were commonly thatched with straw, **täckte
med halm,** in the manner before described at Little
Gaddesden (T. I. p. 202 *orig.*). This *straw-thatch* was
here made very high and very steep, so that the rain and
wet could not stand thereupon, but ran quickly off, for
which reason the thatch rotted less, and could consequently stand many more years than a flatter thatch.
They were made also thick enough, viz., sometimes
1 foot and sometimes 18 inches thickness. The walls
of some of the *lathes* were also of flint.

In some places they were now very busily engaged in
thatching.

Râg. Rye was in Kent scarce enough, so that there
were few places where any parcels of land appeared to

---

* *Laith, Lathe, shed, O.N.* Hlatha, *Swed,* Lada, *Dan,* Lade, a barn.
Gloss. to *Studies in Nidderdale.* [J. L.]

† *Lodge.* In Sussex, *an open shed* in a farmyard. [J. L.]

‡ *Stuge,* 'stuggor hvari folket-bodde,' 'cottages in which the
people lived.' [J. L.]

be sown therewith, but in Essex on this border were
nearly as many rye as wheat fields. It was now mostly
fully ripe, and the straw began to be pale enough, while,
on the other hand, the wheat which grew beside it was
only just beginning to fill the ears or to set seed into
grain, **at matas eller sätta kärna til korn,** and was
quite green.

Kyrkan. The church [West Tilbury], which lies
in Essex on a high bank exactly opposite Gravesend,
seemed very old, and was almost entirely built of *Portland
Stone*, which has been described above (T. I. p. 371
orig.)

[T. II. p. 4.] *Sain Foin.* On the hills lay several
meadows which were grown only with *Sain Foin*, which
was now cut, and lay in great cocks.

Höstackar. *Haystacks.*

The hay at the farms was also here set in such stacks
as were before described at Little Gaddesden (T. I. p.
211 *orig.*), and were in shape like *barns* or houses. In
the same way the hay is cut therefrom with a knife
specially made for the purpose.

Vattu-hoar. *Water-troughs.*

At nearly all the farms, as in Kent, so here in Essex,
they had water-troughs either to give horses the water
out of, or also to keep the water in which they would use
for cooking, which troughs were made partly of *Portland
stone*, partly also of lead. The water kept very fresh
therein.

Those of lead were commonly covered outside with
boards, because the soft lead otherwise bent outwards or
inwards, if anyone happened to strike against it.

Handskära. For cutting *Rye* and *Wheat* on this
tract in Essex they do not use a *Scythe*, as at most places

in Sweden, but small *hand-shears;* in cutting *Barley* and *oats,* however, the *Scythe,* **Lja,*** was used.

The iron of the *hand-shears* which they had, was crooked as in ours, but only about half as wide, so that it might so much the easier be able to be stuck in among the crop. On the under side they were not sharpened evenly along the edge, but they had small teeth filed with a fine file quite close together and running obliquely across the edge of the *shears.* There is no doubt that the straw must come off much faster, as well as remain steady when they are cutting it.

On the upper side it was ground quite even at the edge.

[T. II. p. 5.] **Lia.** The *Scythe* that was used here to mow grass with was very large and broad in the blade because it could not otherwise so easily overcome the resistance of the thick grass-growth which there is on a great part of the English meadows.

We measured a scythe whose blade was 3 feet 8 inches long, and $2\frac{1}{2}$ inches wide. In the evening we returned to *Gravesend.*

[T. II. p. 23.] *Essex,* **midt mot** *Gravesend.*

The $\frac{12}{23}$ *July*, 1748.

In the morning we crossed the river to *Essex* to see what there was to be seen.

Åkrar. On the lowland places, near the river Thames, some of the arable fields were now lying fallow. They were ploughed quite flat, but full of water-furrows lengthwise, about 10 feet between two furrows. *The soil* was a *grey clay,* **Jordmon var en grå lera.** Some small *Pebblestones* appeared here and there. In some

---

* The large scythe used in Yorkshire and the north is still called the 'lea.' [J. L.]

places were large plots sown with *Beans*, which seemed to thrive here better than in any place I saw in England. They were sown with open hand, and not in rows.

In several places was sown *Wheat*, which was standing beautiful. The ploughed fields were there arranged in small 'ryggs,'* **ryggar**, or ridges, 4 feet wide each, the ryggs low enough, no *reins* out on the ploughed plots. But of all crops, *barley*, **gumrik** [*Hordeum Hexastichum*, LINN. '*Kegle Korn*,' LILJA, *Skånes Flora*, 1869, I. 46], was here the most plentiful, and now stood beautiful and flourishing; the stalk's length 2 feet 6 inches to 3 feet; two or more plants from one root, in the greater number of ears twenty-seven opposite couples of grains. The ploughed fields lay in *Broad-land*, about 20 feet between the water-furrows.

All these arable fields, meadows, and pastures were separated from each other by dikes, **diken,** so that here also each farmer had his own land separated from his neighbour's, [T. II. p. 24] that he was able to look after and keep it as he best would and could.

Hafre. *Oats.*

We saw at several places in Essex large arable fields which were entirely sown with *white oats*, **hvit hafre**. Of other kinds of oats we found none.

The ploughed fields at this edge of the county were richer in soil, **svartmylla,†** than around Gravesend in Kent. The sub-soil, **jordmon,** was brick-coloured. Very many small *Pebble-stones*, and other small *fragments of flint*, lay on a great part of the arable fields in *Essex*. On some,

---

* RYGGS. "Corn riggs are bonnie."—BURNS. [J. L.]

† '*Svartmyllan*, eller den jorden, som på åkrarna låg öfverst.' (T. I. p. 204.) 'The earth which lay highest on the fields,' the *top soil* ; *lit.* black earth. [J. L.]

however, there was very little thereof. The principal
reason why, in *Essex* as well as in *Kent*, they sow a large
quantity of oats is that they fodder horses therewith.

Gârdar: Hus. *Farms: Houses.*

While we were walking about in Essex to-day we got
to see a great many *Farm houses*, Farmers **gârdar**, which
here had the same appearance as in the other places in
England where we had been, viz., that they resembled
gentlemen's houses more than farmers' houses, **at de
liknade Herregârdar mera än bondgârdar.** The
houses which the farmers themselves dwelt in were
mostly of brick, **tegel,** commonly two stories high,
roofed mostly with tiles, yet there were also a great
many that were content with thatch, which is here made
steep and thick.

The *Day-labourers*, **Dagsverks-karlar,** who mostly
are the same as **Torpare** with us in Sweden, had, in
some places, houses whose walls consisted of cross beams
with oak boards nailed on the outside.

Brick houses were on the outside washed with lime,
and white. Close to the *farm-house* was always the *lodge*
and the *barn*, **Logen och Ladan,** which were commonly
made in the same way as in Upland in Sweden [T. II.
p. 25], viz., all under one roof, the lodge in the middle,
and lathes on both sides, without any walls or divisions
between them. Both the lathes were without floor, **golf;**
but the lodge had a floor of boards to *thrash* upon, which
floor was mostly laid on the bare ground. The lodge had
large doors on both sides, that they could on one side
drive in with a whole load of corn and unload in the lodge,
and afterwards drive out on the other side. The whole
barn, both the lodge and the lathes, had walls of cross-
beams with oak boards nailed horizontally on the outside,
and a high and steep *thatch-roof* covered with straw 1 foot

to 18 inches thick. Beside the lodge, or also sometimes in front of it, they had a little *Skeeling* or *shelter*, **skjul**,* which stood on *posts*, with straw-thatch over it, at times with walls of flakes or wattles,† made of interwoven thin boughs, in which *skeeling* they kept their ploughs and other agricultural implements. Commonly also they had a similar *skeeling* for their *wagons* and conveyances. Against and up the cottage walls were often planted vines which covered the whole wall.

No *hay-lathes*, **hölador,** were used either at the farm or out in the meadows, but the hay was all stacked.

Krita. Those who lived here told us, that here and there on the banks of the Thames in Essex are *Chalk pits* ‡ where they get *chalk*, but that this chalk is not so good as that which is dug in Kent. We saw that in some places they carried out the chalk on to the fallow fields, **på trädes-åkrarna**, which mostly here lay on the hill, and that they shot the chalk there in heaps, where it was yet either unspread or also already outspread, and partly even ploughed in. [T. II. p. 26.] I asked if they used much here to manure the fields with, and how much use it was? They answered that they used it enough for manuring the fields, that it is especially good on cold ground, that when they have once manured a field with it seven and more years may pass before they manure it anew; that they had found it many times better first to burn the chalk to lime and then to carry the lime itself

---

* 'SKEELING. The bay of a barn. The inner part of a house or barn where the slope of the roof comes.' Cooper *Suss. Gloss.* 2 Ed., 1853, p. 75. SKILLING. 'A place called a S., which is what they lay turf up in.' *Chichester Smugglers*, 7th Ed., 1749, p. 14. 'A *Skilling* or outhouse adjoining to the house, wherein lumber and fuel was kept.' *Ib.* p. 41.
[J. L.]

† FLAKES. Tall *wattles*, in Sussex called *Flakes*, still manufactured 1886, in Clapham Woods. [J. L.]

‡ Chalk-pits, *e.g.* Purfleet and Grays. [J. L.]

out on to the fields, but that this is much more costly.
We saw here and there on the ploughed fields which
lay on the low-lying plain near the Thames, that they
had been manured with chalk.

Råg. *Rye.*

We noticed in the course of the day several large rye-
fields in Essex, which were now standing very luxuriant.
I asked the people if they were in the habit of baking
bread of this crop, or why they sow it ? They answered
that no others but poor people use it for bread; but the
principal reason why they sow it is that they carry it to
London where they sell it to merchants, who ship great
quantities of it abroad, to be there sold.

The soil here in *Essex*, which on this edge of the
county is very dry, sandy enough, and full of ' *Pebblestone*,'
seems almost to be more suitable for rye than for wheat.
On the sandy fields the rye stalks were 4 feet long; the
length of most ears 4 to 5 inches.

The beautiful and luxuriant rye was all sown in 20
feet wide *Broadland.*

Trappor. *The steps* which we availed ourselves of,
to mount our horses, and which have been described
before (T. I. p. 297 *orig.*) were here at almost all the
farms. [T. II. p. 27.] They had also similar ones in Kent
almost everywhere. The women had in them the greatest
convenience for mounting their horses.

Gödsel-stackar. *Manure-heaps.*

In the same way as has been before mentioned (T. I.
pp. 251, 252 *orig.*) about manure, that it is laid in heaps to
rot, we also saw to-day near every farmer's house, as well
as often out by the fields, that the manure which is collected *in the farmyard*, was cast together in great four-
cornered heaps to ferment, or rot through into a compact
mass.

Commonly, and for the most part, it was laid alternately with cattle-dung and turf or mould, so that when
they had laid a bed of turf or mould below, a bed
of fresh cattle-dung was laid thereupon, which for the
greatest part was mere *straw-litter*, **halm-byssie,*** and
so by turns turf and dung.

Very often these manure heaps lay along the margin
of some arable field to be so much nearer to hand
afterwards, for it was very seldom laid on the ploughed
fields themselves, but mostly close beside them; whereas
it would seem to have been more profitable to have
spread it on a piece of fallow field so that it might be
once for all exposed to the open air; because the places
which the manure was laid upon would be manured by
the liquid which had run down therefrom. We measured
such a manure heap arranged beside a field and found it
to be 102 feet long, 6 feet broad, and only 3 feet high,
formed alternately of turf and dung.

Genista Spinosa. Raj. *Syn.* 475. [Ulex Europæus]
Furze grew here on the *sand heaths*, **sandhedar,** in
astonishing abundance, so that it covered over nearly the
whole [T. II. p. 28] sand heath. The highest bushes
were 4 feet high. It lay here in many places cut
down, and in great heaps. At nearly every farm, **gård,**
especially at the poorer ones, were large heaps thereof,
which they used instead of other wood as fuel.

Hägnad om åkrar. *Hedges around the ploughed fields.*

The whole country at this side was, in the same
manner as at the other places where I sojourned in England, divided into arable fields, meadows, pastures, commons, &c., each of which was mostly fenced round with
a hedge of hawthorn, in which several other leaf-trees

---

* Byssie. *Mod. Swed.* Boss, *Litter.* [J. L.]

also took up their abode, as elm, oak, ash, sloe, blackberry bushes, **Alm, Ek, Ask, Slån, Biörn-bärs-
buskar,** privet, and others ; yet had the elm at all places
in England * the pre-eminence over other trees excepting
the hawthorn, of which the hedges were.

We saw here, in one place and another, hedges around
some sides of fields which consisted entirely of elm. We
also saw here and there some oak, which in *Kent*, around
Gravesend, is seldom to be seen. Neither *Beech*, **Bok,** nor
Hornbeam, **Äfvenbök** (*Carpinus*), were seen *here*, nor
have I seen any of them in *Kent* ; both of them, however,
grew in abundance in *Hertfordshire*.

In some places only had they any wattle-fencing,
gärdes-gård af sprâtar ihop vriden, such as is described on p. 14 T. II. *orig.* Moreover, the hedges were
in many places poor enough hereabouts, so that they
would not be able to stand against such outrageous cattle,
bångstyriga Kreatur, as we have in Sweden. But
in the places where the hedges were in their proper state
they could always prevent the most turbulent ox [T. II.
p. 29] or horse from entering the arable fields. In
many places they could well have such fragile fences,
because there is on the pasture-lands, for the most
part, such an abundance of good and rich bait that the
cattle need not go to seek better.

Besides that, *Swine* are mostly fed at home at the farm,
and seldom go far from it. Hence it happens that in many
places by the hedges the grass stands in the greatest
luxuriance, and is not cropped by any animal, also the
wayside plants are entirely untouched.

Sain Foin. We saw one and another enclosure,

---

* The elm is specially abundant on the London clay and Gault ; the
oak on the Weald clay ; the beech on the chalk. In the north the elm is
largely replaced by the Scotch plane, *Acer Pseudo platanus.* [J. L.]

täppa, on the hills which was sown with Sain Foin only, which, however, was now cut and carried. Those who lived in this district told us that they do not sow nearly as much *Sain Foin* in Essex as in Kent, because it will not thrive there so well as in the last named district. Can this be because* in *Kent* there are more chalk-hills and chalk-valleys, **kritbärg och kritbotten,** than in Essex? Besides this, we saw also here and there enclosures of only *clover*, which also was now cut and carried. *Sheep*, **Fåren,** were also already turned in thither to feed on the *stubs.*

Bohvete. *Buckwheat.* Here and there appeared large fields which were cropped only with *Buckwheat*. I certainly never saw it more beautiful than here. It stood now in full flower; but had not yet set seed. The soil was a dry *sandy soil*, **torr sandmylla,** full of small *pebblestones*.

[T. II. p. 30]. **Åkrar.** In all the *arable fields* which lay here on the hills, there was not a single ditch; nor were there any 'acre-*reins*' except along the sides of the hedges; but these were so narrow, that no one could go off them without necessarily going onto the ploughed part. Each farmer had his arable fields, meadows, and pastures divided off for himself without having to do with others. Some enclosures were here sown with wheat, others with *Rye*, others with *Barley*, **Gumrik**, others with *White Oats*, others with *Peas*, others were lying fallow.

I did not notice anywhere on these hills that *Beans* were ever sown except near the farms.

The fallow fields were very well cared for, and the *mould* on them was quite fine.

---

* Yes. Sainfoin is largely cultivated on the Chalk, especially on Slopes, where there is nothing but chalk soil proper. [J. L.]

On some *Chalk*, **Krita,** lay spread out, in other places
was *manure*, carried out and shot in heaps still unspread.
On the slope of a hill the fallow fields were arranged in
stitches, **ryggar,** 2 feet wide and 1 foot high, so as to
make it easier to eradicate the weeds by means of ploughing, **körning.***

Ormbunkar. *Brackens, Brakes.*

Pteris, the *Bracken*, 843 [Pteris Aquilina], had the
same bad habit, **oart,** here, as in Sweden, that when
they have once begun to grow in a field they are afterwards difficult to eradicate.† I saw to-day in several
places that it grew as well out in the fallow fields as
amongst the *Rye*, luxuriantly and in great abundance.

Ärter. *Pease.*

We saw in different places large *Pease-fields*. The
peas seemed to be flourishing. They were not sown with
the drill or in rows, but with full hand, as is common with
us. No sticks [T. II. p. 31] or branches, or such like,
were found under them, but they lay on the bare ground.
The pods were already tolerably ripe. I opened some,
but found in everyone an astonishing number of small
maggots, **maskar,** and, as it seemed, not all of one sort.
I reckoned over 170 maggots in one pod. In the most
matured pods the most maggots were found, but in those

---

*Körning, *Ploughing.* Köra is to drive, *e.g.*, the plough. Not to be
confounded with the English provincial word, ' Kerning,' from ' Kern,' a
grain, or corn. "*Kerning ground* is that which, drest well, will produce a
great quantity of *corn*, as gravel does, when others will run more into
straw, and less *corn*." Will. Ellis. *Practical Farmer*, 4th Ed. 1742, 8vo.
p. 169. [J. L.]

† To eradicate *Brackens.* In Abkhaziya the bracken "grows in one
" month to a greater height than a man on horseback. If they mow the fern
" for three years in succession in the spring, when the scythe can still take hold
" of it, then the plant perishes." From the Russian of Vladikin's "Kavkaziya,"
Moscow, 1874. 8vo. [J. L.]

which were little matured few were seen, and in most cases none. Some of the fully ripened pods, however, were also free from maggots.

On one other *Pease-field* where the *Peas* were still very little matured, we could not find any maggots in the pods. It may possibly happen that the insects, which had been the origin of the many maggots just described, had already closed their short life and were dead when these later peas began to flower, and they thus escaped this *vermin*. Lucky is he who so can sow his seed that the insects, which use to cause this damage in the fields and the country, come either too early or too late.

In the evening we returned home to Gravesend.

GRAVESEND.

[T. II. p. 5.] **Mjölkens Ansning, &c.** *The Dairy.*

Here in *Kent* the farmers or husbandmen keep only a few *cows*, so that they have not any more milk than they require for their own households. When the milk is newly milked, they sile* it in four-cornered boxes of lead. The length of such a milk-box, **mjölk-låda,** is about 2 feet to 2 feet 6 inches. Sometimes they are of the same length and breadth, the depth about 4 inches. When this box is siled in the morning nearly full of milk, it is left to stand so for twenty-four hours, or till the next morning, when the cream is skimmed off, **då gräden skumas af,** but the remaining *sour milk* is used either for the people, or, as mostly happens, it is given to the swine.

In the same way, the milk that is siled one evening is skimmed the next, so that in the summer they never leave it to stand longer in the box than twenty-four hours,

---

Sile, a milk strainer. Sile, v. *to strain*, as fresh milk from the cow, v. n. to sile down, to fall to the bottom, or subside. North. & Lincoln ; Grose, Prov. Gloss. [J. L.]

but in the winter they allow it to stand for thirty-six
hours, so that of the milk that is siled in the morning the
cream is not taken off before the evening of the next day.
From this cream *butter* is afterwards churned.

I related to the English women how long we in
Sweden let the milk stand before we take the 'curds,'
filet, off it, when they answered that we could not in
this way make such [T. II. p. 6] good butter as they.
For they said they had proved that when one churns
butter of such a cream as is taken off so sour a milk, the
butter, has not one-half of the delicious and agreeable
flavour, **smacken,** that the English generally has. A
butter churned from so very thick a milk they here called
girughets Smör, 'rank butter,' *lit.* 'butter of avarice.'

They believed also that as much butter can be made
of *sweet cream* as of *sour.* They never let the milk stand
here in England so long that it becomes like our
filbunkar [flat wooden dishes of curdled milk] with so
thick cream and milk. Moreover, they do not know
here what a **filbunka** is. They said that they use
leaden vessels to sile the milk in, because in summer it
keeps fresher therein. I asked if they did not use *wooden
vessels* to sile milk in ? They answered, 'no,' because an
acid settles in the wood and corrupts the milk, which
acid they cannot so easily wash away.

The leaden vessels are well washed with warm water
every time they are used, so that not the least milk or
acid therefrom is left in them, because it would corrupt
the cream and consequently the butter.

Very little or no *cheese,* **ost,** is made in this part of
Kent.

In *Essex* they have a large number of *cows* and *cattle.*

Kärnan. The *Churn** which they use is a tun lying

---

* The Churn is still called Kern in Yorkshire. [J. L.]

2B 2

horizontally upon a frame, larger or smaller according to
the quantity of milk they have for it, and has narrow
boards set inside lengthwise, full of holes to work the
cream more.   This Churn is turned round with a winch-
handle.

The 7th July, 1748.

Gäss. *Geese.* The story was related to me to-day by
those who said they themselves had seen it, that in
Lincolnshire [T. II. p. 7] and in other places in England,
once a year, viz., in the summer-time, nearly *all the
feathers and down are plucked off living geese,* which after a
time again get new down and feathers in the place of the
old ones ; although they will look disfigured enough at
first, when they are newly plucked.   Those who have
this custom with their geese pretend that the down and
feathers which are plucked off the goose whilst it is living
will have the property that when they are laid in a bolster
and anyone lies upon it so that they become crammed
together, as soon as one gets out of bed, they will
immediately spring up again and expand themselves to
the same height as before, so that it will be scarcely
observable whether anyone has lain in the bed.   Such
elasticity will this down have !   At least there will be a
very great distinction in this respect between those which
have been plucked from a goose while he was alive, and
after he is dead.   Here in *Kent,* as in *Essex,* there are
geese enough bred by the *farmers;* likewise *ducks,*
Anckor.

At få Kalf-Kött hvitt. *To make Veal white.*

Here in England, the county of *Essex* is particularly
noted before other counties for its *Calves,* which have a
very excellent, fat, very tender, and very white flesh.
And that it may become so much the whiter, I saw
during my visit to *Woodford,* that the Farmers, or rustics,

used to lay a great piece of chalk in a trough where they had their *fatted calves,* that the calves might lick it, which in their opinion will have the effect of making the flesh become whiter.

But besides this way, there was to-day related to me another trick, viz.:—If they slaughter a calf, say, at six o'clock in the evening, in the usual way, then they stick him in the neck, and let the blood run so nearly out of him that he is [T. II. p. 8] almost dead. When they see that no great quantity of blood is left, they stop the blood so that it can run no more, and that the calf comes round somewhat ; then let him so live till the morning of the following day, when they always slaughter him. A calf slaughtered in this way is said to have much whiter flesh than if they had slaughtered him in the ordinary way, and killed him all at once.

The learned Dr. Lister also gives an account of this in his Journey to Paris, p.m. 157.

Smör. *Butter.*

In Canterbury, in Kent, butter is not sold by the pound or by weight, as is the custom everywhere else in England,* but it is made rectangular and flat as a board, and is sold by the yard,† **efter alntal.** The butter in

---

* This is not quite accurate. In Plot's *Nat. Hist. of Staffordshire,* 1686, c. III., p. 108, 3 :—"*Limestone Hills.* . . . The butter they buy by the pot, of a long cylindrical form, made at Burslem in this county, of a certain size, so as not to weigh above 6 lbs. at most, and yet to contain at least 14 lbs. of butter, according to an *Act of Parliament* made about 14 or 16 years agoe." There was a Surveyor appointed in consequence of the "tricks and cheats" practised, whose duty it was to probe the butter-pots with a long "butter-boare" to see if they were packed full, "*so that they weigh none* (which would be an endless business), or very seldom." The *Act of Parliament* referred to was passed in 1674, 14 Chas. II., c. 26, "Packing of butter." *Repealed* 36 Geo. III., c. 86, s. 19, 1796. [J. L.]

† In Mexico and California "jerked beef is sold by the *vara* or *yard,* as *butter* is sold at Cambridge in England."—Flack, *Prairie Hunter,* p. 88.
[J. L.]

Essex is said to be a good deal better and nicer-flavoured than that which is made in Kent, at least better than that which is to be had around Gravesend.

Krita til husväggar. *Chalk in house walls.*

At a farm, **en by,** which lies not far from one of the chalk pits, we saw an outhouse whose walls were entirely [T. II. p. 9] built of chalk, which they had cut into quadrangular pieces. It was only at the corners of the house, and at the doors and the window openings that they had built with *brick.* One and another of these *chalk bricks,* **Kritstenar,** if I may so call them, was partly injured by the air, and was beginning to fall to pieces ; but most of them were flat and uninjured. The house seemed to have stood from 8 to 12 years.

Hedera. Ivy. At several Farms *Hedera arborea,* C.B. [H. Helix] grew close against the walls, up which it clambered, and often entirely covered long walls, which, in consequence, looked very pretty. In like manner it clad in many places walls around churches, houses, and gardens. The walls of the before mentioned old church [Denton Church] were for a great part overdrawn with ivy.

Vinranckor. *Vines.*

At very many houses in *Gravesend,* and at a great many of the *Farmers'* and other houses, rich as well as poor, round about the country, they had planted *vines* on the sides of the houses and cottages which looked towards the south, **mot solen,** * and whose walls at this time of the year were almost covered with them.

Kersbärsträn. *Cherry trees.*

Kent is the district that has the name for this, that

---

* "Turn not your vineyard to the setting sun." *Georgics* II., 298, *orig.* 331, *Tr.* Mason, 1810, 8vo. [J. L.]

therein grow not only the best and finest flavoured *Cherries*, **Kersbär,** in England, but also, if anyone will give credit to their account, in the whole world. Whichever way one goes out of *Gravesend*, as well as farther out in the country, one sees almost everywhere near the farms, large fields and orchards, **parcker,** planted only with *Cherry trees.* In other places are found large orchards of *Apples* [T. II. p. 10] and *Pears,* **Äplen och Päron,** either planted separately by themselves or also mixed with Cherry trees. The *Cherry trees* are planted *ordine quincunciali.** The ground, **Marken,** under them lies in some places entirely in grass, **i linda,** and is used either as meadow or pasture.

On the south sidè of *Northfleet* Church was a large orchard of *Cherry trees.* The earth between the *Cherry trees* was ploughed up, made fine, and sown with wheat, which was now standing there as luxuriant and flourishing as at any place I saw on this country side. From the cultivated appearance of the soil it seemed as though they had long availed themselves of this land for ploughing. Several *Apple trees* were also planted here. The *Cherry trees* were now full of *fruit,* **bär.** The soil had apparently been well cared for, because it was not noticeable that the trees made the wheat thinner or poorer immediately under them.

When I was over in that part of Essex which lies immediately opposite *Gravesend,* I remarked that almost everywhere where I wandered about I scarcely ever got to see any *Cherry trees,* much less any whole orchard of them, and not nearly so many as around Gravesend, in Kent. This caused me to ask the people in the villages

---

* *Quincunx.* Adam, *Roman Antiquities* [1791, 2nd ed., 1792], in the 9th ed., 1822, p. 364, figures this *two deep*, that is to five parallel rows wide.

[J. L.]

the reason why they did not endeavour to plant here as many Cherry trees as in Kent, which lies close beside them, only that the river Thames divides them ? They answered that it could not well be done, because the *Cherries in Essex* never attain the same agreeable flavour as in *Kent*. Another said that because the soil in Essex is *Gravel*, **grus**, *Cherry trees* will not thrive there, **ville ej kersbärs träden der fort** ; on the other hand, *Pear trees* flourish there well.

Between *Gravesend* and *Rochester* I also saw [T. II., p. 11] a great number of *Cherry orchards* on both sides of the road, especially towards the *Gravesend* side. The Cherry trees were here planted not *ordine quincunciali*, but all in squares. The distance between two trees was 4 feet. The ground between and under the trees was entirely used up as arable, or also sown with *Sain Foin*, *Clover*, or *Tares*, *Vicia Vulgaris Sativa*, J. B. [Johann Bauhin]. To use these orchards also as ploughed fields seemed, however, to have something incongruous in it, for since the fruit ripened some weeks before the wheat, they were obliged, when they wished to have the use of the fruit, in many places round and under the trees, as well as between them, to trample down the wheat or the crop sown, which we saw happened to all *Wheat*, as well as *Barley* and *Oats*. But where the orchards were sown with *Clover*, *Sain Foin*, and *Tares* (*Vicia*), it was not incongruous, because these kinds of hay were commonly cut and stocked before the fruit was fully ripe. The English fruit-growers, **Trägårds mästare,** maintain that the fruit trees thrive best and bear the most abundant and best flavoured fruit when the soil under and between the trees is kept cultivated, **hålles brukad,** and loose, like a ploughed field, without any crops, grasses, or weeds being allowed to grow thereon. They had shot and hung hosts of dead Jackdaws, **Kajor,** *Rooks*, **Råkor,**

Crows, **Kråkor,** *Magpies,* **Skator,** &c., up in the branches of the trees to frighten away their comrades from coming thither either to scathe the trees or the crops. From these suspended, half-rotted, and stinking birds it was not difficult to know at a distance when some cherry orchard was in the neighbourhood. All through this time of the year whole boatloads of cherries of many sorts are carried from Gravesend * to London.

[T. II., p. 12.] *The 8th July,* 1748.

Åkrar. Many of the *arable fields* which were lying fallow were so full of *quickens,* **qvickrot,** 105, that it was esteemed a pity. I never saw any *ditch* in all the *arable fields* which were in the neighbourhood around Gravesend, or thereabouts, no *water-furrows,* no *acre-reins.* The lowest places were commonly sown with *Barley,* **Gum-rik,** which commonly had 12 to 13 grains in each row.

The colour of the soil also in among the *ploughed fields* was a flesh colour; the mould very loose, with enough small round and flat flintstones and bits of chalk among it. In some places it could be plainly seen that *ditches* were needed, because the water had stood there and formed boggy ground, **stannat och syrts,** so that the wheat was very thin. In many places the fallow fields had not yet been ploughed since the crop reaped on them was carried, but they lay entirely overgrown with weeds.

Vau.† 439 *Dyers' Weed, Weld.* [Reseda Luteola]

---

* The Cherry orchards have long disappeared from the neighbourhood of Gravesend. 1890. [J. L.]

†VAU. *Dan.* Vau, Vouvre ; *Ger.* Wau.—Müller *Dan. Deuts. Wörterb.* 1800 ; *Dut.* Wouw ; *Eng.* ' Weld, a kind of herb whose stalk and root is in great use for dying the bright and yellow lemon colour.'—Bailey, *Eng. Dic.* 1730. 15th Ed. 1753 ; *Fr.* Gaude. *Botan.* Reseda Luteola, *Dyer's Weed.* ' *Reseda Lut.* yields ' Weld' a yellow dye.'—Hooker Stud. Flor. 870. p. 41.

[J. L]

which is cultivated for its yellow colour, was in several places drawn up root and all, bound in small sheaves, **Kärfvar,** which were set one against another in the fields to dry, in the same way as we do with *Hemp* and *Flax.* Its seeds were still not much more than half ripe. It grew here wild, in places abundantly, in other places it was expressly planted.

The 9th July, 1748.

Ängar. The low places in Kent which at high water lay below the level of the water in the river Thames, were divided into meadows and pastures. . . . . . [T. II. p. 13.] . . . . No trees grew on these lowland meadows, but instead of hedges or other fences around them, there were deep dikes about a fathom wide, which now stood nearly full of water.

Arundo Vulgaris Palustris J.B., the *Reed* [Phragmites communis] and Scirpus 39 [S. Maritimus] or the *Sea-rush,* **hafssäv,** grew in the greatest abundance in these dikes and were considered very good fodder.

The *kinds of grass* of which the plants on these meadows principally consisted, were *Alopecurus culmo erecto* 52. [A pratensis], *Gramen Secalinum pratense elatius* (Morison) [Hordeum Secalinum] and *Aira* 67 *syn. Gramen lanatum* (Dalech) [Holcus Mollis].

These here formed the finest, thickest, and most luxuriant grass sward that anyone could wish to have on his meadow. It was now being mown here with all diligence. The pastures were divided into many parts, so that when the cattle went for one week on one pasture, the grass was growing in two or three others, where the cattle had been before : and when the cattle had been here one week, they were moved to the pasture which at the last change had been longest free from their bait.

Hence it happened to a certain extent that the grass grew between the cattle's feet!

In every pasture was commonly a little pond with sloping sides or banks, on one side of the field, that the cattle might get their water : because the banks of the dikes were designedly made so steep that they could not get at the water to drink therefrom.

On the meadows there is not the least sign of moss found, because the thick and luxuriant grass prevents such.

[T. II. p. 14.] In most places the meadows were smooth and flat without any hillocks, **tufva,** but in some places, especially higher up against the ploughed fields, were hillock, **tufvor,** enough, but small. In one and all of them which we dug asunder, was found a multitude of small yellow ants, **myror.** In several places where they had newly and to-day mown hay, we found loose mould in small hillocks, newly, and probably only this week constructed, and resembling a *mole-hill,* **mullvadshög,** but when this mould was scattered, it was found full of the before-named ants. Thus have they heaved up these hillocks, **tufvor.** But we also had the opportunity of discovering another cause for these hillocks in this situation, which was *Juncus acutus panicula sparsa,* C. B. [J. Tenax *Banks.* MS.] This grew in many places in very great abundance, and had the peculiarity of always growing in *tufts* or *tussocks,* **tufvor.** It is not destroyed by any animal on account of its hardness and roughness or bristling exterior ; it takes hold of dust, **damb,** straw, **strå,** and anything that is driven by the wind. Directly this begins to grow on the smoothest ground it makes it in a few years full of hillocks, **tufvor.**

Gödslens förmerande. *A mode of increasing the quantity of manure.*

The soil, which is dug up when the before-named dikes

are made was after some time carried home by the
farmers, where it was laid in the farm yards, alternately
with the *cattle-dung*, in heaps, to lie there and ferment
together with the same, which thus made a choice
manure.

The [Julian]/[Gregorian] $\frac{9}{20}$ *July*, 1748.*

Gärdesgârdar.   Fences.

In some places only we saw *fences*, which were made
mostly of small sprays, **sprâtar,** which wattled fences
are, in some parts of the country, very much used.   They
are made in this way [T. II. p. 15] that, instead of
placing, as we do, two staves side by side, there is only
one set by itself, which generally is not longer than the
height of the *fence*.   Between two staves there is a
distance of about 2 feet.   Instead of 'edder,' **Gärdsel,**
small *branches* or *twigs* of trees are used, which are bent
alternately in curves about the staves in this way, that
when the one *staff* has been left on the left side of the
horizontally placed *runners*, **sprâten,** the next staff comes
to be on the right side of the same, and so on.

Serratula.   Foliis dentatis Spinosis, 662, or **Âker-
tisteln,** [*S. Arvensis*, L., afterwards *Cnicus arvensis* L.
now *Cissium* (Tournefort) *arvensis*] grew in many places
in the greatest profusion in the loose mould on the walls.
In some places it was cut down, that it could not get the
chance of ripening and seeding, and so doing injury to
the neighbouring ploughed fields and kitchen-gardens.

In other places they had the mischievous practice,
common in Sweden, of leaving the *thistle* untouched, by
which it was much more easily enabled to spread itself all

---

* This is the first appearance in this work of the double or alternative
date contemplating the difference of eleven days between the Old and New
Style.—[J. L.]

around, and become injurious to the crops sown, and also
to the kitchen garden plants.

Vägar. *Roads.*

Almost everywhere on both sides of the high roads,
were hawthorn hedges planted, so that one walked or
travelled here as in an *Allée,* or in a garden.

These high roads had not the character, as with us in
Sweden, that the road lay higher than the land around,
but here exactly the opposite is the case—viz., so that
the road goes in most places deep down in the earth, to
a depth of 2, 4, or 6 feet, so that many would believe the
road was only some dry stream-course. There is commonly on one side of the road [T. II. p. 16], if not on
both sides, on the walls or the high sides, a footpath,
gångwäg, on which those who travel on foot go, so that
they are not in danger from those who drive or ride.

That *the roads* are so deep seems to come from this, that
in this country very large wagons, **vagnar,** are used with
many horses in front, on which wagons a very heavy load
is laid. Through many years' driving, **körning,** these
wagons seem to have eaten down into the ground, and
made the road so deep. On the other hand, the hedges
which are planted on both sides of the road had increased their mould, partly from dust which had been fixed
by them, partly from the leaves which they let fall yearly,
partly from the earth which is shovelled up like a little
wall against the roots when the hedge is made or laid
down. But the principal cause, nevertheless, seems to
be due to the wagons, because the arable-fields, pastures,
and meadows on the sides equally in most places lie higher
than the road. *The soil,* **jordmon,** which here consists of
sandy gravel and *pebbles,* **sandgrus och klapper,** and
which immediately absorbs water, causes these roads to
suffer little injury from rain. During heavy rain some

water runs along these roads, but it does not last long,
and, moreover, running water outside the river Thames
is here very scarce.

The ¹⁰⁄₂₁ July, 1748.

Bönor. *Beans.* On whichever side I went out
round *Gravesend* in *Kent*, I always got to see on every farm,
Farmer's **gârd,** some large beanfield. In some places
were whole large arable fields and tracts sown with beans
only. It was commonly the sort which has small and
narrow pods.

In all the places I saw them, they were sown in rows.
The distance or width between two rows [T. II. p. 17]
was uncertain, sometimes it was as much as 2 feet 6
inches, sometimes less, even to only 6 inches—which,
however, seemed too thick. It was not too much when
just 1 foot width was left between the rows.

The distance between each *Bean-plant*, **Bön-stånd,**
and the next in the row was however not the same throughout, but just as if they had been in a hurry when they sowed
them. I saw them stand one foot from each other;
sometimes, however, they had scarcely more than an
inch breadth between them. They commonly stood six
inches from each other, which space they certainly
required, if not a little more. The reason why the
Beans were sown in rows was partly that they could get
at them so much the more readily to clean away the weeds
between them with a hoe, as well as afterwards the
better to be able to pluck off their green pods, which
they send to London to be sold; partly that by casting
up the mould to the stalks they furthered the growth of
the Beans.

After the stalk had attained some length, the top was
cut off that it might shoot no more in length, but turn
all its strength on the maturing of the Beans. They

were sown at different times, whence it happened that when some plots exhibited ripe beans, in other places they were just beginning to strike out into flowers. The principal reason why there are so many beans sown here is that they feed horses and pigs with them in the winter.

The $\frac{11}{22}$ *July*, 1748.

Svartmyllans tjocklek. *Thickness of the soil.*

Near one of the chalk-pits, **krit-groparna,** was an orchard, **trägård,** which consisted partly of [T. II. p. 18] *cherries* and partly of *Walnut-trees.* Here, on one side of the Chalk-pit, they had taken away all the *soil* or *vegetable-earth* **svartmyllan eller matjorden,** which lay upon the chalk. This soil, **matjord,** was not black, but rather more of a flesh-colour. The thickness of the soil **svart-myllan eller matjorden,** was here mostly 21 inches, in some places 27 inches, in other places 18 inches and thereabout. The upper surface of the chalk was however, not horizontal, but went more like waves.

At göra Vin af Russin. *To make Wine of Raisins.*

My landlady where I had my quarters here in Gravesend, had Wine which she herself had made from Raisins, which was so good that those who wish to be thought to be judges of wines had difficulty in distinguishing it from *Madeira* Wine.

The Receipt was given me, how it is made, which was thus :—

To 100 lbs. of Smyrna Raisins are added 45 to 50 pints of water, which is afterwards stirred twice a day, for a period of fourteen or sixteen days.

Thereupon, the raisins are well pressed, and the Wine,

or the expressed juice of the Raisins, is poured into a barrel, **ankare,** which holds about 30 pints, **kannor.** Afterwards a piece of brown paper is taken and stuck full of holes, and laid over the bung-hole, **sprund hâlet.** Some of the wine, or the expressed juice, must be preserved in an open vessel to fill up the barrel, according as it works itself out, or ferments over. It must so stand till the whole of it again begins to ferment. Thereupon three *quarts* of well distilled Brandy, are added, with one pound of the best sugar, the white [T. II. p. 19] of sixteen eggs, and one ounce of alum, which has been boiled in one quart of water. All this is mixed well together, and laid in the barrel, which is well shaken about, bunged, and left to stand so for one year before it is tapped.

On the foregoing it is to be remarked : 1st. That when one begins to blend the Raisins and water together, the water is thrown into a tub, **kar,** or vat, **vatten-så,** which ought to be very clean.

While they are both being agitated together in the same vessel, **käril,** the vessel is covered over with cloths, that earth and such like may not get into it.

2ndly. The sugar and white of egg are whipped before the alum is put in, for if you were to put the alum in at the same time, it would cause the egg to coagulate. The water in which the alum is boiled ought, moreover, to stand till it is cool, before it is thrown into the sugar and egg.

At göra et svagare vin. *To make a milder wine.*

After you have made a strong wine in the foregoing manner, pour anew twenty pints of water on the pressed out raisins, and let it stand one week, after which it is pressed out from the raisins, and is poured into a fifteen-pint barrel; and when it has done fermenting there are put therein half as much Spirit of Wine, Sugar,

White of Egg, and Alum, as in the former. After three weeks' time, it may be ready to be tapped. This weak wine will not keep long, but after it is tapped and bottled, it must be drunk at once. The stronger wine becomes better and more agreeable, the longer it afterwards stands untouched, and that for many years.

[T. II. p. 20.] *Note.*—Wine so made of Red Smyrna Raisins becomes sweet; but of black Smyrna Raisins it becomes like Madeira wine.

Strata Terræ. Immediately west of Northfleet, which lies about a couple of English miles west of Gravesend, there was by the highroad a large pit, **grop**, out of which they had taken partly *Pebblestone*, to lay on the road, partly sand for different purposes.

ft. in.

1. On the top *Pebblestone*, larger or smaller, mingled with a somewhat fine brick-coloured sand, though Pebblestone formed the greater part 2 6

2. A brick-coloured somewhat fine sand, at the thickest 1 foot, but thinner on both sides till it was entirely lost in Pebblestone........................... 1 0

3. *Pebblestone* mixed with a somewhat fine brick-coloured sand, like No. 1; yet the thickness of this *Stratum* was not everywhere the same, for here in the middle it was thinnest, but towards both sides it became thicker 2 0

4. Same sand as No. 2 lost itself similarly in *Pebblestone*, otherwise the *strata* of this sand were always entirely clean and free from *Pebblestone* ... 0 6

5. *Pebblestone*, mixed with quantity enough of the brick-coloured sand 3 0

6. Same sand as No. 2, but we could clearly see that this had not come hither all at once, but by degrees, for it was divided into exceedingly thin *strata* 2 0

ft.   in.

7. A dark brick-coloured or brownish clay.
[T. II. p. 21.]   It lay in some places immediately over the chalk; in other places lay the
sand, No. 6, next above the chalk .... o   4

8. **Krita.** Chalk pebbles. This was the rarest
bed we ever saw in any sand pit. It was mostly
chalk, but nevertheless, mixed enough with small
Pebblestones.   Several pieces of chalk were externally quite smooth, shaped oval or round, and
had the same appearance, **figur**, as *Pebblestone*,
but when they were broken asunder they consisted
of bare chalk. This bed was not of the same
thickness throughout, but thinned out towards
both sides till it was entirely lost 1   3

9. A brick-coloured coarser *sand*, much mixed
with Pebblestones 6   0

10. Chalk mixed with fine light *sand*, small
Pebblestones, together with a number of broken
mussel and snail shells .... 1 ft. 6 in. to o   6

11. A quite fine light sand passing to yellow,
free from all foreign admixtures (*heterogeneis*), 4
feet thick, and who knows how far down? because
the fallen gravel, sand, &c., prevented us from
seeing farther down.

Obs.—That the *thickness* of one and all of these beds
is not uniform, but sometimes thick, sometimes thin,
sometimes entirely lost, as though someone had in former
times tipped these strata out of a wheelbarrow, which
can all be ascribed to varying directions of the currents,
and the unequal movement of the waves, storms, &c.

From this hill it may be 1 or 1½ musket shot to the
nearest *Chalk pit*, **kritgrop**, whose sides consist of bare
chalk, and which is 12 or more fathoms deep, so that
one can thus be sure that the whole of this [T. II. p. 22]

hill just described, with its many *strata*, and which lies higher than the surface of the hills near the chalk pit, most certainly overlies the chalk, **för visso står på krita.** All the hill banks, **strand backarna,** of the Thames, 1½ musket shot below this hill, consist of bare chalk, either pure or mixed with *Flints* and small *Pebblestones.**

Svin. To prevent these animals from grubbing up the ground, and entering the ploughed fields through the hedges, they were, in *Kent* and *Essex*, both ringed in the snout and bore on their necks triangular wooden yokes, exactly in the same way as is done with us here in Sweden.

Alm. *Elm.* When we were walking to-day down by the banks of the river below *Northfleet*, **Nordfleet,** where the river banks consist almost entirely of chalk, with interbedded flints here and there, with *soil*, **svartmylla,** almost of a brick colour thereupon, we remarked how the large Elms which grew in the hedges on the river banks had penetrated with their roots through the soil, which was here 2 feet thick or more, right down to the chalk; but as soon as they met the chalk they very seldom entered it, but then began to run horizontally along the bottom of the soil above the chalk. We remarked this of very many Elms. The chalk is probably too hard for their roots. It was only in one single place that I could see that a couple of Elm roots entered a fissure in the chalk for a depth of 1 foot or 18 inches

---

* The beds here described are now known as the *Oldhaven Pebble Beds* of the Woolwich Series (Whitaker), and the *Thanet Sand* (Prestwich). This section was cited by SIR TORBERN OLAF BERGMAN, (?)ˉorig. work, *German tr.* by L. H. Röhl in *Welt-beschreibung*, Th. I., cap. V., § 39., p. 114 Greifsvald, 1769–74, 8vo. And again transl. into German, incorrectly, by CARL ABRAHAM GERHARD, *Versuch einer Geschichte des Mineral-reichs.* Berlin, 1781-2, 8vo. Erster Theil, § 100, p. 190. [J. L.]

perpendicular. [T. II. p. 23.] The bank had slipped down, or been under-eaten by the water in the river, so that I could see this quite clearly in many trees.

[T. II. p. 31.]   *The* $\frac{13}{24}$ *Julii,* 1748.

Et sätt at rida. *A way of riding.*

In England they are much in the habit of practising a way of riding which is most strange, and not in use among us in Sweden. It is that two persons, the one a man and the other a woman, both sit on one and the same horse. The carl sits in front, guides and governs the horse in the usual way; but the lady [T. II. p. 32], or woman, sits behind him in the same way as women generally sit on horseback, viz., sideways. It is here common to see them so come riding, not only in small places and out in the country, but even in the middle of London; but especially in the summer time when they ride out of town for recreation.

The $\frac{14}{25}$ *July.*

Hö-bärgningen, Hö-stackar. *Hay making, Hay*
stacks.

The meadows were now in most places mown, but in some places they remained still to mow. In the fields the hay was treated in the same way as has been before named in this description of my travels, (T. I. p. 438). When it was quite dry it was set in *cocks*, **vâlmar,** 6 foot high, and down on the ground there were spread cocks from which it was afterwards carried to the place where the stacks were to be made. If the fields lay near the farm, the hay was carried home and stacked, but if they lay any considerable distance from the farm, the stack was made in the field. In the high-lying places the hay consisted mostly of Sain Foin, but in low places, of kinds of grass.

The hay is carried to the stack in wagons, but where
the fields were flat, they availed themselves of a very
handy plan, which consisted in this, that they had a rope
which was fastened to the harness or iron chains with
which the horse drew. This rope was set round about
the cock, and was turned down at the back and passed
underneath it, and afterwards the rope was fastened by a
loop to the chain, when the horse ran the whole cock to
the stack, which was then being made in the field. There
seemed to be little or no hay left behind the cock on the
field [T. II. p. 33], but the cock came almost entire to the
place. Instead of a bridge, they filled the dike with hay,
over which they drove.

Höstackarna, the haystacks are made either round
as in Fig. 1, or oblong, and in the shape of a house, as
Fig. 2.

As the hay-stack was made the hay was trodden down at
once, so that it might lie steady. At the beginning, and
while the stack is still low, they have horses on it to
trample the hay; afterwards, higher up, the trampling is
done by many men. When they have got the stack ready
in one of the aforenamed shapes, the sides L N and M O
in Fig. 1, and E F and C D G H in Fig. 2, are cut with

a knife specially made for the purpose, flat or smooth,
partly that the cattle may not so easily be able to steal
from it, partly that the rain and wet may not fasten
thereon, partly that it might look better.

I will for clearness call the upper and out-sloping
sides A E and A B C D, Fig. 2, and K L, K M, Fig. 1
'thatch,' **tak,** and the lower and in-sloping sides L N,
M O Fig. 1 [T. II. p. 34], and E F, C D G H, Fig. 2,
sides or walls. The stacks are always made so that they
are widest at the thatch-band, **tackbandet,** and grow
narrower afterwards down their sides all the way to the
bottom. This also prevents the water which comes
dripping from their thatch from rotting the walls or sides.
Now follows how the thatching is effected. They are
commonly thatched with straw, which is here taken from
the wheat, as they reckon that the best. Sometimes they
are thatched with hay, but not so often. Then they raise
a ladder against the haystack, so that it comes to lie
along the direction of the thatch. Afterwards they take
the 'baster,'* a small sheaf of straw, **halm-kärfva,** which
is bound with straw at both ends. This is laid down at
the thatch band L M, C D, in this way that it comes to
lie horizontally. Afterwards they stick a 'rick-peg' (*pron.*

---

*BASTER. A long, narrow bundle of straw about as large as one can
span with both hands, still used as described by Kalm, Sept. 1886, also for
laying along the ridge of the stack to make the crest of the straw stand erect.
At Gaddesden Row, Herts, it is *pron.* like 'Master.' Also in the form
‹ BASSE (disyll.) a collar for cart-horses made of rushes, straw, sedge, &c.'
Bailey *Dic.* 1736. *Normandy Patois, Batière,* a *packsaddle,* Fr. Bât, *Ital.*
Basto ; O.N. (*Icel*) Bastari, a *bast binder,* Fr. Bâtier, *Ital.* Bastiére, bastaio, a
pack-saddle maker.—O.N., *Dan., Swed., Ger., Dut., Eng.* Bast 'lime tree
bark made into ropes and mats.' Bailey, *Eng. Dic.* 1736. ' Bass, Bast,
matting, dried rushes or sedges.' Brockett *Northern Gloss.* 3rd ed., 1846.
Dan. 'Bast. *Ger.* Bast, damit man bindet.' G. H. Müller, *Dan-Deutsch
Wört.* 1800.—O.N. (*Icel.*), *Swed.,* Basta to *bind into a bundle,* Dan. Baste og
binde, to *bind up ;* &c. [J.L.]

' reek-peg '), a narrow stick, right through each end of this baster or small straw sheaf into the stack, that the baster may lie steady. On this baster is afterwards laid loose straw about 3 or 4 inches thick, or 6 inches, or even a little more, so that the narrow ends of the straw are turned up towards the top of the stack, and the thick are laid across the above-named baster, **kärfva,** so, however, that the ends project a little beyond the lower sides of the stack, to prevent the water which in wet weather runs down the thatch from pouring on to the sides of the stack. After they have laid the straw thus, they have ready to hand long, narrow, slender sticks [the ' rick-pegs '], which are sharpened at one end. One of them is taken and stuck in with the sharp end down in the stack, on one side of the straw already laid on, yet towards the higher part of the same. The rick-peg is then bent [T. II. p. 35] across the straw so as to lie horizontally. This horizontal part is called ' the rod.' To make it lie still, and at the same time fasten the straw, they have another **sprâta,** ' spray ' of 20 to 25 inches' length, which is sharpened at both ends, and in the middle is slightly cut out on one side, so that it can be bent together, as in the accompanying figure, without breaking off. The ' spray,' P Q R, thus bent is set into the stack in such a way that one end, P, goes in one side, and the other end, Q, on the other side of the ' rod ' or long spar laid across the straw.

The bent spray, P Q R, is then pressed or beaten down till it fastens the end of the ' rod,' and likewise presses the straw and holds it fast. Afterwards new straw is taken, and is laid above this in the manner before described, to fasten in such a manner that the large ends of the new straw come to lie above and to cover the small ends of the straw previously laid below, and the same with the 'rods' which were laid across it. On this new straw no rod was set, but they take still another lot of straw and set it a little higher up, and then it is first fastened with a long 'rod' across, in the same way as has been described before. In this way it is continued upwards till one comes to the top, and there also fastens the straw. After that the ladder is moved a little more to one side, and the thatching is begun again down at the thatch-band, in the manner before described, tight in to that which is already thatched, and is continued so upwards. The row which is thatched every time [T. II. p. 36] from the bottom of the thatch, **takfoten,** up to the top before the ladder is changed, is as broad as the carl can reach to lay when he stands on the ladder. One or two carls are down below, who prepare the straw and give it up to the one who is thatching, who lays this straw near him till he requires it. That he may have the straw so much readier to hand, he has two pieces of stick of 2 to 3 feet long, which he sticks into the stack in a horizontal line, about two feet from each other. Above and against these the straw is laid ; but if it blows hard, he has still beside these, two other sticks, each about two feet long, sharpened at one end, and fastened together by a string, **et band,** at the other, as in the figure.

He sticks these pegs, **käppar,** into the stack, the one on the lower side of the straw, and the other on the upper side, when the string which is between them comes to lie across the straw, and holds it tight so that it cannot blow away. As soon as the carl has laid two rows of straw, or changed the ladder twice, he has a somewhat thick stick, **käpp eller kafle,** about four feet long, with which he beats down the straw to make it lie even, and afterwards smoothes down the straw with it,

beginning above at the top of the stack, and so downwards, when he also sweeps away all the loose straw
which lies on the stack, and makes the straw-thatch on
the whole smooth. After that he continues [T. II.
p. 37] to thatch the upper part of the roof of the stack,
in the manner before described.

The lower sides, B D and C E, never stand perpendicular, but are always made so that the higher they get
the farther they project outwards, so that the stack is
narrowest down at the ground, and broadest up at the
thack-band. Both the round and square have this
peculiar shape, which prevents the water that drips down
from the bottom of the thatch from falling on the lower
sides and rotting them. No pole is set in the middle of
a stack, as with us.

In some places they make very large and high stacks.
When the stack becomes so high that they can no longer
reach to cast the hay from down below up to the carl upon
the stack, there is built on one side of the stack a
scaffold of boards, or a door which lies on two poles, on
which a carl places himself, to whom the hay is first
cast, and who afterwards sends it farther up on the stack.

When the stacks are thatched with bare hay, sometimes also when they are thatched with straw, they are
often made smooth on the surface with simply a rake,
räfsa, so that they, as it were, comb down the top of
the stack with it. The shape of the haystacks and the
manner of making them was everywhere in this district
the same as I have now described. Most haystacks were
here thatched with straw.

Up at the summit of the haystack the spars always
lie bare and uncovered, and thus come to be seen there.
The stacks were always so arranged that the thatch was
very steep, for the rain and wet to be able to run off
so much the quicker. The *pitchforks*, **Järngafflarna,**

they used were of different sizes and lengths. In those with [T. II. p. 38] which they cast the hay up on to the stack, the pitchfork, **järngaffeln,** itself was 1 foot long and 6 inches between the ' grains ' or ' tines,' * **grenarna,** fastened to the handle with an iron ring, as on an ice-pick, the shaft two fathoms long, or as long as one wishes. The small forks, to toss the hay on the meadow, were 6 inches long, and 4 inches between the ' gaffles ' or ' tines,' **gafflarna,**† the length of the shaft at will. The tines or prongs on all these forks were not straight, but slightly curved, **Grenarna på alla dessa gafflar voro ej rake, utan litet krokuta.** A figure of such a *hayfork*, **högaffel,** can be seen in Linnæus's *Skånska Resa*, p. 303, fig. *b* [Stockholm, 1751. 8vo.]. When they here made a haystack, there commonly stood a carl who, with one of the before-named pitchforks, **järntjufvor,** pitched up the hay. One or two carls received it, and spread it out evenly on the stack, as they found it best. Afterwards there were commonly four lads who did nothing else than constantly trample it. The lower sides, or the lower parts of the stack, were made smooth with a rake, and the hay was also raked off, so that the stack in its lower parts might be so much narrower, and wider upwards.

The $\frac{13}{24}$ July.

In the morning we walked from *Gravesend* to *Rochester*, which lies 7 English miles from the first-named place.

Utsigten af Landet. The appearance of the country. We had the whole way a variety of ploughed

---

* ' *Tine* the *grain* of a fork ' (Bailey, *Eng. Dic.* 1736), *i.e. branch* or *brong.* [J. L.]

† ' Gaffle, part of a crossbow.' *ib.* [J. L.]

fields, meadows and orchards, all planted round with hawthorn hedges, in which stood all kinds of foliaged trees, **löfträn**, such as Elm, **Alm,** Elder, **Fläder,** Blackberry-bushes, **Björnbärsbuskar,** Ash, **Ask,** Oak, **Ek** [T. II. p. 39], Dogwood, **Benved,** or Cornel (*Cornus*), Aspen, **Asp,** Ivy (*Hedera Arborea*, C. B.) [H. Helix], Sloe, **Slån,** Privets (*Liguster*), the Spindle-tree, **Alster,** *Euonymus* [Europæus], Maple (*Acer Campestre minus*) C. B.

Here and there lay some beautiful farm. The country here, as in most places where we were in England, was not even and flat, but a continuous chain and variety of somewhat high and long-sloping hills, with valleys between. These hills had all sorts of shapes, sometimes round as rye-bread loaves, sometimes oblong, and of various other shapes. The *inclosures*, or ploughed fields and meadows, lay on the tops and the sides of the hills, as well as down in the valleys, **dälderna.** In some places these hills were steep enough. They all consisted of bare chalk, which had only a coating of soil upon it, of 9 inches, 1 foot, 15 inches, or 18 inches, yet in most places not more than about 1 foot thickness, which we could plainly see the whole way where the high road crossed these hills and they had been digging on the sides of the road; to say nothing of the fact that the same appeared in all the chalk-pits, **kritgropar,** which were dug here and there. On the whole of this walk we could not see the least sign of any flowing and running stream or river, excepting the river *Medway* (Midway) which passes by Rochester. Such running water seems to be very rare on the chalk hills and in their neighbourhood.

The greater part of the *inclosures*, or **täppor** planted round with hedges, which we saw to-day were ploughed fields, sown partly with *Wheat* (*Triticum hybernum aristis carens*, C.B.), *Barley*, **Gumrik,** *White Oats* [T. II. p. 40],

Beans, or *Pease.* I do not know of which ot these kinds there was most, either of Wheat or Barley. It seemed as though there was more Barley on the Gravesend side, and that Wheat prevailed around Rochester. Of *Oats* there was the least. We also saw in some places large hop-grounds, **hummel-gâ.** On the Gravesend side there were extensive inclosures, planted with Cherry-trees; but towards and at Rochester there were not so many of them. When we had come a mile out of Gravesend we came to a little wood which consisted of all the above-named kinds of leaf trees, where we set down as a great rarity two trees which we had not before had the pleasure to see growing wild in England; viz., our *Birch,* **vår Björk,** which stood in a little bog,* **Kärr,** and *Juniper* bushes, **Enbuskar,** of which last we saw several on a chalk-hill, where they grew on the rough chalk, and had scarcely 3 inches of soil upon the chalk. They seemed, however, to be tolerably luxuriant.

Trägârdar af Kersbärs, Äpple, Päron, och Valnöt trän. *Orchards of Cherry, Apple, Pear, and Walnut trees.* I have just said that we saw here a great number of Orchards, planted with Cherries and other fruit trees. The notes I made about the orchards in this district are given above under the 7th July. As far as regards the other trees, we saw likewise a multitude of apple and pear trees, planted either in the same orchard with the cherry trees promiscuously, or also by themselves. The earth under and between them was in [T. II. p. 41] the same condition as I described on the 7th July respecting the cherry trees, ploughed up, and used as an arable-field, or grassfield, so that these fruit-trees stood in the middle of crops or grass. They were, nevertheless, much better adapted to have crops sown under and between them,

---

* This certainly fixes the site at Denton. [J. L.]

because the crops ripened as soon as, if not before, the ripening of their fruit, and thus there was no necessity for them to trample down the crops while gathering the fruit. At the sides of these orchards, and often at the sides of the ploughed fields, and at home at the farms stood plenty of large walnut trees, there planted, and now full of fruit.

Strata Terræ. I remarked a little above, that nearly all the hill sides, **backar,** between Gravesend and Rochester consisted only of chalk, **af bara krita,** with only a thin *stratum* of soil, **svartmylla,** lying upon it; yet we saw in 2 or 3 places that some of these chalk-hills, **kritbärg,** had above and upon them not chalk, but a hill of sand, **en backa af sand,** at times mixed with small *Pebblestones,* which sandhill lay upon the chalk, which was beneath it, and it was remarkable that the chalk-hills which had such a sandhill or collection of sand upon them, were commonly the highest hills of all we saw along this road. But how this sand in former ages came there, either by some river, or in what way, I cannot say. We found, however, that the sand in such a hill upon the chalk, was not of one kind only, but consisted of many sorts which lay alternately upon one another. I will give their position *in one of these hills,* **backar,** *through the middle of which* the highway ran.

[T. II. p. 42.]

	ft.	in.
1. *Svartmylla.* On the top, *soil* of 9 to 12 ins. thickness, but sandy enough............................	1	0
2. A yellow fine sand, with just coherence sufficient to form lumps **hârdt i klimpar hop-sittande fin sand.**............................	2	9
3. A light-yellow quite fine looser sand	3	0
4. A very fine *grey sand*	3	0
	9	9

and who knows how much more, because the bottom of the pit prevented us from getting farther down, but, that it could not go a very great depth, could be concluded from this, that the hill-sides on both sides below, consisted of bare chalk, as we saw on both sides of the high road, which was dug in them. Here and there in each of the above-reckoned sand-strata, there were some small pieces of, I know not what I shall call it, which looked as if it had been a nail rusted away.*

Hägnad om åkrar, ängar, &c.

Around nearly all the enclosures, such as ploughed fields, meadows, orchards, &c., were planted hedges of hawthorn, but they were in some places worthless enough. In only a few places were there any ' Raddles,' or wooden hurdles, **Ris-gärdes-gård**; at times, but seldom, one got to see such *wattled-hurdles*, **sprât-gärdes-gård**, as were described above (T. II. p. 14, *orig.*).

Åkrarne. *The ploughed fields* we saw to-day, lay both on the tops of the hills, and on their sides. I have recently named (T. II. pp. 39, 40, *orig.*), the kinds of crops that were sown on them. There were no dikes or water-furrows ever seen on or near them—both of which, however, would be of little use here, because the chalk soil seems to absorb all the water [T. II. p. 43], in respect of which we did not see the least flowing water all along this road. I saw no ditches by the road-side, which is a sign that the water cannot possibly remain there long. If by the side of any single hedge, there was sometimes found a ditch, this seemed only to be made to get earth out of, to make a bank on which the hedge had been planted, and to get mould to cast up on to the roots of

---

* At Poling Wood, Sussex, where the Reading clays are dug for the pottery, these pieces of "what-you-may-call-it" are called by the workmen "Rock." [J. L.]

the hawthorn of which the hedge had been made. There were no acre-reins out on the ploughed fields, but only very narrow ones at the sides of the fields, close to the hedges. These were so narrow that one could with difficulty walk upon them still less mow any hay there. In most places these ploughed fields lay full of small *Pebblestones*. The land was ploughed quite even and flat, that which was sown with wheat as well as that with other kinds of crops, but there were some riggs or stitches. There were very many weeds on a great part of their fallow fields. Some were thus full of quickens, which had been sown there ; others full of wild poppies, **Vallmoge,** various kinds of Thistles, **tistlar,** and other weeds, **ogräs.** But it was not to be wondered at, because the ploughed fields in such places at this time of the year were left untilled.

With such agriculture, **åkerbruk,** it is not difficult to understand why their *Wheat, Barley, Oats, Pease* and *Bean-fields,* stand so full of wild Poppies and other weeds, viz. : partly because they manage the ploughed-fields so badly, and leave the weeds all freedom to run to seed and sow themselves. I remarked that they used frequently to drive horses, sheep, and cows, to bait on the same, but [T. II. p. 44] while they meant to reap a profit, they caused themselves double loss ; for while, it is true, they commonly ate up the wild poppies, yet several of the other rank weeds were left (such as thistles, &c.), mostly to stand untouched by the cattle. Such a fallow-field was often left to lie two or three years uncultivated and as a pasture.

Though it happened, truly enough, that when the earth got as it were a coating of grass-sward, **gräsvall,** over it, the number of thistles and other weeds diminished ; yet as soon as such a pasture was again ploughed up, the earth loosened, and cultivated as a ploughed field, and sown with seed, the manifold seeds of weeds lying in the

earth also got new life, came up to the day, grew,
grodde, and in many places smothered the crop; for
their seed has the property, that if the ground is hard,
and unfit for them to come up, they can lie many years
down in the ground without growing or taking harm, but
quicken as soon as the earth is moved and turned over.
From this we see how necessary are many courses of
ploughing during the summer in a field confounded with
weeds.

The *Pease* in these fields were partly sown in rows and
the earth ploughed up between : the weeds uprooted, and
the mould moved on to the roots, so that the stalks are
on a hill. We also saw the *Pease-land* sown in the same
way in rows, but never cleared of weeds, or the earth dug
up between, but the weeds were entirely smothering and
taking the life out of the Pease. In many places the
Peas were sown *broad-cast*, as with us, and there the
weeds and the Pease had to fight with each other for
existence, as they best could.

The Pease were nowhere furnished with sticks.

[T. II. p. 45.] Of the *Harrow* and *Roller* here used
there is nothing particular to record; they are mostly
like ours. The *Plough*, **Plogen,** in Kent has this advantage, that the ploughshare, **vändbrädet,** can easily be
changed to whichever side of the plough one wishes.
But in other respects it merits no recommendation,
because it is very heavy and unwieldy.

The soil, **jordmon,** on all these ploughed fields was
of so loose a nature, that they could in the greatest
drought plough it up when they wished. In such a loose
earth they nearly always set three pair of horses, as large
as the largest Dragoon horses, before this plough ; then
one full-grown person was required to hold the plough,
and a boy, **gåsse,** to drive the horses : we sometimes
saw even as many as five or six pairs of such large horses

set before one plough. Such an earth, for whose ploughing up they laboured with three pairs of horses, we could at all times in Sweden with the *Westmanland* plough, and especially with Baron Brauner's, without doubt equally well and finely plough up with one pair of horses, if not with a single one. The *Kentish plough* has this peculiarity that it ploughs deeper than most other ploughs. We saw however, in some places to-day, fallow fields, which lay quite well farmed and ploughed up, so that the earth was friable and fine as the best new-made bed in a garden. Beans were mostly sown in rows, and treated in the same way as described above (T. II. p. 16 *orig.*) yet they were also here and there sown, as with us, *broad-cast.*

[T. II. p. 46.] **Vägarna.** *The roads* here were good enough. Although the ground was chalk, and therefore firm, yet they were not satisfied with that, but *coarse sand* and small *Pebblestones* were everywhere carted on to them, because Chalk in wet weather is slippery enough. On both sides of the road there were mostly hedges, and the road went, especially in hills, deep down in the ground, even to eight or ten feet. There were no ditches beside the road.

Väderqvarn. *Windmills.* Here and there on the hills, appeared some Windmills, built in the usual way. At Rochester was a Windmill which pumped up the water for the use of the town.

Västanvind. *The west wind strong in England.* That the west wind in this part of England must be one of the longest lasting, and strongest winds appeared clearly from this, that in the plantations, **Trägårdar,** which nevertheless, lay quite even, and not so especially facing this wind, the trees bent over from the west, with the upper part considerably over towards the east side, which oblique and leaning growth was without doubt caused by the aforesaid west wind.

2D

Kyrkor. *Churches, the ancient ones mostly of Flints, &c.*
I have mentioned above (T. I. pp. 479–80), that nearly
all the old Churches in this part were built of Flints,
as *Chadwell* in Essex, *Northfleet* west of Gravesend,
and several others in Kent. To-day also we saw that
many Churches in *Rochester* were for the most part built
[T. II. p. 47] of bare flint, **Flinta,** only that they used
some Portland stone among them.

We went after-
wards from the high
road up to a hamlet,
til en by, where we
saw an old Church
which they used as
a *malthouse,*＊ **höllo
på at göra til et
mälthus.** This was
similarly almost en-
tirely built of Flints,
only that the window
frames and mullions,
**fönster karmar
och ramar,** and the
door-posts, **dör-
trän,** were of Port-
land stone. The
windows were quite

*West Front of Ruined Church at
Ivy Cottage, Shorne, 1887.*

small. There appeared, truly enough, bricks, **tegelstenar,**
in the walls in one place and another, but it could at
the same time be plainly seen, that the wall had there
been broken, and that the brickwork was the work of
later times.

＊ In lane to Shorne. Kalm was the first writer who notices this ruin.
The *Kentish Traveller*, 4th Ed., 1790, has a paragraph, p. 116: "On the

We saw afterwards another Church [the description applies to Shorne Church], which similarly, was for the greatest part built of Flints, **flintor**, yet that *Portland* stone was here and there built into the wall. The window frames and tracery as well as the door-posts were always, in all such old Churches, of Portland stone; also frequently the angles of the Church walls and the tower. The windows were mostly small enough. For which

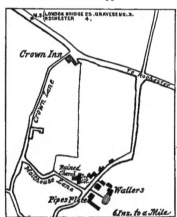

west side of the lane opposite to the house marked Mr. Maplesden's in the Map, the traveller will probably notice an ancient Chapel or Oratory. There can be no doubt of its having been a sacred edifice, because in digging for the foundation of the contiguous building a stone coffin and many human bones were discovered. In Mr. Thorpe's *Antiquities* is an engraving of the North-West view of this Chapel, but it is left to the researches of future antiquaries to ascertain when and by whom it had its original, no deed or other historical evidence having yet been met with relative to its institution or endowment." The Map referred to in the above note is on the scale of one inch to a mile in the *K. T.* Mr. Maplesden's house is now called *Pipes Place*, and a little cross-lane into the above lane from the west and passing south of the ruin is called ' Malthouse Lane.' I have not been able to find the alleged view in any of the thirteen plates in Thorpe's *Antiquities*. On August 10th, 1887, I visited the ruin, when Mrs. Cheesman, æt 84, told me that when she was young it was always *called* 'the Malthouse,' but that she did not know that it had ever been used as such. Kalm's description is accurate. The windows are all two-light, but the mullions are gone. This was a true Church; A *Piscina* and two *sedilia* are to be seen on the south side interior. The architecture is pure Early English, probably early 13th century. The curious history of the extinct Merston Church close by, leaves room to suppose that this too was once a parish church. This venerable ruin forms part of a modern residence known as Ivy Cottage, and seems to be totally unknown to modern Archæologists. [J. L]

reasons we may conclude : (1) That the brick kiln, **Tegel-bränneri,** in former times seems to have been little known, or at least not specially used in this district. (2) That the use of Glass, **Glasbruken,** also in those times was not very great.

On the south side of *another Church* there have formerly been three large doors side by side; but they were afterwards built up with flints, and made only into small windows.

Some of these old churches now stood deep down in the earth so that their floor was much deeper down than the outer surface of the Churchyard—a sign of their great age. Thus, either the Church has sunk, or the earth in the Churchyard has been raised by [T. II. p. 48] the corpses and coffins buried there, with other earth that had been carried there, or all these causes together.

I also noticed that in most places in this district, and also in Essex, they used the churchyards where they buried their dead as pastures for horses, donkeys, or pigs, but especially for horses. In some places the churchyard, **Kyrkogården**, was used also as a hayfield or meadow, so that they mowed the grass before the cattle were driven in thither.

Rochester is a beautiful town, tolerably large, and very old, lying on both sides of the river *Medway,** about 27 English miles from London. Here about are several hills, and part of the town also lies upon them, but still it is mostly down in the valleys by the river side. The houses are mostly of brick, some of them quite beautiful. There are several churches here, some of antique architecture, **gammal modig byggnad.** Over the river

---

* *On both sides of the river.* Strood occupies the left bank opposite Rochester. [J. L.]

Medway runs a large stone bridge,* which is reckoned
to be one of the finest in England. In the town is
a Cathedral and Bishop's Palace. A short distance
below the town lies the famous *Chatham*, where the
English men-of-war are partly built, repaired, and kept.

In the evening we came back to Gravesend.

The $\frac{16}{27}$ *July*, 1748.

Brunn i fasta Kritbärget. *A well in the solid
chalk.* Between two of the chalk-pits at Northfleet there
ran a wall or projection of [T. II. p. 49] bare chalk,
which they had left untouched, from 8 to 9 fathoms wide.
On both sides of this wall of chalk were great chalk-pits
of 6 or 7 fathoms deep. The sides thereof were perpendicular. Near one side of this wall they had dug a well,
en Brunn, down in the dense and solid chalk. This
well was round, 3 feet 6 inches diameter, and *steined*
with brick. I measured its depth, and found that from
the surface of the ground down to the upper surface of
the water in the well was 57 English feet. The water
which was taken from it was very clear, and tasted as
nice as the best **Käll-vatten,** spring-water, and was also
very refreshing, **lätt druckit.** Those who live hereabouts take from it all the water they require for cooking,
family drinking, brewing, boiling, washing clothes, and
for punch, tea, &c. Besides this, 8 horses and 4 cows
were watered daily with the same well-water, for although
the river Thames is close by, yet they do not give its

---

* *Rochester Bridge.* For its history *see* Lambarde, *Peramb. of Kent*, 1576,
4to, pp. 303-314; Stow, *Annales*, 1615, fol., p. 335; J. Harris, *Hist. of Kent*,
1719, fol., pp. 259-262, &c.; W. Wildash, *Hist. of Rochester*, 2nd Ed., 1817,
8vo., pp. 35-49, with a beautiful engraving of Rochester Bridge, Castle, &c.,
from Strood Quay. From whence (p. 41) is gathered that " In what year
the present stone bridge was begun cannot accurately be determined ; it was,
however, *compleated* in the fifteenth year of Richard II., 1392." [J. L.]

water to horses or cattle, because it is very salt, as the
Floodtide, **Floden,** *refluxus maris,* brings up salt water
from the sea, and if the horses and cattle drink of this,
it is said to make them ill. Although this is a dry
summer, it has never been remarked that the water has
diminished in this well. I asked whether the people who
drank of it felt well after it? They answered that better
water cannot be than this, and that they never feel
ill from it, or are in any way subject to illnesses more
than other people. I now drank freely enough of it,
without experiencing the least inconvenience afterwards.
I have also during the whole of my visit [T. II. p. 50] to
Gravesend, as well as elsewhere in England, never
experienced in the least degree such an effect as some
ascribe to the chalk water, **kritvatnet,** viz., that one
unaccustomed to it will at first have diarrhœa until he
becomes used to it. Most, and probably all the wells in
Gravesend are dug in the bare hard chalk; so that the
water which I drank at meal-times and when I was
thirsty the whole time I was there, was no other than
that which had filtered through the chalk, **silat sig
genom Kritan,** but I have not noticed the least
change in the body in consequence.

The ¹⁷⁄₆ July, 1748.

Strata Terræ. On the south side of the Windmill
Hill, **Väderqvarns backen,** which lay near Gravesend,
was a large pit from which they took sand. Here we
saw what the hill on the south side consisted of, and
measured the *strata,* which were as follows, beginning at
the top :—   Ft. ins.

1. Svartmylla, *soil* 1   0

2. Soil and a fine sand mingled together. These
together produced a yellow colour 1   0

3. A light-grey fine sand. In it were here and
there ochre or rust-spots 1   6

Ft. ins.

4. Light ochre-coloured sand, which went in waves 0 0½

5. Light-grey sand, same as No. 3 .... 1 6

6. A rust or dark ochre-coloured sand........... 0 1

7. A fine, very light sand 2 6

8. An ochre-coloured fine sand 0 0½

9. Fine very light sand, the same as No. 7, which went down to the bottom of the pit, **gropen**, and who knows how far down ?

_____

7 8

Higher up on the hill was another _sandpit_, **sandgrop,** the bottom of which was higher than the top, **Kullen** [T. II. p. 51], of the foregoing. There the beds, **hvarfven**, were in this order :—

Ft. ins.

1. Svartmylla, _Soil_, about 1 foot, but a good deal mixed with a fine brick-coloured sand and small _Pebblestones_ 1 0

2. _Pebblestones_ 2 6

These _Pebblestones_ were mostly the size of marbles, **knäckar**, coal-black, round or oval, quite smooth, as though they had been ground or polished. When such an one was broken it was found to consist of bare flint. No angular ones were seen at all.

3. An ochre-coloured fine sand..................... 2 6

4. A fine white sand 0 3

5. An ochre-coloured sand 0 1

6. A fine white sand 0 2

7. The ochre-coloured sand 0 2

8. The fine white sand 0 2

9. A grey clay falling into cubes, **En grå i tärningar fallande lera** 0 0½

10. The fine white sand 0 2

11. The grey clay 0 0½

		Ft.	ins.
12.	The ochre-coloured sand	0	2
13.	The fine white sand	0	1
14.	The grey clay	0	1
15.	The fine white sand	0	$0\frac{1}{2}$
16.	The grey clay	0	1
17.	The fine white sand	0	3
18.	The ochre-coloured sand	0	1
19.	The fine white sand	0	2
20.	The grey clay	0	1
21.	The fine white sand	0	3
22.	The grey clay	0	$0\frac{1}{3}$
23.	The fine white sand, full of rust spots	1	0
24.	[T. II. p. 52.] A light grey sand	0	1
25.	The fine white sand	0	9
26.	The ochre-coloured sand	0	1
27.	The fine white sand	6	0
28.	The ochre-coloured sand	0	1
29.	The fine white sand	0	6
30.	The light grey sand, full of rust spots	2	0
31.	The ochre-coloured sand	3	0
32.	Pebblestones, mingled with a light yellow sand	1	6
33.	The fine white sand	4	0

$$27 \quad 4\frac{5}{6}$$

No more could be seen on account of the depth of the pit. Whether all these *Strata* came into their present shape at the sin-flood or on any other occasion, I leave others to divine. The whole of this high sand-hill, **Sandbacken,** does most probably stand upon solid chalk, because all the country round about consists of bare chalk with a thin crust of earth upon it.*

---

* These sandpits may still be seen, but are now occupied by gentlemen's houses. [J. L.]

Mâssa. *Mosses.* On the hardest chalk hills, it is true, some fine *Hypnum* sometimes appeared; but we nevertheless remarked that this district around Gravesend was not especially favourable for *mosses.* There was no sign of these seen, though I looked carefully for them, either on the arable fields or *inclosures* which were sown with Clover, Sain Foin, &c., not even once on the *reins* by the hedges.

The Woodlouse. *Oniscus* cauda obtusa integerrima. *Linn.* *Fauna Svecica*, 1256, occurs in multitudes everywhere on the chalk, that it has as it were taken up its quarters in these places [T. II. p. 53.] When anyone came near it, it drew itself together, so that it lay perfectly round, and looked like a very small, black, shining egg. This is larger than our ordinary Swedish *woodlouse*, **grâsuggor** (plural).

The $\frac{18}{29}$ July, 1748.

Phalæna subulicornis spirilinguis; alis superioribus subcœruleis, punctis sex rubris, inferioribus omnino rubris. Linn. *Faun. Svec.* 814 [Anthrocera Filipendulae, *Burnet moth*]. This beautiful *moth*, **Fiäril,** which made quite a show with its beautiful red colour, had in particular taken up its abode in old Chalk pits overgrown with small bushes, where it flew in multitudes; but outside them it was very rare. It flew very slowly, and not so fast as the other *butterflies*, **Fiärilar.** It sat very much on the flowers of *Scabiosa pratensis hirsuta* C. B.

Aranea abdomine fusco ovato, linea exalbida pinnata, cauda bifurca, Linn. *Faun. Svec.*, 1223 [A. labyrinthica] occurs here in multitudes, on the chalk hills as well as in other places. I saw it also in Essex. The accurate description which Linnæus gave in his Fauna Svecica (*loc. cit.*) of the manner in which it makes its house, **bo,** relieves me from the necessity of repeating this, because this *spider*, **Spinneln,** makes it here in England almost in the same way. The difference is only this, that we found his subtle house and snare not only laid out over the grass, but also on the sides of sloping banks, **backar,** when the earth had fallen down; and on these places he commonly chose his house, where some little pit of a hand's breadth [T. II. p. 54], and depth ran into the bank. There he made his cylindrical house down in the aforesaid hole, above which he spread out his net on all sides, that it looked like a great funnel, **tratt,** especially if there were some small bushes in the neighbourhood, on which he made fast some ends of his net. A fisher-man setting his bownets, **Ryssior,** cannot set them more cleverly. He had often made his house up in the bushes, where the threads of his net extended a couple of ells on every side from his cylindrical hole, so that no insect could come near the bush without being snared in the net. He himself always sat either at the bottom, or opening of his cylindrical hole, so like an open purse, ready to spring **til vägs,** forward, as soon as there was any booty to win. When any insect was caught, he sprang at once upon it, and bit it several times in the head, then carried it into the entrance of his nest, where he ate it up. It was enjoyable to see what work he had with the *Curculionidæ* beetles; for as these are covered over with a hard shell he could next to never reduce them to order. As soon as they came on his net he seized them, but they were so clever that they drew in the feet and head. He then bit them well on the shell, but without effect; then, as soon as he left them they again began to crawl, when he sprang up again and bit them : but equally in vain, so that he at last became tired, and let them go their way. He had always down in the bottom of his house a hole through which, when pressed by necessity, he could have his escape, and not

be caught, when he always sought [T. II. p. 55], his
safety behind some twig, or down in the earth, when anyone chased him, but directly one again became quiet, he
' crope,' **krop,** through the hole into his house, advanced
to the opening to see whether any further danger was
brewing, or if all was quiet. I sometimes tore their house
asunder, when they commonly, after one or two days,
had it ready again.

Svin. In *Kent* the farmers generally have no more
pigs than they require for their own use, so that they
seldom come to sell any of them ; but in and near *London*,
the Distillers keep a great many, often from 200 to 600
head, which they feed with the lees, **drank,** and any
thing that is over from the distillery : and after these
animals have become fat enough, they are sold to the
butcher at a great profit.

In the same way, and with the same object, a great
number of pigs are kept at starch factories, which are fed
and fattened on the refuse of wheat, when the starch is
manufactured. The house where the swine are kept, is
cleaned and washed every day.

Âkrar, Hvete, Korn, etc. *Arable fields, Wheat,
Barley*, etc. Several old and enterprising farmers in this
district, told me that when the arable fields are well prepared one can get a return from wheat of 20 times the
grain, and sometimes a little more, but the fields must
then be well managed. Similarly they can get 20 times
the grain from Barley, on a well-cultivated field. The
kind of crop is changed yearly [T. II. p. 56] viz., when
the fields have lain one summer fallow, they are sown
either with *wheat* or *turnips*, after that with *Beans*, then
with *Barley*, or *Oats*. The fallow fields are commonly
ploughed three times during the summer ; if they go so
far, they are ploughed 4 times, and harrowed and rolled
between each ploughing. Chalk is also used here for

manure, on the ploughed fields, and when a field has once been manured with it, it is not necessary for them to manure it again for 10, 14 or more years.

På styf lergrund sades Kritan vara skön.

On a stiff clay soil the chalk was said to be good.

Among other ways of manuring arable fields, it is reckoned as the best to fold sheep on them in the summer, during the night in a little narrow fold, so that they stand quite close together. One and another enterprising farmer said he had himself tried to sow wheat in rows, and ploughed up the earth with a horsebreak, a little neat plough which is drawn by one horse, between the rows ; but it had not turned out well for them. Nevertheless, they thought that it might be done, otherwise the horsebreak is much used here to plough and clean away the weeds between the rows sown with Beans and Pease, since it lightens the labour very much.

Turnips are also much sown here in Kent for sheep, swine, and oxen to feed and fatten them with.

The Farmers said that they found the best time to sow wheat here, to be within one month before Michaelmas (after the *Old Style*) many, however, sow it one month after, but this plan is not held to be so good.

Ängs-skötsel. The management of *Grass-land, Sain Foin, Clover,* &c. Most of their grass fields in this district are sown with some [T. II. p. 57], particular kinds of hay, such as St. Foin, Clover, Tares, *Vicia,* Lucerne, &c.

Sain Foin is said to thrive very well on the chalk hills, **Kritbackar,** which we also found to be everywhere evident. For 30 years back they had not known so much of it used as now. They learned to use it from France. *Sain Foin* is an excellent food for horses, but for cows it is, when dried, not so good as good hay. When it has once been sown, it can sometimes stand for 16 or more

years before it need be sown again. It is either given to
the horses whole, as it is, or it is chopped up in a chaff
cutter, **i en hackelse-kista,** stalk and all, very small,
and so is mixed with oats, baiting, **agnar,** beans or
pease, and is afterwards given to the horses, who thrive
perfectly well on it. They cannot cut the *Sain Foin* here
more than once in the summer. *Clover* is also very much
sown here, but it does not last so long as *Sain Foin*,
because it must be sown with wheat or something else,
and a parcel of land is sown time about. They hardly
ever carry more than two cuts, **slåttar,** before it is sown
again, nor is it worth while to let it stand longer, for
when one has cut it two years or two summers, it loses,
tyner af,[*] so much after that that they can scarcely go on
to it with the scythe, **lian,** therefore when they have mown
it two summers, and very often only one, the field is
ploughed up anew, and sown with *Clover,* but although
it cannot stand long before it must be sown again, yet it
saves a great deal of inconvenience, above all in this
district, where no ordinary kind of grass will [T. II. p. 58]
thrive; because this *Clover,* the first summer it is mown,
gives such a very great abundance of a rich and good
hay. As a food for horses it is most excellent, but not so
for cows, although it is true they milk a good deal
from it, yet the milk acquires some particular flavour in
consequence, and is not nearly so agreeable as the
cows are fed with good grass. One can particularly
easily recognise this *Clover-smack* in the milk, if the cows
are allowed to go out in the summer and eat the green
clover. At that time one must take care that they are
not allowed to eat as much as they like of it, for the
clover tastes so nice to them, that they cannot stop, but

---

[*] 'TINE, to *lose v.* JAMESON. Tine, tyne, and *Suppt.* Tine.' J. T.
BROCKETT. *Gloss. of N. country words.* NEWCASTLE, 1846. [J. L.]

sometimes they eat it so greedily that they swell up and die. The *Clover* has in one respect the advantage over other kinds of hay, that it can commonly be cut twice in the summer. Some have also now begun to sow *Lucerne*, but it is still uncertain how it will succeed. [This is a very interesting notice].

TARES. *(Vicia vulgaris Sativa, J. Bauhin)* are also sown here by some for fodder, and the Farmers knew scarcely any kind of hay on which the cows give so much milk, and when they have eaten it, especially if it is green, the milk also has a nice flavour; nevertheless, it is found that cows give the best flavoured milk when they eat good grass. In very many places here in England they mow their meadows twice in the summer, sometimes also three times, but they seldom drive the cattle in to feed there, either in Spring or Autumn. Nevertheless, the farmers said that the hay of the *aftermath*, **af den senare slåtten,** was not so good as that of the first crop.

[T. II. p. 59]. **Bönor.** *Beans* are much sown here, and used as food for horses and swine. They also give them pease for food.

Krita. *Chalk.* It is not known to me whether chalk is used for any purpose in gardens, **trågårdar,** but in *hop-grounds* **hummel-gårdar,** it is used by some as a manure, when it is first mixed with other manure.

Ost, Smör, etc. *Cheese, Butter, etc.*

Nearly every County (Province) in England has something special, which it produces more plentifully and of better quality than any other county. Thus *Kent* commonly yields better hops and cherries than other counties; *Hertfordshire* better *flour*, **hvetmjol;** *Cheshire* and *Gloucestershire* better cheese; *Suffolk* better butter, etc. In connection with this, it is remarkable that the county which gives the best butter, cannot produce such good cheese, and *vice versd*. The reason seems to be that for either butter or cheese the best and fattest milk is required. Where they make butter they also make cheese, but they use first to churn the butter from the milk, and afterwards they make cheese from the same, which cannot be good, because most of the quality, **mästa kraften,** of the milk is already taken away.

Råg. Rye is also sown here in *Kent* by some who partly sell it, partly use to mix it with wheat, to grind and make bread of it. The straw, **Halmen,** is sold to *Watermen,* **Roddare,** and those who go backwards and forwards with boats and yachts to and from *London,* who use to lay [T. II. p. 60] the straw on the bottom of the boat, and on the seat, so that passengers may sit so much better, and not soil or dirty their clothes.

The ⅒₀ *July*, 1748.

To-day I went with the *Tilt-boat* to London to hear whether the Captain and the ship I was to cross to America in at once might not be ready for the voyage; and in the afternoon returned with one of the *Tilt-boats* down to Gravesend.

Kritans nytta. *The use of the Chalk.*

On the fields which lie in the neighbourhood around Gravesend they use very seldom or next to never to manure their ploughed fields with chalk; because the soil which is there mostly a mould is already so loose and dry that it ought not to be any looser: but farther away from thence where they have wet, low-lying arable fields, consisting of clay, they manure them from time to time with chalk. All the agricultural labourers, **åkermän,** and Farmers hereabout, agree unanimously in this, that the principal use of chalk as a manure on a ploughed field, is on such land as consists of stiff clay and cold soil,

for it unbinds the clay, and makes it fit to produce crops
in abundance.   It is also on this account that the Farmers
in Essex where there is no chalk to be found, even those
who live a long way off, come hither down to the banks
of the Thames, where there are chalk-pits, to buy here
many loads of chalk, and carry them a long way over
land [T. II. p. 61], to manure their arable fields with it,
when they consist of a stiff clay.   Those who live farther
in Kent, and have a similar clay soil, improve it in the
same manner, with chalk.   In sandy soil chalk is said
not to be of any use.

Thus those who live both near and far away from here,
avail themselves of this chalk for manure for their arable
and grass lands.   From Essex, Middlesex, Surrey, and
very many other places in the English Provinces which
either lie near the Thames, or else on the sea coast, all
kinds of provisions, such as wheat, barley, oats, butter,
cheese, &c., are carried to London in small vessels.
When the same small vessels return home from London,
they will not go back empty ; therefore they come to
some one of these chalk pits, ballast their vessel with
chalk which they can have here for a small price, and
carry it home, where they either burn it first to lime,
before they lay it on the arable fields, or lay it on the
fields as they get it.   Foreign ships also on the home-
ward voyage often take from hence a great quantity of
chalk with them.

The bases of the walls and banks on both sides of the
Thames are made of this chalk, partly because it binds
well, and partly because they have no other kind of stones.
It is arranged there both in layer and smaller pieces.
[T. II. p. 62].   The outhouses in different places were
built of bare Chalk.   The principal use to which chalk
has been put, is, that in several places, they burn lime of
it-- of which more a little farther on.

In the Comedy House in London, the *rope-dancers*, **Lindansare,*** and those who walked on the rope and lines, used to rub their shoes thickly underneath with chalk, so that they should not slip. The rope also was chalked to a certain extent.

The 20/31 July, 1748.

Notes on the Chalk and Chalk hills at Northfleet, and other places in Kent.

Northfleet is a village which lies a short English mile West of Gravesend, on the same side of the river. Here, and all the way to Gravesend, all the hilly banks of the river Thames, and the land around, consist of bare chalk, only that a thin soil lies upon it. Here, near the banks of the Thames, one great chalk pit succeeds another, both of considerable extent, and of great depth. These chalk pits are for the most part quadrangular, and their sides are perpendicular. The depth of these pits from the upper surface down to the bottom is 8, 12, 15, or more, fathoms. They do not belong to one and the same person, but there are several who have shares therein, who are gentlemen living in London, but who have, nevertheless, people here who live near the chalk pits [T. II. p. 63], to see that the work goes on well and properly.

That the chalk has been quarried for many centuries back, can be concluded, besides what one has from old historians, also, partly from the number of the pits, and their very great size and depth, partly from the considerable number of old pits, which are now to a great extent refilled with rubbish and overgrown with all kinds

---

* In the Prologue written by Dr. Johnson, and spoken by Garrick at the opening of the Theatre Royal, Drury Lane, 1747, line 46, ' Here Hunt may box, or *Mahomet may dance*,' refers to a celebrated rope-dancer. [J. L.]

of trees and weeds. Some of the chalk-pits where they
were now breaking up and burning the chalk were near
the river; others again some musket-shots therefrom;
for they had taken away all the more suitable chalk from
nearer the river so that there was nothing left, but high
heaps, full of the earth they had sifted when they took
the chalk, and the soil which had lain upon it together
with pieces of flint, chalk, bricks, and other rubbish. In
these chalk-pits we had a very good chance of seeing how
thick the vegetable soil and the mould is which lies upon
the chalk, as well as all the various beds and *strata* of
chalk, with what is found in it, etc. At the top of the
pits, and upon the chalk, lay the vegetable mould or soil,
matjorden eller svartmyllan, commonly to a depth
of 15 inches, mixed with small pieces of flint, which
resembled those which lie on the open plain, and the
sun has bleached and made white. The colour of this
soil was brown. Yet the soil was not everywhere along
the top of the pit the same thickness; for just [T. II.
p. 64] as it was 15 inches thick, so it went down in a
bow or curve to 4 feet perpendicular depth. Neither
was the breadth of such a *sinus*, **vigg,** everywhere the
same, for sometimes the upper part was 10 or 12 feet
wide, sometimes scarcely 2 feet. The depth of such
hollows was also unequal—now more, now less; yet the
soil was commonly, beyond and above these pockets,
15 inches.

Below that came the chalk. It was not quite pure at
the top, but to some small extent mixed with the brown
earth for a thickness of 3 feet.

This mixed chalk thus looked dirty, and was also
charged with *pieces of flint* and full of small *Pebblestones*,
which, both flints as well as pebbles, exactly resembled
those which lay up to the day and were bleached by the
sun, which seems to indicate that these parts of the chalk,

which are now 4 feet perpendicularly under the upper surface of the soil-crust, **jordskårpen**, formerly lay up to the day and the sun. We dug into the bank and found everywhere such bleached flint fragments and *Pebblestones.* When these bleached flint fragments which lay in the bank were broken, they often looked inwardly like flints which have been in the fire, but nevertheless, have not been so hard burned as to have run to glass.*

At times were found at 8 feet perpendicular depth in the chalk itself large spots or pipes, **fläckar,** of [T. II. p. 65] one to two feet diameter, which consisted entirely and solely of such brown mould as lies on the surface, and is the same as we call **svartmylla.** In these "*pipes*" as well as in the chalk around them, were plenty of small *Pebblestones.* We found similar pipes in many chalk pits. In some places they were obliged to throw away the vegetable soil, flint fragments, Pebble-stones, and other mixed earth, for a depth of 6 feet perpendicularly, before they could get pure chalk to use for lime burning.

I will now give the notes I made in one and another of the chalk-pits in order that I might see *how* the beds lay in them, and what the walls consisted of. In one of these *Chalkpits*, the *nearest to Gravesend,* the strata were in this order :— ft. in.

1. Highest, and on the chalk was soil, **Svart-mylla eller matjord,** which here in colour was mostly brown, about one foot thick more or less... 1 0

It was not everywhere of the same thickness, but sometimes went down in curves or pockets, **viggar eller kilar,** in the chalk to a depth of two, three and four feet, but unequal breadths.

2. Next to that a chalky mixture of Pebblestones

---

* Of course this is the effect of oxidation. [J. L.]

Ft. in.

and some of the aforenamed soil, **Svartmylla,**
principally chalk—one foot, more or less   1   0

This chalk was somewhat loose and not so
[T. II. p. 66] hard as the perpendicular walls of
the chalkpit.

3. Afterwards came a nearly horizontal stratum
of bare roots, about ⅛ to ¼ inch thick. It consisted
of nothing but small roots, the largest of which
were the size of a quill pen; but one could not
distinguish what kind of roots these had been.
They were not particularly rotten. I imagine that
they were fine roots of Hawthorn, **Hagtorn,**
which had run so far down, and then they had
found under this stratum a harder chalk, and
could not go farther down in the earth, but afterwards ran horizontally upon the same, and consequently time after time had formed this. What
made me think so was (1) that the chalk which
lies immediately under is very hard; (2) That I
found fresh and growing Hawthorn roots, of the
same thickness as recently named, which ran just
horizontally among the other roots in this stratum.

4. Hard chalk, 3 fathoms. What it was like
further down I cannot say, because the fallen
gravel and mould, **grus och mullen,** prevented
more being seen below.

In one of the *Chalk-pits* which were *close to Northfleet
Church,* the strata of the chalk were in this order :—

ft. in.

1. The soil and vegetable earth, **Jordskårpan
och matjorden**.....   1   0

2. [T. II. p. 67.] Hard Chalk about 58–60 feet. 60   0
Pieces of flint were here and there mixed in it.

3. A stratum of bare flints, laid quite close
together—3 to 6 inches thick...........................   0   6

Ft. in.

4. The hard chalk 9 0

5. A *Stratum* of flints... .... 0 1½

The flints here also lay quite close together, but the pieces of flint were very thin, like small thin tablets. There often lay a couple of such thin bits on one another.

6. The hard chalk 18 0

7. A stratum of flints exactly like No. 3.

8. The hard chalk 4 0

And who knows how far down, because the bottom of the pit prevented me from seeing deeper.

———————

92 7½

Note.—In the chalk bed, **krithvarfen,** below No. 3. some flints only appeared here and there.

In another of these large chalk-pits nearer to *Gravesend* the strata were thus :—

ft. in.

1. On the top, soil, **Svartmylla,** about 1 0

but mingled with chalk, that the colour of this earth was very like bricks.

2. Chalk 12 0

3. A stratum of flints, quite horizontal, as if they had been designedly laid level 0 6

4. Chalk about........................... 30 0

5. [T. II. p. 68.] A stratum of flints, arranged in the same way as No. 3 .... 0 6

6. Chalk 3 0

7. A bed of flints like the preceding............. 0 6

8. Chalk one fathom and perhaps much deeper, because the fallen earth prevented me from seeing more 6 0

———————

53 6

Obs. 1.—That these *strata* of flints consisted only of

one single bed of flint, and not of many piled one on the
other. It seemed as if there had been a flat, even, and
level plain of bare chalk, whereon someone had spread a
stratum of single flints so close together that one touched
another, and then laid chalk on it.

Obs. 2.—The flint which lay in these beds was in some
places thicker, up to 6 inches thickness, in other places
thinner, even to a thin plate of $\frac{1}{4}$-inch thick. Between
these strata of flint there seldom appeared any flints in
the chalk itself, only some isolated ones here and there.
In the chalk, but very seldom, was some little *Pebblestone,* sometimes oval, sometimes spherical.

In the afore-named *strata* of Flints, the flint is surrounded by chalk quite close, as if the chalk had been
soft, **blöt,** when the flint came to sink down in the chalk,
and afterwards some more soft chalk came to lie thereon.
[T. II. p. 69.] These *strata* or beds of flints among the
chalk are peculiar. The flint stones lie here as horizontal and as close to one another as if they had been
designedly thus arranged by human hands. How did
the Flint stone first come there in such an order ?

The whole hill, **backen,** near the river Thames
west of Gravesend, consisted of bare chalk ; but at its
base, even with the water surface when the flood-tide is
highest, was such a stratum of flints as just described,
which lay in the same way, quite horizontal, as if it had
been arranged on the dead level. The pieces of flint
lay here entirely in the same plane. This flint stratum
could be seen at low water for nearly half an English
mile along the river bank.

The colour of these perpendicular walls in the chalk-
pits is, for the most part, snow-white. In other places it
had acquired a yellowish tint, viz. : where there was soil
and trees above, from which some wet occasionally
trickled down and ran over the sides. In the places

where there are many *lime-kilns*, **kalkugnar,** the perpendicular walls are, from the quantity of coal-smoke,
nearly black. In some places where the chalk had newly
fallen down, it was full of *black specks*, the size of a small
pin's head, just like as if a Lichen had begun [T. II. p.
70] to grow there. In one piece and another were large
rust spots, which in some places ate into it to some
extent.

The perpendicular sides or walls of the chalk-pits are
commonly full of fissures, **springor,** which go sometimes perpendicularly, sometimes horizontally, and cross
each other at right angles. The width of such a fissure
is not always the same, being sometimes so narrow that
one can scarcely thrust in the blade of a knife, but sometimes they are wider, that one can easily get in a finger.
I cannot just say of which kind, perpendicular or horizontal, there occur most, yet the horizontal seem to be the
most numerous. When I call the fissures perpendicular,
it is not to be understood that they were so according to
mathematical rules, but they stood sometimes exactly
perpendicular, sometimes nearly so. The same remark
applies to the word horizontal.

In the old chalk pits they had in some places dug
large holes like caves, **hvalf.** Those who lived close by
said that they thought they had been in former times
used as cellars, **källare.** The cave within had not taken
any particular injury from time, nor had the walls ; yet it
seemed that pieces of chalk had from time to time fallen
down from the roof. The chalk in these old cellar walls,
which were perpendicular, was full of fissures which ran
both perpendicularly and horizontally, and even obliquely.
I mean [T. II. p. 71] by oblique that which is a *medium*
between perpendicular and horizontal, or tolerably near
thereto. These oblique fissures were everywhere very
few, and not nearly so many as the others. The distance

between the horizontal fissures was nothing less than the same throughout; for when the one *stratum*, if I may so call it, was thick, the next was often quite thin.

In the old cellars the distance between the planes of the bedding was mostly 6 inches, sometimes, however, more; often 1 inch, and sometimes only half an inch, or a narrow strip, **en smal rimsa.** Nor was one and the same stratum always of the same width between the fissures; for although it commonly maintains the same width, it sometimes happens that when it has been for a time of one and the same width, it then by degrees grows narrower, and at last terminates in an *angulum acutissimum.* Neither did the fissures always behave the same way: for *now* a fissure might run exactly horizontal, as far as the face of the chalk-pit went; *now*, just as it had gone for a little horizontally, it stood obliquely, and another horizontal fissure began in it, 1, 2, 3, or more inches, either above or below, and so on.

When one gently drew out a piece of chalk, which lay between two horizontal fissures both [T. II. p. 72] the under and upper sides thereof were a *planum*, or plane without lumps or projections, and commonly of a little darker colour than the chalk within, a sign that air and water had entered the fissure. The coal-smoke which comes from the limekilns, which occur in nearly all these pits, is however able to have caused the same dark colour. After running for some time straight as a line horizontally, it bent off and ran obliquely.

Among the horizontal joints or bedding-planes, there were commonly some master-joints, which mostly ran the whole way across the face of the quarry, and were larger than the others. The distance between them varied—2, 3, or 4 feet, seldom less than 18 inches, but the space between them was often divided by small horizontal fissures.

Neither are the perpendicular fissures of the same description throughout, for sometimes they go in a straight line right up the wall. Sometimes when they have gone a certain distance, they stand obliquely, and then another begins a little on either side, and runs up in a straight line. The width of such a fissure behaves in the same way, as has been said of the horizontal ones. The distance between the perpendicular fissures, as with the horizontal ones, is not uniform, but sometimes wide, sometimes narrow, often only 1 inch and even less; but sometimes 2, 4, 6, 8, and 10 feet wide.

[T. II. p. 73]. These perpendicular fissures, or 'joints,' commonly preserved a certain direction, for they mostly ran from E. to W. and from N. to S., or about, it might be, a slight curve from W. to N. and E. to S., as well as from S. to W., and from N. to E. But this was so slight, that it could scarcely be noticed. Yet there were at times some seen which departed from this rule, and ran for example from S.E, to N.W., from N.E. to S.W., and so on. Nevertheless, this curvature happened seldom enough. They commonly lay, as was first noted, and this in chalk pits, which were a whole English mile from each other.

When pieces of chalk were drawn out of the rock, their sides facing the perpendicular fissures were quite plane, and as smooth as if they had been cut even with a knife drawn along a *rule*.

The chalk walls which have been longer exposed, and on which both the sun, air, and rain have operated longer, are far more full of perpendicular, horizontal and oblique fissures, than that which is newly quarried. At least the former could be more plainly seen: for an old chalk, which has been longer exposed, is nearly cracked all to pieces, while in a newly fractured surface one can with difficulty see any cracks.

Sometimes in the larger fissures it is seen that thin and flat bits of flint, like thin pieces of Schist [T. II. p. 74], had filled up the fissure. Can it have been formed there, after the chalk had been so cracked to pieces? Thus, it is evident, that chalk rocks have their fashion or quality of cracking to pieces, just as 'granites,' **grâbärgen,** with us.

When the chalk has lain its time in the open air, under sun and rain, there are often very small holes, on the upper surface, so that it becomes as it were cellular. The depth of the holes is, however, seldom over 1 or 2 geom. lin. $= \frac{1}{12}$ or $\frac{1}{6}$ inch.

The flints which were found in the chalk had no certain shape, but were nearly all formless pieces, just as when one smelts metals or some ore, and lets it run on the ground in any chance form. The largest pieces of flint are about 2 feet long, though one seldom sees such large ones. Most are about 9 to 12 inches. Nearly all flints, here in the chalk pits, are black; though some lightish pieces occur here and there.

On the banks of the river Thames there lie in some places plenty of flints, but although the strand for six hours stands under water, and for the next six in the open air, still they have not suffered any other change on that account, than that some are externally of a white colour, or also sometimes slightly inclining to blue, such as flints are wont to be when they lie on the hills in the open air, and the sun shines on them and bleaches them. Otherwise most of the flints here were as clean and black, when they were broken, as those which are newly taken out of the solid chalk. [T. II. p. 75]. The flints sometimes had on their surface, as it were, a rust-eaten or ochre-coloured crust, and in such flints rust-eaten places often occurred. The figures were such as before described, as those assumed by an ore, smelted and run on the earth as it would. The pieces were commonly oblong, and at the same time full of lumps and irregularities. They also frequently resembled fingers, feet, pegs, human bodies, part of a hand, a goat's-horn, a small calf-horn, etc. Inside they were commonly black, but also frequently more or less full of lighter spots.

The *Heterogenea* and foreign or less common things, which are found in these chalk pits, either in the chalk or the flints are in particular these :—

1. **Strålflinta,** as I call a kind of stone which lies like a sponge upon the flint, is broad and flat, consists of parallel threads hard-petrified, which run perpendicularly to its flat side, exactly like the *Amiant*-like **Strålgips,** [*fibrous gypsum*] in Prof. Wallerius's *Mineralogia,** p. 55, only that this is somewhat denser. In colour it is white or light grey. Still it is a kind of flint, because it strikes fire with steel. It lies not only in the flint, but also sometimes in the chalk.†

2. **Musselskal,** *Bivalve shells*, occur firmly fixed in corresponding cavities in the flint, as well as in the chalk.

3. Crystaller, *Crystals*. Often when one breaks a flint to pieces, there are found inside small rock crystals, **bärg crystaller** [T. II. p. 76] closely packed. There is generally an empty space left with them.

4. **Klotrunda flintbitar,** or the so-called *chalk-eggs*. These are frequently found firmly united to the flint. Externally such a chalk, or, more strictly, flint-egg, is covered with a white chalky crust of the thickness

---

* Wallerius (Johann Gottschalk). *Mineralogia.* Eller Mineral Ricket indelt och beskrifvit af J. G. W. *Stockholm,* 1747, 8vo. The first of a long series of Mineralogies. [J. L.]

† **Strålflinta.** Thin *plates* or *scales* of fish exhibiting a transverse fibrous structure are common, especially in fragments, in the upper chalk, and in the flints. [J. L.]

of a half *line*=$\frac{1}{24}$ inch; but when it is broken one gets to
see that it consists mostly of bare flint. They are
generally spherical, **klotrunda,** but sometimes slightly
oblong, sometimes they are quite solid and bare flint,
but sometimes hollow, when in the centre there lies a
little chalk, either attached to the flint, or loose, so that
when it is shaken, the chalk is heard striking against the
sides within. From such internal space there is no hole
or passage to the outer periphery, but the flint is solid
round about the hollow space within. These are as
small as swallows' eggs or bullets, and also as large as
cannon balls.

In some chalk pits the men used to sit and flake the
flints there gathered into small pieces to sell to travellers
and others to strike fire with.

[Omit 8 lines on p. 76 and 5 lines on p. 77.]

[T. II. p. 77.] Some old chalk pits are now left
desert, and stand full-grown with all kinds of trees and
weeds. Among the trees are particularly Privets,
Viburnum, Guelder-Rose or Wayfaring tree, Thorn-
bushes, *Cornus fæm.* [Cornus *sanguinea, Cornel*] in very
great abundance.

[Omit 4 lines.]

When the sun shines, while one remains in a chalk-
pit, it costs the eyes a good deal to look at the white
chalk.

Rabbits, **Caniner,** had their holes and dwellings in
several places in the loose fallen earth and chalk, where
in the evenings they are seen in great numbers.

Tattingar. *Sparrows* had their nests in the excavated
caves.

In one of the chalk-pits was laid out a beautiful
orchard full of different fruit trees, together with all
kinds of kitchen garden plants and vegetables.

In the chalk-pits near *Rochester* which lay 1½ Swedish

mile from those just described at Northfleet, the chalk-walls had entirely the same structure as those described above, viz., that they went in similar horizontal [T. II. p. 78] and perpendicular fissures, contained the same *heterogenea*, had precisely similar *strata* of flints, laid close to one another, and 1, 2, 3, or more fathoms of chalk between every such *stratum* and the next. In the chalk between these *strata* there were also some flints here and there.

How they burn lime from chalk at Northfleet and elsewhere in Kent.

I have before remarked that all the country around *Northfleet* consists of bare chalk, in which they have dug deep pits and taken out of them both chalk and flint, partly for sale abroad, and partly to burn lime from the chalk. The method of burning lime here practised is the following, which I will relate in the order in which it happens :—

They break off with a crowbar large pieces from the sides of the chalk-pits, and cause them to fall down to the bottom of the pit. They begin this quarrying at the top of the pit, after they have first removed the mould and earth, which lies upon the chalk, and so continue downwards right to the bottom ; but not more at one time than will suffice for burning for one or two weeks. All the other walls in the chalk-pits which they have left off quarrying are mostly perpendicular, but the walls where they are working are sloping enough, so that they can go up and down the same frequently. The pieces which have fallen down, and are still very large, are hewn asunder into smaller pieces with an iron pickaxe.

[T. II. p. 79.] After that, the chalk, so reduced into somewhat smaller pieces, is laid on a lump or block of chalk which they have made for themselves, and with a pick, which is like such as we use to pick millstones with, only that the edge of the pick does not go parallel with the handle, but at right angles to or across the shaft, as in a scarf-cutter, **skarf-yxa,** they hack the chalk into still smaller pieces, so that the largest bits of chalk are seldom larger than a clenched fist. The pick is about two inches wide in the blade. The flints which are found among the chalk are collected and laid in a heap, to be preserved and afterwards sold. They next have a 'Riddle,' 'Fiddle,' or sieve, **et Rissel,** of about 30 inches diameter, whose bottom is made of small iron wires, the 'bars' and 'slashers,' bound round with very fine iron wires, or 'whippings.' These iron wires, *i.e.* the bars and slashers, are set as usual in the sieve so as to make it full of four-sided holes or squares. Every side of such a square mesh is $1\frac{1}{2}$, $1\frac{3}{4}$, or 2 inches. This 'Riddle' or 'Fiddle,' **Rissel,** was held by one person, while another with a shovel cast the chopped-up chalk therein, when it always happened that the pieces which were smaller than the hole in the bottom of the fiddle passed through and fell out, together with the chalk which in the process of chopping had been reduced to powder. The pieces of chalk which were left in the fiddle were cast out into baskets, which were carried to the limekilns to be burned to lime; but the smaller pieces which fell out through the holes of the fiddle [T. II. p. 80], together with the fine meal, was left lying on the bank, and was not carried to the lime kiln. The reason why they will not use this is said to be that it puts out the fire in the limekiln because it is so fine.

Skåfveln, the shovel which they took up the bits of chalk with, was slightly concave, exactly like such shovels as are used in granaries and salt-houses, only that it was somewhat broader. The breadth, or *latitudo transversa,* of the shovel blade was 22 inches; *latitudo perpendicu-*

laris, or the length, was 10 or 11 inches. At the bottom and round the edge it was shod with iron.

Korgarna, the baskets which the small pieces of chalk were cast into, and in which they carried the chalk to the limekilns, were made of willow boughs or shoots, in shape like a large Goblet, or Beaker, *Pocal* **eller Bägare.** Their height was 13 inches, the diameter at the base rather over 6 inches, the diameter at the top 15 to 16 inches.

After they had filled the baskets, of which there was here a very large number, they were carried by women to the limekilns, where there was a carl who received the basket, cast or tipped the bits of chalk out of it over or on to the limekiln, yet in such a manner that he slung them with such direction that they did not come to lie on each other, but were spread evenly about beside each other.

The limekiln was built of brick. When it was empty, and one looked down into it from above, it was in shape like a beaker [T. II. p. 81] or goblet, as round as if it had been drawn with a pair of compasses, but narrow at the bottom and widening upwards. The internal diameter of the kiln at the base or bottom was 66 to 72 inches, but at the top at the surface of the ground the diameter was 13 feet, some a little more. The perpendicular height inside from the bottom to the highest rim, 22 feet 6 inches. Down at the bottom the kiln was externally built perpendicular for a height of 6 or 7 feet, above which level its shape afterwards on all sides looked like a parasol. They had there laid horizontally on the top of the perpendicular wall, beams, or balks, on which they had set other smaller balks, which all sloped outwards like a parasol. Immediately within the balks were laid large lumps of chalk, and immediately inside these the brick wall of the limekiln, which leant against and was supported as it widened out by these closely-laid, parasol-shaped balks, or struts; for if these struts had not been there, the upper part of the kiln would not have been able to stand. These balks so arranged were fastened by their upper ends to other horizontal balks, which were shaped into a frame adapted for that special purpose, whereon a platform was made on which they could go and walk around the kiln, and carry chalk, coals, and any-thing that was necessary for the same. Down at the bottom the limekiln had four openings, or mouths, **ugns-munnar,** through which the fully burned chalk could be taken out, and by means [T. II. p. 82] of which the wind always found access to play in and heat up the coal in the kiln, so that there was always a strong draught.

Each kiln-mouth, **ugnsmun,** which was square, was 30 inches broad and 2 feet high. The perpendicular part, *i.e.,* the lower part of the kiln, was externally an octangle in this way, that starting with one of the sides that stood perpendicular, the oven's mouth was in the next, in which the upper part of the side stood quite as far out as the perpendicular face, but afterwards went more and more in, the lower it got, till at the bottom of this inwardly sloping part was the kiln-mouth. They had in most cases built a screen of boards round the kiln with two entrances, one on each side, to prevent the too excessive blasts of the wind. This screen was on the outside of the kiln, for on the other side, the bank with its perpendicular sides, against which the lime-kiln was built, performed the same service. The bottom of the bank where they were now getting the chalk was horizontal with the upper surface or the edges of the lime-kiln. When they burn chalk to lime in this kiln, dry brushwood or sticks are laid on the bottom to light the fire with, then a thin stratum of coal, then a stratum of the broken pieces of chalk, again a thin stratum of coal and so alternately until the goblet or beaker-shaped kiln is full. The fire is lighted at the bottom, and spreads itself more and more upwards according as the coal down below becomes burnt up. [T. II. p. 83.] The chalk is generally burned to lime, although it holds together in the same bits as it was when it was put in.

As the chalk becomes full-burnt, the pieces are taken out down below, at the bottom of the kiln, through the above described kiln-mouths, when the chalk which is above, successively sinks down into its place. And that this may proceed with more certainty, they have a long either single or forked fire-poker, which they thrust here and there down into the kiln from above, and stir about, when the bits of chalk sink down all the faster. The bits of chalk are shovelled out of the fire with the above described broad shovel. The fuel they use for this purpose is only and solely coal, except that when they first light up a kiln they have at the bottom fagots to light up with, because the coal will not otherwise so easily take fire. A little way from the kiln lie large heaps of coals, but before they are used they are broken with an iron hammer into quite small pieces, little larger than the end of a little finger. A great part is as small as dust. The carls give as a reason that they burn better and more evenly in consequence, and do not become caked because a thin bed of such is sufficient to heat up and burn the stratum of bits of chalk which lies upon or under it. As soon as the carl has broken into very small pieces as much coal as he considers to be sufficient for a certain number of baskets, he takes some water in a bucket and throws it [T. II. p. 84] thinly over the same fine-broken coal, partly by this means to prevent them from being blown away by the wind, since they are now in part like mould, partly also because they will heat stronger when they come thus into

2F

the kiln. Thus prepared the coal is carried by women
in the above-described baskets, and is set around the
sides of the kiln, where the carl takes them, and throws
them into the kiln as he finds necessary.

No one must think that the beds or strata of these
coals in the lime-kiln are so thick that when they have
laid such a bed upon the white chalk, the chalk can be no
more seen, but only black coal. By no means, these coal
beds are both thin and very porous. Two or three or four
such baskets, as have been before described with the
chalk, suffice for a stratum up at the highest edge of the
kiln, where it is widest. In the same way it is true of
the stratum of chalk, that the bits of chalk do not lie so
close, but that one can nearly everywhere see the bits of
coal between them. Someone may perhaps think that
the lime which is burned from this chalk must lose much
of its white colour, by reason of the black coal which is
mixed alternately with it; or also may enquire whether the
coal is afterwards separated from the bits of chalk ?
The answer is that the coal is not separated from the
bits of chalk after the chalk is burned, nor would it admit
of this, because, as was said before, the bits of coal are
quite small, and a great part [T. II. p. 85], of them like
mere dust, but they remain and are blended together with
the chalk ; but it ought to be noted that when the coals are
burned they have lost all their black colour, and acquired
a light one, so that the chalk as far as regards its white-
ness takes very little harm on that account. Besides
that, they assert that a lime burned from chalk, which is
blended with powdered coal ashes will be much more
binding in the walls, than all other lime-mortars, which
quality they attribute to the coal-ashes.

At every kiln there are six persons, three men and
three women. Two of the carls have the charge of
breaking the chalk loose, and of hewing it into small

pieces, as well as of lifting the baskets on to the women's shoulders; but it often happens, nevertheless, that the women also get helping to hack the chalk into small pieces. Both the carls and all three women help to fill the baskets with the bits of chalk, when the carls commonly *screen* the bits of chalk in the fiddle, and the women throw them into the baskets. The women are obliged, almost alone, to carry the baskets on their heads and shoulders from the place whence the chalk is taken to the lime-kilns. Likewise they are obliged to carry coal-baskets from the place where they were filled to the lime-kiln. The third of the three carls is constantly at the lime-kiln, where he takes the chalk baskets from the women's heads and shoulders, and throws the chalk into the kiln. Similarly he throws the coals in their turn into the kiln. In short, he performs all the duties which are carried on at the lime-kiln itself, besides that he helps [T. II. p. 86], when he has time, to break up the coal into small bits, **at boka sönder stenkålen,** etc.* Every woman always carries three baskets each time, namely, she has a piece of board of about 8 inches broad, and about 1 foot long, on which is a rope or band, one end of which is fastened to one end of the piece of wood, and the other to the other. This band is laid by a noose over the upper part of the head, so that the piece of board comes to lie across the shoulders, when one basket is set to rest upon the piece of board, and the other two beside it on the head, whilst the woman inclines her head a little as she walks. On the head they have an old man's-hat, and under the piece of wood and the band a bunch of hay, that the piece of wood and the cord may not injure the back.

---

* **Boka,** *see Glossary* to *Studies in Nidderdale,* p. 240, *s.v.* 'Bukker,' also *Stud,* p. 28. [J. L.]

When these lime-kilns are once lighted up, they are said
to burn the whole year night and day, only being allowed
to go out during Yuletide, on the principal feast days. But
as soon as these are past they are lighted up new, and are
continued in that state night and day till the next Yule.

The chalk which is laid in the morning in the kiln to
burn, is in it, sometimes two, sometimes three days,
before it passes through the kiln, and becomes full-
burned. For the most part they reckon three days for
its burning. While it is thus passing through the kiln
its burning goes on, not only from the beds of coal which
lie next to it, but [T. II. p. 87] also from the brickwork
in the kiln, which is very hot from the long continued
burning. The heat of the kiln is so strong that pieces
of flint which have accompanied the chalk fragments
into the kiln are converted into a white glass.

As soon as the chalk laid in the kiln is full-burnt, and
has got through the whole kiln, so that it is now at
the bottom, it is taken out of the kiln with the above
described shovels. The ground outside round about the
lime-kiln near the kiln-mouths is [paved with] broad
square flat bricks, **tegelstenar.** The burned bits of
chalk are laid in such places as are in the *skeeling or*
shelter, **skjulet,** which is round about the kiln, and
when they have got all the corners, **vrår,** so full that no
more can be accommodated there, it is carried thence in
large carts, **kärror,** down to the banks of the Thames,
which runs close by, where it is laid unslaked in vessels
or barges, and is carried up to London to be sold. Otherwise when they take a portion of this burned chalk, and
throw a little water upon it, it begins by degrees to
smoke and becomes so hot that one cannot hold the
hand upon it. At length the bits fall to pieces into a fine
meal, exactly in the same way as happens with another
unslacked lime from limestone.

When the chalk is full burnt, it is considerably lighter, than it was before, and full of small fissures, like as when one has laid potters'-clay in the fire. The colour on the surface is greyish, which without doubt is due to the coal and smoke. If such a piece be broken asunder, it is not [T. II. p. 88] so white within as it was while it was still unburnt.

Pieces of flint of 5 inches long and 1 inch diameter, which have come to be cast with the chalk into the lime-kiln are burnt through, and snow white all through so that they look like white Dutch ware, **krus.**

The burned pieces of chalk are so cracked to pieces and full of cracks that they fall into small bits when one takes hold of them.

The parts of these pieces which have been against the cracks are also darker in colour than that which has been midway between the same cracks, because some coal smoke has without doubt penetrated into the cracks.

That the slacked lime might not be spilt when it is thrown into the barge, they had a trough of boards knocked together, of 4 or 5 feet wide, and about 8 feet long, which they set sloping against the side of the boat and tipped the bits of chalk out of the barrow into this trough, when they fell down into the vessel. Such a trough or slide is always used at boats when unburnt chalk is loaded in them.

I have said before that around all these kilns on the lower side is built a screen of boards, partly to prevent the wind from blowing too strongly on to the kiln, partly and principally that those within it might be able to keep the burnt pieces of chalk, which they take out of the kiln before they are carried down to the barge, **Fartygen,** or yacht, **Jackten,** which conveys them to London. This screen is in fact of boards, but its foot is in some places to a height of 3 feet of brick. For a roof over [T. II.

p. 89] this skeeling is the *altan* or balcony, as I may call it, which goes round about the upper edge of the kiln. Between the kiln-walls at the bottom and the screen, **skrank eller plank,** the distance is commonly 6 feet. The screen has two openings, one on each side of the kiln, where they load the burned bits of chalk on to the cart.

The limekiln is always built close in to the place where they break the chalk, that they might not have too long a distance to carry the baskets and the chalk, therefore there are seen standing here and there unused old limekilns, which they have left since they had quarried away all the chalk near them, and it began to be too far to carry the chalk-baskets.

The women receive each about eightpence a day, for which they work exceedingly hard, for they mostly labour like slaves.

They said they were paid in this way, that a woman gets one penny when she has carried sixteen baskets of chalk to the limekiln, and for this penny she had also broken up a good deal of chalk. The man who had charge of them, confirmed what the women had said, that they receive one penny for sixteen baskets carried, at which rate they can earn twelve, fifteen, or eighteenpence a day, according as they are industrious. The men, **Karlarne,** get either nine or ten shillings a week. Food and everything they must find for themselves.

A little way from *Rochester* on the Gravesend side were several Chalkpits, out of which they took chalk, which was loosened with crowbars, **järnstörar;** hacked still farther to pieces with iron-hackers, **järnhackor,** or picks, and was finally beaten [T. II. p. 90] with iron pounders, **järn-knöster,** into small lumps and bits, which were afterwards carried to the kiln, where they were burned to lime.

After they had pounded a heap of chalk fragments into smaller bits, all the pounded chalk was not carried to the limekiln, but they laid it first in a coarse 'fiddle' and screened away that which had gone to powder, which they did not take. The flints which were found in the chalk were separated therefrom, and were cast together in a heap, to reform the ground, as they were obliged to do. The limekilns were here built entirely underground, so that the upper edge of the limekilns was horizontal with the surface of the ground. The kilns were, however, here one-third part smaller than those which are at *Northfleet*, and getting on for half the size; but in other respects nearly of the same form, excepting that at the bottom there is only one draught-hole, **drag-hâl,** instead of several as in those at *Northfleet.* They also went through at once down to the same draw-hole, like a tar-mill with us in Osterbotten. In other respects, the walls are all built of brick. The Carl said that the chalk, which he lays in the kiln the one morning, can be ready burnt to take out the following morning. The lime they burn here is not carried to London, but is all used up at *Rochester* and in that neighbourhood.

The chalk is burned, in other respects, here in exactly the same manner as at *Northfleet*, viz., alternations of coal broken into very small pieces, and bits of chalk, etc.

The 1st August, 1748.

[T. II. p. 91.] *Sain Foin* is much used here in Kent. Most people here call it *Cinquefoil* which they have corrupted from *Sain Foin.* When it is once sown, it can stand ten or twelve years, without requiring to be sown again; for which time they can mow it every year. After the time when it begins to be somewhat thin, so that it does not seem to be worth while to mow it, they do not at once plough up the ground it grows upon, but let it

remain two, three, or four years, during which time they
give liberty to cattle, but in particular sheep to go and
bait upon it, by which means the land also becomes
manured. They are obliged to proceed thus with it,
because here in Kent there is very little meadow-land
and pasture for sheep. When they do plough up such
land it is commonly sown the first year with Pease, but
sometimes with another crop, as is found necessary.

For horses *Sain Foin* is an excellent food both in
summer and winter, but if it is given to cows, after it is
dry, they eat no more of it than the flowers that lie on
the top, nearly all the rest they reject and trample under
foot. It has been attempted to sow it, at some places in
Essex, from the seeds which they took from hence, Kent,
but it has not by any means flourished, but grew so
poorly that it has not been worth while to sow it again.
The soil is sand and gravel, at the places where it was tried.

Clover. In this district also much clover is sown.
Spring is commonly the season when it is sown, but they
do not get to mow it before the next [T. II. p. 92]
summer after that. It is hardly ever sown more than
two summers in succession, and very often not more than
a single summer, after which they commonly leave it to
the next summer after it is mown before turning in the
sheep to feed upon it. As was said above, it is necessary
to cause them to be closely crowded on the pasture,
because the farmers then at the same time have the
advantage, that the fields are manured when the sheep
go in to pasture there. The cows eat the clover greedily,
both fresh and dry, stalk and all.

Vicia Sativa. Similarly, in many places hereabout
they sow tares or *Vicia Sat.* as food for cattle. The
principal use to which it is put, is that they cut it up
green at this season of the year, and give it to horses at
home, who eat it very greedily. No more of it is left

standing on the land than proves necessary for collecting
its seed for next year, for this is a *planta annua*, which
must be sown every year, and that in early spring so that
it can by this time, August, be taken up as food for cattle.
At this time of the year, **tid,** they here keep their horses at
home in the stable for the reason that out in the inclosures
they are so much troubled with flies and other insects.

Rofvor, *turnips.* They also sow turnips here as at
other places in England. The season when they commonly
sow them is just about this time. I was to-day
in a large *inclosure* in the afternoon, which in the
morning had been sown with turnip seed. The whole
inclosure was laid out as turnip land. The land lies
fallow all the summer before this time. At the beginning
of July they carry [T. II. p. 93] the manure out on to
this land (see T. I. p. 483 *orig.*) which manure is mostly
straw-litter, **halmbyssie,** such as is collected in the
farm-yard, **fä - gården,** and has there lain under
the cattle, and has become mixed in with their dung.
After this has been carried on to the fields and laid
there by the load, **lasstals,** it is spread out as soon as
possible, and is ploughed down. After that the field
is harrowed and rolled so that it becomes quite fine.
The principal reason why they sow such a quantity of
turnips here is that they feed and fatten both sheep
and oxen with them in the winter.

Åkerbruket. *The Agriculture.* The places which
they make up their minds to sow with wheat in autumn
are such as are either now lying fallow, or also where
beans are now growing, which they plough up in the
autumn and sow with wheat.

The 2nd August, 1748.

Källor mycket *rara* **här på orten.** *Springs very
rare in this district.* I have often before made the remark

that spring-wells and gushing springs with becks flowing from them, **springkällor med springåder och flytande bäck från dem,** such as occur in abundance in Sweden, are sometimes scarce at the places I had pre-viously been to in England. I have also made the same observation here in Kent, and also in the part of Essex which lies opposite Gravesend. The country on both sides consists of high banks and hills with deep dales between, and in some places, particularly on both sides of the river Thames, large low-lying plains, so that many from all this might conclude that in the valleys between the hills and on the low plains immediately under the hills, there would be found an abundance [T. II. p. 94] of running streams, and a plentiful supply of springs here and there, but nothing is more rare. During my visit to Gravesend I walked tolerably well over the country around on all sides, was also twice over in Essex, and there walked assiduously round the country, but for all that I had not the good fortune to get to see a single spring, **källa,** with running water, nor a single running stream, more than immediately west of *Northfleet*.

All the running water I saw here was in the river Thames, the river Medway, which passes by Rochester, and the little beck west of Northfleet.

An Englishman was asked whether there are any springs here. He immediately answered yes, and in addition to that they are beautiful; but when he comes to point them out, it is nothing else than a deep well down in the chalk, which he says has a spring feeder, because the water therein cannot be emptied out, although it lies some fathoms' depth down.

It is certain that the country is here very pretty, to such an extent is this so that through the planting of hedges round all the enclosures it everywhere resembles a garden. Besides this, the continual variety of high

knolls and deep dales without seeing any stones larger
than a boy can throw, greatly increases its charm, but
nevertheless, the pretty effect of crystal clear running
becks, and their murmuring sound in the green dales is
much missed; such a joy no one here knows of. I am
here speaking about the places I was at, for in several
other parts of England there is an abundance of beautiful springs. [T. II. p. 95.] All the water which the
inhabitants require for themselves and their cattle must
be collected either in deep wells in the chalk, or in large
dug-pits and *ponds* in the inclosures, where the rain
water stands, and serves for the cattle, which there
pasture, to drink, for which purpose also such ponds
have always very gently sloping sides, that the cattle
may be able to go down to them and drink. But someone might ask the reason why there are here so very
few, or in short, no springs and becks, where, nevertheless, the country consists of banks and hills, with deep
valleys, though it sometimes rains here heavily? I
answer that I cannot just understand this, but I have
made the following observations :—

1. They have everywhere here deep wells in the
chalk, both near the Thames and far away from it,
wherein is an abundance of water which never fails.

2. The surface of the ground consists of a loose
mould, on which one hardly ever sees any water stand,
however it rains, but it sinks in at once, and the upper
surface is soon dry, at least on the top.

3. When they have dug the pits so deep, that they are
some way down in the chalk, the water stands in them,
and remains for several days before the sun succeeds in
drying it up.

4. When one digs never so little into the chalk, where
it forms a hill, it is quite humid and moist within, and the
deeper one digs so much more humid and wetter it is.

5. In the chalk pits the chalk is found not to lie quite dense [T. II. p. 96] and solid, but is full of both horizontal and perpendicular fissures.

6. If one goes early in the morning into a chalk pit before the sun has dried up the dew, or also on to a field where pieces of chalk are lying, one will find that the chalk is slippery, and almost wetter than any other kind of earth.

From all these observations it seems to follow that the rain and the snow which falls cannot stand in the surface soil because it is too loose ; but it goes down into the chalk; that the chalk has a property of absorbing moisture; that the water filters deeper down, through the many perpendicular and horizontal fissures in the chalk : that very few becks could, on that account, be found on the chalk hills, because they, as it were, swallow up all the water before it has time to collect so as to form a beck ; that crops and pease which grow on the chalk hills, for that reason, do not require to be drained, because the chalk, which lies below, probably absorbs the dew in the night, and in the day is dissolved by the water which lies down in the fissures.

From this want of springs and flowing waters it happens that the cattle, at times in the summer when it is a long and severe drought, come to suffer much. They must often then be driven some miles before they can be watered. I was informed that in some places they had no other water to use for cooking than such as was collected in the chalk pits, which is white and thick, and often so full of small insects that they are obliged both to filter and boil it [T. II. p. 97] first, before they dare use it.

Sain Foin. I have said above that most of the inclosures which here in Kent are used as meadows, were sown with Sain Foin. I saw to-day places were Sain Foin had been cut, harvested, and carried home this year, but as no cattle had been turned in to feed there, it had already so advanced in growth since that time, that it was now 9 in. high, with an abundance of soft and tender leaves striking out from the roots and stalks which, moreover, stood very thick, so that I believe that they might be able to mow it again this summer.

The 3rd August, 1748.

Salicornia, **dess nytta,** *Samphire* its use. *Salicornia herbacea.* Linn. *Flor. Svec.* I.; Rai. *Syn.* 136; grows on the low-lying banks of the Thames, which at every flood tide are overflowed by the salt water of the Thames—for one ought to know that the water in all this part of the Thames which is at and below Gravesend is very salt, because the flood which happens twice a day (of 24 hours) drives the salt water up from the sea. The English women pluck this herb at this season, and pickle it, **insylta,** which is done as follows : The herb is taken entire as it grows, but broken off at the roots. As much of it as is required is thus gathered. It is well washed in cold vinegar, one stalk and plant after another, that all the dust and dirt which had clung to it might be rinsed off. They do not wash it in water [T. II. p. 98] because if it is afterwards laid in vinegar (as it should be) the water which remains firmly lodged in the plant, dilutes the vinegar, so that it becomes weaker, whence it becomes clouded and full of mildew, and thus becomes altogether ruined. After they have thus washed the stalks or the plants clean in vinegar, and laid them on a board for the vinegar to run off a little, they take a stone jar, **stenburk,** of the size which they have enough Samphire (Salicornia) for, lay the plants therein till it is full, pour in the best and quite pure vinegar, just so much as to cover the herbs in the pot. Thereupon they take some mustard, rub it down to a perfectly dry powder, because

it has no efficacy, **kraft,** or at least is not so strong
if it is unground and entire. They then cut a clean
linen cloth to the size round and diameter of the jar
inside, and then another linen cloth of the same size,
hem them round the hedges to a round bag, fill it with
the ground dry mustard so that it is only as thick as the
blade of a knife; then, not only sow up the hole through
which the mustard was put in, but also sow a quilted
network of cross-lines upon the face, just as one stops
a quilt or bodice with 'hards' * and cotton, that it may
lie even. This bag, **påsen,** so filled is laid upon the
Samphire, which not only presses it down so that it all
lies in the vinegar and none above it, but also prevents
it from forming any mildew on the surface. Afterwards
they have a large Chamois-leather, **sämsk-lapp,** which
reaches well over the jar. This is laid over the jar and
tied tight down that the virtue, **kraft,** of the vinegar
may not be lost. [T. II. p. 99.] They let it stand so
for 14 days or a month, and then look whether the
Samphire still retains its green colour, which if it does
then they take some *pinks,* **näglikor,** *Dianthus Caryo-
phyllus,* L. *Clove Pink,* ginger, **Ingefara,** pepper, and
mace, **muskotblomma,** half an ounce of each, and
half an ounce of Jamaica pepper (allspices), boil them
together, let them cool, and then lay them in the jar with
the *Samphire,* tie it up again, after replacing the mustard
bag as before said, and leave it so to stand till they
require it. But if, as commonly happens, they see that
the Samphire has not kept its green colour, but has
changed to a yellow colour, they take it together with
the vinegar it lies in, lay it with the afore-named spices

---

* 'HARDS of Flax and Hemp, the coarser parts separated from the fine
stuff.' Bailey, *Eng. Dic.* 1736. 'HARDENS' or 'HARDEN,' *hemp, hemp-
fabric* &c. Lucas, *Stud.* 1882, *Glossary* p. 257. [J. L.]

in a metal saucepan, and boil all till the Samphire which had a yellow colour when it was put in acquires a beautiful green colour, in respect of which be it noted that it is stirred from time to time while it is boiling. As soon then as it has got its former green colour, which commonly happens in the course of half an hour, although sometimes more or less, they take it off the fire, pour all together into the jar, lay on the mustard bag, tie the Chamois leather over, and preserve it till it is wanted.

They often make them in this way. After they have rinsed them in vinegar when they are newly plucked, they pour pure vinegar on them, and boil them at once with the aforesaid spices; upon which, it is to be noted, that although they are green when they are laid in the metal saucepan, they nevertheless become quite yellow as soon as they are warm, but they must be kept boiling till they regain their former [T. II. p. 100] green colour, after which it is proceeded with according to the previous instructions. They do best of all if they are preserved in a jar in a somewhat warm room. They are used in the autumn and winter season with steak and other food, in the same way as pickled walnuts or cucumbers, without anything else being added to them.

Obs.—The vinegar which they are rinsed and washed in is thrown away after they have been washed.

At insylta Champignioner. *To Pickle Mushrooms.* The women pickled them thus: they plucked them whilst they were still quite small, when they keep best, boil them in very salt water about ten minutes, take them out and lay them in a linen cloth to dry. Afterwards they take vinegar, whole pepper, and mace, **muskotblomma,** boil it all together, and also pour a little white wine into it. When it has boiled a little they take it off, let it cool, lay the mushrooms after they are dry in a glass jar, pour the vinegar and the other spices on to them so that it covers them over, then they have a Chamois leather which they tie over the glass so that it is quite closed, and use it when it is wanted. The large mushrooms are not pickled, but are stewed while fresh. The small ones which were pickled were of the size of finger's-ends, and consisted of the entire *pileus* or hat, and the *pedunculas* or stalk, with the *lamellœ* and all, nothing being taken away. They were not washed before they were laid in the pickle, **saltlakan,** to be boiled.

[T. II. p. 101.] *The 4th August,* 1748.

At midday came Captain Lawson from London to Gravesend, whither the ship had already gone before on the $\frac{30}{31}$ July.

Gravesend is a little spot which lies in a charming place in Kent close to the river Thames, about 22 English miles from London. The houses are for a great part of brick, but some are old and built in a very ugly style. The streets are uneven, irregular, and paved with flints. In the town is a beautiful English Church and a Presbyterian House of Prayer, **Bönehus.** Outside the English Church is this inscription: " Hanc ædem incendio lugubri deletam Georgius II., Rex Munificentissimus, Senatus Consilio, instaurandam decrevit," which at once points attention to the conflagration which this little town suffered some years back, when a great part of it was laid in ashes.*

In and around the town are several kitchen gardens, **kryddgårdar,** whence a large quantity of kitchen garden produce is sent up to London nearly every day, besides what is sold to seafarers, **sjöfarande;** and Gravesend *Asparagus* is especially famous, as it is

---

* 24th August, 1727, destroyed 110 houses and the Church. Pocock *Hist. of Gravesend*, 1797. [J. L.]

reckoned the best in England. The principal support of the inhabitants consists here in selling all kinds of provisions and liqueurs to sea-folk and travellers. All ships which come from abroad to London here take a Custom House officer on board. Here also nearly all ships from London furnish themselves with fresh provisions before they commit themselves to the seas. The ships generally go some days beforehand from London to Gravesend, partly [T. II. p. 102] to furnish themselves afresh, partly to, as it were, undergo from the Custom House officer a new *clearing* before they go to sea, and the captain and passengers commonly come down here 4 or 5 days after the ship.

Exactly opposite Gravesend on the other side of the river Thames, in Essex, lies the fortification called *Tilbury Fort,* which commands the approach to London.

Between Gravesend and London there run daily several small yachts or boats, which convey passengers and other travellers there and back.

[*The 5th August*, 1748.]

[At this point commences Pehr Kalm's 'Travels into North America,' translated into English by J. R. Forster. With Maps, Cuts, and Notes. Warrington, 1770-71. 3 vols., 8vo. The account of the voyage down the Channel is much abridged, and descriptions of points on the English Coast are omitted altogether.]

<h3 style="text-align:center">The 5th August, 1748.</h3>

Resan. *The Voyage.*

At 6 o'clock in the afternoon we went on board the ship *Mary Gally,* commanded by Captain Lawson, and bound for Philadelphia in North America. We then sailed in the Lord's Name from Gravesend, and went a good piece down the river Thames before we cast anchor. We lay there till about 3 o'clock the following morning, when the voyage was continued.

The 6th August.

In the morning we continued our voyage down the river Thames, and so out into the Channel, down which we afterwards sailed under the coasts of England. We could constantly see the shores of England, and were at times in tacking close into them.

All those parts consist of Chalk which are high, steep, and almost perpendicular. Measured by the eye' the height of these steep Chalk coasts, from the water up to the turf, seemed to be 3 to 4 fathoms, in some places [T. II. p. 103] more, in other places less. We could see with the naked eye that in these chalk cliffs also there were such strata of bare flints as have been described above, one of which, just half way between the water surface and the top soil, ran quite horizontal, as though it had been arranged on the dead level, and was visible nearly the whole way along this piece of coast.* Lower down, a little above the surface of the water, another appeared, but the view of it was broken and indistinct. Upon these Chalk hills lay beautiful arable fields, on which the crops which were almost all wheat were just beginning to turn yellow, and were nearly ready for cutting. We could not see any sheaves or cut crops, whereas, at the beginning of the week before, we saw rye sheaves in Essex from Gravesend.

About six o'clock in the evening we arrived at *Deal*, off which we cast anchor. *Deal* is a little spot or town, **fläck eller stad,** lying on the shore at the entrance of a little bay, **vik,** which the sea has made. The houses are nearly all built of brick, and roofed partly with *pantiles*, but mostly with plain tiles.

There is only one church in the town, not large, and almost without a tower, only a little box, **kur,** in its place. The churchyard is tolerably large, and has planted round it an avenue of elms, in which one can go and walk. The inhabitants live tolerably comfortably, and support themselves principally by trade. Nearly all

---

* This has been called by Mr. Whitaker "The Three-inch Band." [J. L.]

ships which come from London, and intend to proceed
through the Channel, or *vice versâ*, lie here one day or
more and furnish themselves commonly with all kinds of
fresh provisions, besides [T. II. p. 104] brandy and other
wines, although they have to pay very heavily for them,
because the people know how to make a good bargain.
A great many also get their living by rowing, in that
they carry passengers from the ships to the land and
back, for which they always make them pay dearly. By
fishing they also make handsome profits, by selling the
fresh fish to the sea folk who come here to anchor. In
the late war most of them followed privateering, **kaperi,**
and thereby accumulated large sums. The haven,
hamnen, is not particularly good, for it is open to the
south and east, from which quarter the storms have
freedom to beat upon this place from the sea, but that
does not make any difference, because it is mostly in the
absence of this wind that the ships lie here in the roads.
Here the ships leave the pilots whom they had from
London to Gravesend. When the south-east gales are
blowing heavily they know it in Deal, because it lies open
to this wind. Here also the ships which are bound for
London take their pilots on board.

The 7th August 1748.

In the morning I landed at Deal, where I was till
towards evening.

Lumbricus Marinus. When the sea-water at ebb-tide
fell off Deal, the fishermen went down on to the lowest
places, which the sea had just left, and which were
covered over with a fine sand, where they dug up
the *sea-worms*, **hafsmaskar,** which have their residence
under the sand on the sea-shore, and are described
by Linnæus in his *Vest Gotha Resa.* p. 189 [T. II.
p. 105], and also in his *Fauna Svecia*, 1270 [1746].

[also in *Systema Naturæ*, Vindobonœ, 1767, 8vo. *Ed.* Decima tertia, 3 T.—T. I. pars. II. p. 1076, 277]. They dug up these creatures, **kräk,** which are a species of earth-worms, **metmaskar,** in this way. They had a little *digger*, **grep,** of iron with three grains or tines, with which they dug up the loose sand where these worms had their residence, when they commonly found them 18 inches deep in the sand. The sign which they had to be able to know where these worms lived is that they creep up out of the sand at high water, and lie upon it, but as soon as it is ebb and the tide goes out they creep down under the sand. Meantime, as far as they have been on the surface of the sand they leave their **träck** behind them, which consists of bare fine sand, and looks like small worms lying in a ring, or of disc-shaped forms, **kringel-lika** *former*, in the other sand. These raised sand-rings indicate to the fishermen the place where the worms live, and by that means betray them. The worms they get are collected in bottles, and are used as bait on hooks for whiting or cod. They call them *Logworms.**

Machine to wind up Boats.

At Deal there is ebb and flood, when the water for six hours rises high up, and for six hours falls very far out, therefore to get up the boats so that they may stand more safely and not be broken by the waves when it begins to be high water, they have on the beach above where the boats stand, *capstans*, with perpendicular axes, with which by means of a rope which is fastened near the bottom of the boat, they wind it up as high as they wish on the beach.

The 8th August, 1748.

Next day at 3 o'clock in the morning we left *Deal,* and

---

* That is Sea-worms. *O. Norsk*, Lögr, the sea. [J. L.]

went with the tidal current from thence along the Channel, but not faster than the stream drove us. We had the English coast at a short distance on our right-hand. It consisted of bare chalk, was tolerably high, and stood for the most part perpendicular.

At 10 o'clock in the morning we passed *Dover*, which is a little spot with a *Castell* above it on a hill. The country here along the coast was in some places quite steep, in other places long-sloping for about half an English mile, above which the high chalk hills came on, **togo emot.** These were not perpendicular, but more sloping, and now over-grown with grass. When the land had gone so long-sloping for a certain distance, it again became steep and perpendicular, so that bare white chalk appeared. In the afternoon the wind blew rather fresh, **blåste en liten kul,** so we luffed (*loverade*)* off and on between the English and French coasts. We were sometimes not far from the French side, so that we could, especially with a glass (*Perspectiv*), clearly see houses, fields, &c. Here, I remember what I read in Camden's *Britannia*, viz., that he says that he early formed the opinion that England had formerly joined on to France† or Flanders, where Dover and Calais now lie, by some small arm, and that the sea had afterwards washed it away, or some other accident now unknown to us, had come to destroy the same arm or ness, **arm eller näs.** I for my part am much inclined [T. II. p. 107] to believe the same when I consider the following facts, viz., that England opposite Calais, between Deal

---

* *Sw.* Lofvera, *Fr.* Louvoyer, *Ger.* Laviren, *Eng.* Luff. Bailey, *Eng. Dic.*, 1736, has " To *loof* (commonly pronounced luff) a term used in conding of a ship, as *loof*, &c., *i.e.*, keep the ship nearer the wind." [J. L.]

† To say nothing of the uncertain conjecture of several writers, Antonius Volscius, Dominicus Marius Niger, Servius Honoratus, Joh. Twine, Guil. Musgrave, and Henry, *Hist. of Btn.*—Pref. [J. L.]

and Dover, forms a projecting point, and that Flanders
near Calais forms a point projecting towards England ;
that both points consist of the same kind of earth, viz.,
of high perpendicular chalk cliffs, **kritvallar**; that the
land on both sides has the same *facies* and appearance ;
consists of a collection of round and long-sloping hills of
chalk, **kullriga och långsluttande högder af
Krita,** so that if one who had seen the coast of England
should get to see the coast of France here, and did not
know that it was such, he would certainly believe that it
was the English coast, **vallen,** and English hills. On
the English coast we saw here and there some beautiful
churches, small towns, &c. The ploughed fields lay on
the hills, but trees were here rare, and we did not notice
that they were divided into *enclosures* by means of
hedges.

In the evening a multitude of Porpoises, **Marsvin
eller Isor,** tumbled about everywhere in the sea around
our ship.

A Burial at Sea.

In the evening, a woman, one of the religious fugitives
from *Pfaltz* in Germany was buried according to the
usual custom of the sea. She was one of sixty men,
women and children, who were now going with us over
to the English colonies in America, to settle there. The
funeral was performed in this way, that after they had
bound her in sailcloth, a quantity of coals in an old sack
were fastened to the feet, when she was laid on a board,
and then plunged from the board into the sea, when she
sank at once to the bottom. Some Psalms were sung
first.

The 9th August, 1748.

Resan. *The Voyage.* At daybreak the ship was
allowed to drive forward with the tidal current as long as

it lasted; but before that, as long as the stream was
against us, we had cast anchor. At daybreak we passed
one of England's promontories, **uddar,** called *Dungeness.*
At 9 o'clock the stream was against us, when we cast
anchor nearly opposite *Fairlight.* On the sea it was now
so calm that the water scarcely moved beyond that the
stream drove it. We could see the English coast quite
easily, which was in some places high, steep, and sloping,
almost perpendicular, and in other places long-sloping.
The perpendicular earth walls near the sea did not here
consist of chalk, but of a light grey earth. We could
nowhere see a sign of chalk in them. The French coast
lay so far from us that we could scarcely see it. At
12 o'clock noon it began to blow somewhat, when we
lifted anchor, unfurled the sails, and with tacking, drew
away.

We were sometimes right under the English coast
near *Fairlight,* which coast did not here consist of chalk
but of a *grey fine sand,* as far as we could discover with
the glass and the naked eye; besides this, Captain
Lawson confirmed the same. This coast also was steep
enough, so that no one could climb up it without a ladder,
stega, or some other instrument, **verktyg,** but in some
places it was long-sloping. The country above it was,
like the rest of England we saw, a collection of hills
[T. II. p. 109] side by side, with dales between. Yet
the hills here were more gently sloping. On them lay
ploughed fields, meadows, and pastures, which were all
enclosed with green hedges and leaf-trees. Here and
there some churches appeared on the hills, with quite
little short and pointed steeples on massive towers, which
had been so built, that the wind which here has a large
field to gather strength upon, might not blow them over.
We could see no chalk cliffs or hills here. Towards
evening we cast anchor for a short time, but as a gentle

east wind began to blow at 9 o'clock, the anchor was again lifted, and the voyage was continued the whole of the following night.

Hafsdjur. *Marine Animals.* [Jelly fish.] We saw also a kind of marine animals floating in the water something like the annexed figure. The colour was mostly violet. It was round and opened itself nearly like a purse, **pung,** when we saw in the midst of it four white rings. It must be some kind of *Medusa.* I could not get a chance of catching any. The sizes were various, some quite small of 1 inch diameter, and the largest about 6 inches across.

The 10th August, 1748.

The voyage was continued the whole of this day with a favourable and delightful wind, which drove the ship quickly, but raised some waves on the sea. In the morning at 7 o'clock, we caught sight of the *Isle of Wight*, which lies outside Portsmouth, and [T. II. p. 110], belongs to England. It, as well as the country round, seemed to consist of chalk, because the cliffs, **vallarna,** were snow white. It is also highland enough.

Färilar. While we were sailing here out on the sea, so that we could only see a little of the English coast a great way off, but not any other land, there came some white butterflies flying over the sea, and sometimes accompanied the ship for a little. Sometimes also they flew before the ship. I could not catch one to see what species it was, but they exactly resembled the snowwhite *Cabbage Butterflies*, **Kål Färilar,** both in shape and size.

I did not see them pitch anywhere on the ship. We also saw them yesterday. All wondered how these frail creatures ventured so far from the shore.

At noon we passed in front of the Isle of Wight, which

was a very high land, but yet near the shores mostly long-sloping. The soil was there of chalk, but this chalk is said not to be so good as that near Gravesend, but harder. On both sides of the Isle of Wight appeared high steep cliffs of bare chalk. The land on the surface of this island seemed to be divided by hedges.

At 5 o'clock in the afternoon, we began to see the Isle of Portland, nearly in front of us at a great distance. We also saw the English coast right opposite us, but a long way off. This was [T. II. p. 111], mostly steep enough, and seemed quite white, but whether it was chalk or some white kind of stone or other, I could not determine, for the long distance.

The 11th August, 1748.

Resan. The Voyage. We sailed quickly the whole of the previous night, and also this day. At 6 o'clock in the morning we saw *Bolthead*, a promontory of England, inside which *Plymouth* (Pleymouth) lies. Porpoises tumbled about here and there in the water. At noon the wind moderated, and almost died away, so that the ship could not travel very fast. Otherwise our ship was a very fast sailer. The captains who were on board agreed that they had scarcely ever seen any ship which sailed so fast. They reckoned it thus, than when other ships in one hour sailed three miles, ours in the same time sailed 5 miles. At noon we left the English Coast, and saw it again no more. **Vi lämnade vid Middagstid Angelska vallen och sågo den ej mera.**

INDEX.

The Figures denote pages.

459

BOTANICAL INDEX.

DIPROSE, BATEMAN & Co., Printers, Sheffield Street, Lincoln's Inn Fields, London, W.C.

CPSIA information can be obtained
at www.ICGtesting.com
Printed in the USA
LVHW040749221119
637982LV00001B/15/P